Queer Opera

Queer Opera

Andrew Sutherland

LEXINGTON BOOKS
Lanham • Boulder • New York • London

Published by Lexington Books
An imprint of The Rowman & Littlefield Publishing Group, Inc.
4501 Forbes Boulevard, Suite 200, Lanham, Maryland 20706
www.rowman.com

86-90 Paul Street, London EC2A 4NE

British Library Cataloguing in Publication Information Available

Library of Congress Cataloging-in-Publication Data

Names: Sutherland, Andrew (Musician), author.
Title: Queer opera / Andrew Sutherland.
Description: Lanham : Lexington Books, 2023. | Includes bibliographical references and index.
Identifiers: LCCN 2023002642 (print) | LCCN 2023002643 (ebook) |
    ISBN 9781666906073 (cloth) | ISBN 9781666906080 (ebook)
Subjects: LCSH: Homosexuality in opera. | Opera. Classification:
    LCC ML1700 .S9487 2023 (print) | LCC ML1700 (ebook) |
    DDC 782.1/09—dc23/eng/20230206
LC record available at https://lccn.loc.gov/2023002642
LC ebook record available at https://lccn.loc.gov/2023002643

For Taryn Fiebig 1972–2021; diva, ally, friend.

Contents

List of Figures

Introduction

Books about opera invariably begin with a discussion of Monteverdi's *L'Orfeo*, the sensitive musician and straight man who would plunge the depths of hell to bring back his beloved wife. Following his failed rescue attempt, the remainder of his life was spent enjoying the sexual pleasures of young men to the extreme irritation of Dionysus. He paid for his choices, and Monteverdi chose to avoid any reference to his bisexuality. Queerness in opera would continue to exist under a shroud of mystery for several centuries – ever-present and hinting to opera lovers of its secret presence, until a brave new world allowed it to burst forth and reclaim the opera space in the name of generations of queer opera lovers who have maintained a steadfast loyalty. This book traces this process and highlights the works in which opera gradually made its way out of the closet and examines a history of queerness over more than four centuries.

For many queers, opera has been an important art form that has formed a central component of leisure time. Attending the opera has been more than simple entertainment; it has been a safe place where like-minded people could meet, a distraction from the heteronormality of wider society and a vehicle for escapism. Whatever codes of heterosocial conduct may exist outside the opera house are in many ways discarded in a place where a nexus of beauty and pathos forms imagined worlds of heightened sensitivity. These worlds are inhabited by people in costume and make-up, many of whom struggle with situations of oppression and in some cases manage to subvert the status quo. For centuries, queer observers have been able to identify with the frustrations of the oppressed, the exhausting obstacles preventing true love and the strength of character to achieve recognition in a society that routinely rejects differences. Simultaneously, being enveloped in the magnificence of the theatre, being lost in the splendour of the music and revelling

1

in the gorgeousness of the visual aesthetic have been an edifying diversion from the monotony of daily life. Susan Sontag reminds us that 'homosexuals have pinned their integration into society on promoting the aesthetic sense'.[1] Opera allows the queer attendee an evening of fabulousness and a moment of safety from a judgemental world.

Since the burgeoning multidisciplinary art form emerged in the final years of the sixteenth century, queers may have loved opera, but the sentiment has not often been reciprocated. With astonishingly few exceptions, queers have struggled to be represented in the art form that they have supported. Prior to the middle of the twentieth century, any form of shared sexual identity with the opera's diegesis has been codified. Queers have a long history of communicating in code, and the ability that opera has of communicating ideas through music may provide another reason for its resonance with queer audiences. While these examples have provided queers with tantalizing glimpses of acceptance, they have provided scholars with endless opportunity to analyse the meaning of the text and music.

With the advent of psychoanalysis and the deluge of social theoretical discourse including feminist theory and, more recently, queer theory, many of these operas have received fresh readings that have explored alternative perspectives regarding socio-sexual relationships in opera. The term 'queer theory' was coined by Teresa de Lauretis in the title of a conference held in 1991.[2] Queer theory emerged as a strong postmodern and poststructuralist critique of identity, echoing the ideas of Michel Foucault (1926–1984). It repudiates the limitations placed on sexual and gender identity from a heteronormative perspective, including the gay/lesbian binary. Since then, a collective understanding of how such a theory might work has evolved, providing a vehicle for legitimate scholarship for understanding the vast world of queer experience. The contributions to the growing scholarship on queer and gender studies by Susan McClary, Elisabeth Wood, Carolyn Abbat, Philip Brett and many others have brought about a renaissance in attitudinal thinking and an alternative to the heteronormative stance that has dominated musicology for so long.

For the purposes of this book, the term "queer" is used as an umbrella term for the many types of queer identity in the rainbow of letters that make up the LGBTQI+ acronym. It is also a helpful term when considering the representative material that I shall discuss. Although the twenty-first century has seen a sudden proliferation of works that show openly queer characters in operas by openly queer composers and librettists, many of the examples I have chosen involve a sexual complexity for which a specific label would be unhelpful. For socio-historical reasons, composers have, in some cases, caged the relationships of potentially queer characters in homosocial situations, with enough ambiguity so as not to arouse the objections of authorities, thereby making sexual distinctions arguable. But argue we shall. Exploring these operas allows us not only to understand the characters' identity and how that informs motivation but also to situate the creative team responsible for the works in their social contexts. This contextualization provides an opportunity to understand the queer experience in the real world and how that informed the operatic diegesis. Conversely, we may observe how the representation of queerness, however coded, impacted society.

Through the research process, it has become clear that much of the material is accompanied by a variety of interpretative perspectives. My emic perspective does not fully embrace every interpretation of the queer theoretical debate, but it generally adopts a position that seeks to understand the way in which queerness finds a voice in the narrative. Musicologist and queer theorist Philip Brett suggests, in addition to finding meaning in music beyond the sung text, that musicologists should 'assert (and exert) the right to propose meanings that are grounded in an inside awareness of the cultural conditions under which homosexual composers in this century and before have functioned'.[3] Music, particularly in the operatic context, can be understood as cultural agency, by actively participating in social change, rather than simply reflecting those that have already transpired. The remarkable sexual revolution that has occurred since the late nineteenth century has progressed, in part, by the ideas generated by experiencing opera. It is no accident that liberal, forward-thinking societies have been socially and geographically close to flourishing opera scenes.

WHAT MAKES AN OPERA QUEER?

Categorizing an opera as queer is as fraught with difficulties as navigating the long list of queer identity labels. I have made judicious decisions about which operas to discuss in detail and make no claims to fully satisfy the full range of diverse opinions regarding my choices. Any discourse generated by this book is welcomed. In popular culture, many creations for the small and large screens have been enthusiastically embraced by the queer community without any identifiable queer representative character. Gay men have frequently found inspiration in strong female characters or women who are simply 'fabulous'. Identifying with a character on the basis of queerness does not always require homoerotic elements but rather a representation of queer ideals. Although some of these ideals may be interpreted as superficial, in terms of a preferred aesthetic, they are often deeply rooted in a desire for acceptance. Other ideals such as melodrama and dark comedy have pervaded queer literature since the popularity of Oscar Wilde's works such as *An Ideal Husband* (1895) in which attitudes of Victorian England are challenged and repudiated. In addition, a fondness of transgressing class and demographic boundaries is a recurring theme and most commonly expressed in the world of cross-dressing, in which the advantaged male adopts the persona of the disadvantaged female.[4] Feminist theorists would ascribe the repudiation of patriarchal attitudes as a central tenant, and as the 'older sister' of queer theory, a similar provocation can be seen to drive queer motivations. Queer narratives can reflect the insufferable and suffocating experience of living in a metaphorical closet and the eventual escape from its imprisonment.

Homoeroticism is not a requirement for queer identity; however, it does constitute an important marker. Since the Stonewall Riots (1969), and subsequent spread of gay pride events around the globe, a celebration of sexual liberation in its many forms has been a defining characteristic of the revelry. Just as Greco-Romans celebrated the pleasures of wine, freedom, intoxication and ecstasy in Bacchanalian festivals, queer festivals make no apology for acclaiming eroticism and the freedom found in expressing it outwardly. In opera, eroticism can be found in the score as much as the libretto and can be used as pointers for sexual subtext. A character may be referred to as a 'friend', but when that friend is considered to have beautiful lips, strong arms, a sensual form or other pleasing physical features, there is a substantive repositioning from Platonic to Apollonian or Dionysian love. Musically, the composer creates sound worlds with a complex system of codified language. Musical markers that determine eroticism can be created through association with previous appearances of a theme or device. Eroticism can also find an association with exoticism, and the choice of instrumentation, timbre, texture or scale device can be an effective conveyor of erotic intent. A queer opera can therefore operate in the shadows, allowing insight into queerness to only the knowledgeable observer. The presence of queer elements can therefore be debated and often is between those who see and hear nothing discernibly homosexual and those who recognize it clearly.

I have structured this book according to themes that I feel reflect a range of character traits found in the chosen operas. In doing so, I have avoided a strictly chronological approach which, although meritorious, would draw focus on the compositions and overshadow the phenomenology of the queer experience. Similarly, I have not grouped the works geographically, as the universality of homosocial and homosexual identity could be diminished. I have also chosen not to include the vast repertoire of largely pre-Classical opera that included cross-dressing for comedic effect, such as Arnalt in Monteverdi's *L'incoronazione di Poppea* (1642/3) and Aristea in Cesti's *Orontea* (1656), or the French tradition of predominantly *haute-contres* performing *en travesti*, such as Pierre Jélyotte, who premiered the role of the nymph Platée in Rameau's *Platée* (1745).

The rich tradition of cross-dressing found in the operas of Francesco Cavalli (1602–1976) is frequently replete with innuendo and cheeky *double entendre*. Cavalli drew upon a collection of stock characters for more than forty operas, one of which is a man playing an older woman lusting after a younger man for comedic effect. In *La Calisto* (1651), Giove is disguised as Diana to seduce Calisto, and in the first season, Giove and Diana were both sung by the bass, using falsetto for the latter role. Operas with prominent roles for a castrato and those that contribute to the great history of operatic trouser roles are not generally included here but not on the basis that they do not represent queerness. The appearance of men in women's costume as a precursor to modern drag has undoubtedly contributed to the feeling of a 'safe place' that queers often experience when attending the opera.

Several other examples of works not included in this book, but that deserve mention here, have contributed to the ongoing scholarship concerning queerness in opera. Any reading of Lully's incomplete opera, *Achille et Polyxène* (1687), that arrived at a conclusion that the leading actors were romantically involved would not be making a huge leap, despite their reference to each other as 'friends'. Lully himself had only two years previously been caught in bed with a man named Brunet, and although he retained his position, he was banned from being in the king's presence. Another example includes the growing scholarship regarding the possible homosexuality of Handel (1685–1759), which has been fuelled by several tenets. Handel's notable lack of interest in women, his preference for socializing in all-male circles, his strict silence regarding his private life and the proliferation of gender-bending and cross-dressing roles in his operas all contribute to academic speculation. One example is the title role in *Serse* (Xerxes, 1738), originally written for the castrato Caffarelli, while two of the other male characters were performed by female mezzo-sopranos, allowing for a confusion of apparent lesbian scenes. Sadly, the music for Handel's opera *Nero* (1704) is lost, although the libretto survives. It includes Handel's only openly gay character, Anicetus. Anicetus is traditionally believed to have killed Agrippina on Nero's behalf and was referred to by the emperor in the libretto as *des Kaysers Mignon oder Liebling* (The emperor's little one, or darling). The historical Nero famously married two men, Pythagoras and Sporus, in legal ceremonies, and Sporus was particularly honoured with permission to wear the regalia worn by the wives of the Caesars.

Richard Strauss (1854–1949) enjoyed exploring the subversion of traditional gender representations as we shall see in his diptych: *Salome* (1905) and *Elektra* (1909). This can also be observed in his next opera, *Der Rosenkavalier* (1909–1910), in which the character, Octavian, is disguised as a woman along the same lines as Cherubino in Mozart's *Le Nozze di Figaro* (1786). Octavian disguises himself as a woman in order to test the fidelity of another man. His role is scored for a mezzo-soprano; however, he is referred to in masculine terms while displaying feminine characteristics. This explains the impetus of Baron Ochs to seduce him. Octavian's gender is undefined, equally credible as either male or female, and representing a genuine example of gender non-binarism.

Also exploring the notion of gender identity was Francis Poulenc (1899–1963) who reversed the gender roles of Thérèse and her husband in *Les Mamelles de Tirésias* (The Breasts of Tiresias, 1945). Although Poulenc's message is ultimately a moral warning of the necessity of procreation, the couple swap clothes and occupational duties – both important gender identifiers in the 1940s. With the husband adopting the role of homemaker, the narrative tests the boundaries of gender stereotypes and serves as a symbol for women's liberation and equal rights. In Act I, scene i, Thérèse sings of her determination to adopt male roles and rejecting assumed duties of motherhood, noting that men have enjoyed such freedom of choice for far too long. Poulenc undermines what he felt were dangerous and selfish sentiments, by providing a despondent underscore, and ultimately the couple happily abandon the experiment in favour of their traditional gender roles.

Wagner's last completed opera *Parsifal* (1882) has been viewed by several observers as a representation of a male, homosexual community, in which women have been rejected. Charles Osborne provided a somewhat acerbic reading of the narrative, stating, 'It is also possible to view Parsifal merely as a sickly, *fin-de-siècle* homoerotic fantasy about a group of knights who allow no woman to invade their realm.'[5] Otto Weininger (1880–1903), author of the book *Geschlecht und Charakter* (Sex and Character),[6] concurred with Plato in *Laws* (c. 356), by rejecting the validity of physical sex between males, but argued that chaste love between men represents the most elevated form of love. The community in *Parsifal* exhibits no physical sexual activity, which ultimately reinforces the homoeroticism of the opera. Nietzsche, a long-time devotee of Wagner, was, however, outraged by the portrayal of sexual abstinence. He called the opera a 'bad work', which preached ideals of chastity which he felt was an incitement to anti-nature and an attempted assassination of basic ethics.[7]

APOLLO AND DIONYSUS

The allegorical nature of the Greek myths and epics provides furtive breeding ground for nurturing queer opera libretti. Not only do Hellenistic tales helpfully include unabashed homosexual content but are also helpful when repressed, conservative society laws and conventions deny overt expressions of queerness, as they have until relatively recently. The historic perspective allows polite, moralistic acknowledgement of queer acceptance under the guise of academic understanding. References to antiquity in relation to queerness provide a veritable nod and a wink to those in the know and as such provide useful material for the practice of coding. David Halperin reminds us that sexuality is a cultural production and that the ongoing ideological discourse is imposed on our physiological capacity.[8] Examining the attitudes to sexuality in antiquity sharpens our modern concept of an individual's sexual behaviour being an expression of their 'sexuality'. Our modern understanding that the manifestation of our 'sexuality' is an expression of our individual identity would have been alien to the ancients who experienced sexual acts as a part of social hierarchy, political standing and Athenian polity.

Queer coding, another modern social construct which would have seemed even more unfamiliar in antiquity, is a fairly recently coined term that has been used out of necessity for centuries in a multitude of artistic forms. Composers have drawn on a range of associative techniques that, while somewhat innocuous to most observers, provide a pointer for individuals familiar with the queer experience. Queer coding is more commonly associated with the cinema and was a useful technique for 1930s film directors wishing to represent queerness in their works while suffering the homophobic Hays Code. Introduced by Republican, William Harrison Hays as a strict set of industry standards, it targeted the portrayal of homosexuals with particular savagery. For decades, actors would, sometimes unknowingly, leave breadcrumbs for queer audiences, often leaving the sanctioning bureaucrats blissfully unaware. The 1995 documentary, *The Celluloid Closet*, directed by Rob Epstein and Jeffrey Friedman, documents the portrayal of queer characters in the Hollywood motion picture industry. Based on the 1981 book, *Homosexuality on the Movies* by Vito Russo, it explores the appalling way in which queer characters were rendered. It also reinforced the practice of codified expressions of queerness, encouraging negative stereotypes and brazenly promoting homophobia.

The Homeric epics and vast majority of major tragedies by Sophocles and Euripides are rich pickings for queers wanting to validate their purpose and practice. The metaphorical use of the two gods, Apollo and Dionysus, is, however, problematic as their specific functions around which cults were formed have been distorted with the advent of Nietzschean constructs. Nietzsche's rejection of opera as a viable, expressive art form is based on his views that the fusion of conceptual and musical ideas results in an unnatural and inartistic experience. He saw opera as involving neither Apollonian and Dionysian elements owing to the conflict for the singer trying at once comprehensible and innately musical. Ironically, it was the fusion of these elements that was thought to revive Greek spectacle at the end of the sixteenth century.

Nietzsche saw the two gods as diametrically opposed. Whereas Apollo represents harmony, progress, clarity, logic and the tenet of individuation, Dionysus represents disorder, intoxication, emotion, ecstasy and unity. The world of mind and order on one side and passion and chaos on the other formed the basis of Greek culture. The Apollonian state of dreaming differs fundamentally from the Dionysian state of inebriation; however, the two states represent the liberations of impulse and elimination of boundaries. For Nietzsche, the combination of Apollonian and Dionysian *Kunsttriebe* (artistic instincts), which Nietzsche called the 'Primordial Unity', forms the dramatic arts and is manifest through frenzied acts that provide an enhanced artistic state.

For queer consumers of opera, the Dionysian qualities of liberation, revolution, excess, ecstasy, dance, sex, orgy, drunkenness, drugs, drama, drag, death and dismemberment offer a particular resonance and through which understanding the queer lifestyle and consciousness can best be achieved. For respectable citizens who revel in order, Dionysus represents terror, but to the disreputable outcast or 'other', he brings inconceivable encouragement. Dionysus is also known as Bacchus, who appeared into Roman culture as an aspect of *Liber* (freedom). Festivals of Bacchanalia, celebrated frequently in Rome, involved omophagic practices of tearing apart live animals and feasting on the flesh to represent the infant death and rebirth of Bacchus. The frenzied feast allowed the god to enter the body of the participant and become one. The Bacchic mysteries were originally restricted to women but were corrupted by an Etruscan-Greek form which invited drunken men and women to shed their inhibitions and enjoy an orgiastic feast.

Bacchus is represented in many operas, including *Bacchus* (1909), by Jules Massenet, and *The Bassarids* (1966), by Hans Werner Henze. Most of the composers to work with Greek tragedy use influences from both Apollo and Dionysus on a relatively equal basis; however, Gluck's *Iphignie en Tauride* (1779) and Tippet's *King Priam* (1962) are particularly Apolline, while Strauss' *Elektra* (1909) and Henze's *The Bassarids* (1966) are distinctly Dionysian. Several operas to deal directly with Apollo include Mozart's *Apollo et Hyacinthus* (1767) and Cavalli's *Gli amori d'Apollo e di Dafne* (1640). Apollo is an attractive figure for queer artists, as he had seven male lovers: Admetus, Branchus, Carnus, Cyparissus, Hyacinth, Hymen and Phorbas of Thessaly. Understanding the heritage of Apollo and Dionysus is important to unlocking the meaning of many representations of eroticism in opera, which for many centuries was obsessed with the Hellenistic traditions.

FEMINIST THEORY TO QUEER THEORY

The development of university gender studies courses followed by queer theory as an academic discipline owes a lot to the foundations of psychology and sexology to the pioneering scholars of feminist theory. Although this book is not specifically focused on feminism, to ignore the importance of the struggle for gender equality would undermine our understanding of the emergence of queer acceptance. Feminist academics developed a framework for understanding gender and sexuality and it is generally considered to have occurred in two waves. The first wave of feminist writers and philosophers included Mary Wollstonecraft (1759–1797), whose *A Vindication of the Rights of Woman* was published in 1792. It focused on the progressive view of gender equality and argued that gender is an artificial social construct. Early feminists sought to address the assignation of roles, responsibilities and respect by authority in daily life.[9] The term 'feminisme' first emerged in 1880s France, spreading throughout Europe in the following decade and making its way to North and South America by the first decade of the twentieth century. Epistemologically, it combines the French word *femme* (woman) and *isme*, referring to a social movement or political ideology.

The second wave, which is associated with the work of Marxist, radical and lesbian feminism, challenged the hegemonic binary of 'normal' male and female characteristics, including physical and behavioural. Women's studies emerged as an academic discipline throughout the Western world which challenged the firmly established patriarchal systems in society. As feminism progressed throughout the twentieth century, it became intertwined with many areas of society, including politics, economics, health, arts, global capitalism, religious fundamentalism and the absence of genuine citizenship rights for many across the globe.[10] An underlying prevailing assumption that gender and sexuality were fundamentally connected and that gender took precedence over sexuality led to an emerging interest in generating a theoretical basis for understanding queerness.[11]

David Halperin discusses the incessant interest in defining and qualifying of the term 'queer' and how queer theorists sometimes inadvertently limit the burgeoning possibilities of queerness to address important issues of intersectionalities such as sexual radicalism and gender fluidity.[12] For many years, the word 'queer' was a derogatory term, causing deep wounds for countless individuals on the receiving end of the slander. It has now been reclaimed and finds its place in the ever-evolving LGBTQI+ acronym despite initial pushback from veteran queers whose memory of the cruel slur had not faded.

When Professor Teresa de Lauretis first introduced the concept of queer theory to the 1990 conference at the University of California, it was deliberatively provocative as the reaction from those present attested. Lauretis sought to challenge the homogenized lens through which gay and lesbian issues were being addressed and to celebrate the diversity of experience as it existed in reality.[13] Ever since, the domination of empirical studies that reductively theorized sexual desire evolved into a somewhat nebulous approach to understanding queerness.

Before anyone really understood what it was or how it worked, queer theory was being embraced by an academic community that appreciated its fundamental ideal of diversity. Not only did it challenge the established ideas of feminist and gay/lesbian identity politics but also provided a credible, academic platform for scholars to discuss diverse and contemporary queer issues. Two texts were written prior to the term 'queer theory' being coined and are widely considered to have provided an important foundation. The first was Eve Kosofsky Sedgwick's *Epistemology of the Closet*,[14] followed by Judith Butler's *Gender Trouble*.[15] Other important writers in the field include Leo Bersani, Sue-Ellen Case, Douglas Crimp, Teresa de Lauretis, Lee Edelman, Michel Foucault, Diana Fuss, Judith Halberstam, David Halperin, Earl Jackson, Biddy Martin, D. A. Miller, Gayle Rubin, Michael Warner, Simon Watney and Monique Wittig.

The early development of queer theory saw an imposed hegemony which labelled any work prior to the arrival of the newly acquired term as anachronistic, and by rejecting identity politics and narrowing the scope of studies, early queer theory operated under a limited interdisciplinary approach. Curiously, queer theory has been normalized and embraced by the straight academic community in a way that lesbian and gay studies failed to gain traction.[16] Such has been the dizzying upward trajectory of enthusiasm for queer theory by our institutions of learning that questions about the readiness of academics to engage with concepts of anti-assimilation, radical politics and fascination with the abnormal and marginalized are being asked of our *episteme*.

The swift rise of queer theory, and the renewed perspective with which sexuality and gender are viewed, has allowed fresh interest in transgender studies as well as challenging previously narrowed perceptions of lesbian and gay identity. Instead, non-normative expressions of gender and sexuality encourage fluidity and a resistance to normativity. Sedgwick argues in her book *Epistemology of the Closet* that the conceptual separations between homo and heterosexuality, as they apply to specific, systemic issues of knowledge and power, are both unhelpful and misguided. Our transhistorical understanding of homosexuality cannot be sharply distinguished from heterosexual history. As a result of these and other transformative ideas, queer theory has provided revisionist historians opportunity to review our collective understandings of the meaning of art works. Many of these new interpretations provide provocative readings, and this is a pillar of the queer theory ideal.

One of the issues surrounding queer theory is that it can be abstracted from the routine lived experience of lesbian and gay individuals in a pursuit of broader application that encompasses generalized notions of queerness. Through the theorization of queerness, the phenomenological nuance of select aspects of the rainbow spectrum can be aligned with the now-antiquated gender studies paradigm despite having considerable importance.

Possibly one of the great strengths of queer theory is the flexibility with which it can be applied to many of the social science disciplines. Previously, academics in fields such as history, classics, anthropology, sociology and religion would apply Deconstruction to their respective discipline by 'queering' them. Queer theory has been used in conjunction with a broad range of topics, one of which is musicology, and in this discipline, much is owed to scholars such as Philip Brett, Susan McClary, Ruth Solie and Elizabeth Wood. The nexus between queer theory and musicology is, of course, what interests me in exploring the rich vein of queer issues found in the growing repertoire of queer opera. In many ways, opera has begun to reflect our evolving concept of what it is to be queer and some of the historical works reflect the dramatic journey that the queer experience has been on.

Feminist theory and queer theory are constructed from the same epistemological framework. They both challenge the perception of gender, sexual/relational and organizational facets of both the individual and society. The two theories are interdependent and share fundamental assumptions. Feminist theory is not anti-male but is focused on concepts of male dominance and masculine attributes such as competitiveness, control, privilege and access. It seeks to disturb the model which attributes males as normal, natural and neutral and females as oppositional, subjected, variant and inferior. Struggling against the rank of second class is a shared basis for both feminist theory and queer theory. Sexual minorities have had to fervently challenge the alpha status of the heteromasculine and associated biases in theory and in practice throughout society, the economy and politically.

There are divergent themes of scholarly discourse between feminist and queer theories. Queer theory has adopted a view that centres on local actions of performative transgression, within which cultural implications largely dominate, whereas feminists aim to address the political and economic concerns from a global perspective. For some writers, the tension between the global versus local perspective on dealing with gender and sexuality has been enough to consider the two theories diametrically opposed. For queers, there are essential, phenomenological features that pervade the discourse such as the experience of being in and coming out of the closet and all of the associated psychological and sociological implications. One such implication is the response to persecution based on sexuality known as 'passing', whereby queers would present themselves in public with convincing traits of a heterosexual. This in turn led to the development of coded forms of behaviour, to allow for interaction without alerting the suspicions of outsiders, and the term 'closet discourse'.[17] Queer theory challenges the artificial, binary categorizations of sexuality and advocates for a more fluid approach to sexual plurality and intersectionality that enhances our understanding of human diversity.

Representations of women and queers in opera have both reflected and informed our understanding of gender and sexuality as it has developed over the last century and a half. Examples of strong, female characters subverting the established patriarchy have produced enduring and popular vehicles for celebrated divas. The 'male gaze', attributed to the male and allowing prolonged scrutiny of the female form in contrast to the expected female behaviour of averting the eyes demurely by looking down, is an example of feminist theory informing operatic representation. Laura Mulvey discusses the phenomenon from a psychoanalytical perspective and argues that it derives from phallocentric behaviours and the 'neurotic needs of the male ego'.[18]

As we shall see, just as queer theory took much longer to emerge, so too did meaningful representation on the operatic stage. Despite the handful of exceptions, which tend to deal with queerness in a codified way, it wasn't until a decade into the twentieth century that complex, non-stereotypical queer characters appeared in significant quantity.

HOUSES OF HOMOSOCIALIZATION

Many opera houses throughout history have garnered a reputation as a meeting place for homosexuals to engage in cultural enlightenment and enjoy the pleasures of fleeting liaisons. In eighteenth-century Germany, venues in which elite social circles orbited were found in opera houses, theatres, aristocratic courts and country retreats. Known as 'Arcadian' academies, those located in Florence and Rome were hives of homosocial activity, and the latter was known colloquially at the time as the 'City of Sodom'. The *Paris Opéra* at the time of Lully was reported to be the first hub of homosexual activity known to Parisians[19] and was replaced as a meeting destination for queers in the late 1970s with the appropriation of the Marais district after migrating from la Butte Montmartre and Pigalle to Saint-Germain-des-Prés, before returning to the right bank, not far from the opera house and around rue Sainte-Anne.[20] Repressed lesbians in the nineteenth century found the opera house to be one of few public spaces that allowed open admiration of other women's bodies. Typically, lesbian opera fans from this period were drawn to the lower female voice of the mezzo-soprano and contralto and the 'trouser' or 'travesty' role.[21] In this way, there is a difference between the way gay men and women experienced opera. For lesbians, it was based primarily on a logical erotic attachment to the performer, but for men, the female diva offered a more tangential connection to queer identity.

Queers have enjoyed an unfair advantage in having access to opera. Unencumbered by the financial and time demands of children, it has been the meeting place for people who have the time and money to spend on such lavish entertainment. Opera houses also offer queers 'a respectable place where gay men can meet and socialize'.[22] Fostering an interest in opera allowed gay men and women into social networks, which consisted largely of upwardly mobile queer socialites. Opera's institutions have provided venues and promenades that were highly regarded for seeing and being seen.[23] They are a transnational nexus of different cultures, class distinctions, ethnicities and sexual identities who gather for the common purpose of fulfilling shared cultural and symbolic needs. This is not to suggest that opera-going represents a great leveller of social and racial disparity. This would be better achieved in the more accessible form of 'ballroom culture' which emerged in the 1970s.[24]

In New York, during World War II, returning American soldiers were provided with accommodation and the means by which they could be entertained. According to Bérubé, 'Male GIs who packed the standing-room section in the Metropolitan Opera House in New York City, which for years had been a gay male cruising mecca, pressed their bodies together several deep against the rail.'[25] In Beijing, during the last century of the Qing dynasty (1644–1911), boys were trained as potential performers in the Beijing Opera in a place called the *tangzi*. The *tangzi* was also a place where men would frequent to enjoy sex with other men and young boys.[26] In London, the Queen's Hall, destroyed during the blitz, was situated at the epicentre of queer subcultures in the heart of the West End. Emerging from theatres in this part of London after a production would provide an environment brimming with the possibility of a homoerotic encounter.[27] When cities like Paris and New York began opening establishments to cater for queer communities, a golden age dawned as they were instantly successful.[28] Paris became the European epicentre for homosexuals to mingle, with artists such as Proust, Colette, Satie, Gide, Diaghilev and Stein, among others, enjoying the growing sense of liberation.

Opera companies can easily lose the goodwill of their queer patrons if they feel unrepresented in a change of direction as The Atlanta Opera discovered in 2007. With the appointment of a fundamental Christian as general director, and a change of venue, it was clear that queers were no longer as welcome as they once were. The former venue, the Fox theatre, while problematic acoustically and with inadequate sight lines, was dripping in history and glamour. It changed location to the Cobb Energy Performing Arts Centre, in the suburban sprawl of eastern Cobb County, a conservative, Republican stronghold which in 2004 voted to ban same-sex marriage and recognition of same-sex marriages. Many of the queer opera devotees chose to make the journey to the Metropolitan Opera, where they could feel entirely welcome in the patrons' lounge.[29]

CODA

The operas included in this book represent a broad range of characters and their variety of queer experiences. In the works written prior to the later part of the twentieth century, the composers and librettist who gave voice to these characters did so under enormous scrutiny and risk of sanction. They persevered and provided countless queer consumers of opera with meaningful opportunities to recognize shared identity and to enter into a world that they could, in part, recognize as a reflection of their own struggles. However, more importantly than finding solace and comfort, queer representation in opera involves agency.

In the 1994 edited volume, *A Night in at the Opera: Media Representations of Opera*, Abel and Palmer observe, 'If gay men often expend erotic energy on opera, we only generate such desire by deflection and sublimation; operatic narrative does not portray our lives.'[30] This statement reflects a time before the trend in queer operas to flourish some sixteen years later but does not fully capture the historical narrative of queer opera or explain the long-standing obsession by queers for it. I argue that opera has always portrayed queerness, but unambiguous expressions are few and far between until the second decade of the twenty-first century. The operas written predominantly from 2010 onwards represent a turning point in queer artistry and one in which all need of codifying representation has been expunged. As such, these works form a part of the queer struggle for space in a crowded market. It is the agency of the unapologetic and the unambiguous, which even Benjamin Britten did not completely embrace, that provides momentum for the queer cause for recognition.

While feminism continues to forge a path in opera and all other art forms, the queer struggle still has much catching up to do. Queer theory is the younger sibling of feminist theory and is approaching adolescence with all of the awkwardness and growing pains of a traumatized teenager. Competing voices in the queer space have divergent views about how the queer community should self-identify and exist in the wider community. In chapter 5, notions of assimilation and acceptance of heteronormative behaviours are embraced by some and repudiated by others. While some have raged for marriage equality and all the benefits it brings, others have repudiated the anachronistic practice completely. José Estaban Muñoz discusses a third way, 'disidentification', whereby a subject neither chooses nor resists dominant ideological ascription.[31] Disidentification seeks to undermine or transform cultural logic from within, creating a change in values that both acknowledges frameworks but challenging the structure. This active approach can be found in many of the operas discussed here; viewpoints are challenged without the need to burn down the house.

Given the long-standing, albeit thorny relationship that queer communities have had with opera for several centuries, it seems that it is finally time for the investment to be acknowledged and for dividends to be yielded. What is being asked for is not a hostile takeover where a sector of the opera-loving community is rejected to make room for the queers but simply recognition, acknowledgement, representation and access. For queers, being unacknowledged in opera is akin to be made to feel like the 'other' in your own home. Without the contribution of countless talented queers who have helped to build and develop opera, the ultra-conservative, narrow view of the human condition would set back the progress of opera to the industrial era. I hope this book serves not only as a celebration of a section of queer history and culture but also as a caution that the story continues to evolve, and queers need to remain an active part of the narrative.

NOTES

1. Susan Sontag, 'Notes on "camp"', *Partisan Review* 31 (1999): 515–530: 529.

2. Rachel Lewis, 'What's queer about musicology now?', *Women and Music: A Journal of Gender and Culture* 13, no. 1 (2009): 43–53.

3. Philip Brett, 'Britten's dream', in *Musicology and Difference*, ed. Ruth A. Solie (Berkeley, CA: University of California Press), 259–280: 259.

4. Selcuk R. Sirin, Donald R. McCreary, and James R. Mahalik, 'Differential reactions to men and women's gender role transgressions: Perceptions of social status, sexual orientation, and value dissimilarity', *The Journal of Men's Studies* 12, no. 2 (2004): 119–132.

5. Charles Osborne, *The Complete Operas of Richard Wagner* (Boston, MA: Da Capo Press, 1993), 271.

6. Otto Weininger, *Geschlecht und Charakter: eine prinzipielle Untersuchung* (Hamburg: Severus Verlag, 2014).

7. Friedrich Nietzsche, *Nietzsche contra Wagner* (Amsterdam: Singel Uitgeverijen, 2012).

8. David Halperin, 'Is there a history of sexuality?', *History and Theory* 28, no. 3 (1989): 257–274.

9. Julie Gedro and Robert C. Mizzi, 'Feminist theory and queer theory: Implications for HRD research and practice', *Advances in Developing Human Resources* 16, no. 4 (2014): 445–456.

10. Susan Moller Okin, 'Gender inequality and cultural differences', *Political Theory* 22, no. 1 (1994): 5–24.

11. Diane Richardson, Janice McLaughlin, and Mark E. Casey, eds., *Intersections between Feminist and Queer Theory* (Basingstoke: Palgrave Macmillan, 2006).

12. David M. Halperin, 'The normalization of queer theory', in *Queer Theory and Communication*, eds. Gust Yep, Karen E. Lovaas, and John P. Elia (Milton Park: Routledge, 2014), 339–343.

13. Cathy J. Cohen, 'Punks, bulldaggers, and welfare queens: Radical potential of queer politics 201', in *Sexual Identities, Queer Politics*, ed. Mark Blasius (Princeton, NJ: Princeton University Press, 2001), 200–228.

14. Eve Kosofsky Sedgwick, *Epistemology of the Closet* (Los Angeles: University of California Press, 1990).

15. Judith Butler, *Gender Trouble* (Milton Park: Routledge, 2002).

16. Steven Seidman, 'Are we all in the closet? Notes toward a sociological and cultural turn in queer theory', in *Matters of Culture: Cultural Sociology in Practice*, eds. Roger Friedland and John Mohr (Cambridge: Cambridge University Press, 2004), 255–269.

17. Alan Stewart, 'The early modern closet discovered', *Representations* 50 (1995): 76–100.

18. Laura Mulvey, ed., 'Visual pleasure and narrative cinema', in *Feminism and Film Theory* (Milton Park: Routledge, 1988), 57–68: 68.

19. Stéphane Leroy, 'Gay Paris: Elements for a geography of homosexuality', *Annales de Géographie* 646, no. 6 (Paris: Armand Colin, 2005): 579–601.

20. Scott Gunther, 'The indifferent ghetto', *Harvard Gay and Lesbian Review* 6, no. 1 (1999): 34–36.

21. Paul Robinson, 'The opera queen: A voice from the closet', *Cambridge Opera Journal* 6, no. 3 (1994): 283–291.

22. Michael Bronski, *Culture Clash: The Making of Gay Sensibility* (Boston, MA: South End Press, 1984), 135.

23. Vlado Kotnik, 'The adaptability of opera: When different social agents come to common ground', *International Review of the Aesthetics and Sociology of Music* 44, no. 2 (2013): 303–342.

24. Malcolm Rio, 'Architecture is burning: An urbanism of queer kinship in ballroom culture', *Thresholds* 48 (2020): 122–132.

25. Allan Bérubé, *Coming Out Under Fire: The History of Gay Men and Women in World War II* (Chapel Hill, NC: University of North Carolina Press, 2010), 109.

26. Shu-yi Yao, 'Tangzi: A gay sex brothel and opera training ground during the late qing' (Beijing: Chinese Academy of Social Science, 2004), 3.

27. Fraser Riddell, 'Queer music in the queen's hall: Teleny and decadent musical geographies at the Fin de Siècle', *Journal of Victorian Culture* 25, no. 4 (2020): 593–608.

28. Leroy, 'Gay Paris', 579–601.

29. Alan Deutschman, 'Cobb Canto: Sex, money, politics and acoustics – The Atlanta Opera's historic move to Cobb County is about more than mileage' (Atlanta, September 2007), 144–145 + 168–175.

30. Sam Abel and Craig B. Palmer, 'Disappearing acts: Opera, cinema', in *A Night in at the Opera: Media Representations of Opera*, ed. Jeremy Tambling (London: John Libbey & Co., 1994), 169–194: 172.

31. José Esteban Muñoz, *Disidentifications: Queers of Color and the Performance of Politics*, Vol. 2 (Minneapolis: University of Minnesota Press, 1999), 8.

Chapter 1

Antiquity

Being a queer figure in ancient Greek mythology was not necessarily one of unadulterated happiness. They enjoyed their share of passion, but jealousy and death were also repeated motifs in the stories of mythical homosexuals, and their love stories rarely ended well. Zephyrus, the god of wind, became insanely jealous of Apollo's beloved Hyacinth and diverted a discuss which struck the young man, killing him and consequently propagating the first flower of the same name from his blood. Hyacinth was also desired sexually by the mortal man, Thamyris, reportedly the first man to have loved another man, according to the Bibliotheca of Pseudo-Apollodorus.[1] Another less-than-cheery tale involves the protagonist found in the formation of opera. Orpheus is well known for his disastrous attempt to retrieve Eurydice from the underworld; however, what is frequently neglected is his decision to give up on women entirely and address his erotic desire to young men. His conversion to homosexuality upset the god Dionysus, who was so infuriated at his rejection of women that he directed them to tear apart his body, dismembering it and throwing his head into the nearby Hebrus river as he continued to sing, even in death. Even Heracles (Hercules in the Roman form), the strongest man in the Hellenistic world, could not protect his homosexual lover, Hylas, who was drowned in a pool by a group of nymphs. Heracles' grief was so profound that he abandoned the quest for the Golden Fleece which he had undertaken with Jason and the other Argonauts. Heracles' other lovers were no better off: Sostratus died young, and Adberus was eaten by man-eating horses.[2]

But rather than strong advocates for queerness, the Greeks seemed ambivalent about same-sex attraction. Such ambivalence was particularly notable when it came to women. Male same-sex unions enjoyed more recognition than women in part because of the greater freedoms they were given.

Lesbianism was not even explicitly defined as a sexuality or category by many of the authors of our extant sources.[3] For example, the philopterid Plato was fickle when it came to his ideas on same-sex love. Initially, he regarded same-sex couples as representing the zenith of idealized relationship structures. In Plato's work *The Symposium* (c. 385–370 BC), the comedic playwright Aristophanes proposed a vision of homosexuality,[4] which was akin to a companionate relationship in which couples have equal status and complete each other through their love. This did not reflect the lived experience of ancient Athenians. Plato's subsequent writings, such as *Laws*, seemed to become contemptuous of homosexual unions, considering them to be unnatural and improper, 'Will not all men censure as womanly him who imitates the woman? . . . at least we may abolish altogether the connection of men with men.'[5] The Greeks gradually sought to regulate all forms of love, imposing increasingly conservative morals throughout the centuries, highlighting the idea that a utopian society in which homosexuality was fully embraced in all its forms is more of an idealized myth than anything based on reality.

In the nineteenth century, when Oscar Wilde launched into his famous 'Love that dare not speak its name' oration in his own defence during his 1895 criminal trial, he tapped into a nostalgic reverence for a time and place free from homosexual intolerance. The infamous phrase, which derived from the poetry of his lover, Lord Alfred Douglas, was assumed to be a coded reference to indecent passions, and Wilde's response has become a much-revered and oft-quoted passage for queer theorists:

> The love that dare not speak its name in this century is such a great affection of an elder for a younger man as there was between David and Jonathan, such as Plato made the very basis of his philosophy, and such as you find in the sonnets of Michelangelo and Shakespeare. It is that deep, spiritual affection that is as pure as it is perfect. . . . It is beautiful, it is fine, it is the noblest form of affection. There is nothing unnatural about it. It is intellectual, and it repeatedly exists between an elder and a younger man, when the elder man has intellect, and the younger man has all the joy, hope and glamour of life before him. That it should be so the world does not understand. The world mocks it and sometimes puts one in the pillory for it.[6]

Wilde references characters from a time and place which he considers a queer utopia. His idealized vision is, for all its eloquence, of course, a fantasy. This does not mean that his thinking is completely flawed, however; his ideas are simply something we are continually aiming to achieve, rather than a period from ancient history to which we are trying to return.

Each of the seven operas in this chapter explores different manifestations of the queer experience in divergent ways and, with more than 330 years separating their dates of composition, reflects very different expectations of

acceptable theatre practice. They are presented in their chronology of composition. Charpentier's *David et Jonathas*, one of only two queer biblical
stories in this book, explores the nexus of a society informed by a strictly
anti-homosexual moral code, with the presentation of a homoerotic story
performed by an all-male cast of adolescent boys. Gluck's *Iphigénie en Tauride* discusses the Greek view of *ephebophilic* and *pederastic* relationships
with notions of the *erastai* and *eromenoi* pairings in relation to Achilles and
Patroclus. Leroux's *Astarté* represented visually on the cover with a picture
of Francisque Delmas (1861–1933) playing the cross-dressing role of Phur
offers a rare account of a Sapphic community during antiquity, with a focus
on the use of exoticism from the French colonial period to the belle époque.
Young Caesar by Lou Harrison also utilizes the exotic influences of the East
by making a distinction between the two cultural-geographical settings of
Rome and Bithynia, the latter being associated with greater acceptance of
sexual fluidity. Rufus Wainwright's *Hadrian* looks at the nexus of love and
politics through the relationship of the Roman emperor Hadrian (AD 76–138)
and his lover Antinous (c. AD 111–130). *Pleasure* by Mark Simpson takes
the Greek myth of Hephaistos (Hephaestus in the Roman form) and recreates
the narrative of rejection and acceptance within the context of a gay nightclub
somewhere in northern England. Finishing with Kye Marshall's opera, *Pomegranate*, we follow two teenagers, Suli and Cassia, who are being prepared
through ritual for initiation into the Dionysian Mysteries and re-emerge in
Toronto in 1984. It explores the pressures of a disapproving family and societal hegemony on a doomed love.

DAVID ET JONATHAS, MARC-ANTOINE CHARPENTIER

For queer individuals who have been emotionally damaged by the failure of
the church to appropriately acknowledge same-sex attraction, the story of
David and Jonathan from the book of Samuel provides some support. People
who want to celebrate their queer identity while concurrently affirming their
faith risk repudiation from organized religious institutions, which brings
into sharp focus a mountain of moral contradictions. Accounts of David and
Jonathan from the Hebrew scripture chronicle a love story of two men, their
souls bound to one another by oath. Their relationship is presented as homosocial, rather than anything explicitly sexual.[7] The book of Samuel states,
'The soul of Jonathan was knit to the soul of David, and Jonathan loved
him as himself.'[8] When mourning the death of Jonathan, David says, 'Your
love to me was more wonderful than the love of women.'[9] These texts offer
a meaningful connection with biblical proof of ecclesiastical affirmation of
same-sex unions.

David represents the biblical equivalent of Orpheus, a singer whose long lament over the death of Jonathan has inspired numerous musical settings. The two met when David, a young shepherd, famously slew Goliath during the standoff between the Philistine army and the army led by King Saul. Still clutching the Philistine giant's severed head, David is brought to King Saul and his eldest son, Jonathan. Jonathan was instantly drawn to David, and it was then that they affirmed their covenant. Scholars have estimated that David was around eighteen at the time of their meeting and Jonathan ten years older. Jonathan removes his clothing and gives it to David on one of the first erotically charged moments of their relationship. David married many women, including Jonathan's sister, Michal; however, there is no mention of his love for her or any of the others as there is with Jonathan. David was seriously rebuked by Nathan the prophet for killing Uriah the Hittite and consequently ordered the death of David's newborn son. In retribution, David gathered an army and sacked all of the Ammonite villages before returning to Jerusalem.

Saul's relationship with David is characterized by petty jealousy. As well as a skilled musician, David, a member of Saul's house, demonstrated that he was a more effective warrior than Saul by a factor of ten. Upon forming an instant connection with Jonathan, who recognized David as God's next anointed king, he ascended to the throne in accordance with God's will. Saul's hatred for David grew and ultimately led to David's defection to the Philistines and a pledge to King Achis. Rather than dwelling on the political intrigue, the plot provides maximum opportunity for spectacle such as dances, the emotional rendering of David and Jonathan's relationship and their respective personal ambitions.

Around twenty-seven centuries later, the boys at the Jesuit *Collège de Clermont* in Paris (now known as *Lycée Louis-le-Grand*) were busily preparing for a performance. The work brought together a five-act play, entitled *Saül*, created by Father François Bretonneau, which was interspersed with operatic material by Marc-Antoine Charpentier (1643–1704). The title of the combined work was *David et Jonathas*. Charpentier was finally able to write and produce operas following the death of Jean-Baptiste Lully (1632–1687), who had until this moment held an iron grip on his opera *privilege*, giving him exclusive rights to all opera production throughout France. The *Collège de Clermont*, an institution attended by children of Parisian aristocracy, had managed to produce four other operas between 1684 and1688 – *Eustache*, *Démétrius*, *Jephté* and *Celse martyr* – and it is likely that a request was made to the king, who expressed support for the Jesuits. The Jesuits and the French nobility were closely connected, even at times of friction between the king and Rome, and his public support for the order was demonstrated further when he declared the *Collège de Clermont* as a royal foundation in 1682.

The *Collège* had become an important training ground for children of wealthy and prominent families at court, and they were taught eloquence, important attributes for Louis' court. As the burgeoning new Italian art form known as opera was growing in popularity in France, associated skills became an important component of a fashionable aristocratic adolescent.[10] According to DuPont-Ferrier, the demographics of the boys at the college ranged from thirteen to twenty in 1677 and twelve to twenty in 1692, the only years the data was recorded. As parts of French society still adhered to the Hellenic model of *erastai* (older, dominant men) and *eromenoi* (younger, passive boys), Charpentier cast David as a tenor and Jonathan as a treble (unbroken voice). This may, of course, have been a matter of casting practicality. David's high tessitura has certainly provided casting difficulties in more recent productions. Finding boys who can sing the character's demanding material is challenging, but even if one could be found, when viewed through a contemporary lens, phrases such as 'Despite the harshness of my fate, at least I can still tell you that I love you'[11] are contextually confrontational between a prepubescent boy and an older man. However, this would have been the case at the *Collège de Clermont*, where the appearance of females on stage was strictly forbidden. In a 2022 production staged in the Royal Chapel at Versailles, one reviewer wrote, 'Caroline Arnaud embodies a Jonathan with a clear voice, evoking childhood.'[12] The risk aversion with which experienced sopranos are cast over young boys disallows audiences to experience the effect of Charpentier's original casting of two male lovers.

Charpentier and Bretonneau would both have been well aware that in seventeenth-century France, sexual acts between same-sex partners were punishable by death.[13] The Jesuits themselves upheld a strict moral position about such depravity transferred to their theatre. However, despite the official enmity towards homosexuality as enshrined in law and church policy, the reality of courtly life suggested a conversely liberal attitude. Although King Louis was reported to exclaim inconceivable horror for the pleasures of sodomy in his court, it was the one matter he chose not to confront. Louis' brother, Philippe d'Orléans, was a vigorous pursuer of men, and because of his heightened status, he and other courtiers not only regarded themselves as immune from punishment but also spoke openly about their pleasures. The prince's vice was something his wife, the Duchess d'Orléans, was expected to tolerate.

David et Jonathas drew heavy criticism on the basis of a lack of *galantrie*, meaning courtliness or politeness, and morality. It was, however, an ideal choice for the boys, as the absence of any female characters avoided the difficult quandary regarding cross-dressing. The cast consisted entirely of men and boys, conforming to the Jesuit rules that excluded women from stage work.[14] When female characters were eventually introduced to Jesuit operas, they were played by schoolboys *en travesti.*

The term 'faithful' reoccurs throughout the libretto. The Bible uses the word 'faithful' to describe the Hebrews in a variety of contexts – faith to the king, faith to a lover, faith to a friend and faith to God. The use of the term in figure 1.1 provides an ambiguity as it could represent all of the above, depending on the chosen interpretation. In his aria in Act I, scene iii, David sings:

Jonathas tant de fois me vit renouveller	*Jonathan has seen me renew many times*
Mille sermens dune amour mutuelle:	*A thousand vows of mutual love:*
Helas il fut toujoûrs Fidelle,	*Alas, he was always faithful;*
Moi seul je puis les violer!	*I, only, I, can violate them.*[15]

Figure 1.1 demonstrates one example of Bretonneau's unreserved choice of language in revealing the intense relationship between the two men. The arrangement of vows, mutual love and the term 'faithful' could easily be interpreted as concerning a marriage. Audiences at the *College* may have understood the strong suggestion of a formal, homosexual union, but ambiguity prevents the libretto from offending Jesuit sensibilities. Jonathan's covenant that takes place before the opera begins includes a pledge of loyalty to the house of David, the anointed king of Israel, and therefore to God. Faithfulness in the context of *David et Jonathas* can conveniently be read according to the perspective of the observer.

In Act II, the *chaconne* celebrates the reuniting of David and Jonathan after David returns from war with the Philistines, and its function has

Figure 1.1 David's Aria, Act I, Scene iii, pp. 47–48. Marc-Antoine Charpentier and François de Paule Bretonneau, *David et Jonathas* [Full score, Urtext version] Nicolas Sceaux (Ed.) (1688). Copyright © 2008–2011, Nicolas Sceaux.

erotic implications. In Lully's *tragedies*, the *chaconne* or *passacailles* typically celebrate marriage and restoration of order. The two exceptions are Lully's first and last operas, *Cadmus et Hermione* (1673) and *Armide* (1686), which are more seductive than celebratory. In *David et Jonathas*, a chorus of shepherds interject with, '*venez, venez tous avec nous joüir des plaisirs les plus doux*' (come, come all with us, to enjoy the sweetest of pleasures). The connection between sweet pleasures and seduction is a common metaphor in the madrigal repertoire of this period, but the word '*joüir*' can actually suggest orgasm. Furetière's *Dictionnaire* offers an alternative definition, 'to have the carnal company of a woman'. Curiously, when *David et Jonathas* was revived in 1706, this particular passage was the only major section of text to be removed, suggesting that the Jesuits found it improper.

In addition to the homoeroticism of the two title characters, the audience was equally shocked by the presentation of Jonathan's death onstage. It was customary for such a moment to occur offstage and to be referenced by dialogue so that the audience was aware of what had transpired. However, Bretonneau embraced the dramatic spectacle of the *tragédie en musique*, with Jonathan dying in David's arms eliciting greater sympathy than Aristotle's theoretical alternative for an offstage death. David's lament of Jonathan in Act III demonstrates the depth of grief he felt for his partner.

DAVID	DAVID
Quoi, je vous perds!	What? I'm losing you!
JONATHAS	JONATHAN
Le jour que je revoi,	The day that I see again
Si je ne retrouvois un Ami si Fidelle,	If I never find a friend so faithful
Seroit en cor plus funeste pour moi.	Would be still more fatal for me.
DAVID	DAVID
Ah! vivez.	Ah! Live!
JONATHAS	JONATHAN
Je ne puis.	I cannot.
DAVID	DAVID
David, David luîmes-me	David, David himself
Va céder aux transports d'une douleur extrême.	Is lost to the transports of an extreme agony.
JONATHAS	JONATHAN
Malgré la rigueur de mon sort,	Despite the rigors of my fate,
Du moins je puis vous dire en cor que je vous aime.	At least I can tell you once more that I love you.
DAVID	DAVID
Ciel! il est mort	Heaven! He's dead.[16]

The story of David and Jonathan provides a transhistorical touchstone for gay identity, claiming space and refuting any argument that queerness is a modern concept in opera. Whether David and Jonathan are viewed as close friends or lovers is a question that scholars have opined about through a range of social and historical discourses. Homo and heterosexual readings of the text both provide valid assessments. References between the characters to attractive, personal physical qualities certainly allow interpretations of 'plutonic' to be extended to 'Platonic' love. If the nature of their relationship was indeed sexual, they provide an anchor for queer identity and an affirmation of theological representation. The diversity of possible interpretations of the relationship of the title characters only enhances its importance in the opera. Regardless of whether their partnership is seen as homosocial or homosexual, its replacement for gallant love is undeniable, and the conflict between love and duty is an essential ingredient for a *tragédie en musique*.

The surfeit amount of historical-theological discourse that exists on the 'were they / weren't they' question marks a stark contrast to the equivalent discussion surrounding Jonathan and David's Greek mythology counterparts (Achilles and Patroclus, Orestes and Pylades, Ameinias and Narcissus, Ganymede and Jupiter and Apollo and his four lovers: Admetus, Adonis, Branchus and Carnus). Certainly, the nature of these Hellenistic partnerships has enjoyed critical analysis, but the transition from myth to biblical character jettisoned Jonathan and David into an orbit of defensive, theological debate that reflects Christianity's difficulty with celebrating universal love. The Bible contains no form of wedding vows, and so the same-sex vows between David and Jonathan, and for that matter, Ruth and Naomi, stand as legitimate biblical models. The tired rhetoric that champions only a plutonic relationship between the two on the basis that, historically, the conservatively religious society would have aggressively repudiated anti-scriptural relations is flawed. It fails to take into account the long list of historical queer people who have flouted dogmatic views imposed by the establishment and proceeded, albeit cautiously in many cases, to embrace love on its own terms.

IPHIGÉNIE EN TAURIDE, CHRISTOPH WILLIBALD GLUCK

Representations of same-sex relationships in ancient Greek art are plentiful. From depictions on vases, reliefs, sculpture, poetry and drama, a myriad of homoerotic depictions has led to countless historians providing views on the enlightened ideals of Hellenic society. The functions of same-sex behaviours for Greek men were a complex and evolving phenomenon. Frequently, boys would enter into manhood via experiences of pederasty encouraged through education, allowing full participation in the *polis*. The proliferation of artistic rendering of the pederastic relationship led to a movement known as the Greek 'miracle'. These relationships were far more than purely physical exchanges but were meaningful components of societies' functions. Although the Greeks were not the first society to allow homosexual interactions, their celebration of such relationships was profuse. From around 630 BC, notions of pederasty in Greek art and literature were endemic, and Greek poets produced copious works that included explicit homoeroticism. The Grecian stage was the exclusive domain of men, a tradition surviving in some societies into the twentieth century, and it can be argued that the Greeks invented drag.[17]

Homer's account of the love between Achilles and Patroclus does not include explicit acts of pederasty; however, this does not suggest that various types of homosexual love were not frequently expressed. There are certainly lengthy passages describing their passionate love, however comradely it might also have been. This relationship draws parallels with Gilgamesh and Enkidu, and David and Jonathan (discussed earlier), and represents honourable pairings of *erastai* (older, dominant men) and *eromenoi* (younger, passive boys). Ganymede, whom Homer described as the most beautiful of the mortals, appears in book twenty of the Iliad. He marks an exception for Homer, whose depictions of same-sex unions tended to be *ephebophilic* (attractions to young men), rather than *pederastic* (attractions to teenagers). Homer's unrestrained adoration of the beauty of the male form is possible because of several important traits of Greek Society. As well as a general lack of religious guilt and no moral or legal condemnation of intimacy between males, athletic nudity, all-male symposia and regulations that encouraged delayed marriage all contributed to a civilization that was largely gay friendly.

The policy of delayed marriage was part of a social revolution that occurred on Crete around 630 BC. Due to the scarcity of productive land on the island and the rapidly expanding upper class, marriage was postponed until thirty and pederasty customarily introduced to limit childbirth. Also, at this time, Spartans instituted the *gymnopaidiai*, a festival in which young boys would dance naked. It is from the term for naked (*gymnos*) that many of our expressions for athletic endeavours derive. Spartans considered the active coupling of unmarried adult males with teenage boys, to stimulate homosexuality, useful in the development of military training. They believed that these unions were an effective tool for educating (*paideia*) future upper-class men and encouraging creativity and self-development. A young man of around eighteen to twenty years old was known as an *ephebe*, a time of growing facial or body hair and thereby past the age of pederastic attraction. Patroclus and Achilles, and Paris and Hector were all still in their youth (*hebe*) at the time of death in Homer's Iliad. From 630 BC, the only one of the major Gods not to enjoy a pederastic affair was Ares. Heroes like Hector, who was in love with Andromache, and also Paris, found their proclivities to be depicted as bisexual in myths and epics written after this time and even into the Roman period.[18]

Gluck's opera *Iphigénie en Tauride* (1779) is based on the play by Euripide, written between 414 and 412 BC. The island of Tauris, from the title, is not mentioned in Euripide's play, and the correct translation should be *Iphigenia among the Taurians*. A mistranslation by Goethe for his play *Iphigenie auf Tauris* (1779), on which Nicolas-François Guillard (1752–1814) based his libretto for Gluck's opera, has led to a belief that it refers to the Crimean Peninsula (*ancient Taurikē*). King Agamemnon has gathered a collection of Greek armies for the Trojan War, but the goddess Diana thwarts their efforts to sail by sending adverse winds. In order to appease the goddess, Agamemnon is advised by the oracle to sacrifice his daughter Iphigenia (Iphigénie) on the altar. Euripides supposes that unbeknownst to her family, Diana saved Iphigénie, sending her to Tauride to serve the enemy Scythians as Diana's high priestesses.

Iphigénie dreams that she murders her brother, Orestes, as well as the deaths of her parents, Agamemnon and Clytemnestra. Two strangers arrive at the island following a fierce storm: Orestes and his companion, Pylades. Thaos, the king of Scythia, demands a sacrifice to appease the gods. Shackled, imprisoned and awaiting execution, the two men are forced to decide who shall live and who shall die. It is an impossible decision, and throughout the second act, it becomes clear that the deep love that binds them makes both men determined to sacrifice himself so the other may live. Following an intervention from Iphigénie, who does not immediately recognize her brother, Pylades agrees to leave the island, to return with a rescue party. He does so in the fourth and final act, killing King Thaos.

Gluck's opera is almost unique by the lack of heteronormative romantic relationship. Although various forms of love are manifest throughout the narrative – brother and sister, priestesses and Diana and even captor and captive – it is the profound and intense love between the two central male characters that is central to the story. Euripides, who had two disastrous marriages, both of which to unfaithful women, wrote few romantic dramas, preferring tragedies. When he was over seventy, Euripides is said to have become attracted to the effeminate poet and playwright, Agathon, whose boyish beauty he widely acclaimed.[19]

During the interaction between Orestes and Pylades in Act II, their love is expressed beyond physical attraction. Orestes sings, '*Je n'avais qu'un ami, je deviens son bourreau!*'[20] (I only had one friend, I became his executioner!). With Orestes indication towards the end of the recitative that he only has one friend, Pylades represents not just one of many casual friends but his whole world. It is clear that the concept of being responsible for his demise is distressing. He also confirms that he was responsible for the death of his mother, Clytemnestra. In the dramatic aria that follows, he sings, '*J'ai trahi l'amitié, j'ai trahi la nature*'[21] (I betrayed friendship, I betrayed nature). The first part of this phrase recognizes that the act of betrayal is reflected in the nature of their friendship. He suggests a depth of loyalty and possibly faithfulness. The second part of the phrase provides conjecture. By nature, he could be referring to the murder of his mother, of which he sang in the recitative. Alternatively, the reference, being linked to the first part of the phrase, his friendship with Pylades, could have implications for the possible sexual nature of their partnership. The phrase 'j'ai trahi la nature' resonates with Montesquieu's title for his chapter concerning sodomy in Book VII, chapter vi of *De l'esprit des lois* (1758) – '*Du Crime Contre Nature*' (The Crime Against Nature).[22]

The phrase, situated in the B section of the aria, after a flurry of string passages, is over quickly, allowing little time for reflection. Orestes is allowing his thoughts on his predicament to be expressed fleetingly and without filter. Pylades immediate response in his recitative is '*Quel langage accablant pour un ami qui t'aime*'[23] (What overwhelming language for a friend who loves you!). Pylade's opening phrase clarifies two things; the first being that the language used by Orestes is overly dramatic. Oreste's self-flagellation over their miserable fate is not warranted, and Pylades is not concerned with applying blame. Secondly, the expression of love at the end of the phrase confirms the mutual feelings between the two men. He reminds Orestes of his love, to provide comfort and reassurance. This marks the ongoing characteristic of the second act, in which both men place their love for each other over their own fatality.

Linguistically, the word '*ami*' (friend) provides opportunity for interpretation, as the concept of friendship had various meanings in the 1700s. Close male friendship was synonymous with the possibility of homoerotic desire, a concept with which contemporary French and German authors were familiar. One of the most comprehensive philosophical writings on same-sex relationships in ancient Greece is *Betrachtungen über die Männerliebe der Griechen* (A Tract Concerning Greek 'Love-Between-Men') which Christoph Meiners included in his 1775 book, *Vermischte philosophische Schriften* (Various philosophical writings).[24] Meiners points out that eroticized friendships were customary among the Greeks and uses Orestes and Pylades as the classic exemplar.

To confirm his steadfast loyalty, he sings these two lines at the conclusion of his recitative: '*Je ne suis pas si miserable, Puis qu'enfin je meurs près de toi!*'[25] (I'm not so miserable, Since finally I die near you!). The opportunity to spend eternity together makes the concept of death not just bearable but also appealing. Gluck's recitatives are notably concise in *Iphigénie en Tauride* and consistently *récitatif accompagné*.

His following aria bears uncanny similarity with '*Che Faro senza Euridice*', from Gluck's earlier work, *Orfeo et Euridice* (1762). Pylades begins with the phrases: '*Unis dès la plus tendre enfance, Nous n'avions qu'un même désir*'[26] (United from early childhood, We had only one desire, figure 1.2).

As well as providing some backstory about their relationship stretching back into childhood (*hebe*), Pylades reveals that their commitment to each other from an early age was lifelong. The language used between the two characters correlates highly with many romantic, heterosexual relationships found throughout the operatic repertoire. They do not explicitly discuss their physical attraction, because it is unnecessary for them to do so. As reflected in so many epics and myths from the ancient Grecian world, the bond between Oresto and Pylades is commonplace. Their attraction is not part of the rite of passage ideas, associated with *erastai* and *eromenoi*, but a partnership with both men on equal footing; they are comrades and lovers equally.

A fascinating example of such homosexual relationships can be found in a group known as the 'sacred band of Thebes', a select group of soldiers consisting of 150 pairs of male lovers who formed the elite guard in the fourth century BC. Second-century Greek author Polyaenus described the army as men, 'devoted to each other by mutual obligations of love'.[27] Denis Diderot's *Encyclopédie, ou dictionnaire raisonné des sciences, des arts et des métiers* (1751–1766) defined the term 'fraternity in arms' as 'the association between two knights for a noble enterprise . . . they pledge to each other to share both the labors and glory, dangers and profit, and not to abandon each other as long as they have need of one another'.[28] Plato described the lover as a 'friend inspired by God'. Around 1590, pederasty was viewed more critically, and homosexual pairings between similarly aged men were increasingly favoured.[29]

Later in Act III, scene iii, after being separated, the two men are reunited prior to what they believed would be their sacrificial death. Orestes runs to Pylades and sings, *Ô joie inattendue! Je puis donne t'embrasser pour la dernière fois!*'[30] (O unexpected joy! So I can kiss you for the last time!). Pylades responds, '*Mon sort est moins affreux puis que je te revois*'[31] (My fate is less dreadful, since I see you again!). Nowhere in the narrative is a reason given for why it would be necessary to separate Pylades and Oreste. The

Figure 1.2 Pylade's Aria in Act II, Scene i, pp. 79–80. Christophe Willibald Gluck and Nicolas-Françcois Guillard, *Iphigénie en Tauride*, Paris: Des Lauriers, 1780. Public Domain.

Minister nebulously mentions 'laws' and 'our gods', but given that Pylades and Oreste were already imprisoned at the beginning of this act, it is unlikely that a law existed on Tauris that prevented male prisoners from being imprisoned together. Perhaps this is a reminder of the constant intrusion of societal values on homosexual relations. Alternatively, the audience could be left to imagine a more plausible explanation for their physical separation.

A 1997 production by Glimmerglass Opera in Cooperstown, New York, portrayed the two lovers as 'classically beautiful, passionately bonded Greek friends who spend a great deal of stage time stripped down to loincloths and chained together'. Artistic director Paul Kellogg explained that the unabashed exposure of the male body and homoeroticism of their relationship were unsettling for some members of the audience. Upon being cast, the two singers were given instructions to begin working out in the gym. The alternative, with a more traditional production, and in a way that many associate with Gluck, is to have the two men fully clothed and singing stock phrases from opposing sides of the stage. In this production, the singers were required to be as unashamed of their near-nudity as the ancient Greeks were of physically expressing love, and the meaning of the text was more viscerally communicated.[32]

The portrayal of women in the opera is worthy of discussion. Gluck had previously written another opera featuring Iphigénie, *Iphigénie en Aulide* (1774), which concerns her father King Agamemnon's attempts to kill her. Both works represent the capacity of the mob to normalize extreme violence through ritual and importantly for women to internalize it. In *Aulide*, Agamemnon is constantly reminded by the Greek people that the future of his rule rests on him sending his ships to fight the Trojan enemy. Iphigénie becomes convinced that her sacrifice, as suggested by the oracle, will bring about a successful campaign. In *Tauride*, the chorus is divided by gender, and the Scythian insistence of ritual sacrifice is a story of women being forced to kill people. The adherence to the barbarous acts is seemingly broken by the purity expressed by the two male lovers, and Iphigénie and the priestesses seem to awaken from a dream with the appearance of Diana. Oreste's sins of matricide are forgiven, and the chorus unites in shared feelings of peace:

Les Dieux, longtemps en courroux,	The Gods, long in anger,
Ont accompli leurs oracle;	Have fulfilled their oracle;
Ne redoutons plus d'obstacles,	Let's no longer fear obstacles,
Un jour plus pur luit sur nous!	A purer day shines on us!
Une paix douce et profonde	A soft and deep peace
Réigne sur le sein de l'onde	Reign on the bosom of the wave
La mer, la terre et les cieux,	The sea, the earth and the heavens,
Tout favorise nos voeux.[33]	Everything favors our wishes.

Importantly, the Chorus of Greeks and the Chorus of Priestesses sing of the purification of the region in the name of Pylades and Oreste. Guillard chose to have the chorus sing about purification in the name of the two male lovers and not in the name of Oreste and Iphigénie. The names of Pylades and Oreste are united in the minds of both their fellow Greeks and the Tauri priestesses to the extent that they are honoured as a pair.

Since its establishment by Jean-Baptiste Lully, The Paris Opéra had been a known nucleus of homoerotic activity. Lully, who famously enjoyed the beds of young men as well as women, was well aware of the proclivities of his social circles. Gluck wrote his operas exclusively for the Paris Opéra, a hotbed for Parisian queers of all persuasions. By the 1700s, the French court acknowledged the Opéra as a venue where homosexual encounters were occurring with impunity. Merrick explains, 'Sodomy seemed both more widespread and less dangerous by the time of Louis XV than it had during the reigns of his Bourbon predecessors.'[34] Gluck and Guillard likely wanted their *Iphigénie en Tauride* to appeal to the queer subculture of Paris, which is manifest in their treatment of Oreste and Pylades' relationship. Furthermore, Gluck made use of characters known for their homosexual tendencies in each opera he created for Paris, such as Orpheus in *Orphée et Eurydice* (1762), Hercules in his revision of *Alceste* (1767) and Narcissus in *Echo et Narcisse* (1779).

While French police attempted to keep homosexual activity under some form of control, the lieutenant general of police in 1775, Jean-Charles-Pierre Lenoir, claimed that in 1725, police had estimated there to be around 20,000 'sodomites' in Paris, but that in 1775 he estimated an increase to around 40,000. This would have represented around 20 per cent of the male population of Paris.[35]

Consequently, when Gluck was invited by the Paris Opéra to set an adaptation of Guimond La Touche's homoerotic play, *Iphigénie en Tauride* (1757), he and Guillard unsurprisingly made no attempt to obfuscate the nature of Pylades and Orestes' relationship but rather venerated it. Nevertheless, Gluck and Guillard understood that Pylades could not admit that he loves Orestes on the public stage of the Opéra, no matter how churlish it seems for him not to respond appropriately. Homoeroticism could only be insinuated but never explicitly asserted. The Parisian audiences interpreted the drama as they chose. The relationship of Pylades and Oreste could be seen as respectable, plutonic companions by conservative opera devotees, but for the aristocratic Parisian male with queer appetites, Gluck and Guillard's romantic tale of mythological male partnership acclaimed the possibilities of the Hellenistic ideal of love between homosexual men.

ASTARTÉ, XAVIER LEROUX

Composed in 1901, Xavier Leroux's second opera *Astarté* is a product of the fin de siècle period and is an example of several important traits found in operas from this time. European art works in the fin de siècle period are characterized by several qualities – *ennui, cynicism* and *pessimism* and a general belief that civilization leads to decadence. As the twilight years of the nineteenth century made way for the geopolitical, new world of the technological twentieth century, a widespread repudiation of the materialism of an increasingly bourgeois society marked the political landscape. Supporters of the fin de siècle movement, which originated in France but spread throughout the continent, embraced a return to emotionalism, irrationalism, subjectivism and vitalism. The fin de siècle coincided with the belle époque, which emerged from the 1880s and remained as a period of peace, relative optimism, economic prosperity and technological and cultural innovations. The apparent diametrical opposition of these two periods created an unusual melting pot, in which French artists developed an intense cultural awareness that produced a period of decadence and fascination with symbolism.

The symbolist movement in French art, another aesthetic development in the late part of the nineteenth century, was a reaction against realism and naturalism and forms a central part of the narrative of *Astarté*. It promoted the 'dream state' while also elevating the reality and grit of ordinary life.[36] One of the characteristics of naturalists that was shared by the decadents was the representation of taboo topics relating to sexuality. These representations, however, were not merely for the pleasure of titillation but also to symbolize the effect that was produced. Méhul's *Mélidore et Phrosine* (1794) is an early example in which the topic of incest between Phrosine and her brother Jule is explored. The decadents also cultivated an interest in the morbid and macabre, which reflected a neo-gothic style. An example is Cherubini's *Médée* (1797), in which Médée murders her two children.

The French colonial period, beginning from the Second Empire and continuing up to the belle époque inspired composers to explore the exotic instruments, melodies and rhythms of distant lands – Eastern Asia, the middle East, Africa and the Pacific region. The *expositions universelles* of 1878, 1889 and 1900 in Paris further inspired librettists and opera composers to explore exotic elements in their works.[37] A shared, codified language of exoticism began to emerge in operas such as Bourgault-Ducoudray's *Thamara* (1891), Lefebvre's *Djelma* (1894), Massenet's *Thaïs* (1893), Lambert's *Le Spahi* (1897) and Hahn's *L'Île du rêve* (1898). One of the central plot elements in these 'exotic' operas is love, and if it exists between two natives, the love would prosper, but love between a native and a European was doomed to failure. In *Astarté*, exoticism is combined with sexual taboo, in the form of an orgy. Paul Milliet from *Le Monde artiste* wrote:

The following two acts are completely successful; the scene of seduction played by Omphale; the religious ceremony where everything else, the sets, the lighting and the staging, is admirably combined to reproduce the phallic and orgiastic cults of Asia; the awakening of the lovers; the prayer to the divine Astarté.[38]

After receiving mixed reviews at the premiere, Xavier Leroux's opera *Astarté* (1901) seems to have disappeared from the performance scene. The two protagonists form opposing factions; on one side is Omphale,[39] a cultist of Astarté, and her Sapphic priestesses. On the other side is Hercules, associated with Vesta, and his army of male soldiers. Symbolically, Astarté as the goddess of war, sexuality and fertility represents the feminist ideal and is aligned with the Dionysian ideals of freedom and sexual abandonment. For Omphale, sex is her power, and she is prepared to wield it in order to protect her society from Hercules. Vesta, who is first mentioned by Iole, who beseeches protection against any threat to chastity (figure 1.3). She sings:

Toi qui voulus rester éternellement chaste,	You who wanted to remain chaste eternally,
Vesta, protège nous!	Vesta, protect us!
Toi qui t'enfuis devant la volupté néfaste,	You who run away from harmful voluptuousness,
Vesta, veille sur nous!	Vesta, watch over us!
Toi que même un désir mauvais met en courroux,	You who even an evil desire makes you angry,
Vesta, veille sur nous![40]	Vesta, watch over us!

Vesta, by contrast to Astarté, was a virgin goddess of the home, hearth and family. Vesta represents the Apollonian traits of order, harmony and reason. A myth, in which she is miraculously impregnated by a phallus appearing in the flames of her fire, further separates the two female goddesses.

Figure 1.3   Iole's Prayer to Vesta, Act I, Scene ii, pp. 10–11. Xavier Leroux and Louis Ferdinand de Gramont, *Astarté* [vocal score], Paris: Alphonse Leduc., 1900–1901. Public Domain.

Hercules, the Duke of Argos, has embarked on a campaign to wipe out the cult of priestesses worshipping Astarté. Driven by his divinely inspired conviction that he is on a crusade of morality, he goads his soldiers by singing, 'Voulez-vous, avec moi, conquérir la Lydie, Et la criminelle cité Où règnent la débauche et l'impudicité?'[41] (Do you want to conquer Lydia with me, And the criminal city, Where do debauchery and immodesty reign?). He travels to Lydia to murder the queen Omphale and takes with him the tunic of the centaur of Nessos, given by his wife. The tunic is a talisman that when worn will prevent him from seduction by another woman. Iole has been tasked by Hercules' wife Deianira to ensure he wears it. When Heracles and his men arrive in Lydia, they gather at the walls of Sardis. Hope for the trapped women appears in the form of Phur, a high priest of Astarté. He has travelled from Lesbos having consulted with an oracle, and the ecstatic reception of the priestesses is imbued with erotic language, praising Astarté's feminine beauty and extolling the pleasures between daughters of Lesbos. They sing:

Déesse aux tresses blondes,	Goddess with blond braids,
Qui verses dans les cœurs les extases profondes,	Who pours deep ecstasies into hearts,
Et courbes les mortels devant ta volonté	And bend mortals before your will
Voici la blanche théorie	Here is the white theory
Des filles de Lesbos, servantes d'Astarté;	Daughters of Lesbos, servants of Astarte;
Chacune vient avec sa compagne chérie:	Each comes with her beloved companion:
Couples charmants qui respirent la volupté![42]	Charming couples who exude pleasure!

The material for the chorus is sumptuous, particularly at the cadence point at the end of the first section, when the basses divide into three parts, giving a warm and rich texture. Astarté may be bending mortals to her will, but it sounds like a pleasant experience. When the female chorus completes the section referencing the daughters of Lesbos, they do so in thirds; they are in total accord. The symbolism of their forced entry into the female enclave of Sapphic priestesses, complete with their phallic spears, is thinly veiled. The masculinity of the conquering force with their dismissive view of the cultist women is expressed by one of Hercules' followers, Euphanor, who sings, 'Des formes, en effet, se montrent à nos yeux, Mais ce ne sont point des guerriers: ce sont des femmes!'[43] (Forms, in fact, show themselves to our eyes, But they are not warriors: they are women!), to which the male chorus respond, 'Des femmes! Des femmes!'[44] (Women! Women!). The libretto by Louis de Gramont (1854–1912) makes heavy use of explanation marks, but its use after both utterances of the word 'women' by the men is important and allows for two interpretations. The first is that they are shocked by finding their mission involved defeating the fairer sex, and the second is that the mere thought of a group of sexually active women aroused their base instincts.

Given what transpires, which is that the women invite the men into the city under the guise of mass seduction, the second option seems apposite. The ruse is far too easy for the women, who sing:

Les Guerriers Ténors	The Tenor Warriors
Oui, nous cédons à vos charmes	Yes, we give in to your charms
Prenez emportez nos armes,	Take away our weapons,
Mais cédez à notre amour!	But give in to our love!
Les Femmes	The women
Venez, ravis d'allégresse,	Come, delighted with joy,
Venez goûter tour à tour	Come and taste in turn
A la coupe de l'ivresse,	At the cup of drunkenness,
A la coupe de l'amour.[45]	With the cup of love.

It is in this act, Act II, where Leroux makes use of his 'exotic' orientalism. The foreign land to which Hercules and his men have travelled is represented musically as 'other'. The opening of the act is dominated by a recurring chromatic theme, which explores a series of alternate diminished and minor chords. With moments of counterpoint, no clear use of melodic phrases and overt use of *leitmotivs*, the work is conceived along Wagnerian lines. The chromaticism foreshadows serialism; however, the twelve notes are not strictly ordered. This work, and many others like it, occupies a space in between Wagner and the Second Viennese School. One such *leitmotiv* is heard as the voyage to Lydia is underway and is a clear example of this hint of the serialism ideals that are to come.

When Hercules returns to find his men missing, he asks Hylas for an explanation, who responds, 'Vers eux des femmes sont venues, Aux captieux discours, aux gestes éhontés, Versant des vins troublants, offrant leurs gorges nues . . . Et les voilà domptés!'[46] (Women came to them, To captious speeches, to shameless gestures, Pouring disturbing wines, offering their bare throats . . . And here they are tamed!). As if to further taunt the would-be conqueror, the women respond by singing to their new captives, 'Venez, ravis d'allégresse, Venez goûter tour à tour, A la coupe de l'ivresse, A la coupe de l'amour'[47] (Come, delighted with joy, Come and taste in turn, At the cup of drunkenness, With the cup of love). At this point of the opera, the symbolism is clear; the power of Astarté's virility and sexual abandonment has easily defeated Vesta's ideals of chastity. For contemporary French audiences, this reflects the ideals of the fin de siècle movement, emotionalism, irrationalism, subjectivism and vitalism, which are not only embraced in the narrative but powerful enough to defeat the army of the hero, Hercules. In Act III, Hercules enters Omphale's palace, and after initial bluster, including the phrase, 'Ton corps luxurieux sera mis en lambeaux'[48] (Your lush body will be torn to shreds), Omphale removes her veil and Hercules is immediately bewitched by her erotic beauty and completely pacified. Amidst the groans and cries of the chorus, who seem to have begun their amorous engagements, Omphale continues to seduce Hercules, assaulting him with terms of erotic femininity, singing:

Mais quels sont-ils, tous ces crimes que j'ai commis,	But what are they, all these crimes that I have committed,
Ces forfaits attestant la noirceur de mon âme?	These packages attesting to the darkness of my soul?
Est-ce ma faute à moi, si la Divinité	Is it my fault that the Divinity
M'a fait le don fatal d'une rare beauté;	Has given me the fatal gift of rare beauty;
Si de ma chair s'exhale un troublant parfum d'ambre,	If a disturbing scent of amber exhales from my flesh,
Et si des Rois sont morts sur le seuil de ma chambre,	And if kings died on my doorstep,
Pour avoir entrevu ma rose nudité?[49]	For having caught a glimpse of my pink nudity?

As the seduction continues, Omphale changes tac and adopts a dominant role over Hercules who has completely succumbed to her entrancement. Hercules explains, 'C'est l'ambre de ta chair, c'est l'or de tes cheveux, Et c'est ta gorge aux pointes roses que je veux'[50] (It's the amber of your flesh, it's the gold of your hair, And it's your pink tipped throat that I want), to which Omphale responds, 'Et si je ne veux pas te les donner?'[51] (What if I don't want to give them to you?). Initially Hercules states that he will take her by force, but through a process of careful manipulation quickly has Hercules prostrate before her, begging to be humiliated and to be treated as her slave. This act of complete sexual submission conjures erotic practices or role-playing involving bondage, discipline, dominance and submission and sadomasochism. Hercules abandons Vesta and embraces Astarté, which Omphale, Iole and the priestesses celebrate with a ceremony. Hercules succumbs to the effects of a potion he was given to drink and falls asleep, and as he does, the women celebrate his total humiliation with a Bacchanalian, lesbian orgy. They sing:

Omphale	Omphale
Il cede au magique breuvage. Il dort!	He gives in to the magical brew. He is sleeping!
Que par tout à présent la joie immense éclate!	Let immense joy explode through everything now!
Chorus	Chorus
Astarté! Pour célébrer ta victoire,	Astarte! To celebrate your victory, let's sing!
Chantons! Buvons!	Let's drink!
Aimons![52]	Love!

Omphale	Omphale
Aux clartés de la flamme écarlate	In the light of the scarlet flame
Chantez, buvez, aimez-vous librement:	Sing, drink, love each other freely:
Omphale, cette nuit, prend un nouvel amant.	Omphale, tonight, takes a new lover.

The dream-like state, associated with the symbolist movement, is evident in this Dionysian scene which is likely the first physical depiction of lesbian sex in an opera. The women sing, '*Livrons-nous à la joie, Chantons, aimons, buvons ! Si l'amour le baiser, le plaisir, est un rêve, Ah ! sans trêve, Rêvons !*'[53] (Let us indulge in joy, Sing, love, drink! If love kiss it, pleasure is a dream, Ah! without truce, let's dream!). Theroux and Gramont were not hinting at an orgy through implication and code. The stage directions at the beginning of Act III, scene iv, indicate, 'As the orgy reached its climax, Omphale has disappeared, followed by Cléanthis.'[54]

In Act IV, Iole finally arrives to deliver Hercules his tunic. Rather than stealthily providing her master with the protection he needed against Omphale's powers of seduction, Iole falls under the same power and quickly submits to Omphale's control. Iole is dressed as a boy, an act that would provide an element of sexual appeal for lesbian audience members, but Omphale sees through the disguise, recognizing the beauty of Eros in her. An extant colour photograph of the baritone, Delmas playing Phur and dressed in an opulent sliver and pink dress, replete with magnificent head dress and an impressive beard, suggests that the ruse was somewhat flawed in its application. Iole is powerless against Omphale's persuasive charms, and Hercules is quickly forgotten by both women as shown in the following scene:

Iole	Iole
Je vais consentir et céder à vos vœux,	I will consent and give in to your wishes,
Omphale	Omphale
Dis-moi: «je consens,» Dis le moi, je le veux,	Tell me: 'I agree', Tell me, I want it,
Iole	Iole
En vous laissant baiser mon front et mes cheveux!	By letting you kiss my forehead and my hair!
Douce est la voix, qui m'implore.	Sweet is the voice, which implores me.
Je ne résiste pas! Ah !	I can't resist! Ah!
Omphale	Omphale
Et laisse-moi baiser ton front et tes cheveux!	And let me kiss your forehead and your hair!
Cède à la voix, qui t'implore.	Yield to the voice, imploring you.
Ah! ne résiste pas!	Ah! do not resist!

Iole	Iole
Malgré moi je chancelle, Et sous votre baiser,	In spite of myself I stagger, And under your kiss,
Je me sens tressaillir.	I feel myself flinch.
Omphale	Omphale
Demeure, enfant, demeure au prés de nous.[55]	Abide, child, abide near us.

Now, with the protection of his talismanic tunic, Hercules watches Omphale's seduction of Iole and he rages at her malicious trickery. In the process of trying to tear off the tunic, which seems to be attached to his flesh, he tears it off, causing a fire in the process of his frenzy and causing his own death. The stage directions read, '*L'incendie se déchaîne avec fureur et envahit toute la scène*'[56] (The fire broke out with fury and swept the whole scene). The destruction of Hercules is the final representation of victory of Astarté over Vesta or Dionysus over Apollo. It is also clear support for the growing feminist movement which, at the turn of the century, saw an emboldened group of women challenge traditional marriage arrangements and undertake gender role-defying employment while continuing the struggle over the patriarchal view of the role of women in society. Following the destruction of the temple, the women leave the palace, and in the final scene, they arrive at the island of Lesbos and at the foot of the statue of Astarté, worshiping and adoring her.

Leroux's wife, Meyrianne Héglon-Leroux, sang the role of Omphale in the premiere with cast members, Louise Grandjean, Albert Alvarez and Jean-François Delmas, each of whom was celebrated opera stars with established, international careers. The season achieved twenty-three performances, indicating a degree of commercial success.[57] Despite this, there is yet to be a revival of this neglected work.

In this opera, the women were not the instigators of the conflict. There was no provocation but for Hercules' determination to seek out and destroy an ideal that offended him. He arrived at their home, seeking to penetrate their world and end their Sapphic practices through slaughter. In a manner found in Berg's *Lulu*, the women were forced to use what they had at their disposal for self-defence – their cunning and their femininity. The men are portrayed as laughably weak; Hercules is reduced to a desperate, sex-crazed little boy who has bitten off more than he can chew. Omphale's dalliance with Hercules can be seen as an ephemeral disruption to a utopian existence of exclusive femininity.

YOUNG CAESAR, LOU HARRISON

Stories from antiquity form a useful resource for narratives exploring queer themes. They provide many appealing qualities, but foremost is the ancient

Greeks' and Romans' acceptance of homosexuality as an integrated part of the sexual activities of their citizens. Added to that is the degree of respectability afforded Classical subjects in art works that allow the observer to contextualize homoeroticism at a distance. By removing sexual 'perversions' safely away from our immediate history, audiences shaped by a conservative perspective can understand the representation of queerness from a detached perspective, like watching a dangerous zoo animal behind safety glass. This has been the practice for several operas such as Charpentier's *David et Jonathas* (1688), Gluck's *Iphigénie en Tauride* (1779), Leroux's *Astarté* (1901), Strauss' *Salome* (1905) and *Elektra* (1909) and Szymanowski's *King Roger* (1926). Lou Harrison's *Young Caesar* (1971) joins this list, but queer opera themes would not return to antiquity for inspiration for nearly half a century, with Mark Simpson's *Pleasure* (2016).

Harrison was a proud and openly gay man, fighting for gay rights well before Stonewall in 1969. When he was summoned by the draft board in 1942, he informed them candidly that he was gay, classifying him as 4-F, which prevented individuals from military service on the grounds of unacceptable physical, mental or moral standards. He explained, 'They didn't want me, and I didn't want them.'[58] He and his partner Bill Colvig were members of the Society for Individual Rights (SIR) in California which operated between 1964 and 1977. SIR fought to publicly affirm gay and lesbian identity, eliminate victimless crime laws, provide a range of social services (including legal aid) to 'gays in difficulties' and promote a sense of a gay and lesbian community. Harrison stated, 'Our fight for civil rights was done on a political level from the beginning. Even though SIR eventually collapsed, we had done our job: to get these politicians to commit themselves to gay rights.'[59]

Whe *Young Caesar* premiered at the Californian Institute of Technology (Caltech) in Pasadena, several of the patrons withdrew their support in protest at the openly gay storyline and the symbolic 'eroticon' scene, representing the courtly orgy by use of several flying phalluses. Music critic David Stabler wrote, '"Young Caesar" may have worked with puppets, but it definitely does not with people . . . Not even during the orgy scene that had nearly naked men walking politely back and forth while everyone else appeared to be at a political fund-raiser.'[60] He reworked the opera with seven additional arias in anticipation of a performance at the Lincoln Center, but the event was cancelled in 2000. It is the revised performing edition that I reference here.

The opera was written just a year after Tippett's *The Knot Garden* (1970) and two years before Britten's *Death in Venice* (1973), and Harrison was clearly forging a new path in representations of queerness in American opera, but in several ways, *Young Caesar* represents a polite cautiousness in comparison to what would follow decades later. The original version was devised as a puppet opera, a medium that had fascinated Harrison since encountering de Falla's *El Retablo de Maese Pedro* (Master Peter's Puppet Show, 1919–1922) and further inspired by the ancient puppet dramas and shadow puppetry found in China and Indonesia. Portraying physical homoeroticism through the medium of inanimate objects rather than real men may have been a necessary first step for America's first foray into queer opera. Wanting to rework a Native American story for his kachina puppets, used by the Hopi to represent sacred, natural and supernatural forces, the composer was unable to find a suitable story. Instead, he took Colvig's suggestion, 'Why don't you do a gay subject?'[61]

Harrison's love of Eastern aesthetics was formed as a child. His family Portland apartment was filled with Chinese carved teak furniture perched on Persian rugs, colourful Japanese lanterns dangling from the ceiling, cloisonné objects on the mantel and rooms covered in Japanese grass wallpaper boasting artefacts from Asia and the Middle East. Hawaiian music dominated the radio broadcasts the year he was born, which inspired one of his compositions around eighty years later, and he admitted that by recreating the music of Asia, he was trying to recapture the lost treasures of his youth.[62] Travelling to Korea on a Rockefeller grant, Harrison studied the piri flute with Lee Hye-Ky, earning the right to teach it in the United States. Upon returning, he made his own, as well as a zheng, a large Chinese string instrument analogous with a zither.[63] His instrument building with his partner Bill culminated with the construction of 'Old Granddad', a metallophone orchestra for use in their Chinese ensemble, and ultimately deployed in the ensemble for *Young Caesar*.

Caesar is depicted as bisexual, reflecting historical understanding and helping to diminish the horrors of sexual deviancy for a conservative audience. In the opera, he is betrothed to Cossutia, a woman of considerable dowry but whose weight and size Caesar fears. With a change in fortune, he instead marries Cornelia, whose skills as a horse rider are admired by the teenage boy. In these opening scenes, there are only coded glimpses of suspicious queerness. Caesar's opening aria includes a lament of the things he will need to forgo in order to submit to his father's choice of a bride. He bemoans the inevitable sacrifice of favoured pastimes, such as poetry and plays to be replaced by 'serious plans, of soldiery and politics and devious ways'.[64] Equally subtle is his Aunt Julia's statement regarding his betrothal, 'I say you must be what you are, Gaius. You must say what you think and feel what you feel.'[65] It is the discourse with his slave, Dionysus, that offers a clearer hint at queerness in the young adolescent. The choice of name for the slave offers a clue regarding the disposition regarding sexual behaviour, and the repeated use of the endearment 'sweetheart' is suggestive both of campness and also familiarity. Dionysus, or Dio, is excited about the possible revelries that are

on offer at the court of King Nicomedes to whom they must pay a diplo-
matic visit. In anticipation, Dio places a small phallus around Caesar's neck.
Caesar has more trepidation about his mission, 'But he's a king, Dio. And I
have had so little experience. I could easier scale those walls right now and
surprise the enemy than know how to please a man and a King.'[66] The notion
that he needs to be able to please a man suggests that Nicomedes' reputation
precedes him; however, Caesar is clearly not revolted by such thoughts but
simply concerned about his relative inexperience.

The death of Caesar's father following his opening aria is a pivotal moment
in the unfolding drama. Caesar's fortunes change suddenly, and he sings of
the profound loss of a father figure. The moment sets in motion a series of
events which lead to the journey to Bithynia and his queer encounter. In 1962,
the first study to explore a causal link with homosexuality and the absence of
a male role model proposed the 'weak father' theory, otherwise expressed as
a distant or hostile father.[67] This stemmed from the 'family of origin theory'
espoused by Bowen.[68] Although further research supported this concept,[69]
there were critics of the psychodynamic perspective who found that no compelling evidence could be found.[70] More recently, new research that adopted
a broader, quantitative data collection found support for either the absence of
a childhood male role model, in particular concerning intimacy and relationships, or the dissatisfying emotional connection with the father for a healthy
sexual identity.[71] Given Caesar's youth, the subconscious need for a symbolic
father replacement figure is compelling when considering the age difference
between him and the king.

The role of the narrator operates with sung vocal lines and spoken text as
do many of the characters. In Act II, he explains the initial meeting of the
king and his guest from Rome, 'The King embraces Caesar with a kiss, as had
his representatives earlier at the dock. Only the kiss of the King is long and
tender, and bespeaks not of formality but of passion.'[72] The kiss has unsettled
Caesar, who says, 'What if he greets me with another kiss? That was such a
strange kiss: So unlike Cornelia's, or even Dio's.'[73] We can only imagine that
the strangeness of the kiss concerned the passionate exchange, but the word
'even' when describing the kisses he was used to with his slave, further suggests the customary Roman practice of using a slave for sexual gratification
was adopted by Caesar. In Caesar's next aria, he sings, 'Beneath a crown, his
eyes. Beneath his robes, a King. Now I become Ganymede and Dio was right,
I'll know what to do.'[74] Ganymede symbolizes youthful beauty and pederasty
on account of the myth in which he was abducted by Zeus to be his cupbearer,
and Caesar was to be sexually abducted by King Nicomedes. In the evening,
at the banquet held for the visiting envoy, the king, who is, according to the
narrator, 'enamored of Caesar's appearance and naiveté',[75] is enchanted with
the appearance of Caesar. He has emerged wearing the diaphanous white

tunic of the former cupbearer, confirming his passive role as Ganymede in the ensuing relationship.

In scene x, the entertainment begins with a fast-moving dance which sets a G-minor melody in the solo violin against a four-note ostinato played on the guzheng and harp. This is followed by the 'eroticon', played faster than the previous section, in which the upper woodwind employs a pentatonic melody antiphonally with the strings, over the top of a sustained five-note chord: C, D, F, G, B natural, played on the sheng and the organ. Although the tuning system for Gamelan differs from Western music, this chord is suggestive of the *slendro* tuning system in Javanese music which consists of five, roughly similar intervals. He referred to this process as 'aural imitations of the generalized sounds of gamelan', an imperfect procedure but one in which he avoided any harmonic modulation.[76] The transparency of the structure of this music, and indeed the whole opera, echoes the minimalism influences of John Cage, with whom Harrison worked closely for many years. Harrison's use of Eastern instruments and techniques was considered by musicologists as 'exotic', and the perceived correlation between exoticism and eroticism formed the basis of the prevailing discourse on the 'queer aesthetic' in music. The modern 'queer aesthetic' emerged during the time of Harrison's boyhood and the period of American decadence, characterized by an affirmation of 'otherness'.[77] Another exotic element is the treatment of the spoken text, where the composer borrowed a technique from Chinese operas he had seen as a boy. The text is punctuated with percussive interjections, which combined with the underlying percussive ostinato used in Japanese Noh theatre provides a feeling of suspense and anticipation to the drama.

Scene xi, the bed scene, begins with Caesar lying awake in the arms of the snoring Nicomedes. The ensuing aria by Nicomedes, in which he urges Caesar to stay with him, rather than hastily returning to Rome, is seductive and tempting. Nicomedes takes his young lover on a tour of his realm, enticing him to enjoy the pleasures of his hospitality. By means of dramatic tension, three of Caesar's men, Marcus Verres and two other Romans, plead with Nicomedes to allow them to take the agreed provision of ships back to Rome. Verres says:

> Your highness, I will not venture to suggest what a king's routine should be –
> but we must soon return to Rome. We cannot afford to dally like children, or
> partake iondefinitely [*sic*] of the . . . unusual ways of your court. We are also
> anxious to return to our wives and to our manly duties, unlike Gaius Caesar.[78]

The patent slight on Caesar's pleasures with the king, and the questioning of his manhood and maturity, establishes a symbol of opposing ideals; one in which war and the much-needed military advantage of the ships is espoused by Verres, and the other of peace, championed by the king with his penchant for sleeping in late, banquets, entertainments and orgies. The year 1971 was two years before America withdrew from its war in Vietnam, and Harrison's strong pacifist agenda is reflected in Robert Gordon's libretto, with the familiar trope of the age, 'make love, not war'. The three Roman soldiers mock Caesar: Marcus Verres – 'He is frivolous', Second Roman – 'He is perverse', Third Roman – 'He is unfit to be a king'.[79] The Second Roman continues, 'It's a disgrace that a Roman citizen should behave in such a manner, especially in public',[80] and the Third Roman adds, 'Believe me, such scandalous conduct will not go unreported. They will hear of this in Rome.'[81] Marcus Verres spits, 'Catamite!'[82] which has its etymological foundation in Ganymede, to which the Second Roman responds, 'Look at the Queen of Bithynia!'[83] and finally, the Third Roman, 'Look at the boy in the petticoat. The inner partner of the royal bed!'[84] According to Roman historian Suetonius (AD 69 – c. AD 122), such slants levelled at Caesar were prevalent; however, they were vigorously denied.[85]

In addition to the opposing ideals of war and peace, another dichotomy is presented in *Young Caesar* in which the presentation of East and West correlates with notions of exoticism and sexual 'other'. Part I takes place in Italy, around 86 BC. Notions of sexuality are limited to heteronormative practices, and Harrison limits his orchestral palette to instruments commonly associated with Western music, such as flutes, oboes, trumpet, trombone, harp, Western percussion instruments, organ, prepared piano and strings. By contrast, Act II is set in the ancient country of Bithynia, the exotic East, and it is here that queer 'other' flourishes. It is also here that Harrison introduces the Eastern instruments into the timbre. Bithynia was an independent kingdom for two-and-one-half centuries, from the death of Alexander the Great until 74 BC, when King Nicomedes willed it to Rome. The practice of 'othering' through use of 'exoticism' was employed by Leroux in his opera, *Astarté* (1901), and many other works.

The importance of *Young Caesar* in the discourse on queer opera cannot be overstated. Until now, queer American composers had avoided the risk of exploring queer themes in their operas. It is one thing to include coded symbols in musical works, but when same-sex relationships are embodied and displayed, the possibility for backlash from a conservative public and the related hostility could certainly be dangerous. The evolution of *Young Caesar* from a puppet opera into a live performance version for a large chamber ensemble with arias and male chorus follows the reluctant acceptance of queerness in the American psyche. Harrison did not consider his activism as heroic but just something he felt compelled to do. This opera provided reassurance for queer composers to follow, that giving voice to persecuted minority groups in the arts now had precedence. In the few short years that followed Stonewall, queers were now claiming space on the operatic stage.

PLEASURE, MARK SIMPSON

The title of Mark Simpson's opera *Pleasure* (2016) is layered with meaning. Set in a hedonistic gay club of the same name, in an unidentified city in northern England, the clear reference to the Bacchanalian revelry that takes place there suggests a narrative focused on eroticism and a celebration of the beauty of youth enjoying the liberation that alcohol and dancing encourages. All of this forms a component of the plot, but as the drama unfolds, it becomes apparent that such pleasures are sought as an antidote for the pain of rejection, internalized homophobia and self-loathing. There are four characters in the seventy-minute opera: Val, a fifty-something toilet attendant and self-appointed confidant to the patrons at the club; Nathan, Val's lost son and resentful of his abandonment issues; Matthew, a young man with an insatiable appetite for male beauty and looking for romance; and Anna Fewmore, a charismatic, aging drag queen impresario with her own history of family abandonment.

Melanie Challenger's libretto draws on the Greek myth of Hephaistos as a foundation for the theme of rejection of 'other' by the family. The tragedy of Hephaistos is taken from Homer's 'Iliad' and the 'Odyssey'. He is depicted with a hammer and an anvil, as the Greek god of blacksmiths and an array of other crafts. Homer contests that Hephaistos is the son of Zeus and Hera, who during a quarrel threw him from Mount Olympus. Whether he was born with a club foot or as a result of his fall, his physical impairment was a source of intense shame and disgust for his mother. The boy was rescued by Thetis and Eurynome who sheltered him in a cave for nine years while he plotted revenge on his mother. He constructed a beautiful golden throne for Hera, who became completely bound by the many delicately fashioned cords invisible to anyone's eyes but Hephaistos. He only released Hera from her imprisonment when Dionysus got him drunk, after which he ascended to the status of a god.

Hephaistos is embodied in Nathan, and the parallels are scattered breadcrumbs throughout the text. He establishes himself as an outsider when he appears in the club, singing, 'I don't belong here.'[86] His physical form is instantly the source of lustful admiration from the patrons, a reaction with which he was unfamiliar. The chorus of clubbers sing, 'What a beauty. Something wild in his eyes. His skin as pale as violet. His eyes as wild as a pricked bull',[87] to which Nathan responds, 'It makes them so happy just to see my body. I've never been looked at like this. I've never been wanted like this.'[88] Hephaistos developed a powerful physique from his life as a blacksmith, and Nathan explains to Matthew that his scars resulted from his job as a welder. Hephaistos was rejected by Hera; however, Val explains in the penultimate scene that Nathan had been taken from her: 'When they took my son, I closed my eyes, slipped inside a seed of pain.'[89] The opera concludes with her determination to finally share her story with her estranged son. Whereas Hephaistos is distracted by the effects of Dionysus' liquor, Nathan is distracted by proclamations of love and adoration from Matthew, which are initially confusing. Nathan sings, '"Dance with me" says that young man. Strange . . . unexpected.'[90] The damage caused by Nathan's rejection is most clearly expressed in scene two, set to a dark, slow and menacing tempo, during which he sings of the reason for his 'gift' of a throne to his mother, 'Violence grows in the mind of someone denied the pleasure of touch in childhood. As the violence thrives, feelings of pleasure are crushed.'[91] The opera unfolds under a wary tension triggered by the prospect of Nathan's fragile state and propensity for violence.

The theme of rejection, which forms the basis of the opera, reflects a distressing reality for many members of the LGBTQI+ community. Queer individuals are prone to the regular array of life stressors such as illness, injury, death of a loved one and job loss, but additional stressors specific to having a minority sexual orientation can compound problems with mental health. Meyer's minority stress theory[92] considers four domains of specifically queer stressors: prejudice events such as harassment, violence, discrimination and rejection; expectations of prejudice events; concealment of identity; and the internalization of negative societal attitudes and beliefs such as internalized homophobia.[93] Rejection from family members is a frequent experience for many queer youths, and a common reaction to rejection is concealment. The effects of negative internalization of oppression relating to sexuality can lead to severe depression and anxiety.[94]

For Nathan, his experience of rejection has brought him to 'Pleasure', where he intends to confront Val. The chorus immediately noted there being 'something wild in his eyes',[95] and this is confirmed by Matthew who has seized on the opportunity to get closer to him, 'This one's got a weird look of pain.'[96] Matthew's frequent patronage of 'Pleasure' where alcohol and beautiful, young men are in plentiful supply typifies the aspirations of many young gay men, seeking love in eroticism in a package of idealism. He sings, 'Young male beauty is the guiding principle of this place.'[97] Matthew's intense attraction to men, 'The beauty of the male form hangs like a lantern above me',[98] presented him with the courage to attempt the seduction of Nathan. For Matthew, the notion of love with Nathan is like ambrosia, but his determination is countered by Nathan's initial reluctance. Matthew sings, 'I think I'm falling for you',[99] to which Nathan responds, 'You don't know me',[100] claiming the space of 'outsider'.

If Nathan represents Hephaistos, then it stands to reason that Anna embodies Dionysus. Anna Fewmore, cast as a baritone, is another fixture of the club, and her friendship with Val stretches back for many years. Dionysus was also borne of Zeus, from his thigh specifically, but his mother was Semele, making him the only god with a mortal parent. As the god of wine and fertility, his areas of special concern are mirrored in Anna's role as the club's impresario, 'Come, all you exquisite creatures, blessed booze-soaked and beautiful men! Follow me! I will take you to my band of worshippers. The god of booze! The god of letting go!'[101] Anna's dual gender identity is expressed in another of his calls to Dionysian worship, 'Come, all you exquisite creatures, ladies and gentlemen and those of you above the trivialities of gender.'[102] She later describes her character when reminiscing with Val of her own familial rejection, 'Beautiful, two-formed, mad-sounding, mad-making queer queen of the dole. A rag bag of man and woman.'[103] Anna was rejected by her sister and mother, presumably as a result of her gender fluidity, but it was Val who lifted her out of her self-loathing. Anna describes the pain that she constantly hides from society, 'Inside a heart beats a wounded one, its dark twin.'[104]

Val's incarnation of Hera is revealed initially through her position as bathroom attendant at 'Pleasure'. She sings in the first scene, 'I can't leave',[105] suggestive of some form of imprisonment. The irony of a bathroom in a busy nightclub being considered as luxurious, 'This is my palace, my throne',[106] is in stark contrast to the realities of such a workplace but reveals the connection with Hephaistos' revenge. Val reveals her need to give support, advice and love to the many regular patrons who visit her bathroom, a need which seems to grow with each exchange. Her desire to provide a maternal role for the young, gay men stems from the loss of such a role when her son was taken: 'Here I can give what I could not give before.'[107] Val reminisces on the violent behaviour of Nathan's father and worries that her son may exhibit the same tendencies, 'What if the likeness hides another likeness?'[108] The link with Zeus' violent outburst which saw Hephaistos thrown from Mount Olympus is clear. Val's character was inspired by a real conversation Simpson had with a bathroom attendant in a Liverpool club, and the conversation exhibited maternal characteristics which allowed him to speak openly about his life.[109]

'Pleasure' represents a place of escape for people burdened by deep-seated issues that cause anxiety. Pre-recorded crowd noise and distant clubbing music are used as an effect at various points throughout the opera to establish context. Superficially, the queer community appears to be celebrating and having fun, but ultimately the stressors need to be addressed in order to foster mental health. The gay club enables a microcosm of queer groups that are plural, temporary, fluid and usually elective, an example of neo-tribalism in which shared lifestyles, values and understandings of what constitutes appropriate behaviour bind the collective identity.[110] According to Maffesoli, shared social identity through group membership creates a sense of solidarity and belonging which is frequently enacted in hedonistic cultural rituals.[111] There are, however, complex interactions between the individual and the tribal membership, as individuals can be simultaneously reminded of their personal isolation through seeking shared, social belonging, providing an oscillating paradigm of coinciding dependence and freedom. Each of the four characters in *Pleasure* is desperately seeking a connection with someone to fill a void in their lives. Anna's warning to Nathan, 'You'll grow old, dancing beside your own image. An appetite for life's empty secret will turn you into a god',[112] may have been an unwanted, acerbic observation; however, it serves as a clear metaphor for Hephaistos as well as wise council against the trappings of hedonistic pleasure while searching for meaningful companionship.

Simpson's lyrical score is imbued with memorable vocal lines and an accessible musical palette which approaches musical theatre while acknowledging contemporary operatic styles. Simpson's music is usually typified by more complex, postmodernist techniques; however, his aim with *Pleasure* was to avoid providing an alienating or abrasive sound world. *Pleasure* offers a window into the harsh reality of a queer community that is brought together to escape the stressors of being 'other' and is a contemporary account of the complex, tribal ritual of hedonism used as a façade to avoid confronting their damaged past. The metaphor of Hephaistos serves to remind us that these issues are age-old; however, the added layer of trauma shared by a community familiar with various kinds of rejection makes *Pleasure* a distinctly queer tragedy.

HADRIAN, RUFUS WAINWRIGHT

Emperor of Rome from 117 to 138, Hadrian's many and varied accomplishments form part of a familiar discourse for history enthusiasts. As the builder of Britain's Wall, and what is now the Castel Sant'Angelo in Rome, his frequent travels around the vast Roman Empire and imposed military discipline, his reign is viewed among the most successful of Rome's many leaders. His personal characteristics such as his obsession with Greek culture, being the first emperor to sport facial hair and his love of a Bithynian boy named Antinous all contribute to our image of the man. Despite this detail, the only two significant accounts of his life are both tardy and scant. The first is a biography written in Latin which forms part of a series of imperial biographies known as the Historia Augusta, completed around 250 years after Hadrian's death. The second, written in Greek, is a simple summary of his achievements from a portion of Cassius Dio's 'History of Rome' from the early part of the third century. Any other narrative accounts have not survived and so the gaps are filled in from excavated materials.

As a renowned Grecophile, Hadrian fulfilled the embodiment of his predilections through the ultimate Hellenizing act of falling in love with a beautiful Greek boy. In the latter half of the nineteenth century, Antinous replaced Ganymede as the popular symbol for homosexuality in German and English literature. As opposed to the young, effeminate *putto* that represents Ganymede, the cult of Antinous as portrayed in art, poetry, cultural history, prose and drama of Wilhelmine and Victorian societies is not only beautiful but also strong, virile and masculine. This cultist revival in Antinous, frozen in time through Hadrian's tributes, reflects a nostalgia for a time and place where homoeroticism was revered and the love of boys was a spiritual concept.

Canadian singer-songwriter Rufus Wainwright, better known for his prolific popular music output, has been a long-time opera enthusiast since he was a child, evidenced by his 1998 song, *Barcelona*, which utilizes lyrics from Giuseppe Verdi's opera, *Macbeth* (1847). *Hadrian* is Wainwright's second opera following *Prima Donna* in 2009 and was a topic of great interest for several years. He worked with Daniel MacIvor who provided the tightly constructed libretto for the premiere production by the Canadian Opera Company in 2018. This production, directed by Peter Hinton, emphasized homoerotic moments in the opera and fully embraced the homosexual themes which were integral to the narrative. In Acts I and II there are erotic sections choreographed for an all-male troupe of dancers. MacIvor was new to the world of opera when embarking on this project but was inspired by the intriguing love story, stating:

> The mystery of why Hadrian's remarkable love for Antinous – underlined by his bottomless grief – has not been celebrated widely as a model of eros points to a fear of same-sex love that has changed little from his age to ours. The deeper I delve into Hadrian's world and his time, the more parallels I see to how we live today.[113]

The death of Antinous, sparking a period of deification on Hadrian's orders consisting of cities, temples, coins, statues and even a star named after him, is subject to speculation.[114] Theories that include suicide as an intentional sacrifice, accidental drowning and murder contribute to the mystery of their love story. Local myths considered that a gift to the Nile River would prolong the ailing emperor's life. In this version, Wainwright and MacIvor have chosen murder for the untimely end of the beautiful Bithynian youth. The violence is certainly in step with the traditions of nineteenth-century grand opera and may also echo Wainwright's experience as a fourteen-year-old, when he was sexually assaulted and robbed in London's Hyde Park. The incident led to Wainwright's paranoid fear of contracting AIDS, which was then rampant throughout queer communities, and seven years of self-imposed celibacy.[115]

The work adopts the trappings of a traditional grand opera at three hours in length, and it includes a comprehensive orchestration, a large mixed chorus, numerous characters and the nexus of politics and censured love. Wainwright's musical language, while thoroughly tonal, provides memorable musical phrases and a variety of colourful timbres that convey the period with specific use of percussion and harp and moments of modality that conjure a Classical sound world.

The opera opens with Hadrian musing on his soul while lying on his deathbed. Lavia, the maid of his wife Sabina, Hermogenes, his physician, and Fabius lament his broken heart as Hadrian chimes in with the name of his lover, Antinous. Lavia notes that Hadrian expressed no such grief for his wife, Sabina. Fabius considers the ambiguity surrounding Antinous' death, and three senators provide the alternative rumours – either by accidental drowning, suicide as a sacrifice for Hadrian or murder. Lavia expresses her thoughts regarding Hadrian's foolish relationship with Antinous homophonically with Hadrian who repeats his lover's name against an ever-present, ominous tritone.

The scene anticipating Hadrian's death is interrupted with the arrival of two spirits, former emperor Trajan and his wife Plotina, who had supported him as an emerging political entity. After sharing his grief with them, he pleads with Hermogenes to kill him, but his physician is unwilling and the discussion alerts Turbo, the commander of his army, who insists Hadrian stops his urgent request for a hastened death. Hadrian posits that Turbo, who does not recognize his tears, does not really know him. The scene is too much for Hermogenes who stabs himself in the heart so as not to witness Hadrian's unconscionable entreaty again.

Throughout Act I, each of the characters who enters either passes judgement on Hadrian's relationship with Antinous or urges him to consider the political unrest that continues with his absence. For Hadrian, there is only one thought, and the heartache from his loss of Antinous haunts him. Attempts to remind him of Sabina are dismissed as noise by the dying emperor and the long notes provided whenever he sings the name Antinous permeate the business of the texture as a recurring motif of love and grief. In contrast, Turbo's material with fast, syllabic recitative matches the seemingly insignificant affairs of state which concern him, as does the homogenous moments from the three senators. Hadrian once again brings the discussion back to Antinous, 'You saw him not as I did. The sun in the sky.'[116] The senators have eagerly been awaiting some form of direction from Hadrian who, much to their astonishment and disappointment, proclaims, 'Sirius will now be Antinous. The sky shall be his dominion.'[117]

Act I closes with Plotina bargaining with Hadrian. She urges him to sign the document which will abolish Judea and with it those who favour monotheism. In return for preserving their pagan universe, Plotina promises Hadrian two nights with Antinous who will live again, allowing him to learn the answer to the question of Antinous' death. Trajan questions the wisdom of such a deal, to which Plotina responds in speech that learning the truth will first lift Hadrian up and then finish him, after which the Act concludes suddenly. The non-linear chronology of the narrative, along with the appearance of two ghosts that seek to influence the sequence of events, adds recognizably operatic devices to the work and further indicates Wainwright's familiarity with operatic conventions.

In Act II, Plotina and a revived and invigorated Hadrian find themselves seven years in the past. Hadrian is reunited with Sabina, and the perfunctory nature of their relationship is displayed when he refers to her as his wife; she retorts, 'Wife? Been years since you've called me such. Have you a fever?'[118] In scene iii, in an aria full of frustration of her unrequited love, she sings, 'I'm your wife. Do you see? Will you look at me?'[119] Wainwright uses his address to his people to emphasize Hadrian's love for all ancient Greek culture, 'My Hellenic brothers, you honor me with praise. But praise to Greece a home to my spirit.'[120] Hadrian's documented infatuation with Hellenic culture also represents a connection with a society in which homosexuality was afforded relative dignity and freedom. Hadrian's relationship with Antinous was, however, not a traditional arrangement of pederasty as Antinous is depicted as a fully developed man albeit with youthful and feminine features in many of the contemporary sculptures. He is cast as a tenor against the deeper vocal register of Hadrian's baritone.

Antinous had slain a boar that had been charging at Hadrian during a hunt and the youth is brought to the emperor as the chorus suspend an E major sixth with added seventh chord over several bars in the middle of a word; time stops for the meeting of the two lovers. Hadrian observes Antinous' form, 'A boy yet not a boy. A beard soon comes, I almost feel it here.'[121] Hadrian is famously remembered for being the first Roman emperor to sport facial hair and as he projects his physical predilections onto the young man, the encounter has a clear homoeroticism borne out by Hadrian's languid phrases and the stirring heterophony in the strings. As Hadrian touches Antinous' cheek, a dorian-mode 'lyre theme' created by composer Michael Levy[122] is played by a harp in the pit and accompanies the exchange. The stage directions indicate, 'There is electricity between Hadrian and Antinous, it's almost too much for Hadrian. Hadrian worries he will give the game away and removes his hand.'[123]

Turbo suggests that 'there are many here more boy than he',[124] an indication that a traditional pederastic relationship would be more suitable, but Hadrian is oblivious to the offer. Continuing to downplay Antinous' worth by diminishing his achievement during the boar hunt, Hadrian quizzes, 'Not

hunting then what?'[125] to which the young man responds, 'Let us say Love.'
Hadrian concurs, 'Let us say love. From this day, Antinous The Lover.'[126]
Standing close to one another, they both ask if what they are experiencing is
a dream. The scene reinforces the mutual love developing between the two
characters despite the power imbalance that characterizes the relationship.
Levy's 'lyre theme' and sustained chords in the string add a dream-like quality and a sensuality to the unfolding scene.

As the cast gather for the sacrifice of a lamb, Hadrian sets Antinous with
the task of counting the stars. Antinous sings to Hadrian, 'This night with
you from here unspools forever',[127] and Hadrian sings of their shared future
together. A disapproving Turbo remarks that Hadrian 'develops more and
more Greek tastes',[128] and other characters chime in with similar concerns
about the elevation of the young man in addition to Hadrian's emerging
homoerotic feelings for him. The couple sing to each other amidst the
interweaving vocal textures, oblivious of the criticism, with phrases that
gradually develop in intensity such as Antinous' passage, 'With you this
night eternal. Gentle as you wish or as you will, fate makes me yours
forever.'[129]

Act III begins with the embodiment of Hadrian and Antinous' sexual
attraction, and over a static C major chord provided by strings and percussion, their sexual act takes place. As the scene develops, the texture becomes
gradually more complex, and the growing orchestration becomes busier,
bolder and with greater use of extreme registers. The stage directions state:

> We are out of time. A world between worlds. We see Antinous. He has trans-
> formed from a coy youth into a fully grown man, a powerful, sexual being.
> Hadrian appears. They begin to make love. Tenderly at first, then with great
> passion. There is a sacredness here. An iconic love. Slowly around them grows
> their location. A curtained bedchamber. As their lovemaking climaxes it is clear
> that Antinous is the dominant sexual partner. After some moments Hadrian rises
> from the bed.[130]

In the post-coital serenity that follows, Hadrian sings of their sanctuary in
Tibur, where their metaphorical and perhaps literal garden will be in bloom.
Words of devotion continue as Hadrian sings phrases such as 'You have my
heart'[131] and 'Tonight I'm yours'.[132] Antinous is considered with a great deal
of distrust in Daniel MacIvor's libretto, and this is heightened in Act III,
scene iv, when several characters prompt him to share his thoughts regarding the Jews. His response is alarmingly sympathetic and unaligned with the
prevailing view that they should be eradicated, going so far as to admire the
saviour's supposed miracles and attempting to emulate walking on water.
Turbo is outraged by this behaviour and churlishly retorts, 'Perhaps he will

since he can turn master into slave.'[133] He sings to Sabina that Antinous is now the new empress.

Sabina had been aligned with Turbo's desire to sacrifice Antinous for the benefit of the emperor but, observing his dedication to Hadrian, has a change of heart. Antinous is poised on the edge of the barge, willing to sacrifice himself for Hadrian, but Sabina intervenes and explains that he has been misled, insisting that he return to Hadrian. Turbo is outraged by her deceit and has her taken away. He then approaches Antinous and after kissing him on the mouth, he takes his face in his hands and suddenly snaps his neck. Hadrian watches as Turbo dumps the limp body into the river and collapses with grief. Following Hadrian's death, he is reunited with Antinous who appears in full Egyptian regalia as the Gods gather to begin their recessional. In the final scene, the chorus divide into three delineated groups of Jews, Christians and Muslims, representing the outcome of all of the political machinations. Turbo's final words are an acknowledgement of Hadrian's sincere love.

The death of a queer character in opera is a familiar convention – expunging that which is not acceptable. The difference in Wainwright's opera is that Antinous was not seemingly murdered for his queerness, rather from a perception that his influence was corrupting ultimate authority. Turbo disposed of Antinous as a matter of political expediency rather than revulsion by his sexuality. The symbolic kiss prior to his murder as indicated by the stage directions provides ambiguity with regard to Turbo's own feelings towards the handsome youth. This may have been a fleeting display of repressed homoeroticism or perhaps a parting gesture on behalf of the emperor to his one true love. Certainly, MacIvor leaves no uncertainty of the depth of Hadrian and Antinous' passion, as the lines of text in which mutual devotion is deeply expressed dominates the opera. Wainwright provides a sensual score in which moments of sexual and romantic love are treated with lightness and space and long, sensuous vocal phrases contrasting with the busy, pecking rhythms of the minor characters obsessed with their personal, political desires. Ultimately, we are left with the moral lesson that love is one of life's greatest achievements, even for those as revered as Hadrian.

POMEGRANATE, KYE MARSHALL

The notion of a 'lesbian opera' likely means different things to different people. On a foundational level, an opera containing coded references understood by the lesbian community could easily fit into the subgenre category. As more overt representations of lesbianism such as the principal characters identifying as lesbian or scenes with physical sexual acts become more mainstream in the opera world, the definition is able to expand. An inert understanding of the nature of lesbian relationships and the hegemony that attempts to define or restrict it seems essential in creating a narrative that provides meaningful interpretations of gay women. In Kye Marshall and Amanda Hales' opera, *Pomegranate*, which bears the epithet 'a lesbian chamber opera', the central characters struggle against the oppressive forces that seek to separate them, but their relationship is also under pressure from the personal differences between them. The other characters are seen from their point of view and in many ways from a constructed, universal lesbian perspective. This, perhaps, could be a defining characteristic of the subgenre known as the 'lesbian opera'.

The creative process for developing *Pomegranate* took place over several years. The earliest structure of *Pomegranate*, which consisted of five songs, was presented on International Women's Day in 2014 at Toronto's Heliconian Club. Mount Helicon in ancient Greece is believed to be a favourite haunt of the Muses. Fittingly, this club was founded in 1909 to provide women in the arts and letters a space to meet and exchange ideas. The initial draft was later workshopped in 2016 by Tapestry, an underground opera company in Toronto which seeks to nurture new works and support emerging creators and artists. Hales' libretto was developed by Marjorie Chan and this version incorporated five of Marshall's melodies, written for the harp to evoke the sound of a lyre in the first act, with more contemporary idioms influencing the material in the second act.

Hale explains the origins of her inspiration, 'I had been to Pompeii in the early 2000s and my inspiration for *Pomegranate* was the frescoes that I saw in the Villa of Mysteries there.'[134] Archaeologists remain uncertain as to what the frescoes depict, but they are widely considered to involve a form of Dionysian ritual involving women. Hale continues, 'The images stayed with me so I formed a story for myself about two young girls falling in love. They're teenage girls, they're innocent, and the setting is sort of a Roman girls boarding school.'[135] Worshipping Isis was one of the unofficial religious traditions practised in Roman antiquity, and we are introduced to a temple of Isis, functioning also as a refuge for girls in need, led by a temple priestess.

The opera begins without an overture or significant instrumental introduction, and Cassia, wearing modern dress, is introduced immediately on a cobbled street amidst the ruins of Pompeii. As she sings, she reveals that she has travelled back in time and longs to be reunited with her love. Reminiscing, she sings, 'I take your head upon my belly[,] comb your lustrous hair with my gentle fingers[.] Blood fever rising to your touch, I watch the painter fill her brush and I remember where we have been.'[136] The lover is, thus far, genderless, perhaps to allow the presumptions of those observers unaware of the opera's content to manifest.

The following scene, in which the first of several time jumps takes us back to AD 79, Cassia, Julia and a priestess are singing to the goddess, Isis. The sparse orchestration, coloured by harp and three celli (cello is Marshall's instrument), with simple, repetitive patterns, underpins a somewhat homo-erotic text in which Isis is extolled in secrecy and ecstasy for her beauty. As Mount Vesuvius begins to erupt, Cassia appears in a toga, befitting of the time. She appeals to the priestess, who admits her refuge in the temple, where 'we honour the ancient Mysteries vested in our bodies we the women of Pompeii'.[137] Julia leads her to the Villa of Mysteries and in scene iii, she encounters Suli, remarking, 'How soft your touch',[138] and laughing. As the two are dancing together, Julia enters and addresses Suli, revealing her name to Cassia for the first time. Her name triggers some kind of memory to the confused Cassia and she begins to be entranced by Suli. Julia beckons them both to prepare for the rituals of the Mysteries which serve as a rite of passage for young girls to become women.

In scene iv, Marcus Quintus enters, praying to Apollo. This is the first appearance of a male character, and the positioning of his character as aligned with Apollonian philosophies is juxtaposed with the Dionysian characteristics of Suli's yearning for freedom, dancing, flirtation and rebellion. Established immediately as the foe who wishes to destroy the cult of women worshipping Isis, Amanda Hale's libretto initiates the major source of conflict for the narrative. Quintus sings simultaneously of his fervent desire for a woman to love him and his desire to eliminate the feminist, Dionysian cult, an irony that is highlighted by his phrase, 'Pray send a maiden to love and cherish me[,] I hunger for affection.'[139] His text does not include any indication of reciprocal love or cherishment.

Cassia's memory of Suli returns fully in scene v, when she sings, 'She calls my name, her voice like honey, the voice I remember.'[140] The moment is interrupted with Quintus entering the villa and disrupting the ceremony. He takes in the beauty, that is the young Suli, 'Her name fills my mouth. Come Suli, dance for me, dance for me pretty[,] I'll have mercy on you.'[141] Having recognized the priestess as his long-lost sister, he beseeches her to let him keep the teenage girl. In the following scene, Suli and Cassia have baskets of pomegranates, some of which are split open, and they use them sensually while dancing around flirtatiously with each other. They sing canonically as Cassia teases, 'Will you wed the Centurion?'[142] to which Suli responds, 'No man will catch me!'[143] They continue to seductively feed each other pome-granates, 'Fermenting fruit, its juice on my lips.'[144] They are oblivious to the other characters who discuss the issue of Quintus' return for Suli, as they kiss and embrace each other.

Cassia sings, 'When Suli runs her tunic flies like winged Pegasus',[145] and Suli responds, 'No-one will sting you but me.'[146] The prepared harp imitates the sound of bees with thin pieces of paper placed in between the strings. The harp carries the lion's share of the orchestration which comprises flute, oboe and three celli, providing imitative effects for several moments in which the natural world is referenced in the text. Marshall adds to the evocation of the ancient world with fleeting moments of modality, which appear but are then frequently resisted by the intrusion of tonality. Later in the scene, Cassia declares, 'O Suli my love for you[,] my pledge to Isis equal in my breast',[147] as the bees continue to swarm, evoking an erotic metaphor in which they are 'throbbing at branches cleft'.[148] Once again, Quintus interrupts the sensual pleasure, brutally hijacking the bee imagery, 'Suli, my maiden sweet honey mead you will make for my pleasure.'[149] The two girls escape after throwing a hove of bees at him, which proceed to sting him.

Suli and Cassia make a pledge to each other in scene vii as they hide from Quintus. Cassia sings, 'I have loved you for so long I could not bear to lose you.'[150] Their duet develops into a passionate and urgent musical episode as the two begin to make love behind a wine press. Suli sings, 'Fingers laced with mine as one-handed we move our hips to the rhythm of the wine press.'[151] The duet concludes with the two women singing intimately and in unison prior to the pledge. Cassia begins, 'I Cassia pledge to hold myself for you[,] Suli my hillside fox and quick bite of sharp desire.'[152] The stage directions in the score outline the following sex scene:

> Lovers are gripped with passion but in the sudden realization of it become immediately shy with each other. Throughout the scene they go back and forth between desire and shyness or fear. So slight build ups then pullbacks. Towards the end of the scene they finally let passion overtake their fears, building to a climax.[153]

The music that accompanies this scene is characterized by upward-moving arpeggiated figures and oscillating triplet patterns, with sequential, antiphonal motives between the flute and first cello.

Nowhere is the stark contrast of the Apollonian and Dionysian conflict in parallel with masculine versus feminine sensibilities more apparent than Quintus' phrase in which he urges his sister to return to Rome. He sings, 'You must marry and bear sons[.] Women are for breeding.'[154] Hale makes a close alignment of feminist and queer theories throughout the libretto and the comparisons are not explored through subtle subtext. Marshall creates a sound world through her orchestration as well as her harmonic, rhythmic and melodic material cast the brutish Centurion as the unwelcomed outsider. His character is not afforded notable associated musical context, with the possible exception of a semi-quaver cello ostinato, with off-beat tenuto crotchets in a strict 4/4 as his soldiers are marching, and his text is frequently at odds with the phrases he sings.

Following Quintus' triumphant exit and Cassia's grief for the loss of Suli, the priestess invests Cassia with the power of divination. During the process, Cassia is frantic with anxiety, 'Suli my life, my love, my home[.] I thought we would be together forever[.]'[155] The ever-present and ominous rumblings of Vesuvius finally explode, bringing the first act to a close as Cassia screams Suli's name. With the delineation of epoch between the two acts, Hale doubles each role. Silenus (companion and tutor to the young Dionysus) becomes the uncle, the Priestess is Mother, Julia the initiate and handmaiden to the Priestess becomes Jules, the bartender.[156]

Act II transports us to the present, the time when we first encountered Cass; however, rather than walking the cobbled streets of the ruins of Pompeii, she is in downtown Toronto. The orchestration shifts slightly with the flute being replaced by alto saxophone. We are introduced to Jules, the bartender of a lesbian bar in 1984. The stage directions indicate that she removes her jacket to reveal 'dyke clothes',[157] as she straightens up proudly. Cass is sitting at a table in an angry exchange with Suzie, a reincarnation of Suli. Suzie is outraged that Cass wants her to be a 'closet dyke';[158] however, Cass insists that it is purely for the benefit of her mother. The issue of cohabitation becomes heated and Cass storms out of the bar but returns to Suzi with two pomegranate cocktails which seem to aid in a reconciliation and a passionate embrace.

The following scene explores the details of their first date, and throughout the intertwining phrases references to the ancient city of Pompeii and the explosion of Vesuvius pepper the narrative, including their school trip to the ruins. They reflect on the longevity of their three-year relationship, unaware that they were lovers in a previous life. The lesbian bar represents a safe haven for the couple, where they can freely express themselves and have nothing to hide. The psychological protection that the bar provides is challenged by a contemporary nemesis in the form of Suzi's uncle. Once again, the presence of a man in the lives of the two women represents a sinister, unwelcomed threat to their world. Cass warns, 'Nowhere is safe for lesbians.'[159] In scene xvi, Jules sings of her failed relationships that explains why she stays away from love, 'We were oh so in love till she ditched me for another[,] broke my heart in a thousand pieces.'[160] The melodic motif of this scene is derived from her 'I see it all' material – her commentary on the fragility of lesbian relationships.

With the entry of the uncle in the following scene comes the same homophobic disruption of the space that he has permeated, and his language, as with Quintus, is immediately at odds with the musical setting, 'I will make you marry[,] learn to be a woman.'[161] Resulting in the disapproval of her queerness by her mother and uncle, Suzie is forced into deciding whether to remain with her family or to continue her relationship with Cass. The quartet of characters pull at Suzi's emotional sense of belonging until she finally relents into her mother's arms. With this decision, Suzi's mother sings to Cass venomously, 'You'll never see her again!'[162] Cass shouts to Suzi as she leaves the stage, 'Suzie! I'll wait for you! . . . the villa . . . the frescoes.'[163] The opera concludes back in Pompeii, in the alcove, behind the wine press in the present day. Suli and Cassia are reunited once more on the eve of the revelation of the Mysteries, and they use the metaphor of the pomegranate as a symbol of their erotic love, 'Together we squeeze our pomegranate opens seeds bursting the bloody fist . . . One by one you feed me the years plump seeds spurting[.] Fruit of the dream world seeding our bodies with memory.'[164]

With the constant, ominous presence of Vesuvius on the verge of eruption, the opera is given a context in which the characters are in imminent danger. With the convention of time travel, the contemporary threat, although altered, remains when the characters find themselves in 1984 Canada. Despite the relative acceptance of queerness, lesbians are still experiencing deeply held views that view their relationships as a threat to heteronormativity. The danger comes in the form of patriarchal figures whose reactions to the two women being together are guided by self-interest; their relationship is an inconvenience. The bigotry and homophobia of the two men are secondary to their general lack of empathy. Much of the messaging from *Pomegranate* promotes feminist concepts more directly than queer concepts. Hale explains, 'I hope people will leave the theatre with an expanded feeling of women's experience across the centuries, and with a feeling of our endurance in the face of challenge.' She continues, 'I hope our audiences will be prompted to think too of how hostage we are to Nature, and how quickly all our plans can be scooped by an event like the eruption of Mount Vesuvius.'[165] Their love spawns disapproval for the interruption of expedient heteronormative functions, rather than a revulsion of queerness. Sadly, the relationship buckled, reminding us that we must try harder to protect that love which we strive so hard to achieve.

NOTES

1. John Corvino, ed., *Same Sex: Debating the Ethics, Science, and Culture of Homosexuality*, Vol. 70 (Lanham, MD: Rowman & Littlefield, 1999).

2. David M. Halperin, 'How to do the history of male homosexuality', *GLQ: A Journal of Lesbian and Gay Studies* 6, no. 1 (2000): 87–123.

3. Christine Downing, 'Lesbian mythology', *Historical Reflections* 20, no. 2 (1994): 171.

4. Giulia Sissa, 'Agathon and Agathon. Male sensuality in Aristophanes' thesmophoriazusae and plato's symposium', *EuGeStA. Journal of Gender Studies in Antiquity* 2 (2012): 25–70.

5. Thomas L. Pangle, ed., *The Laws of Plato* (Chicago: University of Chicago Press, 1988), 233.

6. Jonathon Goodman, *The Oscar Wilde File* (London: W.H. Allen and Co., 1989), 114.

7. Dirk Von der Horst, *Jonathan's Loves, David's Laments: Gay Theology, Musical Desires, and Historical Difference* (Eugene, OR: Wipf and Stock Publishers, 2017).

8. 1 Samuel 18: verse 1.

9. 2 Samuel 1: verse 26.

10. Andrew Sutherland, *Children in Opera* (Newcastle Upon Tyne: Cambridge Scholars Publishing, 2020).

11. François Bretonneau, *David et Jonathas* (Paris: Claude Thiboust, 1688), and François Bretonneau, *David et Jonathas* (Paris: Louis Sevestre, 1706), 38–39. 'JONATHAS: Malgré la rigeur de mon sort,/Du moins je puis vous dire encor que je vous aime'.

12. Steve Boscardin, 'David et Jonathas de Charpentier à Versailles: un Opéra à la chapelle', *ResMusica*, 13 November 2022.

13. Justin Henderlight, 'Marc-Antoine Charpentier's David et Jonathas: French Jesuit theater and the tragédie en musique' (PhD diss., University of British Columbia, 2017).

14. Theresa Angert-Quilter and Lynne Wall, 'The 'spirit wife' at Endor', *Journal for the Study of the Old Testament* 25, no. 92 (2001): 55–72.

15. Bretonneau, *David et Jonathas*, 12. 'Jonathas tant de fois me vit renouveller / Mille sermens d'une amour mutuelle: /Helas il fut toûjours Fidelle, / Moi seul je puis les violer'!

16. Bretonneau, *David et Jonathas*, 38–39. 'DAVID: Quoi, Prince, je vous perds! JONATHAS: Le jour que je revoi, / Si je ne retrouvois un Ami si Fidelle, / Seroit encor plus funeste pour moi. / DAVID: Ah! Vivez. JONATHAS: Je ne puis. DAVID: David, David lui-mesme a ceder aux transports d'une douleur extréme. / JONATHAS: Malgré la rigeur de mon sort, / Du moins je puis vous dire encor que je vous aime. / DAVID: Ciel! Il est mort'!

17. Monica Silveira Cyrino, 'Heroes in D(u)ress: Transvestism and power in the myths of herakles and achilles', *Arethusa* 31, no. 2 (1998): 207–241.

18. William Armstrong Percy III, 'Reconsiderations about Greek homosexualities', *Journal of Homosexuality* 49, no. 3–4 (2005): 13–61.

19. Steven Robinson, 'The contest of wisdom between Socrates and Agathon in Plato's Symposium', *Ancient Philosophy* 24, no. 1 (2004): 81–100.

20. Christoph Willibald Gluck, *Iphigénie en Tauride: Tragédie en quatre actes* [Full score] (Paris: Des Lauriers, 1780), 72.

21. Gluck, *Iphigénie en Tauride*, 75.

22. Charles-Louis de Secondat Montesquieu, 'De l'esprit des lois (1748),' *Œuvres complètes* (1964): 1949–1951.

23. Gluck, *Iphigénie en Tauride*, 78.

24. Christoph Meiners, *Vermischte philosophische schriften*, Vol. 1 (Weygandschen buchhandlung, 1775).

25. Gluck, *Iphigénie en Tauride*, 78–79.

26. Gluck, *Iphigénie en Tauride*, 79–80.

27. Anton Adămuț, 'Philosophical aspects of homosexuality in Ancient Greek', *Philosophy, Social and Human Disciplines* 2 (2011): 11–22.

28. Brian Joseph Martin, *Napoleonic Friendship: Military Fraternity, Intimacy & Sexuality in Nineteenth Century France* (Hanover: University Press of New England, 2011), 20.

29. Steven Eric Soebbing, 'The portrayal of male homoeroticism in selected early classical operas' (PhD diss., The University of Nebraska-Lincoln, 2012).

30. Gluck, *Iphigénie en Tauride*, 127.

31. Gluck, *Iphigénie en Tauride*, 127–128.

32. Anthony Tommasini, 'Realism unvarnished for Gluck's bonded males', *The New York Times*, 3 October 1997, 1, http://www.nytimes.com/1997/10/03/movies/realism-unvarnished-for-gluck-s-bonded-males.html.

33. Gluck, *Iphigénie en Tauride*, 205–211.

34. Jeffrey Merrick, 'The Marquis de Villette and Mademoiselle de Raucourt: Representations of male and female sexual deviance in late eighteenth-century France', in *Homosexuality in Modern France*, eds. Jeffrey Merrick and Bryant T. Ragan Jr. (New York: Oxford University Press, 1996), 30–53: 30.

35. Soebbing, 'The portrayal of male homoeroticism', 2012.

36. Yumnam Oken Singh and Gyanabati Khuraijam, 'Aestheticism, decadence and symbolism: Fin de siècle movements in revolt', *Journal of Literature, Culture & Media Studies* 4, no. 7/8 (2012): 71–84.

37. Valeria Wenderoth, 'The making of exoticism in French operas of the 1890s' (PhD diss., University of Hawaii, 2004).

38. Paul Milliet, 'Astarte', *Le Monde artiste* 8 (February 24, 1901): 115–117.

39. Omphale was originally performed by Leroux's wife, Meyrianne Héglon (1867–1942).

40. Xavier Leroux, *Astarté* [vocal score] (Paris: Alphonse Leduc, 1901), 10–11.

41. Leroux, *Astarté*, 32.

42. Leroux, *Astarté*, 140–141.

43. Leroux, *Astarté*, 167.

44. Leroux, *Astarté*, 168.

45. Leroux, *Astarté*, 175–177.

46. Leroux, *Astarté*, 180.

47. Leroux, *Astarté*, 181.

48. Leroux, *Astarté*, 201.

49. Leroux, *Astarté*, 213–215.

50. Leroux, *Astarté*, 223–224.

51. Leroux, *Astarté*, 224.

52. Leroux, *Astarté*, 276–281.

53. Leroux, *Astarté*, 289–290.

54. Leroux, *Astarté*, 299.

55. Leroux, *Astarté*, 413–415.

56. Leroux, *Astarté*, 429.

57. J-G. Prod'homme, 'Les Musiciens Français à Rome (1803–1903)', *Sammelbande der Internationalen Musikgesellschaft* (1903): 728–737.

58. Leta E. Miller and Fredric Lieberman, *Composing a World: Lou Harrison, Musical Wayfarer*, Vol. 543 (Champaign, IL: University of Illinois Press, 2004), 189.

59. Tom Ellison, 'Lou Harrison centennial birthday celebration: 1917–2017', *The Diversity Center of Santa Cruz*, 24 April 2017, accessed 12 September 2021, https://www.diversitycenter.org/lou.

60. Leta E. Miller and Fredric Lieberman, *Lou Harrison* (Champaign, IL: University of Illinois Press, 2006), 34.

61. Winston Leyland and Peter Garland, 'Winston Leyland interviews Lou Harrison', *A Lou Harrison Reader* (1987): 70–84: 79.

62. Bill Alves, Brett Campbell, and Mark Morris, *Lou Harrison* (Bloomington: Indiana University Press, 2017).

63. Brady Joseph Spitz, 'Lou Harrison's "old granddad": A composer's guide' (PhD diss., Rice University, 2019).

64. Lou Harrison, *Young Caesar: Opera in 14 Scenes* [Full score, Revised Performing Edition] (New York: Peermusic, 2021), 16.

65. Harrison, *Young Caesar*, 51.

66. Harrison, *Young Caesar*, 97.

67. Irving Bieber, Harvey J. Dain, Paul R. Dince, Marvin G. Drellich, Henry G. Grand, Ralph H. Gundlach, et al., *Homosexuality: A Psychoanalytic Study of Male Homosexuals* (New York: Basic Books, 1962).

68. Murray Bowen, 'Family therapy and family group therapy', in *Treating Relationships*, ed. David H. Olson (Lake Mills, IO: Graphic, 1976), 219–274.

69. Joseph Nicolosi, *Reparative Therapy of Male Homosexuality: A New Clinical Approach* (Northvale, NJ: Jason Aronson, 1991).

70. Bertram J. Cohler and Robert M. Galatzer-Levy, *The Course of Gay and Lesbian Lives* (Chicago: University of Chicago Press, 2000).

71. Ray A. Seutter and Martin Rovers, 'Emotionally absent fathers: Furthering the understanding of homosexuality', *Journal of Psychology and Theology* 32, no. 1 (2004): 43–49.

72. Harrison, *Young Caesar*, 109.

73. Harrison, *Young Caesar*, 115.

74. Harrison, *Young Caesar*, 116–117.

75. Harrison, *Young Caesar*, 120.

76. Leta E. Miller and Fredric Lieberman, 'Lou Harrison and the American gamelan', *American Music* (1999): 146–178.

77. Niall Munro, 'American decadence and the creation of a queer modernist aesthetic', in *Hart Crane's Queer Modernist Aesthetic* (London: Palgrave Macmillan, 2015), 16–40.

78. Harrison, *Young Caesar*, 143.

79. Harrison, *Young Caesar*, 143.

80. Harrison, *Young Caesar*, 144.

81. Harrison, *Young Caesar*, 144.

82. Harrison, *Young Caesar*, 144.

83. Harrison, *Young Caesar*, 144.

84. Harrison, *Young Caesar*, 144–145.

85. Josiah Osgood, 'Caesar and Nicomedes', *The Classical Quarterly* 58, no. 2 (2008): 687–691.

86. Mark Simpson and Melanie Challenger, *Pleasure* [Full score] (London: Boosey & Hawkes, 2016), 206.

87. Simpson and Challenger, *Pleasure*, 169–170.

88. Simpson and Challenger, *Pleasure*, 170–171.

89. Simpson and Challenger, *Pleasure*, 385–387.

90. Simpson and Challenger, *Pleasure*, 229–230.

91. Simpson and Challenger, *Pleasure*, 125–127.

92. Ilan H. Meyer, 'Resilience in the study of minority stress and health of sexual and gender minorities', *Psychology of Sexual Orientation and Gender Diversity* 2, no. 3 (2015): 209.

93. William J. Hall, 'Psychosocial risk and protective factors for depression among lesbian, gay, bisexual, and queer youth: A systematic review', *Journal of Homosexuality* 65, no. 3 (2018): 263–316.

94. Gregory M. Herek, J. Roy Gillis, and Jeanine C. Cogan, 'Internalized stigma among sexual minority adults: Insights from a social psychological perspective', *Stigma and Health* 1 (S) (2015): 18–34.

95. Simpson and Challenger, *Pleasure*, 169.

96. Simpson and Challenger, *Pleasure*, 173.

97. Simpson and Challenger, *Pleasure*, 186.

98. Simpson and Challenger, *Pleasure*, 163–164.

99. Simpson and Challenger, *Pleasure*, 310–311.

100. Simpson and Challenger, *Pleasure*, 311.

101. Simpson and Challenger, *Pleasure*, 156–157.

102. Simpson and Challenger, *Pleasure*, 132–134.

103. Simpson and Challenger, *Pleasure*, 294–295.

104. Simpson and Challenger, *Pleasure*, 316–317.

105. Simpson and Challenger, *Pleasure*, 56.

106. Simpson and Challenger, *Pleasure*, 59.

107. Simpson and Challenger, *Pleasure*, 70–72.

108. Simpson and Challenger, *Pleasure*, 277.

109. Jennifer Chamberlain, 'Composer Mark Simpson on his debut opera, pleasure', *The Skinny*, 22 April 2016.

110. Sarah Riley, Yvette More, and Christine Griffin, 'The "pleasure citizen" analyzing partying as a form of social and political participation', *Young* 18, no. 1 (2010): 33–54.

111. Michel Maffesoli, *The Time of the Tribes: The Decline of Individualism in Mass Society* (London: Sage, 1995).

112. Simpson and Challenger, *Pleasure*, 338–340.

113. Sean Michaels, 'Rufus Wainwright to compose opera about Roman emperor Hadrian', *The Guardian*, 3 December 2013, accessed 15 December 2021, https://

www.theglobeandmail.com/arts/theatre-and-performance/how-rufus-wainwright-is
-turning-a-roman-emperor-into-a-coc-opera/article15677143/?page=all.

114. Dag Heede, 'Antinous: Saint or criminal?,' *Lambda Nordica* 22, no. 4 (2017): 17–39.

115. 'Rufus wainwrights rape tragedy', *FemaleFirst.co.uk*, 1 March 2005, accessed 15 December 2021, https://www.femalefirst.co.uk/music/musicnews/Rufus +Wainwright-3238.html.

116. Rufus Wainwright and Daniel MacIvor, *Hadrian* [Full score] (London: Chester Music ltd., 2021), 80.

117. Wainwright and MacIvor, *Hadrian*, 92.

118. Wainwright and MacIvor, *Hadrian*, 30–31.

119. Wainwright and MacIvor, *Hadrian*, 64–65.

120. Wainwright and MacIvor, *Hadrian*, 40–41.

121. Wainwright and MacIvor, *Hadrian*, 85–88.

122. Levy specializes in compositions for recreated lyres of antiquity, which he describes as 'new ancestral music'.

123. Wainwright and MacIvor, *Hadrian*, 90.

124. Wainwright and MacIvor, *Hadrian*, 90.

125. Wainwright and MacIvor, *Hadrian*, 94.

126. Wainwright and MacIvor, *Hadrian*, 95.

127. Wainwright and MacIvor, *Hadrian*, 124.

128. Wainwright and MacIvor, *Hadrian*, 128.

129. Wainwright and MacIvor, *Hadrian*, 129–130.

130. Wainwright and MacIvor, *Hadrian*, 1.

131. Wainwright and MacIvor, *Hadrian*, 22–23.

132. Wainwright and MacIvor, *Hadrian*, 28.

133. Wainwright and MacIvor, *Hadrian*, 104.

134. Jenna Simeonov, 'A lesbian chamber opera to span centuries: Pomegranate', *Schmopera*, 8 May 2019, accessed 5 January, https://www.schmopera.com/a-lesbian -chamber-opera-to-span-centuries-pomegranate/.

135. Simeonov, 'A lesbian chamber opera'.

136. Ky Marshall and Amanda Hale, *Pomegranate* [Vocal score] (Unpublished score, 2019), 6.

137. Marshall and Hale, *Pomegranate*, 41–43.

138. Marshall and Hale, *Pomegranate*, 62.

139. Marshall and Hale, *Pomegranate*, 101–102.

140. Marshall and Hale, *Pomegranate*, 109–110.

141. Marshall and Hale, *Pomegranate*, 148–150.

142. Marshall and Hale, *Pomegranate*, 199.

143. Marshall and Hale, *Pomegranate*, 199.

144. Marshall and Hale, *Pomegranate*, 213.

145. Marshall and Hale, *Pomegranate*, 239–242.

146. Marshall and Hale, *Pomegranate*, 244–245.

147. Marshall and Hale, *Pomegranate*, 248–249.

148. Marshall and Hale, *Pomegranate*, 251–252.

149. Marshall and Hale, *Pomegranate*, 264–265.

150. Marshall and Hale, *Pomegranate*, 295–296.

151. Marshall and Hale, *Pomegranate*, 303–304.

152. Marshall and Hale, *Pomegranate*, 310–313.

153. Marshall and Hale, *Pomegranate*, 314.

154. Marshall and Hale, *Pomegranate*, 346–347.

155. Marshall and Hale, *Pomegranate*, 381.

156. Amanda Hale, 'Pomegranate: How my self-published chapbook became an Opera', *Write* 44, no. 2, Summer (2016): 14–15.

157. Marshall and Hale, *Pomegranate*, 397.

158. Marshall and Hale, *Pomegranate*, 406.

159. Marshall and Hale, *Pomegranate*, 464.

160. Marshall and Hale, *Pomegranate*, 477.

161. Marshall and Hale, *Pomegranate*, 497.

162. Marshall and Hale, *Pomegranate*, 541.

163. Marshall and Hale, *Pomegranate*, 542.

164. Marshall and Hale, *Pomegranate*, 572–576.

165. Simeonov, 'A lesbian chamber opera'.

Chapter 2

Passing and Coding

In this chapter, I have combined two processes that have unique applications to the queer community. Both are based on the notion of hiding in plain sight. The practice of 'passing' has become a necessary one for queer individuals throughout history, in order to protect themselves from authorities, backed by legislation, to incarcerate and even execute those found to be actively homosexual. Passing requires the adoption of identity traits commonly associated with a privileged group in order to deceive a member of the privileged group into believing the pass.[1] For those societies with more enlightened legal frameworks for sexual liberty, the pernicious presence of vigilante homophobes, looking to teach a lesson to those who express queer physicalities, is a constant threat, providing further the need to blend into a heteronormative background.

Logically, passing involves the individual to hide their identity to ensure their identifiers of sexuality become invisible. Much of the theory linked with identity formation is fundamentally informed by the logical connection with visibility. Science-based research such as Victorian physiognomy and the emergence of psychoanalysis such as Lacan's mirror stage, or Foucault's philosophical discussions of the Panopticon, rely on a degree of epistemological confidence in our ability to observe visual markers. The act of passing subverts these visual certainties, replacing them with anxieties related to visibility, invisibility, classification and social demarcation.[2] For public figures, this exhausting display becomes particularly important when every mannerism, choice of clothing and turn of phrase can be scrutinized by those determined to see through the pass. The process of passing depends on the disposition of the observer; what may be considered gender 'abnormality' in some cases may indicate the presumption of heterosexuality on the basis of a lived understanding of hegemony in other cases.

Passing occurs within the contemporary queer community, underlining the perpetual need for a better understanding of sexual fluidity and variation. Bisexuals sometimes feel the need to identify as being gay or straight, finding greater social acceptance in the safety of the firmly claimed sexuality poles. They are frequently derided as being promiscuously curious or for adopting a label which is easier to wear than 'gay' for closeted men, leaving bisexuality nebulously occupying an unspecified space between two poles of identity. Lesbians form judgements of other lesbians who sleep with men. So-called 'straight' people who enjoy rare moments of queer behaviour repudiate any hint of queer identity.[3] All of which highlights that the theoretical nexus of physicality, sexuality and community offers a complex view of identity made even more intricate when it is hidden through the act of passing.

Another form of hiding in plain sight is the process of coding. Coding allows the queer-identified individual to draw from the archive of shared linguistics and other forms and create an algorithm that is understood by the queer community but covertly incongruous to those outside. Representing homosexuality on the stage was long regarded as an unmentionable vulgarity by a hegemonic society; however, the enthusiasm with which the queer community embraced the theatre as a form of escape provided a conundrum in which agitators sought to allow queers their space without provoking retribution. During the 1920s, the mainstream nightclubs in Times Square would regularly stage 'pansy acts' which were popular acknowledgements of the existence of queerness. The year 1927, however, saw the introduction of the padlock bill, which prohibited theatres from 'depicting or dealing with, the subject of sex degeneracy or sex perversion',[4] which put an end to the 'pansy acts'. Both Broadway and Hollywood then created a set of coded characters, vulgar stereotypes though never directly categorized, which allowed the middle class an opportunity to witness the strange manifestation of the abhorrent degenerate.[5] Queers were either seen as untrustworthy villains or weak and ineffective subservient members of the lower class.

In Bedřich Smetana's *Dalibor*, the carefully coded queer relationship between the fifteenth-century knight, Dalibor, and his recently executed 'friend', Zdeněk, provides an intriguing insight into the perceptions of an audience based on sexuality perspective. The term 'friend', given a heterosexual reading, may suggest a platonic companionship; however, it is important to remember that prior to any meaningful categorization of homosexuality as distinct and accepted form of sexuality, such a term provided little in the way of helpful assessment. In Strauss' *Salome*, the small role of the Page of Herodius, who is enamoured with Narraboth, would likely have gone completely unnoticed when given a straight reading, but for those able to understand homoeroticism and loving devotion between two men, *Salome* provided yet another reason to shock an unsuspecting audience. Benjamin

Britten chose libretti that were often ambiguous in their depiction of queerness, and he made every effort to disguise his gay characters to all but the astute queer intelligentsia who found little difficulty identifying the clues. Combining his mastery of musical techniques and his love of classical literature, Britten's portrayals of Claggart in *Billy Budd* and Peter Quint in *The Turn of the Screw* were sufficiently obfuscated notions of queerness so as not to draw unwanted attention from the authorities. Ricky Ian Gordon explored coding in *27*, an opera concerning the life of Gertrude Stein, through the changing social fabric of the queer community in early-twentieth-century Paris. Finally, in *Fellow Travelers*, Gregory Spears highlights the need for queers to pass, in order to survive the appalling period of McCarthyism which targeted gay men in a process known as the 'lavender scare'. Each of these operas provides a range of historical perspectives; however, it would be naïve to assume that coding is a bygone practice.

DALIBOR, BEDŘICH SMETANA

In 1961, during the communist regime (1948–1989), a new penal code was introduced in Czechoslovakia, decriminalizing homosexual acts. Previously, such acts were defined as crimes against human dignity and were punishable by a prison sentence of up to one year. The change in law was celebrated by the gay community and visitors of *T-klub*, one of two gay establishments in communist Prague, who enthusiastically sang an aria from Bedrich Smetana's opera *Dalibor* (1868) as a queer anthem in celebration of the progress.[6] This choice of music must have resonated with the gay community in Prague, still living a relatively underground existence. For opera music to become anthemic, such as Puccini's *Nessun Dorma* from *Turandot*, Leoncavallo's *Vesti la Giubba* from *Pagliacci* or Wagner's *Ride of the Valkyries* from *Die Walküre*, the music must be of such quality as to inspire spontaneous reproduction and must provide meaning that surpasses the opera from which it came. In the case of *Dalibor*, Smetana managed to achieve both, despite its status as an infrequently performed work. Unfortunately, like many nationalistic operas from this time, the story did not resonate meaningfully with foreign audiences.

Much of the reason for Smetana's *Dalibor* being less frequently performed than his excellent music deserves is the stilted and almost comedically bad libretto. Good Czech librettists were thin on the ground in the 1860s, but Ervin Špindler (1843–1918) was tasked with translating Josef Wenzig's (1807–1876) original German libretto. Its German origins, as well as comparisons with Wagner's *Lohengrin* (1848), drew sharp criticism following the premiere at the New Town Theatre on 16 May 1868. The problematic libretto makes use of clumsy rhyming schemes, which once translated into

English is difficult to take seriously. Furthermore, the title character, based on a fifteenth-century knight, who dissented against King Vladislaus II of Hungary's authority and executed in 1498, comes across as impulsive, rather than heroic. He is rescued from prison by Malida, disguised by dressing as a boy, who becomes immediately enraptured with him, and declarations of marriage are made within moments – a development that is highly unconvincing in its briskness. Also, the opera lacks a genuine nemesis, as the actions of King Vladislav seem to be based on reasonable and genuine impulses.

The strongly insinuated homosexual relationship has taken place prior to the commencement of the narrative and is illuminated through Dalibor's detailed and constant reference throughout the opera. The first act takes place in a great hall in a Czech castle. Dalibor is on trial before the king, for the murder of the burgrave (count) of Ploskovice, which was an act of revenge for the execution of his friend, Zdeněk. Zdeněk was a violinist, the national instrument of Bohemian cultures, and although he does not appear in the opera, he is represented by passages for solo violin. It is during the trial that we hear Dalibor's thoughts about his friend Zdeněk in Act I, scene iv. He sings:

Vždy odolal jsem čarozraku žen.	No female charms ever have me bewitched!
Po příteli můj duch toliko toužil.	To have a friend was my heart's one desire!
Mé přání splněno, přátelství sen	My wish was granted me, I lived sweet
jsem snil, u Zdeňka v ňader tůň se	friendship's dream in Zdeněk's company and
hroužil.	knew no ire.
Když Zdeněk můj ve svatém nadšení	When Zdeněk mine in sacred ecstasy
zvuk rajský loudil v mysl rozháranou,	With music sweet chased all gloom from my
rozplýval jsem se v sladkém toužení,	heart,
povznesen tam, kde hvězdy jasné	I felt transported there, in daring fantasy,
planou.	Where the stars in heaven their journey do start!
Však slyš! Již dávný čas jsem vedl	But hear! For many months I stood in quarrel
hádku	With the local council's stupid vainglory
s litoměřickou radou zpyšnělou	And now and then I took to arms,
a opět v boj jsem šel, po boku	with me was Zdeněk,
Zdeněk,	
můj drahý Zdeněk, nerozdílný druh.	My dearest Zdeněk, always close to me.
Boj zuřit počal hněvem.	Embittered fighting then flared up and captured
Zdeněk pad' v nepřátel moc	was My Zdeněk. A passion monstrous, inhuman
mně pak v potupu ji narazila na	Had him beheaded.
hradbách na kůl.	Then to my horror,
Hrůz obraze,	They impaled Zdeněk's head upon a spike!
který jsem pníti	That dreadful sight I had to behold
tam musel zříti!	there thus exposed!
Tím zděšením	That dreadful sight
nevím, zda bdím!	There thus exposed!
Marně oko slze volá,	And no amount of clement tears
by si ulevila ňadra má![7]	could diminish my pain so fierce!

Figure 2.1 shows a section of the aria, in which Zdeněk is represented by the mercurial semiquaver passages from the solo violin.

So much is suddenly revealed about the relationship between Dalibor and Zdeněk that there must have been an audible gasp from any queer opera devotees present at the premiere. The phrase, 'No female charms ever have me bewitched!'[8] (*Vždy odolal jsem čarozraku žen*), a particularly clumsy translation that does not match the rhyming scheme, reveals that Dalibor has not yet had heterosexual, romantic relations. This seems an entirely unnecessary confession for the courtroom, and such an admission for a fifteenth-century knight would have been alarming. Another rather incredible phrase from this passage seems to reveal the sexual nature of the relationship: 'When Zdeněk mine in sacred ecstasy'[9] (*Když Zdeněk můj ve svatém nadšení*). It is at this moment, the solo violin enters, playing jubilant scalic figures to accompany Dalibor's vocal line and suggesting that despite Zdeněk's lack of physical presence, the two are still very much united.

Dalibor's arrival is heralded by a glorious fanfare, and Milada becomes instantly attracted to him. Dalibor's testimony is one of the most incredibly beautiful tenor arias in the repertoire, and it is easy to imagine that this is what was sung in the T-Klub in the early 1960s. Thanks in part to Smetana's masterful writing, Milada's desire for revenge for murdering her brother is quickly replaced with unqualified love for this man who she has not met before. There is a discernible note of resignation to his fate throughout

Figure 2.1 Dalibor's Court Scene Aria, Act I, Scene iv, p. 47. Beidrich Smetana, Josef Wenzig and Ervín Špindler, arr. Vaclav Juda Novotny, Dalibor [piano reduction], Umělecká Beseda, 1923. Public Domain.

Dalibor's appearance in the trial. He accepts the certain punishment of death, without a hint of regret. He sings:

Ničím je mi život,	No meaning has my life
co Zdeněk můj kles',	Since Zdeněk is away!
vše jedno, zda zemru	What matters if I die
snad zítra či dnes![10]	Tomorrow or today?

His melody is set in a gleeful G major, with a jaunty 6/8 meter. This cheerful disposition comes from a man who is blissfully awaiting to be reunited with his lover. He later sings to his friend in 'heaven's regions' that through celestial visions, he can still see and hear Zdeněk. He embraces the prospect of death so that 'once again I drink your magic tones, Sweeter than here does your song sound there!'[11] (*Již piju, opět piju strun tvých čarozvuky! Slavněj než zde zní píseň tvoje tam!*). Unexpectedly, Dalibor is sentenced to life imprisonment, rather than death, and it is not until the beginning of Act II that we once more hear of Dalibor's love for Zdeněk.

A plot is established by the comedic lovers, Jitka and Vítek, to free Dalibor. It involves Milada entering the prison under the ruse of finding employment and dressing as a boy. She charms the jailor, Beneš, into gaining access to the prison dungeons but takes with her a violin for which he had been pleading. Dalibor is delirious, and when Milada appears, he mistakes the 'boy' as a reincarnation of his murdered lover. He begins singing a short recitative, followed by an aria in sections of contrasting moods:

Nebyl to on zas? Nebyl to zas Zdeněk?	Was it he again? It must have been Zdeněk!
Nezaslechl jsem zvuky zlatých strun?	His golden strings, did I not hear them playing?
Kde meškáš, Zdeňku? Zjev se, příteli!	Where art thou, Zdeněk? Show thy face to me!
On jde mě potěšit, ve snu se blíží,	He tries to comfort me in dreamy visions,
nemůže jinak ke mně, Zdeněk můj.	For there's no other way – Zdeněk mine!
Ó Zdeňku, jedno jen obejmutí,	Oh, Zdeněk, just one fleeting touch of hand
a žalář bude rájem mi.	and paradise would here to me descend.
Chci volnost, všechno zapomenout,	Oh, freedom, thee and wealth would I resign
zasvitne-li sem pohled tvůj!	For Zdeněk's friendship one sweet sign!
Leč hrobu stíny nás od sebe dělí,	But the grave's darkening shadows do us part,
ty trůníš tam a já zde hynu v celi.	divide!
Ó Zdeňku, že mi nelze obraz tvůj,	In heaven thou and I must here abide!
když v mysli mi tane, kouzlem	Oh, Zdeněk, why, oh why can I not keep
učarovat na věky!	by some magic power, thine image dear for ever,
Ó Zdeňku, ó Zdeňku!	Oh, Zdeněk, oh, Zdeněk!
Ó kéž bych jenom housle měl,	Could I only have a fiddle which here at least
bych aspoň tóny ty zas přičaroval,	those tunes would conjure up those days and
po kterých sladce blouzním den i noc![12]	nights change into blissful dreams!

The opening of this section of text is set to a wistful melody underpinned by gentle and simple homophonic accompaniment. The vocal style is clearly bel canto, and there is a touching moment of *sotto voce* singing when he pauses on his second utterance of 'O Zdeněk'.

The phrase that follows, 'Oh, Zdeněk, just one fleeting touch of hand, and paradise would here to me descend' (*Ó Zdeňku, jedno jen obejmutí, a žalář bude rájem mi*),[13] may translate more accurately as an embrace, but nevertheless, there is further suggestion of a physical relationship beyond some form of platonic comradeship. When Milada, symbolically dressed as a male, appears, Dalibor grasps for the violin without so much of a glance at her. After singing Zdeněk's name three times, he finally turns his attention to the boy and asks for his name. After discovering Milada's true identity, the following exchange is baffling. Despite continued pronouncements to Zdeněk, he instantly falls in love with the smitten Milada, and suddenly declarations of unending matrimony spring forth, followed by a passionate duet.

Ó Zdeňku můj, teď chápu, proč jsi přišel,	Oh, Zdeněk mine, I know now why you came,
své hry čarovným zvukem chtěls	Your tunes, enchanting tunes were meant
ohlásit příchod spasitelky mé,	To herald this, my sure salvation,
která má v ňadrech mých tě nahradit.	This lady fair who has to take your place.
Povstaňte již, Milado!	Stand up, fair Milada!
Vy žena jste, která přemohla mne.	You are the one who has conquered me.
chci být vám bratrem, přítelem a vším!	It's me who killed your dearest brother!
Sem na srdce k věčnému svazku duší![14]	Be you my sister, friend and lover!
	Here, to my heart, for union eternal!

The final passages suggest that the relationship could have arisen out of Dalibor's sense of honour rather than a sexual attraction. At this point, the plot to free Dalibor is about to transpire. Before he is marched from his cell to the scaffold, he sings of his impending reunion with Zdeněk.

Již přijdu, Zdeňku, a ve krátké době	I'm coming, Zdeněk, and I expect that soon
i Milada se vrátí zpět k tobě,	Shall Milada also come to assume
ta dívka svatá, pro kterou jsem žil.	Her place amongst us, our grave to brighten.
Nuž dál, jen dál! Smrt duši nepoleká,	Let's go, let's go! Death my soul cannot frighten!
já znám ji z bitev. Zdeněk na mne	Too well I know it, Zdeněk has known its
čeká!	sting!
Krev smyje vše, čím jsem se provinil![15]	Oh, may my blood reconcile everything!

Dalibor's wish to repair the damage of bloodshed through his own mortal end is revealed. Smetana's vocal lines for the title character are reminiscent of Belini, and the absence of any *leitmotivs* in the piece leaves the stylistic comparisons with Wager wanting. There are even moments that echo Beethoven, and similarities with plot elements of Fidelio are apparent. When Budivoj, commander of the castle guard, arrives to take Dalibor away for execution, Dalibor refuses to reveal Milada's conspiracy, referring to her as 'the boy', as Budivoj still believes a young man was responsible for the plot. Dalibor's maintenance of Milada's anonymity is a chivalrous gesture to ensure her safety, but the symbolism of her transgender manifestation would not have been lost on queer audience members. During the entire scene in which Dalibor and Milada declare their sudden love for one another, the vision is of a man embracing a boy.

The king has acquiesced to the advice of his council and ordered Dalibor's execution. The tolling bell, signalling the start of the execution, triggers the conspirators, including Malida, who storm the castle. She is fatally wounded and dies in Dalibor's arms. As she lies dying, his mourning for her is intertwined with his desire to be reunited with Zdeněk, in what can only be imagined as some sort of celestial *ménage à trois*. Dalibor's final words fall just ten bars before the close of the opera. He reiterates his joy at being in an endless three-way relationship with Zdeněk and Milada, singing, 'Sweet now shall be my end, my end! With Zdeněk there'll Milada be!'[16] (*Sladké teď bude mé skonání! Čeká mne Zdeněk s Miladou!*). In the original version, he was stabbed to death by Budivoj. One of the three alternative endings devised sees Dalibor executed before Milada could rescue him.

Any reading of this story through a heteronormative lens would see the declaration of love scene as the defining moment of the opera. The duet involves some wonderful music, but in attempting to create the image of a passionate couple, the frequent and repetitive utterances about Zdeněk with sadness and desire, rather than expressions of unambiguous attraction for Milada, create a confusing and unconventional scene.

Dalibor only enjoyed a limited number of performances during Smetana's lifetime and upon his death in 1884, he believed that the work was a failure, despite being one of his favourite operas. However, it was revived two years later and is now considered staple repertoire in the Czech Republic. Mahler introduced the work to the Viennese in 1892, and it has subsequently been revived several times in Austria and Germany.[17] In 1956, fresh from filming to productions in Bulgaria, Václav Krška returned to Prague and created a screen adaptation of Smetana's opera.[18] It was entered into the Cannes Film Festival that year, but the *Palme d'Or* went to *The Silent World* by Jacques-Yves Cousteau and Louis Malle.

Although the Czech Republic still struggles with the concepts of acceptance and respect for members of the LGBTQI+ community outside of the large cities, it has managed to forge a level of enlightenment which is seen as a beacon of hope for queer reformists in eastern Europe. The Czech Republic seemed ready to become the first of Europe's post-communist countries to approve a bill, fully recognizing marriage equality for same-sex couples in 2018, but at the time of writing, the law remains stuck, leaving the queer community banging their heads against a rainbow wall. Much needs to be done to allow characters like Dalibor and Zdeněk to fulfil the potential of their union. In the meantime, may the music of Smetana's *Dalibor* live on as the anthem of gay Prazan.

SALOME, RICHARD STRAUSS

Richard Strauss (1864–1949) completed the first version of his one-act opera, *Salome*, in 1905, before making an alternative French version two years later. The libretto is a German translation by Hedwig Lachmann (1865–1918) of Oscar Wilde's (1854–1900) French play, published in 1891. Wilde's play included homosexuality and incest at the court of King Herod, in addition to an act of necrophilia, which did nothing to quench the scandalous reputation of the English playwright when his infamous trial for indecency took place only four years later. For Wilde, *Salome* represented an opportunity to reject the rigid, British cultural traditions and turn to Greek classicism, which embraced verbal music, Aristotelian dramaturgy and an anti-Christian perspective.

The process of translation from Wilde's original text into the multiple forms of Strauss' libretto is important when considering *Salome* from a queer perspective. Wilde explained in a French interview, 'To me there are only two languages in the world: French and Greek.'[19] Wilde considered *Salome* 'like a piece of music'[20] with its many leitmotifs, refrains, alliterations, assonances and other features found in contemporary French Symbolist literature.[21] The English translation by Lord Alfred Douglas (also queer), with illustrations by Aubrey Beardsley (1872–1898), appeared in 1894, and Wilde disapproved of both. He felt the translation failed to sensitively retain the musicality of the original and had an archaic, historicizing fairy-tale style. Lachmann's translated edition of the play into German was generally considered a success; however, it follows the English version closely. The result is a rougher, less-refined version. However, Lachmann utilized a more modern form of German in contrast to the pomposity of the English translation with its Elizabethan pronouns.

Strauss had initially wanted Anton Lindner, the music critic who had previously published Lachmann's translation, to create the libretto. However, with the premiere of *Pelléas et Mélisande* in April 1902, Debussy had proven that the librettist could be successfully dispensed with. Strauss continued without the customary libretto, setting Lachmann's text directly to music. The result was an adherence to the original text but with a reduction of roughly half.

Strauss was frequently drawn to sexually charged material in his compositions. His operas are dominated by women to an extent that men seem limp
and trivial by comparison. Strauss preserves Wilde's eroticization of John the
Baptist, whom Salome venerates with awakening sexual passion. She relishes
the sight of his white body, commenting on his hair and red lips. The pres-
ervation of the male gaze leitmotif in the score is underpinned by shimmer-
ing, harmonically ambiguous material, over which Narraboth declares, 'Wie
schön ist die Prinzessin Salome heute Nacht!'[22] (How beautiful is the princess
Salome tonight!'). This admiration is juxtaposed with an exigent warning by
his Page, not to look at Salome with such lustful intent (figure 2.2).

The Page also comments on the moon, which looks pale and dead – another
literary and musical leitmotif. In the play, it is clear that the Page of Herodius
is enamoured with Narraboth. This comes into sharp focus when Narroboth
is later found murdered, and the Page exclaims, 'He has slain himself who
was my friend! I gave him a little box of perfumes and ear-rings wrought in
silver, and now he has killed himself!'[23] Strauss' decision to remove this text
could reasonably be viewed as logical expediency of unnecessary dialogue
from a minor character, however, along with his decision to cast the Page as
a contralto, minimizes the opportunity for conjecture relating to his homosexuality. Strauss was one of the last composers to routinely make use of
the travesty role, or trouser role, although the Page was not his last. He created two demanding roles with Octavian Graf Rofrano in *Der Rosenkavalier*
(1911) and the Composer in *Ariadne auf Naxos* (1912).

The last decade of the nineteenth century was one in which homosexual
identity was emerging in many European cultures. *Salome*, under Oscar
Wilde's pen, is a product of an awakening and gradually increasing daring
that was emerging in several arts circles. Strauss, despite being exclusively
devoted to his wife, responded to a milieu in late-nineteenth-century German
societies, in which gay desire was expressed more freely than in most others.

Figure 2.2 The Page's Warning to Narroboth in the Opening Scene, p. 8. Richard
Strauss, Hedwig Lachmann and Alfred Kalisch after Oscar Wilde, Salome Op. 54 [Piano/
vocal score by Otto Singer], Berlin: Adolph Fürnster 1905. Public Domain.

The play is imbued with a homoeroticism that many viewed as perversity. *Salome* was however not the only object of Herod's physical admiration. Upon discovery of the recently suicided Syrian, he questions why he would do such a thing, given his beauty (figure 2.3).

'Fair' is a perfect fit, syllabically, but does not convey the same meaning as 'beautiful'. The play involves several layers of transgressive sexuality, connecting the relationships between the characters. Salome is as infatuated with Jokanaan the prophet as Narraboth the Syrian is enamoured of her, who then kills himself out of unrequited love from her. Salome's lust for Jokanaan culminates in her kissing his severed head, and she engineers the execution by exploiting her stepfather Herod's lust for her. Furthermore, her mother Herodias' marriage to Herod (who murdered his brother, Herodias' first husband and Salome's father) is condemned by Jokanaan as incestuous. The intensity of these debauched infatuations invokes an unfavourable picture of a degenerative society at odds with Victorian sentiment. The Jewish setting, and in particular, one infamous section consisting of five squabbling Jews, supports claims that Strauss intended to emphasize anti-Semitic assumptions about Jewish sexuality. Strauss certainly had supreme contempt for religion and despised John the Baptist, dismissing him as an 'imbecile'. In the libretto, even Jokanaan's lyrics dwell on homoerotic details of the soldiers' attire and physiques.

Wo ist sie, die den Haupt leuten
  Assyriens sich gab?
Wo ist sie, die sich den jungen Männern
  der Egypter gegeben hat, die in feinen
  Leinen und Hyacinth gesteinen pragen,
  deren Schilde von Gold sind und die
  Leiber wie Riesen?[24]
	Where is she, whom the captains of
	  Assyria possessed?
	Where is she who hath given herself
	  to the young men of Egypt, who
	  are clothed in linen, whose shining
	  helmets are of silver, whose shields of
	  gold and whose bodies are brawny?

The translation here is curious and reflects a compromise to favour syllabic suitability. *Riesen* is the masculine form of 'giants', indicated by the height of the phrase and the immense interval of a compound major third. In any case, Jokanaan's unnecessary description of these men, particularly their polished helmets, provides further homoerotic language that is unlikely to be an accident.

Figure 2.3 Herod Appreciates the Beauty of a Syrian Soldier, p. 83. Richard Strauss, Hedwig Lachmann and Alfred Kalisch after Oscar Wilde, Salome Op. 54 [Piano/vocal score by Otto Singer], Berlin: Adolph Fürnster 1905. Public Domain.

In Wilde's Britain, all homosexual acts were made illegal by the Labouchere Amendment of the 1885 Criminal Law Act. Dellamora (1990) suggests that Wilde's transgressive aesthetic anticipated contemporary theoretical critiques of subjective depth such as deconstruction and postmodernism. *Salome* certainly reflects this position. Several academics have viewed the role of Salome as a code for gay desire, in the way she abandons expected societal norms, to embrace her physical lust. Queer audiences are far more likely to identify with Salome's 'perverse' attraction to a beautiful, semi-naked and restrained man than the misogynistic King Herod. Jokanaan continually references Salome as the 'daughter of Sodom', compounding ideas of unfettered lascivious behaviour.[25] Dellamora considers the Medusa imagery in *Salome* as phallic, even suggestive of impending homosexual fellatio, with Salome as a male cross-dresser. In Beardsley's drawing entitled 'The Climax', the various plant-like shapes pointing up to Jokanaan's head are suggestive of the penis, further suggesting her domination over him is penetrative. The established tradition of performing the role of Salomé in drag was considered, until recently, to have been instigated by Wilde himself.

Strauss made extensive use of leitmotifs throughout the opera, and each important character was assigned one, as well as associations such as Herod's bowl or intangible concepts such as obsession. Harmony also contributes to the establishment of character, and Strauss reinforces the incompatibility of Salome and Jokanaan by attributing dissonant tonal relationships of C-sharp for Salome and C major for Jokanaan. There are three groups of characters with more general harmonic characteristics; Jokanaan and the Nazarenes have a diatonic framework, with slow and simple material suitable for the faithful followers; Herod and the Jews are given shrill and exceedingly dissonant music; and Salome sings mellifluous phrases underpinned harmonically with a mid-romantic style. With an orchestra of over one hundred musicians, some of the vocal passages are deliberately indiscernible over the frenzied milieu.

Salome is a work, steeped in queer history. In addition to the foundation laid by Oscar Wilde and Lord Alfred Douglas, Maud Allan would add her own transgressive reputation to the piece. Allan had been accused of lesbianism, and being a spy, for which she unsuccessfully sued for libel. Her brother was hanged in 1898 for the murder of two women in San Francisco. Her production entitled *Vision of Salomé* opened in Vienna in 1906, and her version of the *Dance of the Seven Veils* furthered her infamy, and she was billed 'The Salome Dancer'. Her court case involved obscenity charges and even necrophilia as depicted in Wilde's play, and associations with her brother brought forward arguments of sexual insanity in the family. Over a century later, Matthew Tennyson performed the role of Salome in a production by the Royal Shakespeare Company, marking the fiftieth anniversary of the decriminalization of homosexuality in Britain.

BILLY BUDD, BENJAMIN BRITTEN

Theodor Uppman (1920–2005) was not Britten's first choice to play the intensely attractive, boyish sailor, in the title role of his new opera, *Billy Budd* (1951). Britten created the role with Geraint Evans in mind; however, the tessitura was too high and he was recast as Mr Flint. Uppman was a thirty-one-year-old from California, blonde, tanned and muscled from hauling barrels of oil in an aeroplane factory when he was invited to audition for the role. Upon meeting Uppman for the first time, Britten remarked, 'Well, you certainly look like Billy!'[26] He was to personify youth, beauty and goodness when he took to the stage in Covent Garden.

Britten (1913–1976) worked with two librettists, E. M. Forster (1879–1970) and Eric Crozier (1914–1994). Crozier was predominantly involved in researching British naval history. Both Britten and Forster included markers of queerness in a variety of forms in their respective musical and literary creations, but queer themes needed to be presented cautiously, mirroring their own situations. One of the shared themes in Britten's operas is the way in which queerness is destroyed. Billy and Claggart both meet their ends in *Billy Budd*, as did Quint and Miles (discussed in this chapter) and Aschenbach (see chapter 5). Britten's choice of literary works provides a possible insight into the composer's perception of the viability of homosexual love, which he chose to extinguish rather than allow to blossom. Britten's cautious approach to coding queerness in *Billy Budd* involves processes of interpretation and allegorization to peel back obfuscating layers of censorship and social oppression. This is a closet-queer opera by necessity, which explores the dangers of closeted individuals in the face of unobtainable homoerotic beauty.

Set in 1997, on *The Indomitable*, a Royal Naval vessel during the war with revolutionary France, the all-male cast of seamen is governed by the master-at-arms, John Claggart, a brutal sadist, who is responsible for discipline. Samuel Johnson (1709–1784) considered the penal-like conditions of being at sea during this period and quipped, 'Being in a ship is like being in a jail with the chance of being drowned.'[27] Winston Churchill noted the homosocial environment created in the absence of women, remarking, 'The traditions of the Royal Navy are rum, sodomy, and the lash.'[28] The strict naval regulations, imbued with a sense of moral authority reflective of late-eighteenth-century attitudes to sodomy, mirror the sexual oppression of 1950s Britain, where the constant need for deniability governed the opportunity for queer representation in celebrated public institutions such as the Royal Opera. Britten's codified representation of queer eroticism is, like much of his work, based on a Socratic logic and frequently takes the form of confrontation and transformative dialogue.[29]

The homosocial world of the ship enables the traditional structures of heteronormative society and reproductive imperatives to retreat and for the relationships between men to dominate the narrative. In Act I, scene iii, the crew perform a shanty which fleetingly references two female figures: Anna and Susannah; however, their banter quickly turns to the physical aesthetics of Billy, 'She'll cut up her Billy for pie, For all he's a catch on the eye.'[30] The men are able to celebrate and derive pleasure from male beauty in the self-contained male world.

Billy is an outsider to this world, arriving in the story well after the cast has established themselves in the setting. He is the third prisoner to be presented for duty on the ship, a 'foundling', raised by a 'poor old man', and with no home. Britten's operas often cast queerness in the guise of the strangers, whose appearance challenges the established norms and authority. Strangers share an enlightened view with the other protagonists, challenging the status quo and usually treated as either a threat or consolation.

For Britten, codifying homoerotic behaviour took several forms, but two techniques reoccur with notable frequency in his compositions. The first is in the evocation of sensuality in his vocal lines, and the second is symbolized through knowledge exchange. Claggart declares his secret erotic desires for Billy in his soliloquy in Act I, scene iii. He sings repeatedly, 'Handsomely done, my lad. And handsome is . . . as handsome did it, too',[31] and as the chorus have dispersed for bed, and he is alone, his phrase develops into 'O beauty, O handsomeness, goodness'.[32] Safe in the knowledge that no one is listening, he references the 'depravity'[33] to which he was born. This is an example of Britten's knowledge exchange between him and the audience, through Claggart. The meanings of such phrases are designed to operate on different levels. For those familiar with queer knowledge, the understanding of Claggart's lament has deeply understood resonances with the closet experience. Those with a different perspective may be more inclined to dismiss such a theme.

Britten cautiously presents love scenes symbolically, through the exchange of erotic knowledge, rather than by physical gestures of intimacy. Another example is in Act I, scene ii, in which Captain Vere summons a boy to pass on a message. The boy exits without singing, but the words that immediately follow from Vere are 'Plutarch, the Greeks and the Romans. Their troubles and ours are the same. May their virtues be ours, and their courage.'[34] When viewed through a queer lens, the juxtaposition of the boy's appearance did nothing to advance the narrative but provided a sexual context to the historic reference. The Greeks and Romans had many virtues that Vere may well have wanted to share, but for the queer observer, Britten was providing a wink subtle enough that it could easily be refuted.

In the final scene of Act I, Billy is conversing with Dankser. Dankser begins by acknowledging him, 'What's the matter Beauty?',[35] his nickname for Billy, to which Billy responds by mentioning the 'queer things' that the Novice had said. By the time Herman Melville wrote the sexually ambiguous novella, *Billy Budd* in 1891,[36] the term 'queer' was being used in the nineteenth century for a range of meanings. Among the entries for 'queer' in the 1811 'Lexicon Balatronicum' are: 'Queer as Dick's Hatband'; 'Out of order without knowing one's disease'; 'Queer Bitch'; 'An odd out of the way fellow'; 'Queer Ken'; 'A prison'; 'Queer Mort'; 'A diseased strumpet'; and 'Queer Rooster.' An informer that pretends to be sleeping and thereby overhears the conversation of thieves in nightcellars. By the early 1900s, Gertrude Stein was using the term to describe members of her own community. If Melville used the word 'queer' to suggest homosexuality, it would be a very early example of its etymological transformation.

At the beginning of Act II, the ship is enveloped in mist, which causes visibility problems. The mist also symbolizes the lack of clarity and confusion which has descended over the characters in light of Claggart's machinations to destroy Billy. Claggart brings his slanderous accusation to Vere, to which the captain demurs, 'Don't come to me with so foggy a tale.'[37] As the formal proceedings are set in motion, Vere curses the enveloping fog, 'creeping over everything, confusing everyone. Confusion without and within.'[38] The mysterious 'mist' theme in the orchestral interlude immediately follows. The protagonists are confused about what the deviant knowledge emerging from Claggart's self-confession represents, and the surety with which the patriarchy has hitherto enjoyed is now compromised. There must be a process of self-alienation, before they can recognize what has been ever present, but hidden from view. When Claggart is dead, Vere notes, 'The mists have cleared.'[39]

Vere confronts Claggart in Act II, scene ii, and here, the characters are separated into a clearly delineated good versus evil dichotomy. Billy has always represented purity and goodness, and now Vere labels Claggart, 'Claggart, John Claggart, beware! I am not so easily deceived. The boy whom you would destroy, he is good: you are evil.'[40] In this case, it is Claggart who embodies queerness, not Billy. Claggart, Quint and Aschenbach all represent notions of malevolence. Claggart seeks to destroy that which is good, Quint wants to corrupt innocence and take it for himself and Aschenbach is engaged in constant self-flagellation over his guilt for desiring Tadzio. Each of these three characters also shares the trait of being strangers, as mentioned earlier; Billy is a late admittance to the ship's crew, Quint appears outside of windows and in shadows, waiting for an opportunity to enter the physical domain, and Aschenbach has travelled to Venice on holiday. Britten's cautious approach to queerness in his operas includes this process of vilifying queerness, treating it as an 'outsider' and ultimately destroying it before it can manifest physically.

The relationship between Vere and Billy is another example of innuendo and vague suggestion. In Act II, scene ii, Billy is summoned to Vere's cabin where he is invited to occupy the post of Captain of the Mizzen.[41] This is a much-coveted promotion for Billy and acknowledgement of his skills as a seaman; however, it is not the position itself that is what excites Billy, it is the opportunity to be closer to Vere. He sings, 'To be near you. I'd serve you well. You'd be safe with me . . . I'll look after you my best. I'd die for you.'[42] Whether the observer chooses to read this as a marker for homosexual attraction or simply non-sexual adoration is left as a question of interpretation. Britten's librettists often suggested that he make homosexual elements more overt, but the composer would tend to err of the side of ambiguity. Playing with ambiguity and double meaning was a favourite endeavour for Melville also.[43]

With the decriminalization of homosexuality in 1967, a dramatic shift in the willingness of the media to write openly about queerness is evident in this review of the 1966 BBC-2 production:

> There was no question of the glamorous super-boy, no worrying equations of goodness with beauty; Billy was simply our well liked and respected Peter Glossop *without so much as a hint at homosexual undertones*. This rather tended to deprive the sinister Master-at-Arms Claggart (Michael Langdon) of a motive for destroying the hero. Without any ambiguities of frustrated desire he had to fall back on the sheer badness he actually professes. Similarly, benign Captain Vere's failure to speak up for Billy is meaningless unless he is understood to be over-compensating for an illicit infatuation he suspects in himself.[44]

The flagrant use of the word 'homosexual' in print is not as surprising as the unambiguous disappointment in the disguised queerness of the characters which undermines the strength of the narrative. This review may seem unremarkable by modern standards; however, it represents a candour which flew in the face of contemporary journalistic conventions.

Several variations between Melville's text and the libretto from Crozier and Forster, and reviewed by Britten, reveal important elements of characterization, particularly with respect to the homoeroticism of Billy. Feminizing elements attached to Billy only during Claggart's spurious report to Vere of Billy's mutiny are missing in the libretto. In the Novella, Vere asks Claggart whether he intends to condemn 'Billy, the Handsome Sailor, as they call him?' to which Claggart replies, 'The same, your honour; but for all his youth and good looks, a deep one. Not for nothing does he insinuate himself into the good will of his shipmates . . . You have but noted his fair cheek. A mantrap may be under the ruddy-tipped daisies.'[45] The libretto refines this text with, 'You do but note his outwards, the flower of masculine beauty and strength. He is deep, deep. A man-trap lurks under those ruddytipped daisies.'[46] A 'mantrap' can, according to the Oxford Dictionary, refer to a trap for catching trespassers or poachers or the dated expression for a seductive woman. The libretto also replaces 'fair cheek' with a more eroticized version, 'flower of masculine beauty and strength'.[47] Generally, the libretto avoids overt references to Billy's remarkable strength, which is notable in Melville's rendering. The libretto limits any indication of his strength to Claggart's warning to Squeak, that Billy will kill him if he is caught messing with his kit. Billy 'floored' Squeak, which communicated his physical dominance.[48] Britten's pacifism likely influenced the suppression of any hint of brutishness that Melville may have conveyed.

The nexus of homoeroticism and grief for death of a young man is recounted in a tradition of literary works, such as David and Jonathan (see chapter 1), Achilles and Patroclus and Apollo and his mortal male lovers. The notion of transformation from physical to ethereal is heralded by angels of grace and statements of love. In Vere's epilogue, he sings, 'But he has saved me and blessed me, and the love that passes understanding comes to me.'[49] Another of Britten's vague markers, the phrase is instantly recognizable from its use in the Christian context from Philippians 4:7, often chosen as a fitting doxology. However, it also has a meaning from a different context, 'the love which dare not speak its name', from the poem *Two Loves* (1892) by Lord Alfred Douglas, and likely in reference to Oscar Wilde. Written one year after Melville died, leaving his novella unfinished, Douglas clearly did not inspire Melville's text, but it is unlikely to have been lost on Britten, who revelled in literary references. Both references are equally fitting. Billy's epiphany during his final hours, characterized by a departure from the astonishing naivety he exhibited throughout the narrative, is comforted by an apparent spiritual vision, 'I've sighted a sail in the storm, . . . I've seen where she's bound for',[50] to which he adds a blessing for Captain Vere. Having heard the story of Christ's passion, 'the good boy hung and gone to glory',[51] Billy now becomes the young, male sacrifice, achieving a transcendent, invulnerable status. The blessing, an action that is the epitome of Christian forgiveness, is also a symbol of his continuing love for the man in the face of death.

In the epilogue, Vere answers the questions he posed in the prologue, 'Who has blessed me? Who saved me?'[52] – indications of confusion and the recurring theme of being 'lost'. With the answers provided by Billy in the lead-up to his execution, Vere now confirms, 'He has saved me, and blessed me.'[53] Love provides the salvation from the hostility of being 'lost on the infinite sea',[54] a symbol both for the inhospitable world and the fate which delivers misfortune to those 'others' who are not welcome to participate in it.[55] The notion of doomed fate is embodied in the wretched Novice, condemned in Act I to an underserved flogging and then used as a pawn in Claggart's scheme to entrap Billy. The Novice laments:

Why had it to be Billy, the one we all love?
Why am I in this cruel and hateful ship instead of safe at home?
Oh, why was I ever born? Why?
It's fate, it's fate. I've no choice.
Everything's fate.[56]

Billy reflects during his remaining hours of the cruel fate of his stammer which disallowed him to provide a defence. And Captain Vere, a symbol for patriarchal authority, is equally resigned to the fate provided to him by the strict maritime code. It was Billy's love for Vere that allowed him to answer his questions and to bring his sense of being 'lost' to an end.

THE TURN OF THE SCREW, BENJAMIN BRITTEN

In March 1954, Benjamin Britten (1913–1976) was interviewed by Scotland Yard. Although there was a gentlemen's agreement with members of the leisured class, it was tenuous at this time when the constabulary sought to apply further scrutiny on men indulging in sodomy and related anti-social behaviours. The notorious trial that saw the imprisonment of Lord Montagu, Michael Pitt-Rivers and Peter Wildeblood had been concluded for less than a week before Britten began work on *The Turn of the Screw* (1954).[57] It is in this context of the demonization of homosexual behaviour that Britten approached Henry James' 1998, gothic horror novella. According to the librettist Myfanwy Piper (1911–1997), 'Neither Britten nor I ever intended to interpret the work, only to recreate it for a different medium.'[58] Indeed, much of the narrative remained intact, but the wordless ghosts are given voice by Piper and Britten, changing their mysterious malevolence into something more sinister and presently dangerous.

James' work has been reproduced in numerous guises, as have the characters in each rendering. The two ghosts, Peter Quint and Miss Jessel, the innocent children, Miles and Flora, along with the unnamed Governess and the housekeeper Mrs Grose have haunted criticism of each adaptation for well over a century. As well as Britten's operatic version; William Archibald's 1950 Broadway play entitled 'The Innocents'; John Frankenheimer's 1959 American televised account starring Ingrid Bergman; and Netflix's 2020 adaptation, 'The Haunting of Bly Manor' have all given alternative readings of the nature and intent of the characters. Additionally, the homoerotic content of the narrative has been the subject of analysis for a number of writers, who have debated the substantive existence of the ghosts and their intentions with the respective children.[59]

Michel Foucault (1926–1984) considered sexuality in Western cultures in relation to identity, knowledge and power and understood the increasingly sexualized network of relations from the eighteenth century to exist in four categories: the hysterical woman, the precociously sexual child, the Malthusian couple and the perverse adult. The characters in *The Turn of the Screw* represent three of these figures.[60] The first is manifest in the Governess, the second is the children, but in particular, Miles, the third, is unrepresented, and the fourth is unambiguously Peter Quint. With the advent of queer theory, a subversive view of the characters and their relationships has challenged the hitherto long-standing, moralistic stance in which Quint is seen to represent the worst kind of evil and the Governess as unadulterated goodness. The reconsideration of society's stance on a variety of taboos allows more nuanced discussion of the implicit homosexual relationship between Quint and Miles in this opera.

In James' story, we learn of the sexualization of Quint's menace through a conversation between the Governess and Mrs Grose, who exclaims:

'He was looking for little Miles.' A portentous clearness now
    possessed me. *'That's* whom he was looking for.'
'But how do you know?'
'I know, I know, I know!' My exaltation grew. 'And *you* know, my dear!'
Mrs. Grose elucidates,
'Quint was much too free.'
This gave me, straight from my vision of his face – such a face!
    – a sudden sickness of disgust. 'Too free with *my* boy?'
'Too free with every one!'[61]

In the opera libretto, she continues,

'But he had ways to twist them round his little finger. He liked them pretty, I can tell you, Miss, and he had his will morning and night.'[62]

Any clearer or more direct representation of 'the love that dare not speak its name' between Quint and Miles would have been impossible to contemplate for either James or Britten, who lived in times where all forms of homosexual relationships were strictly illegal. Quint's obsession with Miles is, however, clearly articulated in Britten's score. The most illustrative example is in Act I, scene viii in which Quint sings the boy's name repeatedly in a series of melismatic phrases. The first of six such phrases is derived from the 'Screw theme', the harmonic framework for the opera, and based on a twelve-tone series that is introduced after the opening prologue.

Quint's material has a unique character, and in this scene, the *sotto voce* style achieved by singing softly and in the higher part of the register provides an ethereal and also seductive quality. These phrases fluctuate dynamically, sometimes forcefully calling and other times seductively beckoning Miles, who eagerly responds with his presence. Quint is always associated with the 'other worldliness' of the celesta and harp, which respond antiphonally with his calls with similarly figured interjections. These passages are largely pentatonic.

Eroticism in music is frequently equated with exotic elements. The association with pentatonicism and exoticism stems from Britten's growing interest in Balinese Gamelan, which is a strong influence in this work and even more so in his final opera, *Death in Venice* (see chapter 5). For Miles, the exotic elements represent 'the opening of magic casements, a world of enchantment and glamour, of preternatural, supernatural, unattainable beauty'.[63] Quint's first vocal entry towards the end of the first act has connective musical tissue with Variation VII, the first overt use of pseudo-gamelan material. Britten was not alone with his experimentation with gamelan-inspired music; Cage, Cowell and Harrison also utilized the structures and heterophonic textures in their work, and a shared understanding developed that gamelan had become a gay marker in American music.[64] The erotic association with exoticism can also be seen with Britten's Oberon in *A Midsummer Night's Dream* (1960). In both cases, the link is ascribed to boy lovers, boy controllers or boy pursuers.

Britten could have chosen the conventional tritone, the oft-used portent of the *diabolus in musica* to represent Quint's wickedness. The composer made effective use of the interval in his *War Requiem* (1962) to represent evil.[65] Instead, Quint's material is a symbol of beauty and of seduction. Quint's words also fail to live up to the sinister reputation he has earned. He sings of desire, adventure, wealth and a degree of duplicity ('the smooth world's double face'[66]), all of which are alluring concepts for a boy approaching adolescence. Quint embraces his desire to exploit the natural desires of the boy and his responsiveness to an older man. Given his position in an all-female household, this last trait is understandable.

From the very beginning, Miles is steeped in mystery and secrecy. He was sent home from boarding school with instructions to 'never go back'.[67] As this is revealed in Act I, scene iii, the Governess asserts that he 'must be bad'.[68] The exact nature of the 'injury to his friends'[69] is never revealed, but at the end of Act I, Miles confirms to the Governess, 'You see, I am bad, aren't I?'[70] Miles' confession is seemingly linked to the tacit disapproval that the Governess displays concerning his relationship with Quint. Her discussions with the boy are predominantly obfuscated by coded phrases and hidden meaning, which further distances her from Miles. In Act II, as the tension between Miles and the Governess continues to grow, Miles observes the nature of their forced relationship when asked of what he was thinking, 'Of this queer life, the life we've been living',[71] and the use of the term 'queer' would not have gone unnoticed by observers.

The relationship between Quint and Miles clearly transcends that of a valet or house servant. As discussed in reference to *Iphigénie en Tauride* and *Death in Venice* (see chapters 1 and 5, respectively), the Ancient Greeks saw concord with respect to education and erotic love between men and boys. Quint was originally charged with the welfare of the children prior to the Governess and entrusted with the responsibility of preparing them for adulthood. The opportunity for initiating Miles into the secret world of adult experience becomes a tantalizing possibility for the obfuscation with which the boy discusses his inner thoughts. In Act II, scene I, Quint and Miss Jessel sing together, and Quint articulates his intentions with the boy. He sings:

I seek a friend,
Obedient to follow where I lead,
Slick as a juggler's mate to catch my thought,
Proud, curious, agile, he shall feed
My mounting power.
Then to his bright subservience, I'll expound
The desperate passions of a haunted heart
And in that hour
The ceremony of innocence is drowned.[72]

Quint wants to explain his passions to Miles particularly and references his passions which are directed towards him. The relationship that Quint describes has Miles as subservient to him; Quint is the *erastes* and Miles is the *eromenos*. The ceremony by which Miles' innocence is drowned points to the physical completion of the pederastic relationship. The same musical material reappears in the final scene, when Quint disappears. As he sings his final lines, he agonizes over his lost opportunity at the relationship that has eluded him; it is the voice of a rejected lover.

The children were not frightened of Quint and Miss Jessel when they were both alive. The Governess is shocked because Miles and Flora maintain the same relationship with them both now that they are dead. For the children, the terror is transferred by the Governess' panic. The discussion that analysts have enjoyed over the existence of the ghosts provides two possibilities: that the ghosts do not exist, in which case, the Governess is actually terrifying the children by having them relive the loss of their friends, or that the ghosts exist, in which case, she is punishing them for their secret, possibly sexual relationships. The children clearly found pleasure in their friendships with Quint and Miss Jessel which the Governess found traumatizing. In either case, her perspective is built on a hypocritical and moralistic set of assumptions concerning sexuality and class that the children, hidden from society, have not yet formed.[73]

Just as in Oscar Wilde's *The Picture of Dorian Gray*, which concludes with the dagger being thrust into the portrait with the intention of destroying the past, but consequently killing the protagonist, so too does Miles' unpitched scream of 'Peter Quint, you devil!'[74] Symbolically, the boy rejects the love of the older male with the resolute pressure from the Governess. If the Governess symbolizes the logic and order of society, her insistence of the boy's suppression of love ultimately delivers him to death, in a way that reflected the situation for many homosexuals in Britain. His simultaneous rejection of Quint's love, and his own desires, does not liberate him, as the Governess believed would happen, but brings to a close his opportunity for love, which has been an allusive prospect for his short life.

Britten's own childhood in the 1920s was not an idyllic time for a young gay boy to be entering into adolescence and anticipating a sexual awakening. Around fifty years before, America was witnessing a rise in anti-onanist writings, which targeted the 'anti-social' masturbatory habits of individuals and their proclivity to share such knowledge with younger children. These moral-purity essayists presented the asexual, homosocial environments of the innocents as being under threat from immoral, older relatives, servants or older siblings, introducing sexual difference and sexual desire to the chaste. These anti-masturbatory views morphed into distinctly homophobic myths associated with the concept of rampant paedophilia which circulated in Britain for decades. Britten apparently shared stories of his childhood with two of his librettists – the first involving him being raped by a school master and the second about him being implicated with his father's latent homosexual interests.[75] Whether there is any veracity to these accounts, the themes of lost innocence which dominate his compositions are difficult to avoid.

27, RICKY IAN GORDON

Artistic presentations of the 'outsider' or 'other' in society are often accompanied with notions of loneliness, oppression and despair. Such characters tend either to struggle against such hegemony, forging space for themselves and their desires where there is seemingly none, or become consumed by the inability to find solace in a welcoming community. For Gertrude Stein and Alice B. Toklas, being Jewish and lesbian presented no such obstacle to happiness, despite living in Paris in the early part of the twentieth century – a time when both Jews and queers were being persecuted. Their lives were marked by love, culture, friends and a steely resolve to defend it all.

27 rue de Fleurus, on the Left Bank of Paris, received new tenants in 1903, when Gertrude and her brother Leo, US expatriates, moved in. Over the years, the two began collecting contemporary art for which they would

become famous. Four years later, Alice arrived in Paris and moved in, and it was at this time that the legendary Saturday evening salons took place. The salons became an important meeting place for notable artists, writers, photographers and musicians. Gertrude, herself a writer, demonstrated an innate talent for recognizing rising stars of the art and literature world. While Gertrude hosted the evenings, Alice would frequently entertain the wives and mistresses of the guests. Alice wrote of her experiences:

> I have sat with wives who were not wives, of geniuses who were real geniuses.
> I have sat with real wives of geniuses who were not real geniuses. I have sat
> with wives of geniuses, of near geniuses, of would be geniuses, in short I have
> sat very often and very long with many wives and wives of many geniuses.[76]

This text appears in Act I, scene iii, of Royce Vavrek's libretto for Ricky Ian Gordon's opera, *27*, and is prefaced with a more pointed statement of Alice's desires; 'Let me be a wife. Your wife among the wives. The wife among the wives.'[77] This phrase articulates Alice's principal ambition as a permanent and meaningful figure in Gertrude's life. *27* is principally a love story, and of all the beauty that Gertrude surrounded herself with, it was Alice that stole her heart. It is easy to see how Alice would have been impressed by Gertrude's rugged individualism, her refusal to be manipulated, her uninhibited acceptance of her identity, her strong views and willingness to face the repercussions of having them and, of course, her adoration of beauty.

However, although Gertrude may have physically and personally dominated proceedings, it was Alice that dominated Gertrude. The two were inseparable, doing everything together as a couple including being co-godmothers to the child of Ernest Hemmingway (1899–1961). Toklas' 'autobiography' was actually written by Stein, who intertwines their experiences together through her wife's voice. Stein's approach to the growing feminist movement is unclear; on one hand she seems ambivalent to the cause, saying, 'Not . . . that she at all minds the cause of women or any other cause but it does not happen to be her business.'[78] On the other hand, she enjoyed following the latest news concerning the suffragettes.

In the prologue, the three male singers adopt the role of a Greek chorus, establishing the setting and the relationship of the two female protagonists. Rather than immediately using an apposite term, the men flounder clumsily, referring to Alice as Gertrude's secretary, then companion, before calling them 'two women',[79] and then finally, with interjections from Alice and Gertrude, they settle on the term 'wife'. Whatever awkwardness was expressed by the three men was not shared by the two women busily preparing for another of their infamous salon gatherings.

The relationship between the two women is characterized by pet names and Vavrek's cheeky *double entendres*. These terms of endearment not only reflect the loving nature of their relationship but also demonstrate the confidence that they held by openly celebrating their union. To be granted entry into this world of emerging geniuses, there was an unspoken rule that acceptance of alternative lifestyles was expected. Vavrek's terms of endearment are given an explicitly sexual treatment:

Wives with my Alica: my lobster, my pussy, my cake . . .
Geniuses with me.
This is the life for Americans, in Paris, Paris . . .
On rue de Fleurus.
Peruse, peruse!
Alice: my kitten, my cherub, my queen,
Snatch the wife![80]

The word 'snatch' had evolved in the early part of the twentieth century into a slang word for vulva, from its previous etymological guise of meaning a hasty sexual encounter. Lobster and cake are not colloquial terms as such; however, the metaphor of woman as dessert, or decadent cuisine, is well established.[81] The origins of the word 'pussy' to suggest the vagina date back much farther, possibly to the thirteenth century, and so Vavrek's use of these terms would be recognized by modern audiences as well as the characters in the opera. These terms also remind us that the women were not just close friends but also physically sexual. The relationship between Alice and Gertrude's brother Leo is not replete with such fond sentiments. Alice sings, 'I do not care for violence, no, no, no. Oh, but I'd stab your brother gladly with my needles.'[82]

In Act I, scene iii, Gordon and Vavrek are presented in a short episode in which the three male singers representing Pablo Picasso, Leo and Henri Matisse, are dressed in drag. Picasso appears as Fernande, Leo appears as Madame Matisse and Matisse appears as Marie. The historical reason for this scene is not based in the autobiographical writings of Alice or Gertrude; however, in an age where occasional liberal venues of tolerance could be found in large cities, drag was emerging in some of the straight cabaret venues to cater for the increasingly queer clientele, such as Montmartre, Pigalle and Montparnasse. Often these venues opened, were raided by police and shut down, only to open again in a cycle of civic defiance. Parisian lesbians had mostly gathered in Montmartre, until Lulu de Montparnasse opened the Monacle[83] on Edgar-Quinet Boulevard, the first and most famous lesbian nightclubs. The portrayal of the 'wives of geniuses' was not a necessary dramatic function but provided a moment of levity caged in the vernacular of 1920s American music.

The first decade of the twentieth century in Paris saw several tentative steps by artists to incorporate queerness into their work. Édouard-Henri Avril (1849–1928) published his book, *De Figuris Veneris* (1906), which depicted pornographic sex acts between ancient historical figures including Emperor Hadrian penetrating his lover, Antinous, and Sappho receiving cunnilingus from a mermaid.[84] The following year, Avril illustrated a lesbian image for a reprint of English author, John Cleland's (c. 1709–1789) book, *Memoirs of a Woman of Pleasure* (1907). Also in 1907, Georges Méliès released his film, *L'éclipse du soleil en pleine lune* (The Eclipse, or the Courtship of the Sun and Moon), in which an anthropomorphized sun and moon appear to be engaging in a gay sex act, possibly analingus. Although these intrepid attempts at queer representation seemed to reflect a progressive and queer-friendly society, the first French magazine for homosexuals, *Inversions*, only released four issues between 1924 and 1925 due to strong prosecution. André Gide, highly influential in the French literary scene and in 1924, defended homosexuality in the public edition of Corydon, for which he was widely condemned.[85] He later considered this his most important work.

So how did Gertrude evade the perpetrators of the Jewish holocaust when so many of her compatriots were being rounded up and sent to their deaths? Gertrude developed a close friendship with Bernard Faÿ, a professor in American civilization at the university of Clermont, Ferrand, and homosexual. Faÿ's meteoric rise through the ranks of establishment, first as chair at the Collège de France and then as one of the chief protagonists of the Vichy regime, coincided with his sympathetic stance. Railing against the modern decadence, he wrote prolifically about the threat posed by the Jews and became a Gestapo agent. Stein and Faÿ shared political convictions and enjoyed a mutual admiration.[86] In an article for the *New York Times*, Stein congratulated Hitler for restoring peace to Germany and asserting that he deserved the Nobel Peace Prize.[87] Gordon and Vavrek deal with Stein's connections with the Vichy regime, but this facet of her life does not overshadow her love story with Alice in *27*.

27 joins a growing list of American operas that focus on historical American stories. Sensing a public fatigue with the tired vestiges of traditional, Eurocentric works, a number of institutions, such as The Metropolitan Opera, and the major companies in San Francisco, Chicago, Houston, Dallas, Minnesota, Seattle and Miami are choosing to combat audience weariness with a more nationalist sentiment. Some argue that this introspective approach risks isolating American opera at a time when international composers are increasingly embracing themes that are predominantly universal. When the Met launched its programme of opera commissions in 2006, it boosted the opportunities for American composers, and the first work to reach the stage was a queer composer presenting queer themes: Nico Muhly's *Two Boys* in

2013 (see chapter 6). *27* was a commission from the Opera Theatre of Saint Louis and was conceived as a vehicle for mezzo-soprano, Stephanie Blythe, who sang the role of Gertrude.

Gordon's ninety-minute score provides an easy-listening experience – working congruently with the light-hearted and amusing libretto, with recurring, memorable themes. There are hints of Delibes' *Lakmé* (1882) and Barber's *Vanessa* (1958), and it moves quickly, in part due to the short, musical cells that make up the lead characters' exchanges. The tuneful, neoclassical approach that also echoes works by Lennox Berkeley (1903–1989) and Aaron Copland (1900–1990) would have been entirely palatable for a 1920s Parisian audience. As a queer opera, it challenges the prevailing approach to representation, by avoiding any sense of identity struggle or sexual awakening that characterizes many contemporary queer narratives, and instead tells an historical love story that just happens to be lesbian.

FELLOW TRAVELERS, GREGORY SPEARS

During the 1950s, the threat of communism in the United States was an ominous presence as the Cold War unfolded. Government officials considered the 'red scare' as a very real risk to national security and sought to systematically root out card-carrying members of the communist party, along with sympathizers known as 'fellow travelers' from all levels of government administration. The figurehead of this process, and vanguard of traditional American values, was Wisconsin Republican senator Joseph McCarthy (1908–1957). His tactics against communist and socialist sympathizers involved public smear campaigns, often unfounded, which has since given rise to the term 'McCarthyism'. Alongside this crusade was the simultaneous drive to remove homosexuals from government positions, known as the 'lavender scare'.

Thousands of suspected homosexuals were investigated, interrogated and dismissed by government officials and private employers on the basis that queer individuals were susceptible to blackmail from foreign agents due to the weakness of their character. McCarthy was a leading figure in popularizing these queer purges; however, in a twist of fate that could perhaps be considered as either *schadenfreude* or *karma*, he fell victim to the same smear campaign he himself promoted. Rumours of inappropriate treatment for his aide, David Schine, who the press suggested was romantically linked to McCarthy's chief counsel, Roy Cohn, contributed to his dramatic loss of support and eventual censorship. The threat of job loss ensured that many queer individuals remained in the closet, and for those interrogated and dismissed, withholding the real reason for being fired was necessary so as not to live in total humiliation within the community and further risk being cut off from support structures.

Many contemporary commentators believed that communists and homosexuals exhibited comparable character flaws, including moral corruption, psychological immaturity and an ability to 'pass' undetected among regular Americans. Communists and homosexuals were considered by some to be connected through the trope of enslavement; homosexuals were slaves to their homoerotic impulses, communists to their Soviet masters. Members of both groups were thought to lack the masculine autonomy necessary for loyalty to the nation.[88] This reasoning provided the framing of McCarthy's relationship with Roy Cohn during the Army-McCarthy hearings in 1954, which was rife with homophobic slurs and accusations.

Gregory Spears' opera *Fellow Travelers* (2016), set to a libretto by Greg Pierce, is based on Thomas Mallon's 2007 novel by the same name. The sixteen-scene opera is set in the period of 1953–1957 and concerns the turbulent relationship between the two male protagonists, Timothy and Hawkins. They meet on a park bench in Dupont Circle in Washington, DC and following an exchange brimming with sexual tension and coded language, the well-connected Hawkins arranges a job for the young, inspiring writer. Timothy had just attended the wedding of Senator McCarthy and was taking notes for a newspaper article when the handsome stranger approached. Hawkins establishes himself as confident and worldly in contrast to the relative naivety of Timothy, who has not long moved to the capital. Both men continue the flirtatious exchange in code while continuing to 'pass' for the benefit of passersby. Pierce's libretto removes much of the political machinations surrounding McCarthy, choosing instead to focus on the relationship of the two men. In doing so, Hawk's character in the opera is given a treatment that is tenderer than the rapaciousness he exhibits in the book.

Hired as a speech writer for Senator Charles Potter, Timothy receives some advice from Tommy McIntyre, who works unofficially for the senator. His suggestive language with phrases such as 'keeping tabs'[89] on people and being 'the first to know'[90] is unsettling, but Tommy also implies some sort of secret bond that they share, which in his naivety confuses Timothy. Wanting to repay his kindness, Timothy buys a book for Hawkins as a gift, handing it to the two women at the front desk of Hawkins' office. After Timothy leaves, Miss Lightfoot reads the inscription and mocks the sentimental language and insinuates, without directly stating it, that Hawkins may be homosexual. It later transpires that she submitted his name to the official investigators responsible for interrogating potential queers working in governmental positions.

In scene iv, 'Timothy's Apartment', Hawkins drops by to thank Timothy for the gift and correctly inferred from the inscription that his amorous advances were welcomed. The romance began with some assertive power play which would characterize the ensuing relationship. Hawk sings, 'I'm your first aren't I? You know what that means? Now I own you. Who owns you, Skippy? I wanna hear you say it. Be my brave boy?'[91] Hawk's intention to dominate Timothy is met with no resistance and within moments, the couple are fantasizing over a secluded, romantic holiday together. This is the only remaining hint in the opera of the sadomasochism elements found in the book.[92] Timothy sings, 'You've probably done this before, lots of times. Once or twice? . . . Sand as white as milk. Miles and miles. Just you and me and the moon. My head on your arm at the end of the day, paradise.'[93] Their vocal lines begin as closely juxtaposed phrases but become homophonically aligned with the phrase concerning the bed, operating mainly in octaves with occasional fifths, 'Under the sheets in a tropical storm you, you, you.'[94] The fantasy concludes with responsive phrases in which they complete each other's sentence, (H) 'The rain finding its way through the gaps' (T) 'in the straw of our roof' (H) 'onto your chest' (T) 'Two little drops' (T & H) 'Two little drops, paradise'.[95]

The scene in Timothy's apartment, including the shared fantasy, represents an imagined world in which the pressures of heteronormative conformity that hangs over them like the sword of Damocles disappear. Without this ever-present concern, the opera might well have been a romance, but instead the ruthless McCarthyist period of homophobic persecution forms the central, voiceless character. Unable to escape the dangers of being placed into and then being brought out of the closet, the relationship is put under extreme pressure from the very beginning. The libretto is peppered with occasional reminders of the unfolding probe, such as Mary's observation, 'They fired Bobby Parker. For being in the wrong Bar.'[96] The Lavender Scare did not simply result in job loss for tens of thousands of individuals but created a silent threat that pervaded the lives of every queer person and came with body count. In 1953, the State Department held a meeting to discuss the prevention of suicide by homosexuals and went to considerable lengths to hide the grim statistics.[97] Newspaper stories were only permitted to report suicides of single government workers for 'no apparent reason'.[98]

Miss Lightfoot's act of whistle-blowing was in response to Hawk's use of his term of endearment for Timothy, 'My Irish tiger cub', which aroused her suspicion. Hawk appears in interrogation room M304, 'These rooms always have such catchy names.' The Interrogator's equally sterile vocal line consists largely of perfect fourths and fifths and articulates the arcane basis for the purge. He sings:

> Let me be frank, Mister Fuller. Eighty percent of these investigations end with an admission of deviant behavior. As you know, the moral perversion and

emotional immaturity of a sexual deviant make him the prime target of black-mail by anyone seeking to undermine the government of the United States.[99]

Hawk responds with apparently undetectable irony, 'I know, I've heard . . . One pansy can pollute an entire government office.'[100] This amusing quip foreshadows the events of the Army-McCarthy hearings of 1954, suggesting that by scratching the surface, the reality of homosexual prevalence will reveal more than expected. With the era of forensic investigation into the sex lives of all government employees, and the public smear campaign designed to engender a shared loathing of anyone deemed immoral by acquaintance with known homosexuals, the chief spokesperson found himself at the centre of allegations. Hawk attempts to explain the situation to Timothy, who expressed his support of McCarthy's 'red scare' policy, 'There. Now I'm Roy Cohn and you're David Schine. Open your eyes Skippy. Why does Schine get the red carpet treatment? McCarthy's in on it too.'[101]

In the final chapter of Foucault's first volume of *History of Sexuality: The Will to Knowledge* (1976), he begins to explore the notions of biopolitics and biopower, arguably one of his most popular and compelling theories. Foucault explains the function of biopower as 'power that exerts a positive influence on life, that endeavours to administer, optimize, and multiply it, subjecting it to precise controls and comprehensive regulations'.[102] The word 'positive' must be considered from its subjective context. Timothy discovered how application of biopower could be a destructive force while working in Hungary and writing of the influence of the Russian regime during the Hungarian Revolution (1956). He sings to Hawk, 'Do you know what they do to men like us in Russia? It boggles my mind.'[103] Timothy's naivety seemed to prevent him from making the connection with the covert use of biopower in relation to the 'lavender scare' in his own country.

Although the interrogation provided a false-negative result, vindicating Hawk, the differences between the two men compounded the social pressure to break up. Hawk's keen survival instincts stretched to the ease with which he embraced a sham marriage in order to 'pass', 'I'm married now, you know: "Lucy."'[104] This arrangement had no impact on his homosexual proclivities, and his suggestion to Timothy that they engage in a *ménage à trois* only added to the fractious contretemps, 'New office boy. Lewis, about your age, dirty blonde . . . should we see if he's free tonight?'[105] Their mutual friend Mary attempted to warn Timothy of Hawk's unrestrained polyamory, 'He's wonderful, you're right about that. But he's a certain kind of wonderful Timmy. I've seen all the people and patterns. It would break my heart to see you become another one.'[106] In the ultimate act of betrayal, Hawk brought any possibility of fruitful reconciliation to an end by giving his name to the Interrogator, 'I think its unwise, for his own sake, and the Department's . . .

If this young man gets the job, he's liable to be blackmailed on account of his tendencies.'[107] Assuming that Timothy would harbour sufficient resentment to sever ties, Hawk put an abrupt end to his employment possibilities in government circles and confirmed that they would never see each other again.

Spears' musical palette infuses a quasi-minimalism with a strong influence from early music styles. There is a functionality to much of the recitative-style bureaucratic dialogue that makes the arioso moments profoundly lyrical by contrast. Underpinned by static harmonies and a gentle pulse of fifths, the vocal line in Hawke's Act II aria, 'Our very own home', sung after Timothy's departure contains baroque-inspired, melismatic ornaments that are hauntingly poignant. That we waited until so late in the work to hear Hawk's character in full flight contributes to the heightened emotion of the scene and the revelation of his deep love for Timothy. Spears also characterizes his score with a distinctly American quality, particularly with his frequent use of open fifths, reminiscent of Copland, and his homage to American minimalism. He invokes archaic dance forms such as a waltz and a sarabande that reflect the superficial formality of the DC circuit. Despite his use of a modern instrumental palette, he favours a vocal style that is patently informed by his adoration of Handel's operatic style.[108]

The pernicious era known as McCarthyism may have come to an end with his removal from office, but fluctuating political discourse concerning the rights of LGBTQ+ individuals provides a continuing concern in many countries. Deep mistrust for the queer community remains a persistent line of reasoning for conservative politicians, and an opportunity to sway public opinion against all forms of queerness is a tantalizing prospect. Fairness and equality in society are fragile social attainments, and McCarthy was not the last zealot to attempt to erase them, as Vladimir Putin has clearly demonstrated.

NOTES

    1. Amy Robinson, 'It takes one to know one: Passing and communities of common interest', *Critical Inquiry* 20, no. 4 (1994): 715–736.
    2. Maria C. Sanchez and Linda Schlossberg, eds., *Passing: Identity and Interpretation in Sexuality, Race, and Religion*, 29 (New York: NYU Press, 2001).
    3. Jessa Lingel, 'Adjusting the borders: Bisexual passing and queer theory', *Journal of Bisexuality* 9, no. 3–4 (2009): 381–405.
    4. New York Times, 'THEATRE PADLOCK BILL REPORTED IN SENATE; Upper House Passes Rent Law Extension Measure and Fort Lee Bridge Bill' (22 March 1927), 10, accessed 25 February 2022, https://www.nytimes.com/1927/03/22/archives/theatre-padlock-bill-reported-in-senate-upper-house-passes-rent-law.html.
    5. George Chauncey and Carolyn Strange, 'Gay New York: Gender, urban culture & the making of the gay male world, 1890–1940', *Labour* 39 (1997): 261.

6. Jan Seidl, *Queer Stories of Europe*, eds. Kārlis Vērdiņš and Jānis Ozoliņš (Newcastle upon Tyne: Cambridge Scholars Publishing, 2016), 192.

7. Beidrich Smetana, *Dalibor* [piano reduction] (Vaclav Juda Novotny, Umělecká Beseda, 1923), 96–116.

8. Smetana, *Dalibor*, 96.

9. Smetana, *Dalibor*, 99.

10. Smetana, *Dalibor*, 130–131.

11. Smetana, *Dalibor*, 145–148.

12. Smetana, *Dalibor*, 347–362.

13. Smetana, *Dalibor*, 356–357.

14. Smetana, *Dalibor*, 380–384.

15. Smetana, *Dalibor*, 515–522.

16. Smetana, *Dalibor*, 574–575.

17. Roger Pines, 'Dalibor. Bedřich Smetana', *The Opera Quarterly* 14, no. 1 (1997): 174–176.

18. Karol Szymański, 'Degeneration of the homosexual phantasm in normalised Czechoslovak cinema: From Václav Krška's the false prince (1956) to Stanislav Strnad's the bronze boys (1980)', *Studia z Dziejów Rosji i Europy Środkowo-Wschodniej* 52, no. 2 (2017): 77–141.

19. Richard Ellmann, '*Oscar Wilde*' (London: Hamish Hamilton Ltd, 1987), 352.

20. Oscar Wilde, '*Complete Works*. With an introduction by Vyvyan Holland' (London and Glasgow: Collins, 1987), 922.

21. Rainer Kohlmayer, 'From saint to sinner: The demonization of Oscar Wilde's Salome in Hedwig Lachmann's German translation and in Richard Strauss' opera', *Benjamins Translation Library* 20 (1997): 111–122.

22. Richard Strauss, *Salome Op. 54* [Piano/vocal score by Otto Singer] (Berlin: Adolph Fürnster, 1903–1905), 5.

23. Oscar Wilde, *Salome* [Libretto] (London: The Bodley Head, 1893), 12.

24. Strauss, *Salome*, 38–39.

25. Richard Dellamora, *Masculine Desire: The Sexual Politics of Victorian Aestheticism* (NC: UNC Press Books, 1990).

26. Telegraph, London, 'Modest baritone made the role of Britten's Billy Budd his own', 26 March 2005, accessed 3 January 2022, https://www.smh.com.au/national/modest-baritone-made-the-role-of-brittens-billy-budd-his-own-20050326-gdl05j.html.

27. Jeffrey Meyers, 'For the love of Billy Budd', *The Gay & Lesbian Review Worldwide* 25, no. 4, July-Aug. (2018): 17–19: 17.

28. Meyers, 'For the love of Billy Budd', 17.

29. Lloyd Whitesell, 'Britten's dubious trysts', *Journal of the American Musicological Society* 56, no. 3 (2003): 637–694.

30. Benjamin Britten, E. M. Forster, and Eric Crozier, *Billy Budd Op. 50: An Opera in Two Acts* [Vocal score] (London: Boosey & Hawkes, 1961), 115–118.

31. Britten et al., *Billy Budd*, 129.

32. Britten et al., *Billy Budd*, 133.

33. Britten et al., *Billy Budd*, 133.

34. Britten et al., *Billy Budd*, 82–83.

35. Britten et al., *Billy Budd*, 159.

36. The novella was not published until 1924.

37. Britten et al., *Billy Budd*, 230.

38. Britten et al., *Billy Budd*, 238.

39. Britten et al., *Billy Budd*, 260.

40. Britten et al., *Billy Budd*, 243.

41. A mizzen is the main mast of a ship.

42. Britten et al., *Billy Budd*, 246–247.

43. Arnold Whittall, '"Twisted relations": Method and meaning in Britten's Billy Budd', *Cambridge Opera Journal* 2, no. 2 (1990): 145–171.

44. Peter Stadlen, 'TV alters structure of Billy Budd', *Daily Telegraph*, 12 December 1966.

45. Herman Melville, *Billy Budd, Sailor and Selected Tales* (New York: Oxford University Press, 1998), 327.

46. Britten et al., *Billy Budd*, 231–232.

47. Britten et al., *Billy Budd*, 231–232.

48. Allen J. Frantzen, 'The handsome sailor and the man of sorrows: Billy Budd and the modernism of Benjamin Britten', *Modernist Cultures* 3, no. 1 (2007): 57–70.

49. Britten et al., *Billy Budd*, 232–233.

50. Britten et al., *Billy Budd*, 311–312.

51. Britten et al., *Billy Budd*, 307.

52. Britten et al., *Billy Budd*, 6.

53. Britten et al., *Billy Budd*, 332.

54. Britten et al., *Billy Budd*, 333.

55. Clifford Hindley, 'Love and salvation in Britten's "Billy Budd"', *Music & Letters* 70, no. 3 (1989): 363–381.

56. Britten et al., *Billy Budd*, 149–150.

57. Philip Brett, 'Eros and orientalism in Britten's operas', in *Queering the Pitch* (Milton Park: Routledge, 2013), 247–268.

58. Quoted by Patricia Howard, in Patricia Howard, ed., *Benjamin Britten: The Turn of the Screw* (Cambridge :Cambridge Opera Handbooks, 1985), 23.

59. Leon Edel and Adeline R. Tintner, 'The private life of Peter Quin[t]: Origins of "the turn of the screw"', *The Henry James Review* 7, no. 1 (1985): 2–4.

60. Philip Brett, 'Britten's bad boys male relations in the turn of the screw', in *Music and Sexuality in Britten* (University of California Press, 2006), 88–105.

61. Henry James, *The Turn of the Screw*, Dover Thrift Editions (New York, NY: Dover Publications, 1991), 49–50.

62. Benjamin Britten and Myfanwy Piper, *'The Turn of the Screw, Op. 54. An Opera in a Prologue and Two Acts'*, Act I, scene v. [vocal score] (London: Boosey & Hawkes, 1955), 54.

63. Patricia Howard, *'Cambridge Opera Handbook: Benjamin Britten's Turn of the Screw'* (Cambridge University Press, 1985), 105.

64. Brett, 'Eros and orientalism in Britten's operas', 247–268.

65. Clifford Hindley, 'Why does miles die? A study of Britten's "the turn of the screw"', *The Musical Quarterly* 74, no. 1 (1990): 1–17.

66. Britten and Piper, *Turn of the Screw*, 85.

67. Britten and Piper, *Turn of the Screw*, 25.

68. Britten and Piper, *Turn of the Screw*, 25.

69. Britten and Piper, *Turn of the Screw*, 26.

70. Britten and Piper, *Turn of the Screw*, 102.

71. Britten and Piper, *Turn of the Screw*, 147.

72. Britten and Piper, *Turn of the Screw*, 107–109.

73. Ellis Hanson, 'Screwing with children in Henry James', *GLQ: A Journal of Lesbian and Gay Studies* 9, no. 3 (2003): 367–391.

74. Britten and Piper, *Turn of the Screw*, 194.

75. Brett, 'Eros and orientalism', 2013.

76. Gertrude Stein, *The Autobiography of Alice B. Toklas by Gertrude Stein-Delphi Classics (Illustrated)*, Vol. 24 (Delphi Classics, 2017), 11.

77. Ricky Ian Gordon and Royce Vavrek, *27: An Opera in Five Acts* [Piano/vocal score] (Malvern, PA: Theodore Presser Company, 2014), 102.

78. Stein, *Autobiography*, 76.

79. Gordon and Vavrek, *27*, 29.

80. Gordon and Vavrek, *27*, 53–57.

81. Eliecer Crespo Fernández, 'Sex-related euphemism and dysphemism: An analysis in terms of conceptual metaphor theory', *Atlantis* (2008): 95–110.

82. Gordon and Vavrek, *27*, 60.

83. Little is known about Lulu, although she famously sported a monocle, after which her bar was named. The wearing of a monocle became a code for Sapphic tendencies.

84. Marguerite Johnson, 'Eighteenth-and nineteenth-century Sapphos in France, England, and the United States', in *The Cambridge Companion to Sappho*, eds. P. J. Finglass and Adrian Kelly. Cambridge University Press, (2021), 361–374: 361.

85. Scott Manning, 'Revelation and dissimulation in André Gide's autobiographical space', *The French Review* (2004): 318–327.

86. Barbara Will, *Unlikely Collaboration: Gertrude Stein, Bernard Faÿ, and the Vichy Dilemma* (New York, NY: Columbia University Press, 2011).

87. Charles Bernstein, 'Gertrude Stein views life and politics', *New York Times Magazine*, May 1934; 71.

88. Andrea Friedman, 'The smearing of Joe McCarthy: The lavender scare, gossip, and Cold War politics', *American Quarterly* 57, no. 4 (2005): 1105–1129.

89. Gregory Spears and Greg Pierce, *Fellow Travelers: Opera in Two Acts* [full score] (New York: Schott, 2016), 56.

90. Spears and Pierce, *Fellow Travelers*, 56.

91. Spears and Pierce, *Fellow Travelers*, 92–93.

92. Fred Cohn, 'Fellow Travelers', *Opera News*, 17 June 2016, accessed 17 November 2021, https://www.metguild.org/Opera_News_Magazine/2016/9/In_Review/CINCINNATI__Fellow_Travelers.html.

93. Spears and Pierce, *Fellow Travelers*, 93–95.

94. Spears and Pierce, *Fellow Travelers*, 98–99.

95. Spears and Pierce, *Fellow Travelers*, 99.

96. Spears and Pierce, *Fellow Travelers*, 130.

97. Julia DaSilva, 'Magic, lesbian sexuality, and the "impossible possibility": Reading the early modern witch hunts and the cold war lavender scare for a politics of re-enchantment', *The Undergraduate Journal of Sexual Diversity Studies* (2019): 68.

98. David K. Johnson, *The Lavender Scare: The Cold War Persecution of Gays and Lesbians in the Federal Government* (Chicago, IL: University of Chicago Press, 2009), 159.

99. Spears and Pierce, *Fellow Travelers*, 163.

100. Spears and Pierce, *Fellow Travelers*, 164.

101. Spears and Pierce, *Fellow Travelers*, 182–183.

102. Michel Foucault, *The History of Sexuality: 1: The Will to Knowledge* (London: Penguin UK, 2019), 137.

103. Spears and Pierce, *Fellow Travelers*, 304–305.

104. Spears and Pierce, *Fellow Travelers*, 295.

105. Spears and Pierce, *Fellow Travelers*, 243.

106. Spears and Pierce, *Fellow Travelers*, 248–249.

107. Spears and Pierce, *Fellow Travelers*, 327–328.

108. Thomas May, 'Hip to be hip: When early and new music intersect', *Early Music America* 24, no. 3 (2018): 22–27.

Chapter 3

The Closet

The closet is a contrivance developed in the twentieth century in response to the recognition that homosexuality presented a distinct category of sexuality which homosexual individuals attempted to conceal. Previously, the concepts of homosexuality, bisexuality or heterosexuality were unknown sexual identities. Only individual sexual acts such as sodomy could be considered as 'sins or capital crimes'.[1] The closet remains a rich metaphor that has provided a multitude of linguistic uses – a symbol of confinement, protection, separation and a rite of passage for those who ultimately choose to abandon it in favour of freedom of identity. For many individuals, the process of coming out of the closet is a celebrated occasion, with loved ones supporting and affirming the authenticity of self-identity and the assumption that this will lead to a happier existence. However, for others, such a moment is fraught with the most extreme anxiety, having endured discrimination, homophobia and resultant internalized homonegativity. Research into the effects on health for queer youth points to increased rates of depression, suicidal ideation, substance abuse and risky sexual behaviours.[2]

The process of coming out is unique for each individual. For many, the need to suppress their sexual orientation is felt so vociferously that engaging in self-destructive behaviours becomes a psychological response. Conversely, others celebrate the ability to craft a new identity based on their newly acquired freedom of expression.[3] Many young, queer people alter their behaviours, concealing any trace of identifiable sexuality markers, including intimacy avoidance and dating someone of the opposite sex, to deflect unwanted attention to their authentic sexuality.[4] Even after the coming out process, decisions are often made on the basis of gaining acceptance within heteronormative, hegemonic contexts. Kjaran and Jóhannesson identified four strategies for openly gay men to achieve social acceptance among young, queer Icelanders: distancing, embracing, achieving and accommodating. Distancing involves either the embodiment of perceived masculinity or the repudiation of the binary gender system. The embracing strategy manifests as an extroverted display of stereotypical, flamboyant queerness which invites polarized reactions to challenged perceptions of masculinity. Achieving uses a deflection tactic whereby success through hard work within a chosen field can provide opportunities for respect. Such overcompensation is a common attempt to redirect feelings of inferiority. The accommodating strategy allows openly gay men to conform to expected heteronormative social conventions in a rejection of stereotypically queer traits. This form of identity requires discipline and is often regulated through social networks when observations about appearance and mannerisms are presented.[5]

Each of the operas discussed in this chapter deals with the closet from an adult perspective, and the respective characters are uniformly compelled to remain in the closet because of the dangerous alternative of coming out. Three of the four narratives occupy a space based on geographical and historical reality, and one creates a dystopian world in which leaving the confines of the closet would be undoubtedly fatal. In each case, it is the nature of the ultra-conservative hegemony that keeps the doors of each closet firmly shut. Peter Eötvös' epic opera based on Tony Kushner's Pulitzer Prize-winning play shows the dangers of a closeted homosexual existence during the height of the AIDS crisis, while including the perspective of the partners who were oblivious to their surreptitious homosexual activities. Leslie Uyeda's opera, *When the Sun Comes Out*, paints a frightening picture of a future society in which exiting the closet means certain death. The characters are faced with a harsh reality when considering what is morally just, with what is prudent and safe. Charles Wuorinen's setting of *Brokeback Mountain* explores the inability for two men to enjoy their relationship because of an unforgiving society that threatens violence to anyone daring to leave the closet. Finally, the closeted existence of Max Aue in Hèctor Parra's *Les Bienveillantes*, in the context of the Jewish Holocaust, manifests in extreme behaviour, highlighting the depravity of Nazi soldiers driven by their ideological convictions.

ANGELS IN AMERICA, PETER EÖTVÖS

For queer communities in the United States, following the hard-fought political and social battles surrounding Stonewall, it must have seemed that the early 1980s heralded a new dawn of sexual liberation and growing acceptance. Around two dozen states had legislated to decriminalize sodomy by 1980. When the mysterious illness that appeared to target homosexual communities emerged, suddenly an entirely new set of issues presented themselves. AIDS was officially recognized in the United States in 1981, but it is likely that a young man in St Louis died of the disease in 1969, just one month prior to the Stonewall riots. The sexual revolution, a result of such fervent struggle to achieve, was now killing the very people who fought to achieve it.[6] By the time President Reagan finally uttered the term 'AIDS' publicly in 1985, 12,000 Americans had died of the virus.

The social stigma that has historically forced homosexual men to seek sexual encounters through anonymous encounters in public spaces promoted risky sexual practice. In the 1970s, as the silent AIDS epidemic swept through urban communities, public sex environments were seen as safe venues for casual sex involving multiple partners. For decades, a secluded section of Central Park known as the Ramble was a popular spot for gay cruising. The park, in particular the area next to Belvedere Castle, was identified as a place frequented by queers as early as the end of the nineteenth century in George Chauncey's book *Gay New York*.[7] By the second decade of the twentieth century, the benches near Columbus Circle became the liaison site of choice, and the following decade saw the Ramble become so popular among homosexual men that it was nicknamed 'the Fruited Plain'. In the 1920s and 1930s, the walkway between the south-eastern corner of the park to the mall was assigned the monikers 'Vaseline Alley' and 'Bitches Walk'. Acknowledging the significance of the park to the LGBTQI+ community, the earliest Gay Pride marches beginning in 1970, known as 'Christopher Street Liberation Day March', followed a course from Greenwich Village and ending in Central Park.[8]

Peter Eötvös' opera, *Angels in America* (2004), which has undergone several revisions, most recently in 2020, is set to a libretto by Mari Mezei. All of the characters are impacted by the early manifestation of the AIDS crisis in different ways, and each deals with not only the devastating reality of death but also the associated stigmas of the disease. Although many of the characters are queer, those who are living in the closet are confronted with a mortal illness that they feel unable to admit to having. Victims of AIDS also impacted those closest to them, and the dual stressor of impending death and admission of a hidden sexual orientation to an unknowing partner was a terrifying experience for many thousands of people worldwide. The fates of the seemingly disparate sets of characters are gradually revealed to be intertwined through their experience with AIDS. Based on Tony Kushner's play, *Angels in America: A Gay Fantasia on National Themes*, Eötvös and Mezei refocussed the emphasis of the narrative as the composer explained, 'In the opera version, I put less emphasis on the political line than Kushner; I rather focus on the passionate relationships, on the highly dramatic suspense of the wonderful text, on the permanently uncertain state of the visions.'[9]

Eötvös integrates influences from jazz, rock and music theatre as well as the invocation of Jewish music in the opening funeral scene. The score provides a dizzyingly eclectic sound world, which through its extreme eccentricity provides a dystopian dream-like experience for the audience. The pivotal role of the Angel as the harbinger of death and other apparitions appear in visions for various characters, and the score serves to highlight the strangeness of the hallucination-like state. The large orchestra, without horns and double reeds, but including saxophones, an enlarged battery of percussion, electric guitars and Hammond organ, is complimented by an inspired use of voices. In addition to the offstage chorus, a trio of amplified voices, soprano, alto and bass-baritone, provide an incessant background accompaniment to the unfolding drama. Sometimes wordless or onomatopoeic and other times highlighting key words or effectively communicating truth at odds with the text being sung by the characters, the close-harmony style adds to the meta-modern effect of the sonic landscape. The same heterogeneity is applied to the vocal material of the characters, also amplified, which oscillates abruptly from lyricism and coloratura to approximated pitched singing and spoken word. The whole effect is highly expressive and impactful while giving a nightmarish quality to the narrative.

Two of the protagonists, Louis and Prior, are introduced in the opening of the opera, at the funeral of Prior's grandmother. Establishing the premise of death, it transpires that Louis has a Kaposi's sarcoma, a dark-purple spot on the underside of his arm, which he reveals to Louis. The physical marker was known to be an indicator of the onset of AIDS and Louis' reluctance to share his secret, 'I could not tell you. I was scared Lou . . . scared that you'll leave me',[10] was prophetic. His boyfriend asks the presiding Rabbi, 'Rabbi, what does the Holy Writ say . . . about someone . . . who abandons someone he loves at a time of great need?'[11] Prior then effectively abandons Louis, leaving him to his fate while seeking further risky sexual activity with other men.

In scene iii Prior appears unexpectedly in a mutual dream scene with Harper, a middle-aged woman, deeply depressed in her sexless marriage and entertaining suicide fantasies. The two characters were strangers, and Prior's presence in Harper's Valium-induced hallucination is surprising. Harper sings, 'What are you doing in my hallucination?',[12] to which Prior responds, 'I'm not in your hallucination, you're in my dream.'[13] Harper is confused by Prior's use of make-up, prompting him to explain that he is homosexual. Harper declares, 'Oh! In my church we don't believe in homosexuals',[14] allowing Prior a satisfying retort, 'Oh! In my church we don't believe in Mormons.'[15] Within the dream sequence, both characters are able to cross the 'threshold of revelations',[16] unveiling unknown truths about the other. Harper observes that Prior is sick, and Prior reveals that Harper's husband, Joe, is homosexual. Harper's news comes as a shock. She asks, 'Do homos . . . take,

. . . like . . . lots of long walks?',[17] and Prior confirms her worst fear, 'Oh yes, we do. In stretch pants with lavender coifs, up and down the avenues of Sodom and Gomorrah.'[18]

Joe's closeted secret was something he was unable to admit to his wife, but in a moment of vulnerability, as he found himself 'observing' the loitering men in Central Park, he phones his mother, Hannah, 'Mom. Momma. I'm homosexual. I'm homosexual. *(Pause)* Mom? Please, momma. Say something.'[19] Hannah is a devout Mormon and after the shocking late-night call from her son, she hurries to see him. Joe seeks the company of a beautiful, young man also loitering in the park, who turns out to be Louis. Louis, like many gay men who frequent public cruising areas for casual sex, was distraught after confirming that he was leaving Prior due to his AIDS diagnosis. The two men return to Prior's home and find comfort in bed together. We first meet Joe when he arrives at the office of Roy Cohn, a conservative, corrupt lawyer, who values the superficiality of perceived power and adamantly refuses to admit, to his last breath, that he is homosexual. Roy is also the only historical figure in the opera. On his death bed, Roy is visited by the vengeful ghost of Ethel Rosenberg, a woman sent to her death on the electric chair thanks in some part to Roy's connivance.

Throughout the opera, Prior's condition worsens. When he arrives in hospital, and still unknowing that Louis has left him, he is cared for by the transvestite, Belize. Belize is a nurse and his ex-boyfriend who also attends to Roy when he is admitted to hospital. Prior's connection with reality becomes increasingly tenuous, and he begins to envision an angel who addresses him as a prophet. The Angel assigns him a 'great task' which will involve him saving the world, acknowledging that God has long since abandoned heaven and the angels. Presented with the book of the prophets, he is hit by a wave of intense sexual feeling and asks, 'Wait. Wait. How come I have this . . . um, erection? It's very hard to concentrate.'[20] The Angel sings, 'Priapsis, Dilation, Flour, The Universe Aflame with Angelic Ejaculate . . . Holy Estrus! Holy Orifice! Ecstasis in Excelsis!',[21] following which, Prior experiences an involuntary orgasm and ejaculates. The ejaculation represents the unleashing of the potential for chance. Through his contraction of AIDS, Prior's propensity for determination and imagination was emboldened.

Appearing in Heaven, and surrounded by six Angels: Antarctica, Asiatica, Africanii, Oceania, Europe and Australia, Prior refuses the 'great task', stating that he only wants to be blessed by the angels and gain more time on earth. He symbolically throws down the book of the prophets and returns to Earth. Five years later, and in the final moments of the opera, he appears with Louis, Beliza and Hannah at the Bethesda Fountain in Central Park, and sings, 'This disease will be the end of many of us, but not nearly all. We won't die secret deaths anymore.'[22]

The Pool of Bethesda is situated in Jerusalem and is referenced in the fifth chapter of St John's Gospel. In it is the account of Jesus miraculously heal-ing a paralysed man. The pool is described as having five porticoes where large numbers of invalid people would wait to benefit from the therapeutic properties of the water. The Bethesda Fountain in Central Park features an imposing statue of the 'Angel of the Waters', located in the centre of the ter-race. The Angels entrusted Prior with the task of prophesizing that mankind needs to 'stop moving'[23] and to cease progress in order to restore Heaven. Prior believes that his acquisition of AIDS and impending death will force him to deliver the Angel's message; however, he refuses. Instead, he climbs up to Heaven, rebuking the six angels and explaining, 'I'm thirty years old. I want to be healthy again. And this plague, it should stop. In me and every-where. Make it go away.'[24] His rebuke of the Angel's message is delivered in an enraged tirade:

> We can't just stop. We're not rocks – progress, migration, motion is . . . moder-nity. We desire. Even if all we desire is stillness, it's still desire for. Even if we go faster than we should. We can't wait. And wait for what? God . . . *(Thunder)* God . . . He isn't coming back.
>
> And even if He did . . . if after all this destruction, if after all the terrible days of this terrible century He returned to see how much suffering His abandonment had created, if all he has to offer is death, you should sue the bastard, sue the bastard for walking out. How dare He.[25]

The symbolism of the Bethesda Fountain represents Prior's determination to put an end to the deaths at the hands of such a cruel and devastating plague. The 'great work', the struggle for 'more life', marked a dramatic change in fortunes for the global queer community. Since the AIDS epidemic emerged, queers were no longer people to ridicule, pillorize and oppress. They were now dangerous to be near and fearing exposure to the 'gay disease', as many referred to it, created a new level of discriminatory behaviour that could not have been imagined only a decade earlier. The 'great work' of finding a cure for HIV following the development of many effective treatments continues concurrently with the constant need for education. Since 2005, as antiretrovi-ral therapies have become more effective, and more widely available, annual deaths have been in continual decline.

WHEN THE SUN COMES OUT, LESLIE UYEDA

There are several ways in which Leslie Uyeda's opera *When the Sun Comes Out* (2013) is impactful. The economical use of musical forces, which includes a three-person cast and a piano quintet, flute, clarinet, violin, cello and piano, is striking. Chamber operas have the advantage of intimacy over their grand opera rivals, and subtlety of character in portrayal of relationships can often benefit from the immediacy that reduced forces bring. The extreme simplicity of the opera's structure is also notable. There are four scenes, and each of them has a focus of purpose, with the first two scenes each presenting only one character. Rachel Rose's libretto is remarkable for the beauty of its poetic use of metaphor and also for the unabashed eroticism which is so liberated from any confines of convention that it could make Elektra, Salome and Lulu blush.

Commissioned and produced by the Queer Arts Festival in Vancouver, Uyeda's opera occupies the unique distinction of being the first Canadian opera to feature a lesbian relationship. Set in a fictional nation with the not-so-subtle name, Fundamentalia, the severe oppression that governs the sexual function of its citizens determines same-sex relationships of any kind as strictly forbidden and punishable by death. The three characters in the opera are Solana, a rebellious outlaw on a relentless and unfulfilled quest for happiness in the beds of countless women, across many countries. Lilah is a young woman, married and with a child, and for whom a sexual dalliance with Solana represented her first and only experience of erotic pleasure and also extreme danger to her own life and that of her child. Javan is introduced in the fourth scene, the husband of Lilah. It becomes apparent that Javan and Lilah have both been existing in a closeted marriage, and Javan reveals that his great love was a fellow soldier named Azhar, after whom their daughter is named.

The first scene is comprised entirely of Solana's Song, explaining flashes of her backstory – her parents disowning her for being 'different', her transient lifestyle and her relentless use of women as temporary partners. What characterizes Solana most vividly in Rachel Rose's libretto is the confident and brazen eroticization of women, with whom she has had no intention of entering into a relationship. She sings, 'At night, in naked rooms I try on women like other women try on dresses.'[26] For Solana, each encounter offers fresh eroticism, which Rose articulates in delicate prose, 'Hot breath unthreaded, private cottons parted: We unzip against each other, spill like breath, invisible and pure.'[27] Solana confesses to the audience, and to herself, of the manifest utility of each woman and the heartache she leaves in her wake. 'We tell each other naked truths. We look straight into their eyes. We tell each other lies. I stay a night, or a week, or a season. I never give them reasons, roses, bouquets of excuses when I go.'[28]

Despite the preponderance of literature on queer sexuality relating specifically to gay men, there have only been some seminal work on sexuality in lesbian relationships, comprising a fraction of academic output. Nichols

(1990) argues that lesbians frequently interpret sexual attraction as love, and initial stages of a relationship evolve very quickly to a co-habitational commitment. This rapid evolution limits the possibility to examine divergent ideals that would likely lead to conflict, which leads to a high rate of relationship dissolution. The combination of the high value placed on being in a monogamous relationship and the relative difficulty of sustaining a loving commitment beyond the early phases leads to a dissatisfaction with the primary relationship and for an individual to seek other women with whom they can 'fall in love' and repeat the cycle.[29] Whether Nichols' study is an accurate representation of universal lesbian behaviour some twenty-four years later is undoubtedly contestable; however, Solana's sexual behaviour, albeit within the context of a dystopian, sexually repressed regime, does seem to accurately reflect the reported pattern of behaviour.

Solana and Lilah's roles in the relationship are constructed so as to subvert the expected paradigm that might exist between an experienced, older woman and a naïve, younger woman. In Solana's scene, her character is in total control of all her encounters. She decides when to leave each dalliance and her eroticism is almost weaponized, such is her confidence of her powers of seduction, 'I ascend the scale of their cries, kiss their open mouths, play the bone flutes of their spines.'[30] There is something primal in Rose's language that positions Solana as a sexual predator. By contrast, in Lilah's scene, we are presented with a girl who has been seduced, the passive recipient of a dominant figure, 'If only she'd never changed my life. If only she'd never touched me, her language in my mouth.'[31] For all Lilah's protestations and supposed regrets, her desire lurks beneath the surface, but in each phrase, it was desire brought *to* her, not *by* her. As her scene unfolds, her erotic memory takes over her survival instincts brought about by the threat of outside forces, and she recalls their physical pleasure, 'You lowered your face to my perfume and drank me like forbidden wine in the silence of our rooms. Ambrosia. Euphoria.'[32] Lilah reveals that Solana did not always occupy the position of dominance, 'You were the teacher who named a world beyond walls, words for the body's knowledge, and I was the student of fierce appetites. I was the teacher of tenderness, naming with kisses each part of your body in my liquid language.'[33]

In scene iii, the moment that Solana returns unexpectedly, Lilah's mind turns immediately to the danger that she represents. Solana's sexuality is a world of fantasy for Lilah and one in which a dream-like state can cloud her rational judgements. It is in this scene that we are able to witness the relationship in real time, rather than through recollections. Solana begs Lilah for one more night together, and it is at this point that the power shifts. Lilah resists Solana's pleas initially, but Solana's talents for seduction quickly lead to reconciliation. The two women sing in unison for the first time in agreement of 'a single night'[34] together; however, in the following phrase, 'let it be enough to live on forever',[35] although in accord rhythmically, their unison diverges to a major second, suggesting some discrepancy in expectations. They next sing together later in the scene, 'O hopeless was my heart',[36] this time largely in minor thirds. As their homophonic texture continues, the eroticism of the text becomes more urgent, and their vocal lines reach a heightened part of their respective registers in a musical climax underpinned by breathless sextuplets and a screaming *fff* at the end of the section. After this, the text returns to the two women exchanging alternating phrases, which is less erotic and more centred on the practicality of their situation.

The final scene introduces Lilah's husband, Javan. All of the poetic language of the previous scenes gives way to the unfolding tension which arises from Javan's shock at seeing Lilah in bed with another woman. His presence provides a tangible link to the oppressive regime that governs the country. Very few details are given regarding the laws of Fundamentalia, and the audience is left to imagine how oppressive they may be through frequent allusion and Juvan's recount of the brutal murder that was inflicted on his former lover. The limited detail allows the observer to draw patriarchal parallels with their own society and other regions around the world in which same-sex relations are still punishable by death today. Whatever the laws are, the insidious corollaries of extreme forms of hegemony are less tangible but just as damaging. She sings, 'Shame lifts like a butterfly when you touch me. How can that be?'[37] As Lilah oscillates between her fantasy world in which she and her lover can somehow be together and the grim reality she faces in her sexless, sham marriage, she becomes aware of the layers of indignity that society has connected with her lesbianism.

Javan's representation of the oppressive, fundamentalist regime is adjusted, when his own forbidden sexuality is uncovered. He is initially enraged, unpredictable and threatens both women with extreme violence, 'If you try to leave with your lover, I'll kill you both',[38] but as the scene unfolds, his backstory involving his murdered male lover is revealed, allowing the audience to replace revulsion with sympathy, 'What is this tender grief that fills my throat with tears?'[39] The level of eroticism with which Javan recalls his time with Azhar does not match that of the two women, but one phrase provides an indication of intimacy, 'I knew every part of Azhar's body.'[40] His relationship recollections are bound up with grief and as such are more focused on a romanticized ideal, 'I had twelve weeks of joy to last me the rest of my life. Being with him was the deepest prayer I've ever prayed.'[41]

Following Juvan's disclosure, Solana and Lilah eventually manage to convince him to let them both stay in the house and risk the chance of discovery. The symbolic concord between the three has layers of meaning for the observer. Lesbians and gay men are drawn together against the common nemesis of homophobia, but in many regards, there are major differences stemming from ideological stances on the cause of bigotry, accusations of sexism and a range of other issues. Whenever homophobia emerges in the form of injustice to minority groups within the LGBTQ+ community, there is frequently an increased sense of unity. Juvan's change of heart is also symbolic of hope; that change is possible within even the most extreme forms of heteronormative supremacy. The role of Lilah and Juvan's daughter was an important factor in realizing the reconciliation process, suggesting that it is the children who are out hope for the future in bringing an end to homophobic legislation and queer censorship.

When the Sun Comes Out is a tightly constructed melodrama which not only makes an important contribution to queer discourse in the arts but also provides an exceptionally demanding vehicle for the two female voices. Uyeda's compositional style allows for the vocal lines to luxuriate in the femininity and eroticism of their roles. The moments of heightened sexuality are given mellifluous phrases that contrast with the abruptness of the reality they face. The musical language reflects elements of Debussy, with glissandi, occasional tonal clusters, open fifths and a pervading pentatonicism. The opera has proven its commercial worth with numerous seasons that have been announced since its 2013 premiere in Vancouver where it enjoyed full houses and standing ovations.

BROKEBACK MOUNTAIN, CHARLES WUORINEN

When Annie Proulx published a short story in *The New Yorker* magazine in 1997 entitled *Brokeback Mountain,* few could have envisaged the enormity of its success. The adaptation into a motion picture directed by Ang Lee in 2005 was a milestone in queer cinematic representation in part for not only its critical acclaim but also its commercial success. The film was considered at the time 'controversial' as the two protagonists involved in the love story happened to be men. It has been frequently referred to as a 'love story' and a 'gay cowboy film', neither of which is accurate. The two men are married to women and have a sexual relationship, albeit a dysfunctional one, with their wives. Also, they are tasked with herding sheep, rather than cows, and finally, the film is a tragedy rather than a romance in the strictest application of genre markers. *Brokeback Mountain* could more accurately be considered a bisexual shepherd tragedy, although it might not have quite the same ring. The incorrect framing of sexuality of Jack and Ennis reflects the continuing habit of dichotomizing and oversimplifying sexual orientation.[42]

What makes the story of Jack and Ennis so compelling is the geographical and social context in which their relationship is tried and tested. Their love is presented as a universally comprehensible connection; however, the oppression they face is given historical specificity.[43] The setting symbolizes the frontier; the Wyoming mountains are the wild, unpopulated terrain that has not yet been 'civilized' to the point of accepting sexual 'other'. Through representation, *Brokeback* attempts to tame the wildness, and in doing so, martyring one of the protagonists. There can be no progress without sacrifice. The symbolic invocation of the lonely, rugged, cowboy, romanticized through the American icon, the Marlboro man, is embodied by Ennis. The genius marketing campaign that became one of the tobacco industry's winning brand choices successfully targeted men through its rebranding efforts.

One of the great challenges for composer Charles Wuorinen in writing his operatic version of the story was to write for two characters who generally communicate little, in a medium that relies on the communication of text. Additionally, the film characters adopted a stylized form of mumbled speech, which, although contextually appropriate, does not work well on stage over the clamour of an orchestra for those wishing to understand the dialogue. Wuorinen convinced Proulx herself to create the libretto, a medium which she was hitherto unfamiliar. Proulx maintained the themes and much of the detail from her original story but relied on alternative methods of delivery. Certain scenes needed to be clarified, or implied that were missing, such as the moment Alma buys her wedding dress. The score provides much of the geographic and psychological markers, amplifying the emotional content of the sung text. Wuorinen's use of an atonal palette for his score avoids the temptation to borrow from the strong associations the audience may have with Gustavo Santaolalla's Academy Award-winning score for the film.

The opera opens with an evocation of a mountain; bass-heavy and powerfully energetic, it provides a constant presence in the opera in much the same way as Britten's majestic sea music in *Peter Grimes* (1945). The mountain's constant presence is indicated at times with just a single note in the lower end of the timbral palette and is often juxtaposed with more immediately localized scenes that are violent and raucous or tender and intimate. Wuorinen considered his depiction of the mountain as a constantly menacing, deadly force. Another echo of *Grimes* is the use of orchestral interludes that reconnect the presence of the mountain within the respective emotional context.

In Act I, scene ii, the two men have finished their meeting with the trail boss, Aguirre, who tersely explains the rules they must abide by while working for him. With some time to kill, they head to a nearby bar and begin getting to know each other. Wuorinen defines their characters with contrasting vocal material. Jack, being talkative and friendly, is given phrases with a generous range and with larger intervals, whereas Ennis' short utterances are predominantly indicated as *Sprechstimme*, with limited flexibility. As they become more familiar, Ennis' lines evolve into sung phrase, an evolution which continues throughout the opera. Wuorinen considered the contrasting vocal styles of the two characters in relation to the title characters in Schoenberg's *Aaron and Moses* (1957).

In Act I, scene v, Jack and Ennis have their first sexual encounter. The cold, high-altitude mountain air forces Ennis into Jack's tent to regain some body heat. The act itself occurs in the tent and therefore out of the audience's view, leaving the music to imply the action. The two interludes either side of this encounter represent the mountain's awesome presence and unrelenting wild conditions. The pre-encounter interlude creates the conditions whereby the act is enabled; quickening semiquaver string and woodwind passages and high-pitched piccolo reveal the howling, cold wind. The following interlude embodies the enormity of the exchange – the full-textured ensemble with angular intervallic screams, accented and *fortissimo* in syncopated cells. In stark contrast, the next morning, the two men, confused and remorseful, sing of their experience rhythmically concurrent, and yet melodically separate, against a sparse, static accompaniment. Ennis reverts to his speech-singing when he remarks, 'It can't happen again.'[44] When Jack suggests they talk about what took place, Ennis continues his text without singing, 'You better know something. I ain't no queer.'[45]

Wuorinen establishes the conflicting emotions for both characters through the textural arrangement of the material. For moments of fond reminiscing, recalling the extasy and erotic intimacy of their encounter, the two voices interweave melodically. Occasionally, their rhythms correlate in sympathetic major thirds, but these are fleeting and infrequent. When a sudden interruption of logic and the cold reality of their situation erase all other thoughts, Ennis reverts to speech-song and vocalizes by himself, with the same kind of clipped phrases heard at the beginning of the opera.

Act II begins with the reunion of Jack and Ennis after five years. Alma and Ennis communicate predominantly through spoken word, and when the two men embrace, leading to a passionate kiss, the orchestra conveys the moment. The dense texture is rhythmically complex and comprises a series of chromatically ascending cells, each with a crescendo. The ensuing conversation is a mixture of giddy excitement and warm sentiments. It takes the form of a recitative accompanied by inobtrusive and thinly textured flourishes from discrete sections of the orchestra. Ennis sings as melodically and expressively as Jack, but his speech-singing returns whenever he acknowledges the impossibility of their future together.

There is a grittiness in this opera that separates it from the film. Wuorinen's use of atonality maximizes the expressive possibilities of each scene, in particular the tragic conclusion of the opera in which Ennis sings of his regrets with denying Jack his unfettered love over the years; 'I never give you nothin' and I never said what you wanted me to say.'[46] Ennis' concluding phrases, culminating with 'Jack, I swear',[47] are the antithesis of his speech-song phrases from early in the opera and offer up a visceral, full-throated declaration to his murdered friend and lover. The piano, harp and vibraphone accompany this final phrase, with a fully chromatic screaming discord – the sonic embodiment of his anguish.

Jack's brutal and fatal homophobic attack was a watershed moment in the narrative of *Brokeback Mountain*. Suddenly, the oppressive society that the two men worked so hard to appease had the will to murder for representing a sexual 'other'. This was foreshadowed by Ennis' recount of the murder of old Earl, but that was years ago, and surely by the early 1980s, such a thing was inconceivable. In real life, Wyoming demonstrated that fatal homophobic attacks were still occurring in 1998, when the horrific torture and murder of Matthew Shephard (1976–1998, see chapter 6) took place near Laramie. Shephard was beaten so horrifically that his face was completely covered in blood, except where it had been partially cleansed by his tears. Wyoming may have decriminalized consensual sodomy in 1977; however, the repeal left anal intercourse as an indictable offence until it was abrogated in 1982.

LES BIENVEILLANTES (THE KINDLY ONES), HÈCTOR PARRA

For much of the twentieth century, popular forms of Western culture have painted queer characters in two ways: hopeless, ineffective and occupying a low status in society or sinister, evil, untrustworthy and of low moral standards. Queerness was either something to ridicule or something of which to be wary. As the end of the century gave way to the twenty-first, the media softened its tone, and a period began in which the inclusion of a queer character was almost ubiquitous for the success of a television series, and it was not long before leading characters in films were able to subscribe to at least a degree of gender fluidity. This rather extreme change in attitude was mirrored in the opera world, with the celebration of historical queer figures and an exploration of numerous, different forms of queer relationships and identities. Queerness was now being embraced by all forms of the artistic spectrum and held up as a symbol of goodness; the determined struggle against an imposing hegemony pits the queers in 'good' team and the largely homophobic, heteronormative, binary society in the 'bad' team. Queer characters are now expected to reflect caring, loving, individuals just trying to make sense of themselves in the world and causing no harm to anyone in the process.

As with the protagonist in Nico Muhly's *Two Boys* (2011, see chapter 6), Catalonian composer Hèctor Parra has presented in his opera, *Les Bienveillantes* (The Kindly Ones, 2018), a character who is unequivocally evil. In doing so, several questions arise concerning the ontological position that is being adopted. Kim (2017) argues that in order to foster a progressive approach to queer characterization, a multiplicity of identity traits, relationships and scenarios that include queer characters is required.[48] Schildcrout (2005) sets out to establish queer villainy not as a dichotomous position for or against queerness but as a dramatic metaphor for its universality. Through complex, thought-provoking characters, our understanding of extreme evil as manifest in queer individuals allows a broader and arguably more nuanced view of humanity.[49] Belmonte points out that representations of queerness in malevolent characters are often borne out of deep-rooted cultural identity discourses.[50] As such, it is important to consider whether the perpetuation of negative queer stereotypes can disrupt the largely positive gains that have been achieved in cultural narratives in recent decades.

Parra's opera is set to a libretto by Händl Klaus and based on the controversial bestselling historical fiction novel by Jonathan Littell (2006). Following the structure of the book, the opera is organized into seven sections that replicate a Baroque suite – a toccata, an allemande, a Courante, a sarabande, a minuet, an air and a gigue. The design is intended to reflect the love of music that the protagonist Maximilien Aue references at several points in the unfolding drama. Parra's love of Baroque music made the choice of material irresistible, and the score makes use of J. S. Bach's *Passio secundum Joannem* (*St John Passion*, 1724) as a structural model. In addition, there is frequent reference to literary and philosophical works, and other musical works, a signature of Parra, such as Berg's *Wozzeck* (1922), Zimmermann's *Die Soldaten* (1960), Bruckner's Symphony No. 7 (1883) and Shostakovich's Symphony No. 13 (1962). The title of the opera is derived from *The Oresteia* by Aeschylus (c. 525/524 BC), the vengeful goddesses who tormented perpetrators of patricide or matricide. Following the trial of Orestes, and through the intervention of Athena, the Furies are transformed into the *Eumenides* (Kindly Ones). Many of the Hellenic themes, incest and patricide, are imbued in the story but it is the morality of Ancient Greece that provides a lens through which the Holocaust is explored. For the Greeks, it was the commission of the sinful act which is judged, not the extenuating circumstances. Parra also makes frequent use of a Greek chorus throughout the narrative.

Max Aue was a former SS officer of French and German ancestry who contributed to the Holocaust atrocities and was present during several major events of World War II. The terror inflicted by the Nazi regime during the war forms the background of the Max's story, and the narrative is evoked through his perspective. The opera raises questions for the observer of the responsibility each person must take while participating in a process of dehumanization. Max was personally complicit in persecuting and exterminating Jews, taking part in some of the murders himself. In his opening aria, Max explores the process of inculturation that he experienced:

ist ein handgriff bloß ein schrittder	a movement is just a step
womöglich hand in hand	possibly hand in hand
zwar zum tod führt	leads to death
schuldlos schuldig	innocently guilty
am handwerk des tötens[51]	at the craft of killing

This and the surrounding text serve as a warning; Max may be a historical figure, but abominations like him are bound to re-emerge and remind us that history is constantly repeating itself.

Max's homosexuality does not manifest physically in the opera, nor does he discuss his proclivities with any frequency, and it could be possible to dismiss it, as on the surface, it does not seem to directly impact the narrative. Yet, as is so often the case with the burden of queerness in an oppressive, homophobic society, it can be seen as the basis for much of his objectionable decision-making. He mentions fleetingly in his opening toccata of his physical expression of queerness:

ficke ich von zeit zu zeit meine frau	I fuck my wife from time to time
aus gutem haus	from a good house
auf denreisen sind es männer	on the journeys they are men
die mich nehmen	who take me
mich als frau[52]	me as a woman

Importantly, despite the rarity of any discussion of gay sex acts, he articulates the detail regarding being submissive in the process. The words 'men who take me' describe a power dynamic that verges on submission, as it suggests that there may be a degree of freedom in which Max chooses to be dominated.[53] Such physical embodiment of the relinquishing of power is, according to Foucault, exercised by degree rather than totally and can manifest in surprising ways. The binary, gendered associations of submission, receptivity and femininity that oppose domination, insertivity and masculinity are well established in gay power dynamics.[54] For Max, who considers being receptive in anal intercourse, the connection with a lack of power and feminine weakness is expressed in his simile. Max is still profoundly attached to his mother, an obsession that becomes visible through his fantasies about his sister, Una. His own embodiment of feminism is something he finds abhorrent and terrifying. In order to avoid dissolving into his feminine instincts, he projects such characteristics onto the outside world and, in doing so, can attempt to destroy it.

When asked why Max was created as a homosexual character, Littell explained that it was 'for entirely practical reasons'.[55] Max is depicted as an aloof, outsider, constantly attentive of his actions and those around him. The existence of gay men within the ranks of the Nazi regime, such as high-ranking Ernst Röhm, head of the *Sturmabteilung* (SA, the Brownshirts), was often either ignored or refuted. Similarly, Max's incestuous relationship with Una was included for narrative purposes. Max fantasizes that he could be Una, furthering the notion of embodying his femininity, and that his homosexuality masks his intrinsic desires to be a woman and his wish to be violently penetrated. His orgasms represent escape from conscious thought and a temporal reprieve from his masculine self.

In Part Two, *Allemande*, Max recounts a moment with his friend Hans. He begins by placing himself in the location:

ich mochte Berlin für seine orte	I liked Berlin for its places
die kneipen für schwule	the pubs for gays
den tiergarten wo zwischen den büschen	the Tiergarten where the workers are
die arbeiter warten[56]	waiting between the bushes

During the exchange, the two men are relieving themselves one spring evening, and Hans declares that he wants to die. Requesting that Max shoot him with his father's gun, the scene turns suddenly homoerotic. Giving Max the gun, Hans notes that it is loaded. Max sings, '*lutsch daran tief, tief, ich schieße*'[57] (suck it, deep, deep, I shoot), to which Hans moans in agreement and promptly wets his pants and goes home. This fleeting scene explores a broader theme of fluids, which constantly permeates the libretto.

While completing *Les Bienveillantes*, Littell penned an essay entitled, *Le sec et l'humide* (The dry and the wet), focusing on the Belgian fascist politician, Leon Degrelle, commander of the Waffen-SS 'Wallonie' legion that fought alongside German troops on the Eastern Front. Littell's 'dry' and 'wet' dichotomy stems from Klaus Theweleit's work, *Male Fantasies* (1987), which he applied to Degrelle's richly metaphoric text. He viewed the gendered fascist soldier encased in a dry, hard, impenetrable shell, struggling in a wet, slimy and somehow feminized muddy landscape, familiar to his adversaries. Although Aue and Degrelle shared few character traits, they both thrived during the war and were able to recount their stories from the safe comfort of their shrewdly achieved freedom. The metaphor of bodily fluids in *Les Bienveillantes* exists in many forms, such as Max's persistent bouts of diarrhoea and vomiting and imagery such as '*in mir kreist ein schwarzer strom der mich*'[58] (a black stream circles inside me). Parra makes use of a multiplicity of fluid gestures in his orchestral material and important moments to emphasize the theme.

Max's incestual relationship with his twin sister, Una, is unveiled in Part Three – *Courante*. Max discovers that Una has married during the six years since he last saw her and protests, '*Dir bin ich versprochen meiner schwester Una*'[59] (I am promised to you my sister Una). In a flashback, their mother catches the two children naked and in bed together, berating them:

Kleidet euch an	get dressed
Bedeckt die scham	covers the shame
schämteuch zutode	you are ashamed to death
verdorbene brut	spoiled brood
(zu Max) du bist verflucht	(to Max) you're cursed
(zu Una) du bist verflucht	(to Una) you are cursed
Der bruder die schwester	the brother the sister
Die schwester der bruder	the sister of the brother
Aus auseinander	from apart
Genug genug[60]	enough enough

Likening them to monsters, she disowns them both. Later in the scene, and in the narrative's present, Max is introduced to the product of he and his sister's procreation, the two seven-year-old twins, Tristan and Orlando, as well as her husband, the composer, Berndt Baron Von Üxküll. As part of his 're-education' for suspected homosexuality, Max is sent to Stalingrad, where he takes part in the terror inflicted during the siege of the city. He returns to the Üxküll family villa in Part Six, *Air*, and in a drunken fantasy, he enjoys a last, perverse sexual coupling with Una. The scene is sung in French, and they sing of their act:

UNA nous sirotons la pisse (we slurp the piss)
MAX dans des verres en cristal (from delicate glasses)
UNA mangeons du caca (eating from the faeces)
MAX notre caca dans les plats (our droppings on the plates)
UNA savor a petites bouchées (cut pieces take a bite)
MAX avec nos cuillers en argent (with the small silver spoon)
UNA nous essuyons nos lèvres (wipe our lips)
MAX sur des serviettes brodées (with damask napkins)
UNA nous avons mangé (we ate)
MAX nous avons bu (we drank)
UNA ce qui est sorti de nous (what came out of us)
MAX lavons repus nos assiettes (wash fed up with our dishes)
UNA rien de nous n'est perdu (we have lost nothing)
MAX & UNA nous ne laissons aucune trace (leave no trace)[61]

Remembering that the inclusion of an incestuous relationship with his sister was purely for narrative purposes, the depiction of urophilia and copro-phagia seems an extreme extension of an already shocking sexual taboo. In keeping with the persistent reference to bodily fluids, this scene adds another layer of meaning with Max's obsession with his sister. Max understands that he is in part both male and female, the latter being an anathema that he rejects. His twin sister symbolically embodies the other half of his identity, and through the exchange of bodily fluids through regular sexual exchange, and in the more extreme form demonstrated in this scene, he is able to achieve a sense of fulfilment and of completion. Coprophagia is considered an extreme form of paraphilia and can occur as a result of a variety of triggers. It can be a compensation for deficient interpersonal connection, a regression to juvenile modes of oral incorporation, a source of gustatory enjoyment, an indication of disinhibition, an act of submission to authoritative but imaginary figures, a form of penance, an innate need for cleanliness, a sexual arousal or a symbol of psychosis. It presents as a diverse set of emotional responses such as disgust, shame, fear, sadness, horror, anxiety, guilt and enjoyment.[62]

The notion of gender fluidity is further explored shortly afterwards as Max fantasizes once again, singing:

je vois mon corps (I see my body)
dans le miroir (in the mirror)
la robe d'Una (Una's dress)
moi dans sa robe (me in her dress)
Una dans mon uniforme (Una in my uniform)
elle me met du rouge à lèvres (she paints my lips red)
elle me peigne les cheveux (she combs my hair)
met du rimmel à mes cils (brushes my eyelashes)
prend le poing (takes the fist)
et le fourre (and introduces them)[63]

His thoughts are soon echoed by the Greek chorus in a mixture of French and German, another dichotomy represented in the opera:

ALL MEN *tu es* mon frère *schrie ich* (you are my brother)
ALL WOMEN je suis ton frère *schrie* Una (I'm your brother)
ALL MEN et moi ta sœur *schrie* ich (I your sister)
ALL WOMEN et toi ma sœur *schrie* una (you my sister)[64]

Parra imbued Max with humanity despite the process of dehumanization that underpins the storyline. His vocal lines are complex, full of lyricism and coloured by varied orchestral timbres for each part of his vocal range. He is vocally challenged, with phrases that at times reflect a Heldentenor and at other times, a lyric tenor, or even a light coloratura Baroque tenor. He is given sombre, dejected vocalities, articulated by soft colours, breaths, half-spoken passages and the melodic progression of small sound cells. He is vocally complex, delicate and expressive, in contrast to his friend Thomas, who sings with a more homogenous vocal surety that provides a powerful impression suitable for a hardened soldier. Max's vocal fragility provides a disturbing embodiment of a man disposed to such unflinching horror.

The depiction of Max, an invention of Littell and a reinvention of Parra and Klaus offer a disturbing view of the distorted world of Nazi Germany. The protagonist as storyteller necessitates that the audience views the horrors from his perspective. This establishes a challenging conundrum whereby the observer is able to experience a degree of empathy, while simultaneously being horror-struck. Littell frequently reduces Max to his base instincts, dehumanizing him through his perversity, and yet he is given certain virtues attributed to cultivated Germans – intelligence and respect for academic titles, a love of music, especially Bach, and a love of fine wine. His bizarre paraphilia, informed in part by his inner revulsion of homosexual desire and feminized identity, contributes to his psychopathy, allowing a glimpse into the complex world of extreme forms of erotic impulse that are yet to be fully understood.

NOTES

1. Louis Crompton, *Homosexuality and Civilization* (Cambridge: Harvard University Press, 2009), xiv.

2. Joshua L. Boe, Valerie A. Maxey, and J. Maria Bermudez, 'Is the closet a closet? Decolonizing the coming out process with Latin@ adolescents and families', *Journal of Feminist Family Therapy* 30, no. 2 (2018): 90–108.

3. Joanne Greenfield, 'Coming out: The process of forming a positive identity', in *Fenway: Guide to Lesbian, Gay, Bisexual, and Transgender Health*, eds. Harvey Makadon, Kenneth Mayer, Jennifer Potter, and Hilary Goldhammer (Philadelphia: American College of Physician, 2008), 45–74.

4. Liora Gvion, 'Singing your way out of the closet: Young gay men in the operatic world', *Young* 28, no. 4 (2020): 387–403.

5. Jón Ingvar Kjaran and Ingólfur Ásgeir Jóhannesson, 'Masculinity strategies of young queer men as queer capital', *Norma* 11, no. 1 (2016): 52–65.

6. Tim Fitzsimons, 'LGBTQ history month: The early days of America's AIDS crisis', *NBC News*, October 15, 2018, accessed 27 August 2021, https://www.nbcnews .com/feature/nbc-out/lgbtq-history-month-early-days-america-s-aids-crisis-n919701.

7. George Chauncey, *Gay New York: Gender, Urban Culture, and the Making of the Gay Male World, 1890–1940* (Paris: Hachette, 2008).

8. NYC LGBT Historic Sites Project, 'Various locations Manhattan: Central Park', 2016, accessed 13 April 2022, https://www.nyclgbtsites.org/.

9. Schott EAM, 'Peter Eötvös's angels in America at New York City Opera', 1 June 2017, accessed 13 April 2022, https://www.eamdc.com/news/peter-eotvoss -angels-in-america-at-new-york-city-opera/.

10. Peter Eötvös and Mari Mezei, *Angels in America: Opera in Two Parts, Based on the Play by Tony Kushner* [Full score] (Mainz: Schott, revised version 2003–04, 2008/2012), 34–35.

11. Eötvös and Mezei, *Angels in America*, 44–45.

12. Eötvös and Mezei, *Angels in America*, 102–103.

13. Eötvös and Mezei, *Angels in America*, 103.

14. Eötvös and Mezei, *Angels in America*, 114.

15. Eötvös and Mezei, *Angels in America*, 115.

16. Eötvös and Mezei, *Angels in America*, 120.

17. Eötvös and Mezei, *Angels in America*, 124.

18. Eötvös and Mezei, *Angels in America*, 124–125.

19. Eötvös and Mezei, *Angels in America*, 197.

20. Eötvös and Mezei, *Angels in America*, 325.

21. Eötvös and Mezei, *Angels in America*, 327–328.

22. Eötvös and Mezei, *Angels in America*, 441.

23. Eötvös and Mezei, *Angels in America*, 338.

24. Eötvös and Mezei, *Angels in America*, 419.

25. Eötvös and Mezei, *Angels in America*, 40–41.

26. Leslie Uyeda and Rachel Rose, *When the Sun Comes Out* [piano/vocal score] (Toronto: The Avondale Press, 2020), 6–7.

27. Uyeda and Rose, *When the Sun Comes Out*, 7–8.

28. Uyeda and Rose, *When the Sun Comes Out*, 9–10.

29. Margaret Nichols, 'Lesbian relationships: Implications for the study of sexuality and gender,' in *Homosexuality/Heterosexuality: Concepts of Sexual Orientation*, eds. David P. McWhirter, Stephanie Anne Sanders, and June Machover Reinisch (Oxford: OUP, 1990), 350–364.

30. Uyeda and Rose, *When the Sun Comes Out*, 8–9.

31. Uyeda and Rose, *When the Sun Comes Out*, 28.

32. Uyeda and Rose, *When the Sun Comes Out*, 34.

33. Uyeda and Rose, *When the Sun Comes Out*, 38–40.

34. Uyeda and Rose, *When the Sun Comes Out*, 63.

35. Uyeda and Rose, *When the Sun Comes Out*, 63.

36. Uyeda and Rose, *When the Sun Comes Out*, 73.

37. Uyeda and Rose, *When the Sun Comes Out*, 65.

38. Uyeda and Rose, *When the Sun Comes Out*, 96–97.

39. Uyeda and Rose, *When the Sun Comes Out*, 129–130.

40. Uyeda and Rose, *When the Sun Comes Out*, 116.

41. Uyeda and Rose, *When the Sun Comes Out*, 117.

42. Harry Brod, 'They're bi shepherds, not gay cowboys: The misframing of Brokeback mountain', *The Journal of Men's Studies* 14, no. 2 (2007): 252–253.

43. Leigh Boucher and Sarah Pinto, '"I ain't queer": Love, masculinity and history in Brokeback mountain', *The Journal of Men's Studies* 15, no. 3 (2008): 311–330.

44. Charles Wuorinen and Annie Proulx, *Brokeback Mountain: Opera in Two Acts* [Orchestral Score] (New York: C. F. Peters, 2011), 134.

45. Wuorinen and Proulx, *Brokeback Mountain*, 135.

46. Wuorinen and Proulx, *Brokeback Mountain*, 308.

47. Wuorinen and Proulx, *Brokeback Mountain*, 313.

48. Koeun Kim, 'Queer-coded villains (and why you should care)', *Dialogues@ RU* (NJ: Rutgers University, 2017), 156–165.

49. Jordan Schildcrout, *This Thing of Darkness: Reclaiming the Queer Killer in Contemporary Drama* (New York: City University of New York, 2005).

50. Juan Francisco Belmonte, 'Teenage heroes and evil deviants: Sexuality and history in JRPGs', *Continuum* 31, no. 6 (2017): 903–911.

51. Hèctor Parra and Händl Klaus, *Les Bienveillantes* [Vocal score] (Paris: Durand Editions Musicales, 2018), 12.

52. Parra and Klaus, *Les Bienveillantes*, 9.

53. Michel Foucault, *Power: The Essential Works of Michel Foucault 1954–1984* (Penguin UK, 2019).

54. Susan Kippax and Gary Smith, 'Anal intercourse and power in sex between men', *Sexualities* 4, no. 4 (November 2001): 413–434.

55. Klaus Theweleit and Timothy Nunan, 'On the German reaction to Jonathan Littell's Les Bienveillantes', *New German Critique*, no. 106 (2009): 21–34.

56. Parra and Klaus, *Les Bienveillantes*, 26–27.

57. Parra and Klaus, *Les Bienveillantes*, 30–31.

58. Parra and Klaus, *Les Bienveillantes*, 10–11.

59. Parra and Klaus, *Les Bienveillantes*, 141–142.

60. Parra and Klaus, *Les Bienveillantes*, 171–173.

61. Parra and Klaus, *Les Bienveillantes*, 279–283.

62. Nick Haslam, *Psychology in the Bathroom* (New York, NY: Springer, 2012).

63. Parra and Klaus, *Les Bienveillantes*, 291–296.

64. Parra and Klaus, *Les Bienveillantes*, 297–299.

Chapter 4

Hegemony

The dominance of one louder, more forceful group in society over another, smaller, less vocal group is not unique to queerness. The shared experience of hegemony with feminism, racial struggles, religious persecution, cultural identities and class distinctions is a binding force against the privileged components of society which seek to assert and oppress. Exercising hegemonic power is supported through a process of legitimizing ideals, drawing on historical precedent, religion, politics, psychology or medical concepts, to propagate whichever forms of oppression are desired. The ongoing debate about the source of queer sexuality being based on biological or social factors operates on the premise that there is something wrong; we need to discover the root of the problem. Queer communities have been split on this issue, with the rallying cry, 'I didn't choose this', offering succour to the biological discourse that fundamentally feeds into the hegemonic narrative.[1]

Several nineteenth-century philosophers and sexologists proposed a series of biologically based theories which argued for a more tolerant approach to homosexuality. This approach emphasized the notion of same-sex desire emanating from a lack of self-control rather than a positive choice for the individual.[2] In the early part of the twentieth century, operating on the understanding that such biological abnormalities could be remedied, sexual deviancy was treated with a range of horrific stimuli including chemical and electrical treatments to individuals on both sides of the Atlantic.[3] By the 1970s, a wave of autonomous practitioners of psychiatry brought on by the advent of 'nurse therapists' saw a resistance to homosexual law reform, and a counter-psychiatry attracted headlines such as 'Psychiatrists in a Shift. Declare Homosexuality no Mental Illness.'[4]

Throughout many of the operas discussed in this book, the church remains a quiet omnipresence. Although some representations of the church are positive, such as the Pastor in Paula M. Kimper's *Patience and Sarah*, often notions of religion are weaponized against the queer community. One particularly extreme form of religion-based hegemony that seeks to persecute all forms of queerness is the conservative denominations in what is known as the 'bible belt', which occupies West South Central (Texas, Oklahoma, Arkansas and Louisiana), East South Central (Kentucky, Tennessee, Mississippi and Alabama) and South Atlantic (West Virginia, Virginia, Maryland, Delaware, North Carolina, South Carolina, Georgia and Florida) census regions of the United States. In these regions, religious doctrines attempt to divide the perceived conflicting identities of queer and Christian. In such conservative theology, silent thoughts are enough to threaten the possible salvation of the soul. This pernicious concept terrifies those who have no control over basic sexual urges by using an archaic fear of hell as a powerful motivator to heteronormative conformity. This basic psychological warfare is even more horrific when leaders of the right-wing Christian community advocate for an end to any form of queerness by any means available.[5]

This homophobic narrative continues but not unabated with the emergence of queer theology. Rejecting the familiar trope that queer people are sick, evil, perverse, dangerous and sinful, queer theology subverts the message by framing all sexual experiences as natural and created by God. With the position that homosexuality forms a part of a divinely ordained, natural law, it forms part of a normative trait. Much of the early queer theology adopts an apologetic position aimed at reforming the church's endemic, homophobia. John McNeill's book *The Church and the Homosexual* (1976) was a pivotal moment for the Catholic Church, and at a time when ecclesiastical queers were locked firmly in the closet, questions of a long-established kyriarchy were rejected by Rome but provided a sense of hope for countless queer Catholics wishing to enjoy the same Christian values as practising heterosexuals.[6] McNeill argued that by embracing queers into the arms of the church, a process of reclaiming just, moral, ethical and Christian values that had been lost could help modernize the ecclesiastical community. Young theologians now have access to a plethora of queer theology texts with which to frame issues of nationalism, religious violence, civil rights and oppressive hegemony as one of many critical theoretical tools.[7]

Hegemony is explored in this chapter through the lens of six operas. In Jorge Martín's *Before Night Falls*, the story of Cuban artist Reinaldo Arenas explores his persistent struggle for freedom from the Castro regime in Cuba, then from political pressures while in exile and finally from the AIDS crisis. His was a life in which self-expression was crushed under the weight of a state and society which sought to deny his artistic, sexual and political identity. Theodore Morrison's *Oscar* concerns the trial and imprisonment of Oscar Wilde and his refusal to be silenced by the conservative hegemony of

Victorian English society. *As One* by Laura Kaminsky provides an enlightening journey of a transgender individual, struggling with internalized shame and self-loathing inherited from an uninformed community. Iain Bell's *Stonewall* gives an account of the iconic event in 1969 that saw queer rights change dramatically in its wake for communities throughout the world. *The Stonewall Operas*, four short, one-act pieces by Bryan Blaskie, Brian Cavanagh-Strong, Kevin Cummines and T. J. Rubin, use the Stonewall Riots as a provocation for broader issues that continue to confront queers. In each of these works, the bravery of the protagonists reminds us that the many improvements for the queer community have been hard-won by instances of resistance against a range of hegemonic forces.

BEFORE NIGHT FALLS, JORGE MARTÍN

The Socialist Revolution that took place in Cuba in 1959 saw an exodus of men and women due to the extreme homophobic policies of the Castro regime. The introduction of repressive policies meant that any form of expression linked to gay or lesbian identity was rendered impossible.[8] When the AIDS crisis arrived in Cuba, the social values of Castro's regime were revealed. Although the availability of free, universal health care without any prejudicial screening meant that patients could access the best available treatment, anyone testing positive to HIV was quarantined in a state-sanctioned sanitarium. This measure, regardless of whether the individual was sick, forced patients to leave their jobs and isolate themselves from family and loved ones. Those who questioned the draconian measure were deemed 'enemies of the Revolution', thereby relinquishing any possibility for public advocacy on behalf of the victims.[9]

One important literary figure to fall foul of the new Cuban value system was Reinaldo Arenas, who wrote in excess of twenty books in his short life. His publications included novels, short stories, poetry, drama and essays, the success of which was essentially eclipsed with the release of his autobiography, *Antes que anocheza* (Before Night Falls).[10] The text boldly articulates his homoerotic experiences in what represents the first openly queer, Latin American autobiography. It is equally remarkable to have come from a country in which homophobia is utterly ingrained in the societal psyche. Arenas' work, critically acclaimed for its wit, intelligence and creativity, routinely involved queer characters and issues, enabling him to confront notions of traditional gender identities and heteronormativity.[11]

Jorge Martín, also Cuban-born and emigrating to the United States with his family in 1965, instinctively wrote *Before Night Falls* in English rather than Spanish. As well as self-identifying as an American, he felt that authentic portrayals of Cubans should use Cuban Spanisha, and such a choice would create difficult casting choices. Martín was given a copy of Arenas' memoir by a friend and gay English professor living in the same building who was also an opera enthusiast.[12] He co-wrote the libretto with Dolores Koch, also a Cuban American residing in New York. Koch, a friend of Arenas, had already translated his memoir into English. The score was completed in 2005 and revised in 2009. Despite the dark and oppressive themes, the music is imbued with a sunny optimism that distils the country's musical heritage in its material. Martín describes his score as having 'elements of Cuban music, a Caribbean flavor', added to his 'American, tonal, melodic, romantic style'. The Cuban influence, though very subtle at times, is immediately recognizable. It is a work divorced from the modernism of recent times, so austere and minimalist. Quite the contrary, it is exuberant and, essentially, entertaining.[13] Importantly, Castro is not named at any point in the opera, allowing for a more universal reading of the opera's themes.

The opera is imbued with an ambiance of 'magical realism', allowing physical depictions of the settings to be represented through suggestion. Taking a cue from the end of Arenas' memoire in which he addresses the moon, Martín created two muses: the moon and the sea. As well as providing a sense of gender balance in what is a male-dominated cast, the characters interact with Rey at pivotal moments in the narrative.[14] They guide his thinking, providing moments of inspiration such as the decision to smuggle his manuscripts out of Cuba. Martín also created a composite character in the form of Ovidio, evoking the legendary narrator, author of *Metamorphoses* and the *Ars Amatoria*. Ovidio represents the many mentors and friends with associated themes of friendship, betrayal and suicide. He is ultimately destroyed by the Cuban secret police, a metaphorical representation of the death of Cuban literary culture.

Following the orchestral prologue, the curtain rises on Rey's small, fifth-floor apartment in Manhattan. Lázaro is helping Rey as he struggles up the stairs. Rey sings, 'This is the end, Lázaro',[15] as he contemplates his final days suffering the symptoms of late-stage AIDS. Rey reflects, 'We have fought, survived, and escaped tyranny! and although I must die soon, I will be happy to die a free man!'[16] As Rey faces death, the orchestration is characterized by ominous, deep woodwind and brass with a notable absence of strings. All of which falls silent as Rey sings the title phrase of the work, 'Before night falls!',[17] *a cappella*. This metaphor of his impending death marks his urgent wish to complete his final book. We are then introduced to his muses, in the form of the Sea and the Moon.

In the following scene, Rey is back in Cuba and runs joyfully into the arms of Pepe, following a dance with several other boys in which Rey is the centre of attention. The music provides Cuban dance rhythms in the strings with the boys singing a wordless melody with the bassoons. The dance is interrupted by Pepe mentioning the men in the mountains who are fighting for liberty and justice. He asks Rey about his dreams, to which he responds, 'To write poems, free and magical poems, to write a hundred thousand poems, and have a hundred thousand lovers! Each of their bodies a poem, each of our lovings an epic!'[18] The dance rhythms from earlier resume as the two men vow to join the rebels. The score indicates that 'the TREES and NATURE join in the dance which becomes gradually more and more erotic, though never aggressive. The tone is comic.'[19] Rey's aunts appear and are horrified by the display – 'Dirty boys, go away! Filthy boys, keep away!'[20] They chastise him while his friends, including the trees, flee – 'You wild and nasty child! You good for nothing, stupid brat!'[21]

Rey's mother provides an antidote to the bitterness of his aunts and urges him to remember the beauty of Cuba and to maintain hope. Rey considers his mother's beauty to be like that of the land on which he was born; however, his absent father represents a tropical rainstorm over the open countryside. He continues the metaphor, singing, 'I run out naked, and roll around letting the rain run through me.'[22] This imagery reflects the inverse form of Freud's Oedipal complex, whereby Rey has formed an unconscious erotic attachment to his father. As the rain forms a figurative river, he sings, 'I hear the river roar, I want to roar just the same.'[23] His father's desertion of Rey and his mother represents a violent act, and Rey feels a similar desire for destruction. The allegory of the river also doubles as a means by which he can escape to freedom.

Before Night Falls involves a number of set pieces as well as long, arioso sections that allow the material to evolve organically. Martín makes frequent use of jarring juxtapositions to highlight the divergent characters and their associated political adherences. One such example is the rebel camp scene which moves from an optimistic idealism representing the camaraderie of the rebels to the crushing disillusionment that is felt by Rey with the emerging intolerance and authoritarianism. The music is frequently exuberant and contains memorable melodic material informed by distinctive Cuban and Caribbean inflections. Rey's character is onstage almost continuously, but according to baritone, Wes Mason who premiered the role, Martín tempered the demands of the baritone by providing lyrical phrases that provided nothing but support for the singer. The chorus forms a major part of the work and appears in several guises: Castro's guerrillas, enraged prisoners, carousers in New York's Times Square and most evocatively as an offstage halo support to the Muses' sections.

In Act I, scene ii, a group of rebels including Rey and Pepe has assembled in the countryside to proclaim victory. It is New Year's Day, 1959, and their leader is now Victor. Pepe and Rey are horrified by the execution of a boy accused of treason and begin to doubt the glory of the communist ideal, which they had believed would lead to freedom and liberty, rather than punitive killing. In scene iii, the two men secretly pay a visit to the poet, Ovidio, who is in internal exile. He provides a grim account of the situation:

> The state is tightening the noose around my neck. My magazine has been shut down. All gay artists are under constant vigilance. Dictatorships fear sexuality; dictatorships think little of life, hate beauty and invention; dictatorships seek to control everything and everyone, judges and juries, trials, and justice, our minds![24]

Homosexual themes are secondary to that of freedom in the first act; however, after successfully smuggling his completed manuscript out of Cuba, spurred on by his two muses and women's chorus chanting, 'Send it out',[25] he is invited to swim in the ocean by Pepe. 'Think of all the beautiful men there', Pepe sings enticingly. The music that follows, 'Idyll at the beach', sees Pepe, Rey and a group of male dancers in a stylized, erotic dance to a languid and sensual counterpoint for strings, harp and woodwind. The scene is interrupted by a police siren, at which point the music changes suddenly, pivoting to aggressive patterns for wind, brass and percussion. Pepe and the men flee, but Rey is arrested amidst shouts of 'Pervert! ¡Maricón! Damned faggots!'[26] from the police. Rey finally realizes that he has been set up by Pepe.

In prison, Rey is interrogated by Victor, now on opposite sides of the political struggle. Interspersed with accented punctuations from the full orchestra, Victor explains his position to Rey, 'Homosexuals are immoral, a disease that weakens our society, and believe me, we will cleanse ourselves of you!'[27] Having shown Rey a copy of his critically acclaimed, published book, he continues, 'Writers can be dangerous too, like Ovidio and his faggot friends and you.'[28] Victor's rhetoric delivers two devastating blows to Rey who is told that he is arrested for being a sexual pervert, and that Pepe revealed the location of his secret manuscript which Victor burned in front of Rey. With a return to the aggressive orchestral punctuations, Victor sings, 'Now you must tell me the names of those who helped you.'[29] Rey refuses and Victor beats him brutally. In solitary confinement, Victor's chastisement continues as Rey is shown footage of Ovidio confessing his anti-revolution writings and providing several names of other dissidents including Rey. Victor sings the words of the document that Rey signs, including, 'I renounce my life as a homosexual and vow never again to succumb to that disease',[30] allowing him to be released from custody. Free from prison, but not free to live as his authentic self or to write what he feels he must, Rey contemplates his perpetual imprisonment in Cuba.

Act II begins with the chorus singing of the opportunity that has presented itself when a bus crashes into the gates of the Peruvian embassy. Soon after, Rey meets Lázaro, sympathetic to his ideals and declaring 'I'm not gay, you know'[31] but declaring he wants to live with Rey. Lázaro manages to obtain a visa and leave Cuba, and as he bids farewell to Rey, the two sing of their mutual love in a tender duet. In scene iv, Rey is applying for a visa and the visa officer questions his motives, 'Are you a criminal or a mental case? Are you a pimp or a prostitute? Or are you perhaps a homosexual?'[32] Rey acknowledges that he is gay, but the visa officer pushes further with his questions, 'A-ha, another fag – top or bottom?'[33] Rey states that he is a bottom and the officer continues, 'Show me you're a fag. Let me see how you walk.'[34] Unconvinced by Rey's walk, he turns to the chorus who respond with '*¡Maricón!*'[35] repeatedly. He concludes, 'The Revolution is happy to be rid of scum like you!'[36] and informs Rey of his successful visa application.

Having arrived in the United States, Rey is reunited with Lázaro, but he is distraught. He is struggling with a sense of purpose while in exile. He sings, 'The left hates my politics, the right hates my sexuality!',[37] as the chorus chant 'Death to the gays! ¡Viva Fidel!'[38] As Rey laments his predicament, he adds, 'My doctor has told me I've got this mysterious "gay disease"',[39] and he notes wryly that his death will come not from Cuba's tyrants but from his lovers. He prays to Ovidio that he be granted three more years of life to complete his final work. He does, and Lázaro assists his suicide by handing him a bottle of poison. Arenas' life was a constant series of escapes from imprisonment; he escaped the backward-thinking rural province of Holguín in eastern Cuba where he was born, he escaped prison and he finally escaped Cuba. What he was unable to escape from was AIDS. Rey fulfilled many of his dreams related to his literary success, but he did not live to see a free Cuba.[40]

A common characteristic of authoritarian regimes is the inherent distrust of the individual and the threats that individuality pose. Dictatorship states seek to suppress, persecute and punish individuals who seek to innovate in defence of complete control of the population and are routinely prepared to exterminate those who challenge the established order. Agitators are labelled as heretics, social dissenters and political rebels in carefully crafted discourse designed to prevent sympathizers from gaining confidence.[41] Uniformity is the ultimate aim, and individuality is the greatest threat, and Nietzsche considered such states as 'cold monsters'[42] in the desire to stifle culture and manipulate education. The life of Reinaldo Arenas was shaped by a succession of various imprisonments which he battled with continuously; however, perhaps it was this struggle to disseminate beauty that allowed his abilities to thrive from the pressures of a homophobic world. Martín shared several important life experiences with Arenas; however, two important factors separate the two artists: Martín was able to leave Cuba as a child, and he enjoys

a period in which AIDS no longer poses the same threat to the queer community. Arenas' death following a life of persecution is the ultimate tragedy,
but the immortalization of his story in Martín's opera is the ultimate devotion.

OSCAR, THEODORE MORRISON

Descriptions of Oscar Wilde (1854–1900) rarely align with a common concept of heroism, which conjures images of muscular, daring, brave, heterosexual men, rescuing the weak and defending the defenceless. Such images
may have their roots in the Hellenistic age of conquerors, bringing civilization to the barbarians one battle at a time. A more contemporary concept of
heroism has emerged from a growing discourse that has sought to redefine
the term for the modern age. Rousseau[43] considered traits such as 'strength
of soul' and citizenship, while Cameron[44] and Kelly[45] observed that heroism
and morality were not mutually exclusive ideals. Max Weber[46] argued that
charisma is an important virtue which separates heroism from regular individuals. Freud contended that society is desirous of heroes, and that heroes
must not only be powerful and charismatic but also have strong convictions in
an idea to arouse the sentiments of the society. Social heroism involves heroic
action in defence of ideals for which the hero may suffer a loss of social
status, credibility, financial stability and social cohesion, while risking arrest,
torture and death.[47] With these ideas of heroism in mind, we are able to view
Wilde in a new light – a staunch defender of the rights of queer men to love
one another, charismatic, with a strong conviction, and willing to be arrested,
imprisoned and tortured for his struggle. A hero by definition.

During Wilde's life, he was celebrated and then pilloried. His sexuality was
seen as scandalous, and his refusal to apologize for it was shameful. His infamous prison sentence, handed down in 1895, was considered to be the ultimate downfall. During the course of his two-year sentence, he was transferred
from Wandsworth Prison to Reading Gaol, and en route he endured a crown
jeering and spitting at him on the railway platform. He is now celebrated not
only as a literary genius but also as a queer icon of enormous significance.
The process from vilification to veneration occurred as the prevailing views
in society regarding homosexuality changed. Wilde was ahead of his time
by more than half a century, championing his cause for queer acceptance at
a time of intense Victorian conservativism and sexual repression. That he
did so was heroic; that he did so with exceptional eloquence elevated him to
iconic status in queer history.

Theodore Morrison's opera *Oscar* (2013) focuses on the period between
1895 and 1897 that included Wilde's trial and imprisonment. Morrison
intended not to focus on Wilde as a victim but as a tragic hero. The story

presents the perception of his public fall from grace, 'plunging him into a purgatory of social humiliation and physical suffering through imprisonment with hard labor, thence to discard him as a spent husk'.[48] Wilde's sentence of 'gross indecency', the Victorian interpretation of a man loving another man, was a punishment that exercised the fullest extent of the law. Wilde was in love with Lord Alfred Douglas, known as Bosie, his muse and his nemesis, and their public relationship was the cause of his downfall. Bosie is a voiceless character in the opera, presented in dance form, reminiscent Britten's Tadzio in *Death in Venice* (see chapter 5).

Bosie appears to Wilde in the form of visions during his imprisonment. As he forms part of the metadiegesis of the opera, he materializes in several guises: a baggage porter, a French waiter, the prison doctor and, ultimately, death. The audience is aware that underneath these manifestations are all Bosie. Wilde once said, 'If you give a man a mask, he will tell you the truth.'[49] The final vision was prophetic, as Wilde collapsed while in prison, hitting his head and thereby developing a cholesteatoma, a growth in the ear which corrodes the mastoid bone and leaves festering debris in the middle ear. After being released from prison, he fled to Paris and after possibly undergoing a radical mastoidectomy died in 1900.

Morrison scored Wilde's character for a countertenor, providing further Britten comparisons with the sexually ambiguous Oberon in *A Midsummer Night's Dream* (1960). The countertenor voice, the highest tessitura for a broken, adult male voice, connotes a 'queer vocality', in the way that it undermines assumptions about vocal authenticity and concepts of naturalness. The countertenor challenges the heteronormative ideas of masculinity by presenting an extended vocal technique that matches the range customarily associated with female singers, continuing the long traditions of gender-bending roles, castrati and trouser roles throughout operatic history. The perception of the artificial voice and vocal range has provided contrary discourse from musicologists; however, it is the countertenor and the castrato voice that destabilize associations between voice, gender and sexuality within sociocultural and historical frameworks that have most frequently considered as queer vocalities.[50] In life, Wilde was unapologetic for his queerness, and his voice type in the opera, the vehicle by which he communicates and expresses his desires and struggles, is freed from all artificial restrictions on vocal possibilities. In Act I, scene I, Wilde is reflecting on having been refused a room in three London hotels on account of his pending trial. He sings, 'For this love that dare not speak its name, I fear the road will be long, and red with monstrous martyrdoms.'[51]

His metaphorical road reflects his personal fate and that of many other queers who would be victims of a society at odds with a liberal sexual agenda. The angular melody has a haunting quality, beginning with a C major diatonic seventh figure, but being forced into unrelated keys by a series of unrelated intervals, it nevertheless expressively showcases the range of the counter-tenor voice. It is at this moment that Bosie first appears, amidst a spoken chorus spitting insults such as 'sodomite!' at the pair. The overt homophobia is not downplayed in the opera, and the scenes in which Wilde is refused accommodation during the trial seem shocking to our modern sensibilities.

Oscar's wit is on display in the first interaction but dwindles as his predica-ment becomes clear. The unambiguous reference to Christ's nativity scene is reinforced by the detectives in the third hotel who point out the lack of room for Wilde, or his kind, at the inn. The interweaving vocal lines of the detec-tives as they discharge their insults are characterized by accented, descend-ing intervals, the syllabic utterances devoid of any suggestion of beauty or intelligence, in contrast to the beautifully shaped, melismatic phrases sung by Wilde. The symbolic biblical reference helps establish the theme of heroism and martyrdom that ultimately unfolds in the epilogue.

Oscar is presented in John Cox's libretto by the role of Walt Whitman (1819–1892) who acts as a choric interlocutor. Wilde and Whitman met in 1882 during Wilde's tour of America. The two men admired each other, but there is little evidence to suggest they developed a particularly strong friend-ship, and the role of the narrator in this case is less biographical but delivered by a distant and sympathetic enthusiast.[52] In the prologue, Whitman contex-tualizes the narrative for the audience, and as the plot develops, he remains a touchstone, observing, commenting and providing clarity. He is visually static but musically elaborate, reflective of his unstinting personality in life.[53] By the time Wilde met Bosie, Whitman was dead, and the narrative allows him to comment on proceedings from the vantage point of a queer artist of immortal status. It would not be long before Wilde would join the same rank.

The epilogue is a culmination of the theme of heroism that has pervaded the narrative. In death, Wilde is introduced to the panoply of immortal lumi-naries and inducted by Walt Whitman. How Wilde would react to such flat-tery is difficult to imagine, given the line that follows, 'The only mortality I ever desired, was to invent a new sauce.'[54] The chorus of immortals, dressed in togas and beckoning Wilde to join their ranks, was considered a distrac-tion by some reviewers who observed audience members trying to identify the other characters.

Morrison's opera was also criticized for the derivative compositional techniques found throughout the score. The comparison with Britten's opera extends further than the choice of vocal type and general structure and includes the harmonic and rhythmic language which is thoroughly familiar. The prison scenes also borrow from Bartok's use of the octatonic scale that consists of alternating tones and semitones. There are also remind-ers of Samuel Barber, Gian Carlo Menotti, Richard Strauss and Dimitri

Shostakovich. However, Morrison noted that Wilde himself understood that all artists annex ideas absorbed from predecessors. Furthermore, the emotional complexity surrounding Wilde's love for Bosie, despite the extreme problems he caused, is avoided in the libretto. After being released from prison, Wilde wrote to Bosie, 'I feel that my only hope of again doing beautiful work in art is being with you.'[55] Wilde also stated that Bosie 'ruined my life, and for that very reason I seem forced to love him more'.[56] The focus on Wilde's mistreatment, as appalling as it was, and the almost sycophantic epilogue created a one-dimensional perspective of a man, who revelled in life's many contradictions. Humour, one of Wilde's signature trademarks and a technique he used to disguise his subversive agenda, is used sparingly in the opera, leaving the audience with a sobering experience non-reflective of Wilde's personality.

Wilde's final major piece of writing was a letter, his *De Profundis*, recording his experiences in prison and provides explanation of his convictions; however, it was suppressed for many decades while he remained a deeply controversial figure. It was not until the middle of the twentieth century that Wilde's literature as well as his personal life began to be re-evaluated. The 1950s was not, however, a decade of unbridled sexual liberation in Britain, as in 1954, there remained 1,069 men in English and Welsh prisons on sodomy charges. By the end of the decade, however, the pendulum was swinging, and a call to overturn the law responsible for convicting Wilde, Montagu, Turing and many other thousands of queers was growing louder. Lord Arran, one of the major sponsors of the decriminalization act, allowing consenting adult males to engage in homosexual acts in private, quoted Wilde on the day the law passed. He stated to the House, 'Mr Wilde was right: the road has been long and the martyrdoms many, monstrous and bloody. Today, please God! sees the end of that road.'[57]

AS ONE, LAURA KAMINSKY

For transgender people, the word 'transition' has connotations of change from one person to another person. The reality is, however, that whatever part of the process the individual is experiencing, there is one person. The process is one of becoming, stripping back layers of identity, until the person is who they feel they should be. The transgender community occupies a space in the queer spectrum that requires increased understanding, and much work still needs to be done to fully embrace the needs of a small but growing sector of the community. In 2016, just 0.6 per cent of the adult population in the United States identified as transgender, representing around 1.4 million people and not including transgender youth.[58] This number doubled from the same data collection five years previously and may be, in part, due to a more energized discourse.

Laura Kaminsky, a lesbian woman, collaborated with two librettists to create 'As One' – Mark Campbell, a gay man, and Kimberley Reed, a transgender woman. The opera is intensely intimate, requiring two singers, a string quartet and a set comprised of video images, reflecting the intimacy of the narrative. Kaminsky explains, 'It's a very intimate piece in a way, but out of that intimacy comes a lot of power because you're right inside that person's journey.'[59] The two singers play one character, the baritone presents 'Hannah before' and the mezzo-soprano presents 'Hannah after', and at various times throughout the seventy-five-minute opera, they sing together, effectively reconciling their identities as belonging to a single person. Kaminsky was inspired by a story of a New Jersey man whose wife and children supported his decision to become a woman. The legitimacy of their relationship was debated in New Jersey courts, and Kaminsky was struck by the sacrifices required of someone to become who they were meant to be.[60]

Devor (2004) proposed fourteen stages of identity development in his groundbreaking research on transsexual identity. The first three stages involve anxiety, confusion and using sex with others to make interpersonal gender comparisons. These three stages are often marked by interpersonal discomfort, disassociation with available gender identities and explorations of divergent sexual identities. Stages four, five and six involve discoveries of transsexualism, with confusion, and comparisons between this and existing notions of identity, as well as attempts to make connections with other transsexual people. Stages seven, eight and nine include an initial tolerance of transsexual identity, decisions about transition and, finally, relating to others with a new gender identity, managing stigma and involvement in advocacy.[61] Hannah's journey through the opera is broadly reflective of this process, and in Act I, scene iv, 'Sex Ed', they explore difficulties outlined in the initial three stages of Devor's work. They sing, 'We have been separated by gender . . . To learn about sex.'[62]

In this scene, Hannah recounts the familiar moments in school, where sexual education is delivered to students who have been divided into gendered classes, supporting notions of gender binaries. A study by Macgillivray and Jennings (2008) found that textbooks used in teachers' training rarely defined transgender or addressed experiences of transgender people, providing an uncomfortable experience for people with gender dysphoria.[63] The references in the opera to gender as a naturally occurring phenomenon in the animal kingdom and unnuanced descriptions of male manifestations of puberty further isolate and confuse Hannah. Hannah after sings, 'But this boy only wants to be in the other room',[64] and the word 'other' is sung *a cappella* and in a heightened part of the phrase. Kaminsky is able to play with gender and our understanding of her intimate thoughts through her choice of voice for these moments.

Transgender is an umbrella term for people who experience gender dysphoria such that their gender identities defy traditional notions of a binary gender paradigm. It encompasses identities including transmen (female-to-male), transwomen (male-to-female), butch women and cross-dressers and diverges with cisgender or traditional gender identities. Although the media has slowly and relatively recently began to acknowledge transgender people through representation, access to role models of non-traditional gender identity has been difficult, exacerbating feelings of loneliness and isolation. In the final scene in Act I, Hannah sees someone she identifies as being transgender, and her world suddenly and dramatically changes. Upon hearing the 'magical' word that provides a name for what she is silently experiencing, she runs to the library in a desperate search for any material that can provide a connection with the word. She sings, 'To Know' 'the magic word, finally a name for this, that is me, that is my word.'[65]

Hannah devours the contents of the book she finds. She does not utter the 'magic' word, which we assume is either 'transsexual' or 'transgender' as she flips through the alphabetized library card catalogue. The discovery of other people and the realization that she is not alone is given a euphoric musical treatment. Several unworded phrases are sung antiphonally in waves of relief for the protagonist. The general musical treatment maintains the constancy of the post-minimalist context of the score, notable for the absence of sudden changes of mood or fluctuation of dynamics. Kaminsky reflected, 'The joy of learning, of self-discovery and of connection is presented in this scene, and it is done so with both humor and blissful abandon.'[66]

In the scene entitled 'Out of Nowhere', in Part II, Hannah is attacked, providing an emotional climax in this part of the opera. The encounter is precipitated by dissonant chords from the quartet, as they begin Hannah's painful recollection. The male assailant repeatedly demands to know, 'What are you?',[67] replete with casual obscenities and providing an intimidating physical dominance which escalates as she tries to flee and eventually escapes. The man does not question *who* Hannah is but *what*. He reduces her to the position of object – something to not only disapprove of but at which to direct his hatred and violent impulses. He threatens to kill her on the basis that he does not understand her gender identity.

The scene is profoundly distressing and upon arriving home, Hannah begins to research the occurrence of other, similar attacks and is shocked at her discovery. She understands that she is vulnerable, joining a community at risk for being labelled 'other'. 'The Human Rights Campaign' (HRC) emerged in 1980 to fight for LGBTQI+ equality and inclusion and began tracking violent and fatal attacks against transgender and gender non-conforming people in 2013. The year 2020 has been the most violent year since recording began, with forty-four fatalities; however, as many attacks go unreported, this number is likely to be far greater. Often, many victims are misgendered in local police statements and press releases, which obfuscates accurate data collection. Much of the violence is perpetuated by ignorant vigilantes who subscribe to philosophies that align with government legislation that marginalizes the transgender community.

Kaminsky and Reed travelled to Norway, where the final part of Hanna's journey takes place. Reed filmed the seascapes and skyscapes of the Norwegian environment, projected on to the set in lieu of a background for the final scene for the premiere production. Hannah is provided with the stillness and solitude to think and reflect and is able to come to the decision to be the person she was always meant to be. Her phrase, 'Nature doesn't always comply with our wishes. Nature Just is',[68] echoes her experience in sex education class but rejects the misguided instructions of a disinterested teacher. Hannah has evolved, she has become. Despite the engendered markers that society has emblazoned on her understanding of who she was, she managed to peel back the layers of pretence, to reveal her true self, and discovered happiness that she had never before known.

Following initial periods of distress, confusion and exploration of identity, finding labels and gender enactments is an individual process, experienced through the person's sense of authenticity. Gender behaviours and expressions need to correspond with social context, which for each individual provides a unique set of circumstances.[69] In this case, the protagonist is alone, and the final stage of her identity development is not experienced in the opera's narrative. However, Hannah resolves to be happy, and with that decision, she experiences clarity in her daily experiences and is able to solve problems that previously seemed impossible hurdles.

The next morning I rise and make jam again.
This time with better berries.
I fix the hole in the boat.
And even try a yodel.
And I write a dozen postcards . . .
My writing is not like a girl's,
Or like a boy's,
It is mine.
It is free.[70]

As One is a celebration of a journey with a most positive outcome. The libretto is littered with humour and empathy, and Kaminsky's score uses quotes such as Christmas carols during the sequence of holiday scenes and an extract from Grieg at the point when Hannah decides to travel to Norway. There are, however, moments of seriousness and introspection, such as the scene in which Hannah is attacked. The string quartet is required to sing in certain moments, providing a chorused response, 'Unidentified unknown',[71] as Hannah researches transgender victims of violent attacks. The music director speaks, as does Hannah before, who recites a list of names – victims of violence against transgender people globally during the scene that follows Hannah's attack.[72] The post-minimalist style of the string-quartet material provides a connective tissue for Hannah's journey, linking each of the fifteen songs of the three-part narrative, constantly oscillating between major and minor tonalities, and providing a consistent, monochromatic presence. The musical language is dictated by Hannah's personality and her journey, and her persona is given musical form by the viola especially. Kaminsky writes energetic and driving travel music for moments such as the scene in the library but also introspective music such as a blues-derived viola solo.

Being a member of the LGBTQI+ rainbow does not automatically provide individuals with a complete understanding of the complex issues faced by the entire community. To better understand the immense challenges that transgender people face, the queer community needs to take a lead in providing positive role models and creating positive social and cultural images. The scene 'To Know' provides a visceral moment of understanding of the importance of access to community for transgender people experiencing the confusing early stages of becoming. Kaminsky, Campbell and Reed have created an important work with *As One*, not only artistically but also in terms of agency. This opera does not preach or demand a self-flagellating guilt complex but rather presents the audience with access to understanding. The hatred that can be generated through ignorance, as demonstrated by Hannah's assailant, can best be combatted through knowledge – knowledge of the strength required to strip away the layers of engendered hegemony and to become the person that was always meant to be.

STONEWALL, IAIN BELL

For several decades, the 'gay bar' played an important role in allowing members of the LGBTQI+ community to meet with like-minded people in a relatively safe environment. Such meeting places are certainly synonymous with revelry and eroticism, but for many queer individuals who suffered oppressive lives dominated by judgement and a lack of identity, it is unsurprising that the opportunity for psychological and physical release was cherished. In the first couple of decades of the twenty-first century, there has been a significant decline in the number of queer bars, pubs and nightclubs worldwide.[73]

The possible explanations for this are a combination of several factors: a dispersion of former 'gayborhoods' as sexual minorities gain acceptance in certain communities; the arrival of gay dating apps which eliminate the need to meet at a queer venue; and an affordability crisis in larger urban centres such as London rendering several venues economically unviable.[74]

The Stonewall Inn began serving members of the queer community in 1967 and went out of business shortly after the riots two years later. The site has since undergone several changes of ownership but has largely maintained an historical connection to those events. The LGBTQI+ rights movement in the United States certainly did not begin in the early hours of 28 June 1969, as queer activism was already growing in energy in many of the larger cities throughout the 1960s. However, the reasons for the persistent reference to the Stonewall Riots being the catalyst for seismic change in queer rights are in part due to the incredible international attention that the events attracted but particularly for the profound symbolic message that it sent. The term 'no more' articulates the visceral reaction to the police raid on Stonewall that night. The queer community had unexpectedly found its voice as the action unfolded and seemed to understand that through a collective resolve to stand up to intimidation, a wellspring of strength was found that had hitherto not been tapped into.

The Stonewall Inn was well connected with the mafia, known for its dubious drinks policies and was the frequent target of police raids on the basis of alcohol law violations. The police intimidation included expected payoffs known as 'gayola' in exchange for maintaining anonymity of patrons and avoiding arrests.[75] One contested theory for the sudden determination to resist this particular police raid was the recent death of gay icon, Judy Garland (1922–1969). Transactivist Sylvia Rivera explained how she became completely hysterical after learning of the death of Garland and, despite planning a quiet night at home, felt compelled to gather with her queer community at the Stonewall Inn.[76] Although it is unknown who threw the first projectile, shouts of 'Gay Power' began to be heard from the streets outside, followed by customers throwing various objects at hand, at the police. The incidents were occurring simultaneously from an angry mob and the police were caught completely by surprise. The news of the disturbance quickly spread across the city, and the number of demonstrators swelled, forcing the police to retreat to a nearby empty bar. The crowd, made up of the complete rainbow of New York's queer community, managed to outwit the police, now reinforced by the Tactical Police Force, by dispersing and regrouping in a new position. The riots lasted three nights, allowing time for the protestors to distribute leaflets explaining the issues facing the queer community.

When Iain Bell and librettist Mark Campbell began working on their commission for the New York City Opera as part of their Pride Initiative, the looming fiftieth anniversary of the Stonewall Uprising and coinciding seventy-fifth anniversary of the New York City Opera quickly became apparent, necessitating a nine-month completion deadline. The one-act opera comprises of three parts; the first part introduces a number of characters as they make their way to the Stonewall Inn, the second part is inside the Inn and includes the police raid and the third part includes the action that unfolds on Christopher Street. Written for a full, conventional orchestra and a large cast of principal characters, the score is notable for featuring a trans-mezzo who plays Sarah. Although Laura Kaminsky's opera, *As One* (2014, also to Campbell's libretto), concerns the process of becoming for a trans person, Bell's mandate for a trans singer to play the role marks a turning point for the acknowledgement of trans singers. The score also calls for a chorus of drag queens, street kids, lesbians and flaming queens who should be racially mixed and mostly in their early twenties. The role of Sarah was premiered by Liz Bouk, now Lucas Bouk, a singer with a wealth of experience with projects that explore transgender issues. Lucas now performs as a baritone.

In the first section of the opera, during which we are introduced to many of the characters, Campbell focuses on the range of circumstances that made the Stonewall Inn an important refuge for each of them. Each of the roles is entirely fictional, rather than composite characters, and reflects Bell and Campbell's attempt to reflect a range of queer experiences. The first is Maggie, a butch lesbian on her way to the Village by train. She sings of the homophobic slurs she is enduring en route, an experience she seems familiar with and weary of. The nameless man sings, 'Cock-sucking dyke',[77] and she explains to the audience, 'I answer: "With all undue respect, I think you're kinda mixed up."'[78] The ensuing physical altercation is explained in weary tones that express the senselessness of the confrontation as Maggie makes light work of her assailant. The police predictably let the man go and laugh at Maggie, 'What do you expect? I mean, look at you, look at you!',[79] establishing the resentment held towards homophobic law enforcers.

We next meet Carlos, a gay, Dominican-American school teacher who has been fired because of complaints from parents who said, 'It's not good for the boys to be around . . . You know what . . . You and your lifestyle.'[80] As with Maggie, Carlos' brief scene ends with his determination to go to a place where he can be himself and enjoy himself, '*voy a salir Esta noche a la ciudad Bailar con todo. Y despeinarme, Voy a conocer, a chico sexy, Y a singar hasta el domingo.*'[81] (I'm going out to the city tonight. Dance with everything. And dishevelled, I'm going to meet, a sexy boy, and sing until Sunday.) The lights then come up on Andy, sitting on a bench and cruising a nearby man. Concerned that the man is a cop, and that he may expose himself to the risk of entrapment, he engages in identity stereotypes to help discern the man's sexuality. He also recalls the experience of being rejected by his parents because of his sexuality and his resulting homelessness.

The next character to be introduced is Troy, who is in a phone booth, blackmailing a recent lover and arranging to meet him at the Stonewall Inn to exchange 3,000 dollars for his silence. Like his lover, Troy is also a closet bisexual, revealing his marriage and an unexplained, passing reference to his childhood experiences as an altar boy. Sal's character sharply contrasts with the others. His use of homophobic slurs and humour underpins his business model which involves entrapment of gay men followed by extortion, and it is clear that he is Troy's partner in crime. We then meet Leah, who was thrown into a conversion therapy institution by the parents of her girlfriend after being discovered together. The many attempts to 'cure' her were unsuccessful, and she was heading out to the bar in the hope of finding a woman. Next is Edward who is revealed to be the man being blackmailed by Troy. He phones his wife to tell her he will not be home that night. Following Edward is Renata, who is celebrating her eighteenth birthday, and Valerie, two black drag queens who use drag to help them escape the oppression and violence they experience for being 'other'.

We then meet Sarah, who we find sitting on the floor, holding a cupcake with a solitary candle. She is singing herself 'Happy Birthday' to mark the one-year anniversary of becoming a woman. She reveals the breakdown in her relationship with her parents and the connection with her new 'family'. Finally, we encounter Andy who is struggling with a lack of funds and is hoping to find a guy who will take care of him, allowing him a night off from living on the streets. The scene incorporates several ensembles comprised of the various characters, who use their own melodic material in counterpoint to the others, each one growing in texture with the increasing number of characters. The effect echoes Bernstein's quintet from *West Side Story* (1957). Bell created unique material for each of the characters, with distinct Fach categories, techniques and associated orchestral timbres.

With the queer characters introduced, the police prepare their raid, explaining that 'fags are easy'[82] and establishing the lack of resistance they are expecting from the patrons. The second scene opens with Larry, an NYPD Detective Inspector, singing, 'It's a raid. Everybody freeze!'[83] Set inside the bar, Bell is able to reference popular music styles from the period. He avoids direct quotes but creates riffs and harmonic progressions to effect and also created two jukebox songs, 'Today's the Day' and 'Better Days Ahead'. Bell explained, 'It was great fun to experiment with harmonic progressions that one would normally associate with pop music. That was the most fun and thrilling part of it.'[84]

The violence begins with a police officer striking Valerie with his nightstick, producing a trickle of blood from her head. The remaining patrons are threatened with further violence amidst expected homophobic slurs and the ensuing choreographed incursion unfolds over Bell's 1960s-style riffs. The resistance begins with an ATTB chorus chanting 'Gay Power',[85] an oscillating A flat minor/G minor homophonic figure from offstage. The language reflects the power shift of the scene, with the obscenities being issued by the patrons, 'Fucking pigs';[86] however, it is with Maggie's utterance, 'No. Just . . . no. N.O. Not this time',[87] underpinned by an incessant ostinato in the lower strings, that the scene pivots most profoundly. The deeply rooted anger that emerges from Maggie in the following section is reflective of the accumulation of years of targeted police intimidation that she has encountered as a queer person and inspires the other characters who cheer her on while the repeated bass figure climbs. As panic sets in for the police, who are under attack, the three distinct chorus groups chant their respective material simultaneously, 'Gay power! No mafia! OUR bars! OUR village!', 'Resist, refuse. You got nothing to lose' and 'If you ain't gay, Sashay away'.[88] These chants gradually converge into a powerful, homophonic assertion over repeated frantic triplet figures in the upper strings. The scene concludes with an instrumental interlude marked, 'Total violent chaos',[89] a fast-moving section characterized by a determined, unison motif that constantly reasserts itself, and Andy is struck by a nightstick, collapsing immediately.

As the weary protestors gather with the new dawn, sporting injuries and reflecting on the events of the previous night, they sing of the future, asking, 'What now?' and 'What will happen?'[90] The opera concludes with the full ensemble singing, 'Much to be done'.[91] Although there remains much to be done, so much has been achieved since the events known as the 'Stonewall Riots'. As Campbell stated, 'No one is equal until everyone is. We all need to live in a society in which we lift each other.'[92] The period that followed Stonewall can be defined, somewhat simplistically, by two periods: the 'pre-marriage' years between 1969 and 1989 and the struggle for marriage equality that ensued. The first period was defined by the queer community fighting to be protected from attacks and free to live as queer individuals without fear of persecution. Although the first marriage cases in the United States were tabled by couples in three states as early as 1971, the second period saw a shift in emphasis from the queer community from being 'left alone' to being 'let in'. This phase was also greatly influenced by the AIDS crisis that ravaged the queer community and forced a spotlight on the humanity of grieving and persecuted people.[93]

Having an event immortalized in operatic form bolsters its significance in the narrative of a developing society. The fact that *Stonewall* managed to mark the fiftieth anniversary of the events that took place is symbolic but not as meaningful as the creation of a work which celebrates the diversity and strength of a marginalized group that has now found its voice. The concept of opera, being the vestige of the straight, white male, engaged in heteronormative pursuits, is being corroded by a growing number of inclusive works mandating a diverse cast that reflects society. However, opera does not just reflect society, it has agency. Through the creation of the first character to be performed by a transgender opera singer, Bell and Campbell have said 'no more' to the pervasive binarism that has existed.

THE STONEWALL OPERAS

The four operas known as *The Stonewall Operas* are a series of mini-operas to mark the fiftieth anniversary of the events of 1969. They are the culmination of work produced by the Advanced Opera Lab of the Graduate Musical Theatre Writing Program at New York University (NYU). Each work lasts approximately thirty minutes and was premiered as part of the American Opera Projects at the Shubert Theatre at NYU and then at The Stonewall Inn. *Outside* and *Nightlife* concern the Stonewall Riots directly, while *Pomada Inn* and *The Community* explore associated queer themes in alternative contexts. The operas completed the series of events dubbed, 'Stonewall at 50', a commemoration of the legacy of the riots and resultant activism. Each character was performed by professional opera singers from the America Opera Projects, a Brooklyn-based company dedicated to producing new works, and the productions were directed and produced by students from The New School's College of Performing Arts. I will address each opera in turn.

Nightlife, T. J. Rubin

Nightlife explores the lives of four characters who comprise a jazz quartet and have just finished a late-night gig at the Village Vanguard, before walking around the corner to The Stonewall Inn in the early hours of 28 June 1969. Rubin's score utilizes a Jazz-based vernacular in the accompaniment but with through-composed vocal lines set against Deepali Gupta's libretto, awash with 1960s linguistics and a set of tercets for each of the character's arias. The opera begins with the last number of the night for the quartet, and Chick, a closeted lesbian, sings of nameless, eroticized woman and hints at her suppressed desire, 'If I had told her, What would I say to her, How would I ask her?'[94]

Daddy-O, an abrasive man, with little understanding of subtlety, asks Chick, 'So Chick – are you a queer?',[95] a reflection of the times when people were largely considered to occupy one of two binary sexualities. She denies the accusation, which puzzles Daddy-O, who pushes further, 'Then what are you?'[96] For Daddy-O, Chick may sing like a queer, but it is Punk who he determines to be a 'freak'. Punk self-identifies as a 'freak' and during his aria sings of having so much sex, he gives off a strong stench of cum, 'Coke me up and I'll drink your spunk, Until I stink like a skunk, From the funk of your spunk.'[97] Chick and Punk leave for The Stonewall Inn, and they are followed by Daddy-O and Hep Cat. Hep Cat is constantly broke, and it transpires that he is utterly addicted to heroin, which has killed his sex drive as explained in his aria, 'She empties and fulfills me, And will forever, Until she kills me.'[98]

One of the quirkier lines to recur throughout the opera involved a coded description of The Stonewall Inn as a queer venue. Punk initially referred to it as 'kind of a left-handed place'[99] and helpfully explained to Hep Cat, 'This is a left-handed place, And you're a right-hand man . . . You get my point?',[100] to which Hep Cat explains that he can hang with 'any kind of folks'.[101] This codified language reminds us that pre-Stonewall, open discussion of queer proclivities was dangerous, and even close friends and colleagues needed to be fed just enough information that could quickly be retracted or obfuscated. Punk's coded word for queers is 'freaks', a term which he initially rejects but later embraces. Daddy-O sings with his usual brusqueness, 'The real freak is Punk',[102] to which Punk responds, 'Why am I the freak?'[103] Soon after he confirms, 'I'm not freakish',[104] despite Daddy-O's offhand rebuke, 'Funky little freak'.[105] Punk then describes Stonewall as 'a place for freaks'[106] and asks Chick who is still taking the sights, sounds and smells of Stonewall Inn, 'Chick, are you freakish? Are you a freak?'[107] His attitude to the term has evolved, and in his aria, he sings, 'I know what I am, Freakish and queer',[108] followed by an exchange with Chick where the word is used to embrace her into the community, 'I'm a real authentic pervert. And you're a legitimate freak! Are you have a good time?'[109] The final utterance in which Punk whole-heartedly adopts the term as a badge of honour, he addresses Hep Cat, 'We're freaks! And Chick is a freak.'[110]

When Daddy-O finally locates Chick at The Stonewall, he notices a change in her since she encountered a queer-friendly environment, 'I don't recognize you!'[111] This triggers her aria, which operates as her coming-out moment, 'There's a woman, In the mirror, And her face is becoming clearer.'[112] The raid is dealt with curtly and somewhat surreally at the end of the opera, intimated through pre-recorded crowd noises and smashing bottles. Punk sings, 'One last song – And then they cuff us, And beat us, and kill us',[113] before darkly welcoming the possibility of ensuing pain. This leaves the observer with the question of his self-loathing, that he would sing, 'I want it sharp . . . I want it quick.'[114] Each of these four characters has very different reasons for being at The Stonewall Inn that morning, and none could have anticipated the events that would unfold.

Outside, Bryan Blaskie

The difficult and irreversible process of coming out of the closet is based on a
fear of what might happen when facing the world outside. The relative safety
and security of the closet is exchanged for freedom and all of the dangers
that come with belonging to a community so maligned by society that acts
of desperation are commonplace. *Outside*, by Bryan Blaskie and librettist
Seth Christenfeld, serves as a *double entendre* for life after the closet and the
events taking place in the Village during the early hours of 28 June 1969.
The thirty-minute opera is based exclusively in a bar around the corner from
The Stonewall Inn and explores the motivations of four characters as they are
faced with the decision to involve themselves in the violence.

Beginning just as with *Nightlife*, Madam Mister, the drag identity of Mark,
is performing the last song for the night to an even smaller audience than
usual. The abysmal number of patrons is attributed to the recent death of Judy
Garland and the period of mourning that the queer community is observing
for the loss of their great icon.[115] Garland was known to spontaneously visit
many of the bars in the Village and was celebrated as a tenacious diva who
fought tirelessly against the system that sought to contain her. Blaskie makes
several quotes of some of her iconic songs in the score. Madam Mister's
opening aria, as with the remainder of the opera, comes in the style of a
cabaret song, and she concludes with the prophetic advice, 'Don't let the side
that's untrue be the outside, the outside of you.'[116] Mark's bass vocal range
is used to comedic effect when presenting as Madam Mister, and when she
finishes performing, she retires to her dressing room and is soon joined by her
boyfriend, Kenny. Kenny, a countertenor, has just arrived back from the Ohio
and reveals that he has failed to come out to his sister.

Kenny is informed of the police raid the night before, a regular occurrence
and 'Nothing out of the ordinary'.[117] The policeman bribed Mark for not
arresting him in exchange for ten dollars and oral sex, 'Just ten. And maybe
a little extra.'[118] Mark seems resigned to the humiliation, singing, 'I'm not
gonna say it's something I like, but it's nothing that I haven't done before.'[119]
Kenny and Mark join Joan, a 'big, butch lesbian', and Davey, a bartender
who has kept his queerness close to his chest. Davey points out that Judy's
death is an omen, 'Something is going to change. Maybe not tonight, maybe
not tomorrow, but soon. Very soon.'[120] Reinforcing the theme of the opera,
and foreshadowing the events about to unfold, Kenny laments the passing
of Judy, singing, 'I always liked The Wizard of Oz. I always sympathized
with Dorothy, wished for a tornado to take me to the outside world.'[121] The
term 'friend of Dorothy' is still used as a non-hostile expression to indicate a
queer individual. Its origin is likely from the 1909 book, *The Road to Oz*, by
L. Frank Baum in which the word 'queer' is used with remarkable frequency.

The character Polychrome says, 'You have some queer friends, Dorothy', to which she responds, 'The queerness doesn't matter, so long as they're friends.'[122]

Joan's character embraces her sexual identity, using it as a shield against those who seek to judge her. She proclaims, 'I'm not threatened by you ding-dongs and your ding-dongs. You hide in plain sight. I don't hide at all.'[123] Her bravura is impressive, at least to Kenny, and when the phone rings, and she is informed of the riots that are underway around the corner, she is highly motivated to seize the opportunity to take up arms in aid of her people. Kenny is reluctant to involve himself in the riots, owing to his direct connection to the mafia, who have discretely hidden him in the bar to look after it. He worries about the repercussions that would compromise his relatively comfortable situation, 'Uncle Sal's got me here for safekeeping. No one else finds out and all is a-okay. I keep things quiet. I have my bar, the occasional man.'[124] Joan manages to convince him to support the cause, 'What's more important, Davey? The family that hates you or the family, this family that has embraced you? Come outside!'[125]

Mark and Kenny are left alone in the bar. Mark attempts to convince Kenny to join him outside in protest at the unscrupulous police harassment of the queer community, 'I don't want to spend the rest of my life in the back of some shitty bar, paying off and sucking off cops.'[126] The two men sing together of wanting to 'be in the world' together, but as Mark leaves, Kenny remains, choosing to attend to his need to come out to his sister over the phone. He struggles with guilt, knowing that the others are putting themselves in danger, when he couldn't bring himself to face his sexual identity, 'Stop being safe, Kenny. Make a decision. Do something.'[127] The opera ends with the overdue conversation with his only remaining family member.

The juxtaposition of the phone call with the violence taking place on Christopher Street can only be clearly understood from a queer perspective. Whereas one might seem safe and innocuous in stark contrast to the physical violence and threat of arrest, queer people in conservative and oppressive communities can understand the threats faced by outing themselves. The other three characters had been through the process, and although Mark is generally disappointed with fighting the good fight without Kenny by his side, no doubt when the dust settles, the *rapprochement* will provide a new chapter in their relationship, where they can enjoy the freedom of being their authentic selves, outside.

The Pomada Inn, Brian Cavanagh-Strong

The Stonewall Riots were a product of a conglomeration of circumstances that coincided in a specific time and place that cannot simply be replicated, despite how much many may wish. Exploring the freedoms that were achieved through the events at Stonewall and subsequent legislative victories, and contrasting them with the experiences in queer communities in other parts of the world, *The Pomada Inn* allows a retrospective look at how those struggles now afford a vastly improved way of life. Brian Cavanagh-Strong's opera, set to a libretto by Benjamin Bonnema, involves two couples: a lesbian couple living in New York and a gay couple living in Kiev. The events take place in four settings: The West Village in 2016; Kiev in 2016; The Stonewall Uprising in 1969; and finally, London in 2016. Separated geographically, the two couples communicate with one another through the suspension of disbelief.

In New York, Holly and Tara discuss travel options, which are founded on seeing 'Golden domes and shiny cathedrals'.[128] The exchange culminates in a fantasy in which they magically transport to St Volodymyr in Ukraine. They sing of attending a service during which they can secretly hold hands during the Eucharist and 'maybe kiss in front of the organ'.[129] The fantasy ends abruptly with Holly explaining that the propaganda law in Ukraine creates a dangerous environment for queers and one in which 'gay couples in Kiev can't hold hands on the street'.[130] Their conversation segues amusingly into a discussion between Alek and Igor. Igor is eager to go to the bathhouse in Kiev to enjoy 'all the steam and the men';[131] however, Alek is put off by the persistent threat of a police raid. Alek's aria that follows is a heartfelt devotion to Igor, in which he exalts the feeling of safety Igor provides, 'Heaven is the weight of your arm on my chest.'[132] The dream-like section is characterized by ascending and descending pentatonic arpeggios in sextuplets, over which a mellifluous melody takes Alek's tenor range up to a B natural.

Tara inserts herself into the conversation, making her and Holly visible to the two men, and the conversation turns to the inequity that exists for lesbians who may want to enjoy the sexual liberation that can be found in a bathhouse. Alek reminds the others of the jarring experience of being in the midst of an amorous exchange, when a police raid suddenly interrupts proceedings, as they storm in,

fully dressed and out of place,
brandishing their nightsticks,
ready to arrest,
to drag into the street,
to beat you bloody
before you even get the chance to dress.[133]

There is a sudden change in mood in the accompaniment at the moment Alek sings 'when you hear a whistle, a sudden whistle, that means stop what you're doing, put your towel back on',[134] which follows a sudden and profound pause. Tara's slightly naïve response, based on her understanding of the Stonewall Uprising, is to suggest that they consider fighting back, 'In the States, we had Stonewall, which worked because we fought back',[135] to which Igor retorts, '*Durnyy amerykanets*'[136] (stupid Americans). When the scene changes to 1969 New York, Tara is certain that she would have thrown a projectile at a policeman in 1969, but finding herself there, she realizes that her resolve for resistance is more political and rhetorical, rather than physical. 'Tell me which charities to support',[137] she sings, marking her limit of activism she's prepared to contribute in the fight against the fascist hegemony and 'tell me which march to go to. I'll gladly hold up a sign!'[138]

Igor then transports them to the Pomada Club in Kiev. He acknowledges that gay couples cannot kiss on the street, but that the Pomada provides a beautiful sanctuary for queers. He describes the men who show an ultramasculine, heteronormative façade outside, but when inside the club, 'they swish and their voices jump an octave up. They're themselves, for once, in the Pomada Club.'[139] The idyllic portrait is shattered when Igor returns from the bar with news that their friend, Mikhail, was set upon the previous evening when leaving the club and beaten to death. Shortly after, a police raid interrupts their grief. Instantly, Holly suggests a Stonewall-style resistance, 'What if tonight is their Stonewall? Let's get a group together, make a scene, refuse to go quietly',[140] but she is rebuked by Alek who sings, 'It won't be',[141] on a high A followed by a deafening silent pause. He states, 'This is the way things are here. And it's not going to change tonight.'[142] The final and brief scene outside St Paul's Cathedral sees the two girls wondering if the boys are alright.

The Community, Kevin Cummines

The quartet of operas culminates in Kevin Cummines' *The Community* with a libretto by Shoshana Greenberg. Set 400 years into a dystopian future following an apocalyptic event, the survivors, having being plunged into another dark age, are left to contemplate the only surviving artefact from the former civilization – an account of the Stonewall Uprising. The interplay with religious constructs reminds us that the reverence with which we venerate objects, surrounding them with ceremony, is based on historical acknowledgement of the human experience. The layers of meaning with which we currently understand phrases, terminology and social constructs related to the Stonewall Uprising are stripped away and replaced by a detached, naïve perspective with new meanings applied to fill in the gaps of phenomenological understanding.

The Community is led by The High Priestess, who leads an annual ceremony marking the Stonewall Riots. Seymour Pine, the deputy police inspector who led the raid by the New York Police Department (NYPD), is given the status of 'The Prince of Darkness', in The High Priestess' opening aria. In an amusing case of misinterpreted etymology, she teaches the children about 'The Village of the Green Witch' (a play on Greenwich Village), who she believes is the correct title for Martha P. Johnson. Johnson was a self-identified drag queen, who many credited with beginning the riots; however, he consistently stated that he was not present when the action began. Such amusing *faux pas* allow us to question our own religious rituals and the many possibilities of mistaken understandings.

Cummines' score is largely informed by a contemporary music theatre character, with moments of quasi-minimalism in the piano accompaniment which focus on recurring figures exclusively in the upper register. The recitatives and arias avoid any recognizable thematic development, but there is a pervading flippancy throughout, which acknowledges the mystical eccentricity and historical distortion of events. The decontextualization of campness reinserted into religious fervour is most comical with chanting from Jade, Thyst and Rubes while simultaneously effecting a kickline:

We're the queens who dance and drink
We're never going to the clink
And so you know our faith is true
We sacrifice this high-heeled shoe143

Jade and Rubes appear initially as children before emerging later as adults. The two children conflate the term 'Queen' and innocently explore notions of gender, 'Do you think it was a he queen, a she queen, or a they queen?'[144] In 2419, the children are played simulations of a police siren, which they are taught to associate with dread, and when a series of alternating tritones and perfect fourths simulate the alarming sound, they cower behind The High Priestess. When the children suddenly emerge as eighteen-year-olds, Rubes, a countertenor, has achieved the status of 'Primary' or 'Queen'. Despite the strict teachings in the holy book of Stonewall, Rubes has no interest in the perpetuated model of community living and shared sexual partnership, preferring to be alone. He sings, 'What if someone doesn't want a community?',[145] to which Jade responds, 'You need a proper home with you as primary, four secondaries, Two having a uterus, Two having a phallus.'[146] Such an arrangement, sings Jade, is considered optimal and has been passed down for generations.

Jade is the 'Primary' for Thyst; having known each other since childhood, they share their community with Ryea, Tylo, and Nim. However, Thyst has no appetite for a polyamorous life and longs for a monogamous relationship as a couple. Knowing that his urges betray the sacred text, he struggles with the meanings derived from the book and reads it incessantly, 'What is a queen? What is a man? Why can't we live alone? Or as two? What does it say that made our world this way?'[147] Thyst raises his uncertainties with Rubes, asking him to read directly from the book, 'They were tired of being pushed around, tired of being denied their rights, they vowed to persevere until injustice and discrimination came to an end.'[148] The two kiss and vow to run away together and live as a couple; however, unable to leave Jade, Thyst bids Rubes farewell. Rubes is observed leaving, and The High Priestess sings, 'The queen walks toward a foreign sun to find a new sacred text.'[149]

The Community challenges our understanding of liberation and notions of established modes of practice designed to cater for all. The concept of sexual liberation is subverted, and Thyst and Rubes find themselves as outsiders in a community wanting to embrace them. The futuristic scenario offers an amalgam of a dystopian and utopian existence, informed by the lessons learned from Stonewall, in which the characters are given clear, dichotomous readings; police represent everything bad, and queens represent everything good. *The Community* and *The Pomada Inn* suggest a world in which The Stonewall Uprising was an antidote to homophobia in New York and beyond, but the truth remains that the progressive legislative agenda is not uniformly reflected in the experiences on the ground. Queers are still ridiculed, spat at, attacked and marginalized. This is not to diminish the lasting effect of Stonewall, which at least provides a level of recompense against bigotry, but the fight certainly continues. Perhaps by 2419, we will have achieved our ideals of acceptance and love in whichever communities we choose to live.

ORLANDO, OLGA NEUWIRTH

Olga Neuwirth's opera *Orlando* (2019) defies traditional characterization in many ways, most notably by the androgyny of the title character who changes gender in scene vii. The production requires an array of audio and video tools such as pre-recorded film, live cameras, animation, photography, graphic design, stock footage and archive footage. A large rear-screen projection system with six LED screens that are configured to meet the video needs provides much of the background set such that the opera verges on performance art.[150] The work also defied the long, gendered history of the Vienna State Opera, by being the first full-length, main stage work by a woman in 150 years.

Based on Virginia Woolf's 1928 mock-memoir, Neuwirth worked with co-librettist Catherine FilIouz to create the two-and-a-half-hour opera in nineteen scenes. With an appendix to Woolf's book, the opera continues the story of the gender-switching protagonist, Orlando, beyond 1928 and ending instead in 1919, the year of the premiere. Orlando lives for a period of more than 300 years, and Neuwirth's score pays chronological homage to the respective periods, utilizing an array of structures, techniques and quotations. This ambitious integration of numerous styles that incorporates sixteenth-century lute songs, and eventually works its way to contemporary rock, also draws on a range of literary references to contextualize the changing periods.

The opera begins in sixteenth-century England, and we find Orlando as a young boy, being taught by his tutor the masculine art of swordplay by practising with a cricket bat against a punching bag. The spoken voice of the narrator explains, 'The age was Elizabethan and violence was everywhere. He was only sixteen. Yes, HE – for there could be no doubt of his sex, though the fashion of the time did something to disguise it.'[151] The charming favourite of Queen Elizabeth I, Orlando is bestowed land and fortune, in exchange for him promising to stay young forever. The sovereign pulls Orlando to her bosom, holding him there until nearing the point of suffocation, exploring the boundaries of a sexual act and ritual of feminine adoration.

Orlando's age is maintained in a state of stasis and is initially marked by a paucity of companionship, both platonic and romantic. He sings, 'Nobody now asks me to marry; for many years nobody has attempted to seduce me. Though showing off, which is not copulating, is one of the great delights, one of the chief necessities of life.'[152] This loneliness is compounded by an inability to form a meaningful connection with any of his contemporary poets, who treat his work with disdain. He exclaims, 'I am done with men';[153] however, this is not the case. Orlando's despondency causes him to descend into a trance-like state from which doctors are unable to wake, and he is visited by three figures, who announce themselves:

'I am Purity. On all things dark my veil descends! Speak not, reveal not!'
'I, Chastity, rather than let Orlando wake, freeze him to bone!'
'I, Modesty, virgin I ever shall be! Spare, O spare!'[154]

The three spirits then sing together, 'Truth come not out horrid den. Hide! The Truth, nothing but the truth!'[155] They are driven off by the chorus but sing one last prophetic assertion, 'Darkness to all who still desire to know not.'[156] This somewhat obscure ceremony is the catalyst for Orlando's complete physical gender transformation which she discovers upon waking, 'Am I a woman?'[157] The omnipresent narrator confirms the change, 'Breasts. Modesty. Purity. Orlando had become a woman – there is no denying it. But in every other respect, Orlando remained precisely as he had been.'[158]

The observation that Orlando 'remained precisely as he had been' points to the androgyny of his former self and her present self. In Bem and Lewis' (1975) seminal study on psychological androgyny,[159] binary gender roles which subscribe to traditional societal expectations deepen rigid, behavioural restrictions. Alternatively, androgyny is equated with flexibility, a trait which relates to adaptivity and positive mental health. Identity androgyny shares some similar features with psychological androgyny; however, rather than concentrating on the capability of exhibiting both masculine and feminine behaviours or characteristics, identity androgyny explores the self-perception and connection to both gendered groups.[160] For Orlando, her gendered identity remained, while her physical gender changed, providing the opportunity to reconsider her sexuality. The narrator elucidates, 'It is a strange fact, but a true one that up to this moment she had scarcely given her sex a thought. So, Orlando's start as a woman – was of a complicated kind, and not to be summed up at a trice.'[161]

Orlando also finds that some adjustments take some getting used to. She laments the additional requirements society places on women to present themselves appropriately. She sings, 'These are plaguey things to have around one's heels. – Well, and there is the hairdresser, that will take an hour . . . Having to be chaste, year in, year out?'[162] As if to confirm that she has not yet mastered the skill of feminine etiquette, the narrator adds, 'A sailor on the mast nearly falls to his death at the sight of her ankles.'[163] Orlando's reluctance to fully embrace the expected norms of binary behaviour demonstrates that her androgyny identity is firmly established. She establishes the basis for her feminism crusade that is to follow in a series of observations of the treatment of women. Only now, with the gift of a woman's perspective does she fully understand the inequity embedded in social conventions. She exclaims, 'If womanhood means conventionality, slavery and deceit, means denying my love, fettering my limbs, pursing my lips and restraining my tongue, then I would rather turn around with this ship and go back.'[164] The ultimate frustration is that with the inability to operate in a male-dominated hegemony, she cannot be taken seriously as a writer, 'These men will drink my tea, but they will never respect my opinions and see me as a writer.'[165] Conversely, it is a welcome relief not to have to participate in some of the expected activities of the male world, 'But thank heaven that I don't have to ride a warhorse anymore . . . Praise God that I'm a woman!'[166]

Three characters emerge in the opera, whose relationship with Orlando explores different aspects of queerness. The first of these is Shelmerdine, a photographer who emerges during the World War II era. As the two become acquainted, they observe gendered qualities of each other that defy stereotypical norms. Shel concludes that Orlando will bear his child, after which they sing concurrently: Orlando: 'You are a woman, Shel!' Shelmerdine: 'You are a man, Orlando!'[167] The two marry, but Shel is evidently away, photographing various wars and is later seen on screen being blown up. The next character we meet is in 1985, when Orlando is dressed as Boy George and embracing her post-punk, gothic girlfriend. This character is nameless, assigned only the term 'girlfriend'. They share the briefest scene in which they declare their devotion, and then the girlfriend disappears, running offstage. The final character to represent queerness is Orlando's child, an advocate for gender fluidity and non-binary identity. In the premiere, this role was played by Mx (gender-neutral honorific preferred) Bond, a seasoned trans cabaret star from New York. They sing, 'Isn't it awfully nice to be a they?',[168] with a backup chorus singing the praises, variously, of having a 'ding' or a 'vong'.[169]

The appendix scenes add important historical observations of the last century from the gender-fluid perspective. The pro-queer, anti-racist, pacifist message could not be any more overt. The moral advocacy is not hidden behind symbolism or metaphor but explicit. Orlando's child sings, 'We've had enough of hiding ourselves, being compressed into gender roles. Enough of having to continually read about lies by politicians and religious leaders – what they say about us. We've had enough of feeling helpless.'[170] Just as unambiguous is the political commentary surrounding policies of the US administration at the time of the opera's premiere, 'Us first! Make us great!',[171] although the president is not named directly. Despite the importance of the messaging, these post-Woolfe scenes have attracted some criticism for Neuwirth and Fillouz, which points to a less poetic libretto and a score which doesn't match the ingenuity of the previous sections.[172]

The fact that Orland is not portrayed by a male singer at any point in the narrative enhances the notion of gender ambiguity. One moment that encapsulates the opera's theme of gender being an ambiguous, transformative phenomenon is expressed in an exchange between Orlando, her guardian Angel and Orlando's Child:

Orlando: 'Have I changed?'
Angel: 'Identities change . . .'
Orlando's Child: '. . .or are exchanged . . .'
Angel: 'Ev'ry one in its own way. Identities are exchanged.'
Orlando's Child: 'Ev'ry one in its own way. We have changed in our own way.
    Fluid identities. I have changed.'[173]

With subtle reference to 'All we like Sheep' from Handel's *Messiah* (1741), the text represents a liberal reading of gender as an interchangeable, individual mode of expression, with fluidity replacing antiquated concepts of binarism.[174] Orlando's sudden gender transformation results in an immediate lowering of her status, and this theme is given prominence throughout the opera but competes with the many other worthy issues that fight for space. The nexus of androgyny and sexuality is only marginally addressed, with both Shel and 'Girlfriend' given symbolic roles which indicate perfunctory sexual functionality. However, Orlando certainly demonstrates the notions of flexibility and adaptability that are common to androgynous people towards a fluctuating, patriarchal society over the course of around 330 years.

NOTES

1. Shannon Weber, 'What's wrong with be(com)ing queer? Biological determinism as discursive queer hegemony', *Sexualities* 15, no. 5–6 (2012): 679–701.

2. Jennifer Terry, *An American Obsession: Science, Medicine, and Homosexuality in Modern Society* (Chicago: University of Chicago Press, 1999).

3. Tommy Dickinson, *'Curing Queers': Mental Nurses and their Patients, 1935–74* (Manchester: Manchester University Press, 2015).

4. Richard D. Lyons, 'Psychiatrists in a shift. Declare homosexuality no mental illness', *The New York Times*, 16 December 1973.

5. Bernadette Barton, '"Abomination" – life as a Bible belt gay', *Journal of Homosexuality* 57, no. 4 (2010): 465–484.

6. John J. McNeill, *Both Feet Firmly Planted in Midair: My Spiritual Journey* (Louisville, KY: Westminster John Knox Press, 1998).

7. Laurel C. Schneider and Carolyn Roncolato, 'Queer theologies', *Religion Compass* 6, no. 1 (2012): 1–13.

8. Lourdes Arguelles and B. Ruby Rich, 'Homosexuality, homophobia, and revolution: Notes toward an understanding of the Cuban lesbian and gay male experience, part I', *Signs: Journal of Women in Culture and Society* 9, no. 4 (1984): 683–699.

9. Marvin Leiner, *Sexual Politics in Cuba: Machismo, Homosexuality, and AIDS* (Milton Park: Routledge, 2019).

10. Reinaldo Arenas, *Antes que anochezca*. No. 863 A681b esp. (Barcelona: Tusquets, 2013).

11. Francisco Soto, 'A gay Cuban activist in exile: Reinaldo Arenas', *Revista de Estudios Hispánicos* 42, no. 2 (2008): 380.

12. Jorge Martín, 'The book, in my hands', Music by Jorge Martín: A diary of musical thoughts and observations. 8 February 2010, accessed 12 December 2021, https://musicbyjorgemartin.blogspot.com/search?updated-max=2010-02-24T16:20 :00-08:00&max-results=7&start=7&by-date=false.

13. Sebastian Spreng, 'An interview with 'before night falls' composer Jorge Martín', *Knight Foundation*, 16 March 2017, accessed 12 December 2021, https:// knightfoundation.org/articles/interview-before-night-falls-composer-jorge-martin/.

14. Jorge Martin, 'Dreaming Opera: Adapting before night falls', *The Gay & Lesbian Review Worldwide* 13, no. 5 (2006): 24.

15. Jorge Martin and Dolores M. Koch, *Before Night Falls: An Opera in Two Acts Based on the Memoir by Reinaldo Arenas* [Full Orchestral Score] (Atlanta, GA: JMB Publishing, Fort Worth Opera Premiere Edition, 2009), 5.

16. Martin and Koch, *Before Night Falls*, 9–10.

17. Martin and Koch, *Before Night Falls*, 14.

18. Martin and Koch, *Before Night Falls*, 43–44.
19. Martin and Koch, *Before Night Falls*, 45.
20. Martin and Koch, *Before Night Falls*, 49–50.
21. Martin and Koch, *Before Night Falls*, 51–52.
22. Martin and Koch, *Before Night Falls*, 70.
23. Martin and Koch, *Before Night Falls*, 71–72.
24. Martin and Koch, *Before Night Falls*, 116–119.
25. Martin and Koch, *Before Night Falls*, 155.
26. Martin and Koch, *Before Night Falls*, 165.
27. Martin and Koch, *Before Night Falls*, 176–177.
28. Martin and Koch, *Before Night Falls*, 177.
29. Martin and Koch, *Before Night Falls*, 189.
30. Martin and Koch, *Before Night Falls*, 205.
31. Martin and Koch, *Before Night Falls*, 228.
32. Martin and Koch, *Before Night Falls*, 279.
33. Martin and Koch, *Before Night Falls*, 280.
34. Martin and Koch, *Before Night Falls*, 280.
35. Martin and Koch, *Before Night Falls*, 281.
36. Martin and Koch, *Before Night Falls*, 282.
37. Martin and Koch, *Before Night Falls*, 321–322.
38. Martin and Koch, *Before Night Falls*, 322–323.
39. Martin and Koch, *Before Night Falls*, 329.
40. Elizabeth Llorente, 'Tapping the muses: Jorge Martín's creative process for before night falls', *AARP*, 11 June 2009, accessed 7 February 2022, https://www.aarp.org/entertainment/arts-leisure/info-06-2009/tapping_the_muses.html.
41. Emma Goldman, *The Individual, Society and the State* (Chicago, IL: Free Society Forum, 1940).
42. Carol Diethef, 'Nietzsche and nationalism', *History of European Ideas* 14, no. 2 (1992): 227–234: 227.
43. Jean-Jacques Rousseau, *Considerations on the Government of Poland and on its Planned Reformation. In The Collected Writings of Jean-Jacques Rousseau*, Vol. 11; Trans. C. Kelly & J. Bush (Hanover, NH: Dartmouth College Press, 2005).
44. David R. Cameron, 'The hero in Rousseau's political thought', *Journal of the History of Ideas* 45 (1984): 397–419.
45. Christopher Kelly, 'Rousseau's case for and against heroes', *Polity* 30, no. 2 (1997): 347–366.
46. Max Weber, Hans Gerth, and C. Wright Mills, *From Max Weber: Essays in Sociology* (Milton Park: Routledge, 2009).
47. Zeno E. Franco, Scott T. Allison, Elaine L. Kinsella, Ari Kohen, Matt Langdon, and Philip G. Zimbardo, 'Heroism research: A review of theories, methods, challenges, and trends', *Journal of Humanistic Psychology* 58, no. 4 (2018): 382–396.
48. John Cox, 'Truth art and life', *The Santa Fe Opera 2013 Season Program Book* (2013), 76–79: 76.
49. Ruth Behar and David Bleich, *Autobiographical Writing across the Disciplines: A Reader* (Durham, NC: Duke University Press, 2004), 118.

50. Adrian Curtin, 'Alternative vocalities: Listening awry to Peter Maxwell Davies's eight songs for a mad king', *Mosaic: A Journal for the Interdisciplinary Study of Literature* 42, no. 2 (2009): 101–117.

51. Theodore Morrison and John Cox, *Oscar, An Opera in Two Acts* [orchestral score] (New York, NY: G. Schirmer Inc., 2013), 36–37.

52. Gail Turley Houston, '"Oscar" the opera and the high-pitched life', *Victorian Literature and Culture* 43, no. 1 (2015): 182–188.

53. William Burnett, 'Opera advocating for human rights: An interview with "Oscar" composer Theodore Morrison', *Opera Warhorses*, 10 September 2013, accessed 5 January 2022, https://operawarhorses.com/2013/09/page/2/.

54. A line from his first play, *Vera; or, The Nihilists*.

55. Neil McKenna, ed., *The Secret Life of Oscar Wilde* (New York, NY: Basic Books, 2003), 473. Letter addressed to Lord Alfred Douglas, 31 August 1897?

56. McKenna, *Secret Life*, 475.

57. John Cooper, 'Finding Oscar', *The Wildean* 47 (2015): 109–117.

58. Brian Manternach, 'Teaching transgender singers. Part 2: The singers' perspectives', *Journal of Singing* 74, no. 2 (2017): 209–214.

59. Maya Rajamani, 'For a Bronx composer, opera rises out of identity struggles', *The Riverdale Press*, 28 August 2014, accessed 23 November 2021, https://www.riverdalepress.com/stories/for-a-bronx-composer-opera-rises-out-of-identity-struggles,55005.

60. Rajamani, 'For a Bronx composer'.

61. Aaron H. Devor, 'Witnessing and mirroring: A fourteen stage model of transsexual identity formation', *Journal of Gay & Lesbian Psychotherapy* 8, no. 1–2 (2004): 41–67.

62. Laura Kaminsky, Mark Campbell, and Kimberly Reed, *As One: A Chamber Opera for Two Singers and String Quartet* [piano/vocal score] (Brooklyn, NY: Bill Holab Music, 2015), 31.

63. Ian K. Macgillivray and Todd Jennings, 'A content analysis exploring lesbian, gay, bisexual, and transgender topics in foundations of education textbooks', *Journal of Teacher Education* 59, no. 2 (2008): 170–188.

64. Kaminsky et al., *As One*, 40.

65. Kaminsky et al., *As One*, 66–67.

66. David Salazar, 'Q & A: Composer Laura Kaminsky on the development of "as one"', *Opera Wire*, 14 March 2018, accessed 25 October 2021, https://operawire.com/q-a-composer-laura-kaminsky-on-the-development-of-as-one/.

67. Kaminsky et al., *As One*, 129.

68. Kaminsky et al., *As One*, 185.

69. Heidi M. Levitt and Maria R. Ippolito, 'Being transgender: The experience of transgender identity development', *Journal of homosexuality* 61, no. 12 (2014): 1727–1758.

70. Kaminsky et al., *As One*, 190–197.

71. Kaminsky et al., *As One*, 146–147.

72. Salazar, 'Q & A: Composer Laura Kaminsky'.

73. B.R. Simon Rosser, William West, and Richard Weinmeyer, 'Are gay communities dying or just in transition? Results from an international consultation examining possible structural change in gay communities', *AIDS Care* 20, no. 5 (2008): 588–595.

74. Amin Ghaziani, 'Culture and the nighttime economy: A conversation with London's Night Czar and Culture-at-Risk officer', (2019), accessed 4 September 2021, https://metropolitics.org/Culture-and-the-Nighttime-Economy-A-Conversation -with-London-s-Night-Czar-and.html.

75. Nell Frizzell, 'How the Stonewall riots started the LGBT rights movement', *Pink News*, 28 June 2013, accessed 5 December 2021, https://www.pinknews.co.uk /2013/06/28/feature-how-the-stonewall-riots-started-the-gay-rights-movement/.

76. Martin Bauml Duberman, *Stonewall: The Definitive Story of the LGBTQ Rights Uprising that Changed America* (London: Plume, 2019).

77. Iain Bell and Mark Campbell, *Stonewall: Opera in One Act* [Full score] (Bury St Edmunds: Chester Music, 2019), 1.

78. Bell and Campbell, *Stonewall*, 2.

79. Bell and Campbell, *Stonewall*, 5.

80. Bell and Campbell, *Stonewall*, 11–12.

81. Bell and Campbell, *Stonewall*, 18–19.

82. Bell and Campbell, *Stonewall*, 96.

83. Bell and Campbell, *Stonewall*, 109.

84. David Salazar, 'Honoring Stonewall – How Mark Campbell & Iain Bell came together to create an opera celebrating LGBTQ+ community', *OperaWire*, 20 June 2019, accessed 13 October 2021, https://operawire.com/honoring-stonewall -how-mark-campbell-iain-bell-came-together-to-create-an-opera-celebrating-lgbtq -community/.

85. Bell and Campbell, *Stonewall*, 132.

86. Bell and Campbell, *Stonewall*, 134.

87. Bell and Campbell, *Stonewall*, 136.

88. Bell and Campbell, *Stonewall*, 163.

89. Bell and Campbell, *Stonewall*, 176.

90. Bell and Campbell, *Stonewall*, 190.

91. Bell and Campbell, *Stonewall*, 204.

92. Salazar, 'Honoring Stonewall', 2019.

93. Mary L. Bonauto and Evan Wolfson, 'Advancing the freedom to marry in America', *Human Rights Magazine* 36 (2009): 11.

94. T. J. Rubin and Deepali Gupta, *Nightlife* [Piano/vocal score] (Unpublished, 2019), 3–4.

95. Rubin and Gupta, *Nightlife*, 7.

96. Rubin and Gupta, *Nightlife*, 8.

97. Rubin and Gupta, *Nightlife*, 81.

98. Rubin and Gupta, *Nightlife*, 66–67.

99. Rubin and Gupta, *Nightlife*, 61–62.

100. Rubin and Gupta, *Nightlife*, 62.

101. Rubin and Gupta, *Nightlife*, 62.

102. Rubin and Gupta, *Nightlife*, 9.

103. Rubin and Gupta, *Nightlife*, 9.

104. Rubin and Gupta, *Nightlife*, 11.

105. Rubin and Gupta, *Nightlife*, 11.

106. Rubin and Gupta, *Nightlife*, 25.

107. Rubin and Gupta, *Nightlife*, 25.

108. Rubin and Gupta, *Nightlife*, 27.

109. Rubin and Gupta, *Nightlife*, 46.

110. Rubin and Gupta, *Nightlife*, 62.

111. Rubin and Gupta, *Nightlife*, 86.

112. Rubin and Gupta, *Nightlife*, 88.

113. Rubin and Gupta, *Nightlife*, 92.

114. Rubin and Gupta, *Nightlife*, 93.

115. Patrick Stearns, '50 years after Stonewall, classical music still fights the fight', *WQXR*, 5 June 2019, accessed 23 November 2021, https://www.wqxr.org/story/stonewall-50-years-anniversary-classical-music-fight/.

116. Bryan Blaskie and Seth Christenfeld, *Outside* [Piano/vocal score] (Unpublished, 2019), 6–7.

117. Blaskie and Christenfeld, *Outside*, 15.

118. Blaskie and Christenfeld, *Outside*, 17.

119. Blaskie and Christenfeld, *Outside*, 18.

120. Blaskie and Christenfeld, *Outside*, 23.

121. Blaskie and Christenfeld, *Outside*, 26.

122. L. Frank Baum, 'The road to Oz', in *The Complete Works of L. Frank Baum, Part 6* (Hastings: Delphi Classics, 2017), 142.

123. Blaskie and Christenfeld, *Outside*, 30–31.

124. Blaskie and Christenfeld, *Outside*, 44.

125. Blaskie and Christenfeld, *Outside*, 53–54.

126. Blaskie and Christenfeld, *Outside*, 57.

127. Blaskie and Christenfeld, *Outside*, 65.

128. Brian Cavanagh-Strong and Benjamin Bonnema, *The Pomada Inn* [Piano/vocal score] (Unpublished, 2019), 3.

129. Cavanagh-Strong and Bonnema, *The Pomada Inn*, 5.

130. Cavanagh-Strong and Bonnema, *The Pomada Inn*, 14.

131. Cavanagh-Strong and Bonnema, *The Pomada Inn*, 16–17.

132. Cavanagh-Strong and Bonnema, *The Pomada Inn*, 18–19.

133. Cavanagh-Strong and Bonnema, *The Pomada Inn*, 34–35.

134. Cavanagh-Strong and Bonnema, *The Pomada Inn*, 34.

135. Cavanagh-Strong and Bonnema, *The Pomada Inn*, 37–38.

136. Cavanagh-Strong and Bonnema, *The Pomada Inn*, 51.

137. Cavanagh-Strong and Bonnema, *The Pomada Inn*, 50.

138. Brin Solomon, 'In review: The Stonewall operas', *National Sawdust*, 18 May 2019, accessed 27 November 2021, https://nationalsawdust.org/thelog/2019/05/24/in-review-the-stonewall-operas/.

139. Cavanagh-Strong and Bonnema, *The Pomada Inn*, 53.

140. Cavanagh-Strong and Bonnema, *The Pomada Inn*, 65–66.

141. Cavanagh-Strong and Bonnema, *The Pomada Inn*, 67.

142. Cavanagh-Strong and Bonnema, *The Pomada Inn*, 68.

143. Kevin Cummines and Shoshana Greenberg, *The Community* [vocal score] (Unpublished, 2019), 8–10.

144. Cummines and Greenberg, *The Community*, 15.

145. Cummines and Greenberg, *The Community*, 31.

146. Cummines and Greenberg, *The Community*, 32.

147. Cummines and Greenberg, *The Community*, 47.

148. Cummines and Greenberg, *The Community*, 54.

149. Cummines and Greenberg, *The Community*, 69.

150. John Hohmann, 'Orlando: Gender bending and the sound of androgyny in Vienna', *Schmopera*, 27 April 2020, accessed 4 December 2021, https://www.schmopera.com/orlando-gender-bending-and-the-sound-of-androgyny-in-vienna/.

151. Olga Neuwirth and Catherine Filloux, 'Orlando – eine fictive musikalische Biografie', [full score] (Berlin: Ricordi, 2018), 25.

152. Neuwirth and Filloux, 'Orlando', 19.

153. Neuwirth and Filloux, 'Orlando', 131–132.

154. Neuwirth and Filloux, 'Orlando', 138–141.

155. Neuwirth and Filloux, 'Orlando', 156–157.

156. Neuwirth and Filloux, 'Orlando', 161.

157. Neuwirth and Filloux, 'Orlando', 167–168.

158. Neuwirth and Filloux, 'Orlando', 166.

159. Sandra L. Bem, and Steven A. Lewis, 'Sex role adaptability: One consequence of psychological androgyny', *Journal of Personality and Social Psychology* 31, no. 4 (1975): 634.

160. Carol Lynn Martin, Rachel E. Cook, and Naomi C. Z. Andrews, 'Reviving androgyny: A modern day perspective on flexibility of gender identity and behavior', *Sex Roles* 76, no. 9 (2017): 592–603.

161. Neuwirth and Filloux, 'Orlando', 171.

162. Neuwirth and Filloux, 'Orlando', 171.

163. Neuwirth and Filloux, 'Orlando', 171.

164. Neuwirth and Filloux, 'Orlando', 171.

165. Neuwirth and Filloux, 'Orlando', 183.

166. Neuwirth and Filloux, 'Orlando', 171.

167. Neuwirth and Filloux, 'Orlando', 237.

168. Neuwirth and Filloux, 'Orlando', 317.

169. Hohmann, 'Orlando: Gender bending'.

170. Neuwirth and Filloux, 'Orlando', 307.

171. Neuwirth and Filloux, 'Orlando', 336.

172. Fiona Maddocks, 'Orlando world premiere review – A feast for ears and eyes', *The Observer*, 14 December 2019, accessed 5 December 2021, https://www.theguardian.com/music/2019/dec/14/orlando-vienna-state-opera-review-olga-neuwirth-world-premiere-virginia-woolf.

173. Neuwirth and Filloux, 'Orlando', 336–337.

174. Amy Stebbins, 'Dramaturgical oper (an) ations: De-internationalization in contemporary opera libretti', in *Theatre and Internationalization*, eds. Ulrike Garde and John R. Severn (Milton Park: Routledge, 2020), 128–145.

Chapter 5

Assimilation

The act of concealing all markers of a queer identity has been well-practised by generations of queer individuals. In many countries, assimilating into a heteronormative environment is not merely an exercise in identity choice for reasons of expediency or comfort but necessary for safety and relative freedom. In the West, the hazards of incarceration and death are now largely historical, although the realities on the street still necessitate at least a degree of caution for queer people to remain inconspicuous. In the 1950s, members of the Mattachine Society, a national gay rights society in the United States prior to splintering into regional groups in 1961, were engaged in an internal struggle based on notions of assimilation. The debate saw the conservatist, assimilationist faction, guided by the desire to be accepted by society on the basis of shared humanity, argued against the radical faction which viewed the oppressive institutions as the problem and had little interest in downplaying important differences that queerness brings.[1] The tension between accommodation of heteronormative ideals and the assertion of difference remains a fractious and contentious issue.

Several ways in which assimilation is manifested include conversion, passing and covering, and each brings into question the tension between the degree of change that is possible and the degree of change that is desirable.[2] Conversion represents the most extreme form of assimilation, consisting of a complete abandonment of authentic identity in favour of that which is deemed acceptable by a dominant group. Passing requires a more temporary concealment of identifiers of the minority status. Covering is even less obtrusive and involves downplaying any stereotypical characteristics in an attempt to make minority identity more palatable for outside observers. Although sexual orientation conversion therapy was officially rejected by mainstream psychologists and psychiatrists in the 1970s, the practice

has re-emerged in several conservative societies. Despite the general progress with the way in which much of the world views homosexuality, some
sectors refute the notion that a queer orientation forms an acknowledged
form of human sexuality and promote a process of eradicating unwanted
homoerotic urges.[3] The prejudicial phenomenon driven largely by religious organizations encourages internalized self-loathing and self-negation
along with concerns that active queerness will compromise a quality of life
through discrimination, violence, rejection and social marginalization. The
Pan American Health Organization cautioned against the process of 'curing'
homosexuality in 2012, noting that it is a normal and natural variation of
human sexuality.

Assimilation is both a coercive and reciprocal process, as both groups are
actively engaged and because the minority group is forced to adopt the normative standards required of the dominant group. The dominant, in this case
heteronormative group, determines which attempts of assimilation are either
accepted or rejected. A set of survival incentives and concomitant penalties
for the minority group creates a never-ending cycle of coercive bargaining
agreements for admittance into the world of the dominant group. The temptation to assimilate and the desire to be different provide a daily struggle
for many queers. The fear that non-conformity will lead to abandonment
drives many queer individuals to minimize differences for the benefit of the
heteronormative society but simultaneously leads to acceptance based on a
systematic erasure of self-identity.

The six operas in this chapter focus on processes of assimilation in different forms. In Ginastera's opera, *Bomarzo*, the Duke's homoerotic desires for
his brother are revealed only to the audience towards the end of the work,
and his persistent need to conceal his urges ultimately causes his downfall. In
Britten's final opera, *Death in Venice*, a lifetime's habit of assimilation is so
ingrained in Aschenbach that he dies before being able to articulate his latent
homosexual desires to the object of his concealed fantasy. Bernstein's own
life of attempted passing and covering is voiced through François' repudiation of Junior in *A Quiet Place*, by avoiding any discussion of sexual history
prior to him marrying Junior's sister. In Candey's *Sweets by Kate*, a lesbian
couple attempt a mainstream existence in a small-town, suburban setting
before realizing that they missed the sanctity of a welcoming queer community. Lam's unique exploration of the embodiment of queer icon worshipping
takes a gay couple out of their context and the expiration of their relationship.
Finally, in Paterson's trilogy of one-act operas, *Three Way*, alternative forms
of sexuality are explored and gender-fluid, non-binarism is seen to incorporate sexually into a sex party. Here, sexual differences are taught to an uninformed character whose sexuality is hidden from society and only expressed
in the relative security of an orgy.

BOMARZO, ALBERTO GINASTERA

When Argentinian composer Alberto Ginastera (1916–1983) completed *Bomarzo* in 1967, he intended the premiere to take place on 4 August at the Teatro Colón in Buenos Aires. However, de facto president at the time, Juan Carlos Onganía, banned the production for its lascivious content. The opera opened instead at the Opera Society of Washington in Washington, DC on 19 May 1967.

The story is loosely based on the real life of sixteenth-century minor noble, Pier Francesco Orsini (1523–1583), also known as Vicino Orsini, or the Duke of Bomarzo. He was married to Giulia Farnese, and they had several children; their eldest son was Corradino (b. 1545). Orsini's legacy includes a mannerist park in Bomarzo, taking thirty years to build, and for which he commissioned seventeen sculptures and two monuments, following the death of his wife. The park is extant and is known as the *Sacro Bosco* (Sacred Grove), or the *Parco dei Mostri* (Park of the Monsters), or simply, the Garden of Momarzo. Unlike the formal gardens that dominated the period, the layout of Orsini's park is seemingly random. Some believe the outward appearance of informality belies the intention for the visitor to undertake an experience of personal, spiritual change. Cut into one of the stones, the visitor reads, 'Thou, who enter this garden, be very attentive and tell me then if these marvels have been created to deceive visitors, or for the sake of art.'

The librettist Manuel Mujica Láinez (1910–1984) married and produced two children. Despite creating the requisite smokescreen required in Argentinian society at the time, his flamboyancy and homosexual preference were not kept particularly secret. Láinez may well have been projecting some of his own queer identity on his central character, Pier Francesco Orsini, second son of a noble family. A hunchback, he is disfigured physically and psychologically. After being convinced by his astrologer to drink a magic potion, granting him immortality, he experiences a series of flashbacks, recalling important moments in his life. In these flashbacks, he and his two brothers, Girolamo and Maerbale, are represented by boys in speaking roles. Pier Francesco sings:

Me trae el eco de los años idos,	It brings me the echo of years gone by,
de la vida remota, de la infancia,	from remote life, from childhood,
de lo que quise ser pero no pude.[4]	of what I wanted to be but couldn't.

As a boy, he is riddled with self-doubt and shame with his inadequacies. He loathes the sight of himself in mirrors that serve as a constant reminder of his physical impairment. His feelings of hopelessness are compounded whenever he catches sight of himself; however, his self-loathing seems to be based on monstrous characteristics beyond his hunchback, 'All my life has been lived among the monsters who now are but the mirror of my spirit, and I perceive that all this world's endowments amount to nothing, nothing, nothing.'[5]

There are five forms of vocalization in the opera: singing, speech-singing (*Sprechstimme*), speech with relative pitch, speech with musical rhythm and speech with prosodic rhythm. Pier Francesco's vocal line covers almost the entire range of a tenor within a single bar in Act I, scene iii, and the angular melodic writing reflects the largely atonal material in the opera. Ginastera prepares the highest note of a phrase by use of a tritone, exacerbating his discomfort. He provides further glimpses into his secret life in the following scene, 'Looking back on my lifetime, I remember not the great events, not the glorious triumphs, but the course of my secret life that no-one suspected but which weighed so on my spirit.'[6]

Láinez reveals very little about Pier Francesco's secrets in his libretto, other than no one suspecting what they might be, and that they clearly provided a sense of shame. As young boys, his brothers tease him mercilessly, mocking his effeminacy. They boss him around, forcing him to play their games, in which his humiliation plays a central role. Supported by the cajoling chorus, the brothers first dress Pier Francesco as a Jester, mocking his hump. Girolamo then dresses him in women's clothing and, complete with a manufactured tiara and a skirt, forces the unwitting boy to be his Duchess. They are married by the younger brother, playing as Cardinal Maerbale, who sings, *Os consagro marido y mujer, duque y duquesa*[7] (We pronounce you husband and wife, Duke and Duchess). The taunting continues as Girolamo pretends to kiss Pier Francesco, who finally manages to get away, taking refuge on the couch. The humiliation ceases only upon the arrival of their father, Gian Corrado. The imposing figure is carrying a cane and strikes it, insisting to be told the nature of their madness. Pier Francesco, dressed entirely as a girl, is shamefully scorned and blamed for the mockery while the two brothers flee. His father sings, 'What will you do, misshapen effeminate hunchback, tell me that?'[8]

Pier Francesco suffers further humiliation when he is brought to the whore, Pantasilea's bedroom. Despite her attempts at encouragement, he is unable to perform the coital task when he once again sees his reflection in one of Pantasilea's mirrors. He repeatedly calls for his servant, Abul, to remain in the room and explains to Pantasilea that intercourse would be 'impossible'. At this point, it is clear that there is something important that is contributing to his impotence, but it is entirely plausible that it is a case of self-loathing that is preventing him from giving in to Pantasilea's repeated appeals.

Following the death of his father, and then his older brother, Girolamo, Pier Francesco becomes the Duke of Bomarzo. He marries Julia Farnese, but his impotence endures, and his wife later becomes the object of affection for his younger brother, Maerbale. On his wedding night, he once again fails to fulfil his matrimonial duties. Alone, in bed, he experiences first, a vision of Pantasilea, reminding him of what he was unable to do, and then an erotic dream. His fantasy is set to a ballet *'en tempo aleatorio'*.[9] The offstage chorus accompany the dancers with indeterminately pitched sighs, alternating with improvised sections of aleatoric material for each section of the orchestra. The chorus whisper the word 'love', as indicated by Ginastera, 'in all the languages of the world'.[10] The music climaxes with the singers widening their exploration of the chromatic scale with increasing volume and a variety of extended instrumental techniques such as woodwind tapping their keys, brass blowing but without producing a tone, flutter tonguing and pizzicato. All of which intensifies with increasing texture, pitch and intensity with largely improvised material to support the frenzied dancing of the semi-naked dancers. Ginastera stated, 'In the magic world of Bomarzo, dreams and realities are mixed in such a way that the fantasies, desires, memories, and imaginings of Bomarzo become more real than reality itself.'[11]

It is in the twelfth tableau, 'the minotaur', that the Duke's shameful secret is finally revealed. Walking in the garden at night,[12] he comes across the statue of a minotaur from the Vatican Museum. The minotaur's face has broken off, and the Duke projects the figure of his younger brother, Maerbale, onto the lifeless statue. He sings:

¡Minotauro, hermano mío,	Minotaur, my brother,
como yo, desfigurado,	like me, disfigured,
como yo, bello y horrible! . . .	like me, beautiful and horrible! . . .
(Dirigiéndose al Minotauro)	*(Addressing the Minotaur)*
Lo mismo que te rodean	The same that surround you
estos Césares romanos,	these Roman Caesars,
feroces y voluptuosos,	fierce and voluptuous,
inflexibles como el mármol,	inflexible like marble,
con su ronda que en lo oscuro	with his round that in the dark
se extravía, Minotauro,	get lost, Minotaur,
lo mismo a mí me rodean	the same surround me
los Orsini legendarios.	the legendary Orsini.
Andan en torno de mí,	They walk around me
y me queman sus miradas	and their glances burn me
como a ti las de los Césares	like you those of the Caesars
que se encienden en el mármol.	that are lit on the marble.
¡Minotauro, hermano mío,	Minotaur, my brother,
como yo, desfigurado,	like me, disfigured,
como yo, bello y horrible,	like me, beautiful and horrible,
mi atroz espejo, mi hermano![13]	my atrocious mirror, my brother!

As many of the questions regarding the source of the Duke's internalized shame are suddenly answered, a naked couple emerge from the darkness nearby and flee. The Duke then kisses the statue of the minotaur, which possesses the dual qualities of his brother: beauty and passion and deformity and brutality. He sings, 'What other flesh could assuage the ache of my passionate longing? Where could my doubts find a refuge but in your body of marble? Man and monster that you are, do not leave me, dearest brother. We are both beings apart, and our love dies in the darkness.'[14]

The reappearance of the tritone occurs when he pleads with the statue not to leave him. Following this pivotal scene, the Duke witnesses Maerbale enter his wife, Julia's room to seduce her. He orders his servant, Abul, to kill him, which in turn is witnessed by Maerbale's young son, Nicolás. Nicolás then follows the Duke to a giant Hellmouth that he created in the garden and in an act of revenge, poisons him, proving that his supposed immortality was a deception.

The Hellmouth, situated in the monstrous grove, is depicted during the prelude to the opera, and it is here that Ginastera introduces the musical language that will construct the work. Extended instrumental techniques, microtonal pitch inflections, wordless chorus singing and the rich timbre of assorted percussion, mandolin and harpsichord to compliment the orchestral forces create an ambiguous scene, shrouded in mystery. There is a sense of chaos, with musicians asked to improvise simultaneously. The use of the twelve-tone system, rather than being strictly administered, is manipulated to generate vocal lines that have hints of romanticism. It is a unifying feature of the work, with the row being used in a variety of contexts throughout the narrative. Ginastera also includes traditional forms, such as folk tunes, madrigals, courtly dances and church music (such as the *Dies Irae* in the carnivalesque masquerade), to provide reference points.

The offstage chorus add to the mystery of the opera, whispering the name 'Bomarzo' during the Prelude and even moaning extatically with dense, cluster chords. The chorus is placed in the orchestra pit and is used in four different ways: as a traditional opera chorus; as a Greek chorus when it acquires a single personality; as a madrigal chorus; and as a new instrument of the orchestra.[15]

There is little evidence to suggest the real Duke Orsini was homosexual or bisexual. Had he been, however, he would certainly not have been a uniquely gay, sixteenth-century aristocrat. He would have kept such company as George Villiers, First Duke of Buckingham (1592–1628); Cardinal Stefano Pignatelli (1578–1623); Cardinal Scipione Borghese (1577–1633); James VI and I of Scotland and of England and Ireland (1566–1625); Henry III of France (1551–1589), Cardinal Innocenzo Ciocchi Del Monte (1532–1577); Pier Luigi Farnese, Duke of Parma (1503–1547); and Pope Julius III (1487–1555).

Two weeks prior to the premiere, Ginastera and Láinez travelled to Washington, DC and presented a lecture at the State Department Auditorium, entitled 'The Origins of an Opera'. Ginastera discussed the complex sexual neuroses of the protagonist, stating that they reflected 'our time . . . an age of anxiety, an age of sex, an age of violence'. Representing the Duke's sexuality provides much more fodder for discussion. His was not just a homosexual 'perversion' but also one of incest. The desire for his brother seems steeped in something much deeper than a basic, carnal attraction but to be connected with his feelings of inadequacy which manifested in his hunchback. Ginastera's daughter, Georgina, explained in an interview the composer's thoughts on sexual identity in the opera, 'For him it was not so much in the hunchback or the crown, but in a suffering man, like every human being, who loves one woman more than another. Who has, yes, bisexual desires. And in whom his deformity is symbolic.'[16] Ginastera's score is suggestive of highly controlled chaos, characterized by frequent sections of aleatoric material. This structured improvisation acts as an allegory for sexual identity in our own world, where our internal desires are controlled by our own set of expectations and the society that helps form them.

DEATH IN VENICE, BENJAMIN BRITTEN

Although acclaimed as one of the most important queer composers of opera, Benjamin Britten (1913–1976) curiously avoided celebrating homosexuality overtly in his staged works. Some of his operas clearly have queer characters; however, his musical techniques frame the queer character in a way that requires analysis of codified material for surety. Britten's choice of sources tended to adopt an ambivalent or even critical view of the protagonist. Peter Grimes, Peter Quint (see chapter 2), Captain Vere (also see chapter 2) and Aschenbach are all involved in immoral, psychological or physical abuse, including sexual perversion, while concurrently pursuing homoerotic urges. Furthermore, Britten actively reduced much of the overt homosexual content in his libretti, in particular with *Peter Grimes* (1945) and *Billy Budd* (1951), concealing some important queer features but retaining sinister qualities.

Death in Venice (1973) is certainly Britten's most overtly queer opera, based on Thomas Mann's 1912 novella, *Der Tod in Venedig*. Britten worked with frequent collaborator Mary Myfanwy Piper (1911–1997) on the libretto, which was to showcase his partner Peter Pears (1910–1986) in the principal role. In one of Piper's notebooks, an entry states, 'Avoid the obviousness of the homosexual theme by an emphasis on the narcissistic character of beauty . . . his own self-love.'[17] It is quite possible that this was an instruction by

Britten in an attempt to remove blatant homosexual indicators. By contrast, Piper frequently pressed Britten to consider sources with queer themes and to emphasize homosexual elements. Perhaps the potential repercussions were not considered as acutely by Piper as Britten might have.

The protagonist, Aschenbach, is in many ways odious, and his descent into latent homosexual desires marks a severe fall from grace. In the beginning of the opera, he is an accomplished writer (albeit with a case of writer's block), but his journey to Venice, on the advice of a traveller, is predicated on the erotic descriptions that foreshadow Aschenbach's exploits. Phrases such as 'inexplicable longing',[18] 'O terror and delight'[19] and 'a sudden predatory gleam'[20] suggest a heady mixture of carnal desire and forbidden fruit. The journey takes effect before long and the writer finds himself resembling the kind of undignified fop he had hitherto loathed. His fixation on Tadzio, a young Polish boy, holidaying with his family on the Venetian Lido, is so intoxicating that he starts to see the boy as a Greek god.

Britten emphasizes the connection introduced by Mann, of Tadzio with the god, Apollo. He intended to show not only the obsession which brought about Aschenbach's demise but also the electrifying possibility of discovering a love of youthful male beauty espoused in Platonic philosophy. When Aschenbach first notices Tadzio with his family in the hotel, he sings:

Surely the soul of Greece
Lies in that bright perfextion
A golden look
A timeless air,
Mortal child with more than mortal grace.[21]

The connection with Greek mythology had already been introduced during Aschenbach's journey on the gondola, which he likened to crossing the river Styx. His last phrase in scene xi references Apollo as a precursor to the final scene of Act I, 'The Games of Apollo', a contest of Apollonian devotees in an embodiment of Platonic principles evoked by the enchanting Tadzio. Here, Piper's libretto departs from Mann's version, which has subtle undertones of aggression. Mann's version states, 'Now day after day the god with the burning cheeks soared upward naked, driving his four fire-breathing steeds through the spaces of heaven, and now, too, his yellow-gold locks fluttered wide in the outstorming east wind.'[22] Britten's version is less combatant:

No boy, but Phoebus of the golden hair
Driving his horses through the azure sky
Mounting his living chariot shoulder high
Both child and god he lords it in the air.[23]

In a letter from Piper to Britten dated 28 January 1972, she wrote, 'There is no doubt in my mind that Aschenbach was a devotee of Apollo – that Apollo is the God whom he puts up against Dionysus and that Tadzio therefore also can and does represent Apollo in his mind.'[24] The Games of Apollo represent a pinnacle of Hellenistic idealism, a turning point in the narrative, as Aschenbach betrays his desires to develop a genuine relationship with the boy, instead choosing to internalize his desire. Britten confirms the identification of Tadzio's beauty by transferring to him Apollo's theme at the conclusion of the Games. As Tadzio passes Aschenbach on the way to the hotel, he smiles. Aschenbach's torment is exacerbated in this moment. He sings, 'Ah! don't smile like that! No-one should smile like that.'[25] The conclusion of Act I offers the first truly visceral, musical moment in what is otherwise an intrinsically cerebral score. It is an unmitigated crescendo that makes use of dynamics, rhythm, texture and extreme registers to produce a grand climax with abrupt brass punctuations that accompany Aschenbach's wordless cry. The post-coital tranquillity that follows is underpinned by a sustained tritone from the horns before the almost spoken words, 'I love you.'[26]

Staging this scene provided a dramatic problem. Piper wanted a Hellenic and parodic approach, in keeping with Mann's language in which he shifts from detailed realism to a more abstract reflection of beauty. It is also one of the most erotic passages in the novella, and Mann clouded them in a recitation of Platonic references of abstract Greek love. In the opera, the clear representation of pederasty would require either abstraction, and Piper's solution was unpredictably to have the dance performed entirely naked so as to remove it completely from reality.

Tadzio, who remains voiceless throughout the opera, is provided with his own 'Tadzio chord' in Britten's scheme of thematic associations. This is clearly heard at the moment Aschenbach gives a clear and distinct declaration of his Apollonian inclinations, 'When thought becomes feeling, feeling thought',[27] borrowed from the second phrase of Apollo's song. The section concludes climactically with the phrase, 'Then Eros is in the Word',[28] set to Tadzio's theme, making a direct association of the boy to the Greek god.

Britten's intention for Aschenbach to be drawn to the Platonic ideal is supported by one of Britain's early notes on the opera in his red exercise book. In the scene, in which Aschenbach's failed departure of Venice leads him back to his hotel, Britten wrote, 'Aschenbach philosophises – Socrates and Phaedrus – nature of virtue and desire. Thinks of sublimating his feelings for Tadzio in beautiful prose (and of the world's admiration).'[29]

As Aschenbach's embrace of Apollonian philosophies of beauty and boy-love descends into a Dionysian revelry of irrationality and emotional instincts, the life he once led is replaced by a firm obsession with Tadzio and suggestions of an inclination towards pederasty. Aschenbach explains in Act

I that his wife had died and his only daughter has married. Consequently, he has become work-focused and dedicated to a life of self-control and undoubtedly suppression of latent homosexual urges. He makes a series of uncharacteristic, immoral decisions, beginning with his reluctance to introduce himself to the boy, then choosing not to warn Tadzio's mother of the encroaching plague so that the boy might remain with him on the Lido. The possibility of a genuine but sublimated friendship with Tadzio in Act I and the gradual capitulation to lust revealed in Act II show the arc of a man embracing his Dionysian predilections. Apollo and Dionysus are introduced as disembodied voices. They do not appear in the story but help dramatize the Apollonian and Dionysian allegory.

Britten had made use of the twelve-tone system in previous works, most notably in *The Turn of the Screw* (1954). In *Death in Venice*, the series is introduced with the introduction of Aschenbach's vocal line. The first four notes consist of two parallel, ascending whole tones, a semitone apart, and this segment is repeated a minor third higher. The melody is then concluded by climbing to an E and ending on E flat, completing the twelve-tone row. The structure is angular and consists of small steps, providing a sense of restlessness.[30] Britten establishes E as the tonal centre for Aschenbach's world by melodically highlighting the semitones either side of it.

By contrast, Tadzio and his wordless family are represented by mime and dance, reinforcing the distance between him and Aschenbach. Furthermore, Britten's sound world for Tadzio contrasts with the other material in the opera; he is associated with the ephemeral timbre of the vibraphone and a large assortment of percussion instruments. He is also given the tonal centre of A, either major or Lydian, with an emphasis on the lower, whole-tone tetrachord. This use of contrasting keys for central characters is a technique that Britten frequently applied in his operas to delineate groups of characters and to provide a discernible harmonic tension. He also uses orchestral textures and instrumentation to provide character associations without total reliance on the Wagnerian leitmotif approach.

The first production of *Death in Venice* provided a myriad of decisions that would impact the inevitable tsunami of interpretations, opinions and analysis of Britten's final opera. The premiere took place at Snape Maltings on Saturday, 16 June 1973. Peter Pears sang the role of Aschenbach, and Tadzio was performed by Robert Huguenin, who was discovered from the ranks of the Royal Ballet. Britten felt it was important that Tadzio was not portrayed by a muscular, young man, in case Aschenbach's character was interpreted as being a one-dimensional, cruising predator. To provide the sense of Aschenbach being confused by his emerging Platonic aesthetics, Tadzio needed to be boyish – an agent for creative inspiration, rather than an overtly erotic creature.

There was also a strong shared sense from director, Colin Graham, that the production should be unconventional. He wanted to dispense with the straight-line stage under a proscenium, a view that was opposed by the librettist and set designer. This was a favoured approach of Britten's since *Gloriana* (1953), and he experimented with alternative uses of space with his church parables, which were also directed by Graham. The use of dance provided the basis for a more stylized, non-literal style. The set took the shape of a black box, representing an old camera, the opening shutter of which represented the moving colours and images occurring in Aschenbach's mind. To highlight the Hellenistic aesthetic, the dancers were often shown against a white backdrop with different colour quality of light.

It was the 'Games of Apollo' that attracted most of Britten's revisions, as the idea of the Pentathlon, although logical, provided difficulties with choreography and the number of activities somewhat diluted the aesthetic effect of Tadzio as a Greek god.[31] It was not until the production moved to Covent Garden that the full use of technology could be realized. The use of back projections had far greater effect with twenty-five backcloths, compared to the half dozen that could be used on the specially constructed gantry.

The protagonist's burgeoning homosexuality is a central tenant of the psychological realism of the opera. The listener is situated by the music from Aschenbach's perspective, an accomplice to his trajectory of growing homosexual impulses as he pursues the boy through the Venetian streets. We follow his inner dialogue as he gives into his lust, finds inspiration from the beauty of his form, fails to warn Tadzio's family of the imminent plague and eventually surrenders to his desire on the Lido. The audience is simultaneously seduced and seducer. Musically, however, the audience is at times unsympathetic to Aschenbach. Britten relies on persistent phrases, from instruments that caricature and in registers that crudely distance his character, detaching his perspective and positioning the listener into a position in which critical judgement of his exploits can be made.[32] Britten's techniques are at odds with the libretto in that they do not confirm or deny Aschenbach's homosexual identity, neither affirming nor supporting his queerness. In many ways, this reticence to overtly celebrate queerness mirrors Britten's own life.

A QUIET PLACE, LEONARD BERNSTEIN

The year 1983 saw a rapidly divided landscape for the LGBTQ+ community in the United States. Politically, queers were witnessing increasing representation in many levels, with Gerry Studds (1937–2006) declaring his homosexuality on the floor of House, Herb Donaldson (1927–2008) appointed the first openly gay male municipal judge in California, BiPOL founded in San

Francisco as a party for bisexual activism, David Scondras (1946–2020), an openly gay man, is elected onto the Boston City Council and Leonard Bernstein's (1918–1990) final opera, *A Quiet Place*, featuring queer characters, is premiered at the Houston Opera. Despite this period of gradual liberation, the AIDS crisis loomed as a darkening cloud, having only been named as such the previous year by the Centers for Disease Control and Prevention (CDC). The Reverend Jerry Falwell (1933–2007) describes the epidemic as the 'gay plague', and President Ronald Reagan (1911–2004), refuses to acknowledge AIDS publicly.[33]

Bernstein was a major supporter of the fight against the scourge of AIDS in the queer community. He advocated for increased funding for AIDS research and support for victims and their families. Bernstein was a voracious reader of material concerning the epidemic and collected various available resources in the early stages of the crisis. One of his male lovers during the 1970s, Tom Cothran, died from AIDS as the world was still coming to terms with it. He allowed organizations such as the American Foundation for AIDS Research (AmFAR) to use his name in their fundraising and advocacy efforts and donated to causes including People With AIDS Coalition (PWA), Human Rights Campaign Fund (now the Human Rights Campaign) and Lambda Legal Defense and Education Fund, as well as regularly attending and speaking at numerous events. Bernstein gave his support while maintaining an ambiguous public profile regarding his own homosexuality and thereby appearing as a queer ally, rather than being a member of the community.

In *A Quiet Place*, the family of Dinah has gathered for her funeral. Her loss has reignited the considerable tensions that exist between the siblings and their father. One of the siblings is Junior, a bisexual character at the centre of the action and acting as a mediator between the other conflicted characters. Queer-coded subtexts can be found in earlier works such as *Facsimile* (1946), *West Side Story* (1957) and *Songfest* (1977); however, it was not until Bernstein's final staged work that an identifiably queer character was created. Staging such a work in Texas would prove controversial, as although the public knew little of the opera's narrative before the premiere, the political landscape of a liberal district in a conservative state amidst the AIDS crisis provided requisite ingredients for a backlash. This backlash took the form of an anonymously penned handbill, with the title 'Warning: Leonard Bernstein's Operas Spread Herpes' was distributed around Houston:

> Houston has been chosen as the site for the premiere of Leonard Bernstein's new opera 'A Quiet Place'. It is being promoted as an opera about the 'common' folk, in 'common' dress, using 'common' vernacular. One wonders what 'common' strains will be spread by this new 'opera'?

What suckers we have become! It used to be that we did our dirty laundry – germs and all – in private. Now it is put on stage and called 'popular culture' (or perhaps 'popular cultures'). Next we will be told that Leonard Bernstein is preparing a follow-up opera about a man suffering the woes of those nasty sores (how appropriate for Houston, the herpes capitol [*sic*] of the southwest). Maybe he will call it 'Troubles in my Pee-Pee'.

Perhaps Bernstein's new opera should premiere in the Bronx Zoo – grunts and groans, snorts and moans – isn't that fast becoming the 'new American vernacular'? . . . While you may suffer only mental clap by being a 'patron of the arts' and suffering through a performance of Bernstein's opera, the cultural pessimism this kind of 'art' breeds is giving your kids the real thing.

Mayor Whitmire recently issued a call to change the image of the city of Houston. Let us begin by cancelling this opera, proving that Houstonians are not dumb suckers who will bankroll the trash produced by the 'sophisticates'. Let us make Houston 'A Quiet Place'.[34]

In the leaflet, there are no direct attributions of the various sexually transmitted diseases to the queer community; however, in the context of the spreading AIDS virus, the inference is thinly veiled. Symbolic of the terror and anxiety of a paranoid community, the flyer was compounded by phone calls to the HGO office, inquiring about the possible representation of homosexual acts in the production, and a heckler at Bernstein's press conference who remarked:

Classical music in the Renaissance and throughout history has always served to up-lift people. It seems to me what you are doing with an opera of this sort is not to up-lift people at all, but to mire people in the muck of a very rotten situation that many people find themselves in.[35]

Bernstein conceived *A Quiet Place* as a sequel to *Trouble in Tahiti* (1952), in which Junior is mentioned but does not appear on stage. His librettist on this project was Stephen Wadsworth (b. 1953). Originally, the two works were designed to be performed as a double bill, and there are frequent threads of continuity between the two, both musically and in terms of plot. Junior has a condition whereby he speaks in rhyme whenever he becomes anxious or distressed. He has not been home for twenty years, and his arrival at his mother's funeral elicits some observations from members of the chorus, who sing, 'friend?', to which the funeral director responds, 'Well, you know Junior, the one's a crazy queer who skipped the draft.'[36]

The chorus appeared onstage for the funeral scene in the Houston premiere; however, in subsequent productions, they were positioned in the pit throughout the opera and supernumeraries made flesh the guests onstage. The funeral director's response is the first mention of both Junior's sexuality, and his role as the former lover of his sister's husband, François, provides tantalizing gossip for the cortege of mourners. His identity as a queer is conjoined with his conscientious objection to the Vietnam War and his condition described cursorily as 'crazy'.[37] Bernstein compounds Junior's deviant queerness by adding a divergence from American ideals of patriotic militarism as well as masculine, heteronormative associations with guns. Much can be made of Bernstein's inclusion of an identifiable queer character; however, the moment is one of only three utterances of the terms 'queer' or 'gay' in the opera. The funeral director states, 'You know I never understood what you call gay people',[38] to which the analyst cleverly responds, 'I never understood funeral directors.'[39] Junior also mentions the word 'gay' when referring to the bar in which he and François met and again in his final aria.

Sexuality remains largely in the shadows of the opera, emerging occasionally with clues that help reveal the complex relationships that bind the characters. Sam vocalizes his disgust with Junior, but if the reason for this is Junior's sexuality, then it necessitates conjecture. Equally, he later refers to Dede's marriage with François with contempt, snapping, 'You call that married?'[40] We may deduce that he disapproves of the sexual history that François and Junior share, but his retorts are ambiguous, much like the discourse surrounding Bernstein's sexual identity. In Act II, scene iii, we discover that Junior and François had been lovers before François and Dede married. There is a suggestion in François' objections to Junior's topic for discussion that their relationship may have ended technically but that lingering sexual desires have not fully abated. (J) 'Remember when we met?' (F) 'No. Don't do that. You can't just have me whenever you . . .' (J) 'Remember we met in a bar, in a gar . . . in a bay-gar. Love me.'[41]

In case the *ménage à trois* between Junior, François and Dede was not quite complete, we discover in Act II that Junior and Dede had been sexually active together as children. The libretto hints at the possibility that Junior and Dede had been adopted, perhaps due to the infertility of one or both parents; however, this is also obfuscated through a lack of textural clarity. Dede and Junior's sexual experimentation was, in part, prompted by the discord between Sam and Dinah. Junior held his sister 'through the screaming nights',[42] which indicates the general temperature of the marriage and poses questions about the American nuclear family. From the beginning of the opera, the notion of heteronormative, suburban marriage as a utopian ideal is destroyed. Dinah was clearly unhappy in her dysfunctional marriage, the children are estranged from their father and an unconventional three-way relationship involves his two children and an 'outsider', distinguished for his foreignness in the libretto. Throughout the opera, Bernstein challenges traditional gender roles, sexual norms and family ideals, important facets of his own life throughout which he was constantly 'othered' for being the son of immigrants, a Jew and a queer. The metaphor of Sam representing white, heteronormative hegemony, and the children as individuals, damaged by suppression and relentless conformity at the detriment of happiness, is most clearly expressed through François – bisexual but desperately clinging to the binary delineations of conservative domesticity.

When Junior recalls his burgeoning sexual relationship with his sister, François is upset and refuses to listen: (Jr) 'But first I kissed her, my sister.' (F) 'Stop!' (Jr) 'I did. And she was bare, all bare.' (F) 'O.K., enough.' (Jr) 'She was.' (F) 'O.K.' (F) 'Mommy Daddy had their fights.' (F) 'Assez!' (Jr) 'I held her through the screaming nights. And then I touched her. Guess where: there!'[43]

The possibility that following the death of Dinah, after a miserably unhappy marriage, latent feelings of homosexuality in Sam are worth exploring. The two adopted children were not products of successful reproduction attempts by their adoptive parents, and given the general level of happiness, it is easy to consider the marital bed purely as a place for sleeping. The relationship between Junior and Sam is strained at best. Sam expressed his disgust at Junior, without articulating the cause, prompting questions regarding the source of his homophobia. Did he see in Sam something of himself which disgusted him? It is certainly not his appearance, as Sam sings of his 'handsome son',[44] the reutterance of which he prevents himself from completing. As if caught thinking something he shouldn't, he addresses Dede and François, venomously stating that he doesn't understand their marriage. His tirade oscillates between introspective self-flagellation over his failures as a husband and father and vitriolic attacks on the children and François. Scattered throughout, he pleads to be loved, without any clear indication by whom. He then points to Junior, singing, 'You confuse me. How dare you confuse me.'[45] Sam's gym obsession resulted in another argument with Dinah, in which he chose the gym over attending Junior's play. In a flashback in Act II, young Sam is in the gym and sings, 'There's a law about men',[46] in which he incessantly describes the opposing positive and negative qualities about all facets of men but with particular focus on the effect of diet and exercise on physique.

The ambiguity and suggestive sexual language allow for several interpretations of the familial relationships. Junior and Dede's persistent use of the term 'Daddy' could be an innocuous term, but given their status as mature adults, and the frosty relationship they both have with their father, it adds to the milieu of shadowy sexual undertones. In Act III, Junior wants his father to tuck him into bed, and it is at this point that we get the final utterance of his sexuality.

Daddy. Did you come to tuck me in?
Can I have a glass of water?

Sorry, may I have a glass of . . .
Stay some more and sing me the movie song . . .
Olé . . . The way you . . . do . . .
Before the day I gay I go Canada, Bananada.[47]

The text references the movie *Trouble in Tahiti* and infers that Dinah added the 'Olé' for Junior when he was a boy, and that because Sam was unwilling to accept Sam's sexual identity, Junior decided to move to Canada.

Much of the tension in the opera stems from the contrasting voices of Sam and Junior. Both of them frequently leave phrases unfinished, allowing the observer to speculate about the importance of what was not said. Sam is loud in his resentment of being an emasculated and failed patriarchal figure, and Junior is raucous, singing in prolonged streams of quavers in quickly changing, irregular meters. Junior's motif accompanies him throughout the opera in changing forms and has echoes of the trio on *Trouble in Tahiti*, alternating between major and minor tonalities. Both men have difficulty in communicating; Junior becomes flustered and begins rhyming and producing confused sentences, such as the example given earlier, and Sam, conflicted by inner demons, struggles to say the things he knows will reduce tension and encourage reconciliation.

A Quiet Place has been considered by many as a semi-autobiographical construction for both Wadsworth and Bernstein.[48] Both were grieving – Wadsworth for his sister Nina and Bernstein for his wife Felicia. Bernstein was traumatized with guilt when Felicia died from lung cancer, as he had left her to pursue his relationship with Tom Cothran and returned awkwardly to her after the affair with Cothran proved a disaster.[49] Felicia had been Bernstein's rock, supporting him throughout his career, and the connection with Dinah is entirely understandable. Bernstein also experienced a strained relationship with his father, reflected in the tension between Sam and Junior. Such tension may have been familiar to Bernstein, whose family struggled to understand his homosexuality. The invention of Junior and the overt presentation of bisexuality was Bernstein's message to the world, that families in modern America are diverse and complex. Through his own experiences, he demonstrates that helplessly clinging to archaic, heterosocial concepts of the traditional American family needs to be reconsidered to reflect the desires of liberated, sexual Americans.

SWEETS BY KATE, GRIFFIN CANDEY

The struggle for queer acceptance in the society dominated by heteronormativity and binary distinctions may still be continuing in many regions around the world, but for some, the struggle has evolved considerably since the Stonewall Riots of 1969. Legal battles for equality continue on in the courts, and the idea that queers have completely broken their glass ceiling remains a fallacy, and yet it must be acknowledged that for many societies, certain cultural, social and legal battles have been won. For around forty years since Stonewall, members of the LGBTQ+ community throughout the United States sought safe haven in emergent safe zones, known for being queer spaces such as the Castro in San Francisco, West Hollywood in Los Angeles, Boys Town in Chicago, the South End in Boston, Chelsea in New York, the Gayborhood in Philadelphia and Midtown in Atlanta.[50] However, these areas, along with thousands of gay bars, bookshops, sex stores and other gay-focused institutions, have largely disappeared through a process of gentrification and assimilation.

Assimilation, in the queer context, is used from a sociological perspective to describe the normalization of minority groups and is not far removed from the term 'heteronormativity'. A central tenant of the assimilation debate is the issue of same-sex marriage, on one hand an important symbol of equality and on another, the embrace of an archaic institution entirely manufactured for the heterosexual world. Questions arising from the relationship between supressed, minority groups and dominant, majoritarian groups have implications for the very meaning of equality and liberation.[51] The relatively recent process of assimilation of queer culture with the mainstream can be viewed as a victory, with the recognition of the queer community as an irrefutable economic force or as a regrettable loss of lively, community-based culture and transgressive energy which has taken decades to develop. Harris (1997) denounces the assimilation process:

> Although this image [the melting pot] is meant to suggest everything that is hospitable, tolerant, and welcoming about our society, it inadvertently conjures up a picture, not of a lively community of separate cultures, each of which makes a distinctive contribution to an inclusive and well-functioning democracy, but of an inedible ethnic goulash spoiled by too many ingredients, a sludge-like stew of racial and national differences.[52]

Signs that assimilation of queer characters in operas began to emerge from around 2015, when the idea of unguarded queerness became a non-issue. Such characters can openly identify by any queer identity, but the identity has no bearing on the narrative or even of the character themselves; queerness is relegated to a position of irrelevance. For supporters of assimilation, this is a breath of fresh air for a rapidly developing art form that has begun to redress the issue of representation but now needs to show queers as regular people who happen to be queer. For critics of assimilation, this represents a lost opportunity for representation to also contribute to activism, by dealing with the conflicts that have inflicted the queer community. For followers of Foucault, perhaps queer assimilation is simply a new *episteme* that reflects a new mode of thinking, impossible for the pioneering activists of previous decades.

Griffin Candey's 2015 opera *Sweets by Kate* is set to a libretto by Thom Miller and concerns Elizabeth, who returns to the small town to deal with the sudden death of her father. Her return after twelve years brings back the memories of being shunned by the community for being 'other', and now she brings Kate, her partner with her, and confronts the anticipated and continuing disapproval once gain. The gustatory discussions for the narrative between Griffin and Miller did not initially include portrayals of queerness. The two characters are simply people, dealing with a universal theme that is not exclusive to any gender of sexual orientation. The decision for the couple to be same-sex was made later as Candey explains:

> I had been part of a lot of conversations about things that weren't on the opera stage almost at all or very rarely, so when I was talking to Thom, and we started poking around this structure, there was truly no reason why these protagonists couldn't be a same-sex couple or just a non-heterosexual couple.[53]

The fact that the couple are lesbian, rather than a gay male couple, was a result of practicality. Candey, an experienced opera singer himself, was aware of the need to provide female roles for the abundance of female opera singers looking for opportunities to perform. Labonte (2019) asserts that the number of female roles in American operas between 1995 and 2015 was between 42 and 45 per cent, a statistic that is seemingly at odds with the proportion of gender for singers based on anecdotal observations.[54] These statistics do not take into account the contribution to opera made by members of the transgender community, which is of particular importance when discussing *Sweets by Kate*. The role of Elizabeth was first played by Aiden Kim Feltkamp, a transitioned mezzo-soprano who identifies as transgender non-binary. Feltkamp has worked largely in writing and educating, although continues to sing, while chronicling the vocal effects of changes in testosterone levels. Changing *fach* and register during the transition process is of huge importance for the growing community of transgender singers. In addition to playing queer roles such as Elizabeth, Feltkamp has also performed several female roles as well as trouser roles.[55]

Elizabeth leaves the familiar, safe haven of her San Francisco community, to bury her father, Joe. Joe has been poisoned by Carl, a manifestation of a Faustian, devil figure. Carl believes it is he who will inherit Joe's sweets shop rather than his daughter, Elizabeth. The conflict between Carl and the two girls unfolds with the intervention of magic elixirs that change the fortunes of the shop and the community, and through the process of declining fortunes emerges an inner conflict regarding Elizabeth's relationship with her family. Candey illuminates:

> Elizabeth is trying to posthumously square her relationship with her parents and going through this motion that I think a lot of people go through when their parents pass away of putting them on a pedestal and allowing themselves to overlook some of their lesser moments and difficult parts of their character.[56]

The opera is given a flashy, poppy, 1950s American hypercolour ambience, both in terms of the visual aesthetics and the score, which operates in a largely tonal and a lightly swing-influenced vernacular. Candey creates a jingle for Joe's candy shop at the beginning of the first act, which is reflective of the era, without fully embracing a tonic-dominant functionality. Likewise, Carl, the nemesis of the two girls, is treated in a cartoonish way and occupies the position of a bubbly side character, giving way to the less frivolous internal conflict between Elizabeth and her deceased parents. The scene in which Carl poisons Joe and stands by, watching him writhing and twitching in his final death throws, has echoes of Batman's Joker and his startlingly comical reaction to horror. The two female protagonists are undefined by their sexuality within the musical constructs of the opera; however, their characters are given different treatment. Although not in any way chromatic, Elizabeth's material is left somewhat ungrounded, symbolizing her emotional journey. Her material is essentially tonal, but her phrases are allowed to wander, often modulating several times within the space of a few bars. Kate, by contrast, is far more tonally conceived and represents the objective voice of reason in the climax of the narrative.

Elizabeth and Kate's appearance on stage is foreshadowed by short utterances from the gossiping townsfolk. Reminiscent of the gossipy Borough in Britten's *Peter Grimes* (1945), the community is given a collective character, whereby idol gossip gives way to pre-emptive slander and contempt for 'outsiders'. The relative safety of being one of the gossipers is protected by associating difference with some form of moral corruption. In *Grimes*, the villagers attempt to bring violence to the 'outsider' in their midst but stop short when they find him gone from his hut. In *Sweets by Kate*, the intent of violence is prevented at the last moment in Act II, scene iii, with the girls barricading themselves in the sweets shop from the marauding townsfolk.

It is during this scene, entitled *Elizabeth and Kate*, that the network of relationships is explored following the resigned departure of the angry crowd. Elizabeth sings, 'I feel like everything's different, but what has changed?',[57] a phrase with a multiplicity of possible meanings. Carl's malevolent machinations present an external, superficial conflict, which is ultimately of little importance and amicably resolved; however, they agitate and provoke more meaningful issues. Before long, disagreements laden with accusations of an underlying agenda for the sweet shop to fail, so that they can resume their life in San Francisco, are issued. Kate sings, 'I came here for you, and only you. And why did you come here, love?',[58] and confronts Elizabeth with the fact that she is trying to resolve the tension with her parents that led to her leaving twelve years ago. This scene is the least cartoonish in the opera, and the conversation represents the climax of internal conflict which gives way to transformation and resolution. Candey describes the intention behind how the two women are portrayed, 'We didn't want to do a heavy-handed job of representing their relationship on stage, and I think it was important to us that like there was never any gay bashing, any violence towards them. It was just truly a non-contested element of the story.'[59]

Kate and Elizabeth's characters may have assimilated into the heteronormative, suburban culture by discarding any cultural markers and attempting to engage in the local, retail process. Ultimately, they chose to return to the familiarity of their more culturally sympathetic community in San Francisco; their assimilation experiment was unsuccessful. The community which supported Elizabeth's parents was willing to look past the 'otherness' while their endeavours were successful and the reciprocal benefit was appreciated, but as soon as any difficulty arose, they were quick to turn on the couple, turning into a violent mob in a flash. The message seems to come as a warning to queers who attempt to assimilate into communities that do not support difference. In their departing moments, the two women promise to 'return someday. A brighter day. A better day.'[60] Assuming their sentiments are genuine, we can only surmise that their unsuccessful attempt at looking back to the past is a temporal issue, and that next time, some form of transformation will prevent a repeat; either the community will change or the women will.

The presentation of a lesbian couple as the leading protagonists of an opera is a phenomenon of the American independent opera scene that has flourished in recent decades. The number of small, grassroots opera companies, operating throughout the United States, has enabled a new form of opera to emerge. Performing with small casts and reduced chamber orchestras, in non-commercial venues, these companies are free from the crippling overheads that large-scale opera companies are saddled with and are able to offer new material to a smaller audience willing to encounter fresh opera experiences. This movement has heralded a new wave of American opera narratives that is characterized by its diversity of characters and themes. Candey stated:

> I've always vowed to myself, as a white, heterosexual, cisgender male that I would never write an opera about someone like me – not in some sort of flagellating way, but because we don't need anymore. The vast majority of

the canon is about folks like me dealing with upper-middle-class (or higher) 'problems', and tellingly, folks outside of that small ring don't always connect with opera.[61]

Creating two leading lesbian characters, and casting a transgender performer, is the opportunity that is provided by a market unfettered by the need to cater for a demographic of opera lovers who prefer the Eurocentric, nineteenth-century canon. This is not to suggest that the 'A Houses' have not engaged in commissioning new works or attempted to celebrate diversity; however, when *The Metropolitan Opera* included *L'Amour de loin* (*Love from Afar*, 2000) by the Finnish composer Kaija Saariaho in its 2016/17 season, it was the first work by a female composer to be performed by the company since 1903. Although many contributors to the Met's artistic output are members of the LGBTQ+ community, there is scant evidence of any queer characters emerging from any recent commissions, unlike the plethora of diverse queer characters coming from the independent opera sector. *Sweets by Kate* was staged in the iconic venue of The Stonewall Inn, an intimate venue with about as much cultural meaning as a venue could offer and the perfect backdrop for the message of the opera, 'You don't need anyone's permission to live the life that you want to live.'

HEARTBREAK EXPRESS, GEORGE LAM

Not all gay men obsess over female celebrities, considered as gay icons, but many do. For some, the level of obsessive sycophancy can be unhealthy and manifest in unusual behaviour such as hoarding memorabilia. All of the characters in George Lam's opera *Heartbreak Express* (2015) consider country cross-over singer Dolly Parton to be of such iconic status, as to revere her as one would a saint. The word 'icon' derives from its use in describing an image such as a painting or a statue and the semantic extension, 'iconography', with focus on depictions of religious figures. The association with that which is sacred provides an understanding of how female gay icons are worshipped. Gay icons share many discernible features; often beautiful and desirable, and with an experience of overcoming tragedy and hardship, they often have big personalities and forge their own success through a determined resolve to stand up to the patriarchy. Although it is not necessary for them to champion LGBTQ+ causes, it helps.[62] One helpful definition of a 'diva', a term often used interchangeably with 'icon', lists several imperative characteristics,

> A huge voice, an even bigger ego and the balls to use it – throw in a penchant for sparkly dresses, a hint of real-life tragedy and 'my man done me wrong' torch songs and you've got a very loose definition.[63]

Parton's inclusion in the list of gay icons in queer theorist, Georges-Claude Guilbert's book, *Gay Icons: The (Mostly) Female Entertainers Gay Men Love*, is a departure from the predominantly pop-music-oriented women. Parton occupied a space in a music genre commonly considered in the 1970s as a retrograde culture defined by patriarchal, white, homophobic, bigoted, conservative and working-class values. Through her musicality and tenacity, she forged a career that conquered the country scene and then went on to achieve success in the popular music and cinematic worlds. Critic Richard Goldstein wrote in 1973 of the perceived tenets of the country music scene,

> Country music comes equipped with a very specific set of values, which include political conservatism, strongly differentiated male and female roles, a heavily punitive morality, racism, and the entire constellation of values around which is centered the phrase 'rugged individualism'. To me, it is, truly, the perfect musical extension of the Nixon administration.[64]

Despite occupying a space that is inherently at odds with a queer-friendly ecology, gay men are drawn to Parton for several reasons in addition to the broader definitions already stated. She deconstructed her own version of femininity with awareness of class distinctions, a bold, brassy image replete with over-the-top wigs, enhanced cleavage and figure-forming outfits, which she owned through humorous quips, 'It takes a lot of money to look this cheap!'[65] She once joked about her style while performing, substituting the words 'drag queen' in place of 'Jolene' in recognition of her queer fans who frequently attended concerts in Dolly drag. Dolly's overblown femininity expresses a nuance and humour that only gay men can truly appreciate.[66]

Gay icons tend to be heterosexual, with the exception of specifically lesbian icons, and Parton adheres to this through her unconventional marriage which was based on her career coming before any thoughts of children. Despite this, her early hit song, *Jolene* (1974), provided tantalizing suggestions of homosocial behaviour, baiting many interviewers and pundits such as the National Enquirer. Responding with grace to the allegation that she was involved in a lesbian relationship with her friend, Judy Ogle, Parton responded, 'Well, I'm not gay, but if I was, I would be privileged to have Judy as a partner!',[67] only adding to her queer appeal. Typically, songs belonging to the subgenre of the country Cheating Song or Other Woman song address the other woman with menacing tones; however, with *Jolene*, the lyrics begin as an imploration but turn to admiration of her beauty and physical eroticism – addressing her by name, repeatedly and almost obsessively. The lyrics are suggestive of homosocial intimacy and leave space for the listener to overlay meanings of homoeroticism, which many fans did.[68]

Lam's opera, set to a libretto by John Clum, is inspired by the 2006 documentary film, *For the Love of Dolly*, directed by Tai Uhlmann. It involves five characters: Dolly's assistant, written for countertenor, and two couples, two sisters, Darlene and Luanne, and a gay couple, Travis and Don. The couples are 'pilgrims', for whom an audience with Dolly is akin to a sacred rite. They have all been anticipating the moment with unhealthy levels of excitement and have attached such high expectations to the meeting that they each hope Dolly will be able to miraculously solve their problems through divine touch. The assistant points out repeatedly, 'She can touch you, but you can't touch her, OK?'[69] When Travis and Don enter the waiting room, they are too preoccupied with their respective boxes containing a home-made Dolly Parton doll to notice Darlene and Luanne. When they finally acknowledge each other, there is instantly friction with the sisters referring to the men as 'sissies'[70] and the men labelling them as 'refugees from the pageant from hell'.[71]

Travis and Don's relationship is evidently under strain, with their nervous fretting characterized by pecking staccato rhythms and unprepared, angular melodic intervals. In response to the absurd dresses the two sisters are wearing in homage to Dolly, the men unpack their dolls. They intend to show their creations to Dolly, seeking her blessing to manufacture them. Travis reveals that Dolly spoke to him in a dream, promising that the dolls would take care of them. Travis and Don met through their mutual love of Dolly; Travis was entering a drag competition as Dolly in his local gay bar, and Don was playing in a Dolly tribute band. Don explains that Travis is hoping that Dolly's presence can reintroduce the magic of the night they met back into their faltering relationship. Their house has become a shrine to Dolly memorabilia, to the point where they have one of the biggest collections in the world. Travis sings of the price they pay for their obsession, 'You could say we live with Dolly. There's not much room for us anymore. We do love her. Almost as much as we love each other.'[72] Luanne observes, 'It sounds like you've got enough problems. Those dolls aren't going to help you hold onto your man.'[73]

Obsessive collecting of objects provides a window into the psychological profile of the collector. The objects take on a sacred status, unusable in a totalitarian sense, and considered extraordinary. Through the goal of completion and perfection of the collection, individuals project the completion status onto an aspect of their own lives which remains unfulfilled. Collectors often aim to upgrade the collection, reflecting an ideal that only the best will do, and that a complete, unimpaired collection will immortalize them. Collections require purposeful acquisition and retention, unveiling identity traits that are sometimes gendered. Stereotypically, collectors who identify as masculine tend to be drawn historically to collect animal and insect parts, saleable junk, tobacco souvenirs, objects of war, hunting or fishing, game objects (e.g. marbles, tops, kites) and miscellaneous repair and maintenance objects (e.g. nails, oilcans, padlocks).[74] The use of collections allows us to explicate the multiple images that attach to femininity and masculinity. Dolls can be used to mediate three types of gendered images: real-life images, worldly images and otherworldly images. Real-life images are those that exist or previously existed in the everyday life of the collector. Worldly images are expressed directly in the objects in the collection. Otherworldly images are the mythic characters evoked by the collection. The collection can therefore be used to correlate a personal identity through subjective myth.[75]

As the two sisters depart for their highly anticipated meeting with Dolly, the two men consider what life would mean if they had to sell their collection for any reason. Travis sings, 'We'd be getting rid of our life together',[76] to which Don responds by considering the impact of sharing what they had collected together as reducing its meaning, making it seem 'a little crazy'.[77] Travis then catches himself in a slip of the tongue which reveals the level of his obsession, 'But she is us . . . I mean, She is going to see how much we love her.'[78] The divergent meanings placed on the collection seem to be the cause of the growing rift between them when Travis reveals, 'That stuff holds me together. Dolly's songs held my Mama together when my daddy left . . . when father left . . . until Mama.'[79] The trauma that Travis experienced with the loss of his parents has manifested in a mother substitution in the dolls, whereas for Don, the dolls represented a shared passion. The exchange inevitably turns to real children, revealing yet another point of friction.

The meeting with Dolly brings enormous disillusion, and the impossible expectations are shattered when Dolly's perfunctory interest in the dolls instantly destroys Travis' hopes and dreams. Travis sings:

I look at her,
Hoping for a sign,
But this is not the Dolly I prayed to,
The Dolly who saved me.
This is someone else,
And she can't help me.
I'm on my own.
I run out,
Down the hall,
Out the door.
I get sick,
Like I did as a kid.
Scared, alone,
The sissy no one liked.[80]

With the meeting with Dolly ending in disaster, so too does their relationship, and the two men part company. By contrast, the two sisters experienced something of a happy ending, despite the exchange with Dolly also failing to deliver the expected miracles. The opera's score and libretto oscillate between tension and release, dark despair and levity, despondent sobriety and kitsch, reflected in the two opposing outcomes for the pairs of protagonists. This pendulum swing provides a transparent adherence to the central tenet of metamodernism. Fluctuating between the sunny optimism of the modernist movement and the cynicism of the postmodern era, metamodernism can be situated 'epistemologically with (post) modernism, ontologically between (post) modernism, and historically beyond (post) modernism'.[81] The central tenet of metamodernism is that faith, trust, dialogue and sincerity can coexist and limit the effects of postmodern irony and detachment.[82] This concurrent dichotomy is borne out in the material constructed for the two individuals in each relationship, and the juxtaposition of both viewpoints mirrored by the other couple forms the basis of the narrative's tension.

Dolly does not present on stage in any way during the opera and is only referred to by the five characters. In a case of life-imitating art, Lam revealed in a conversation that Parton has to date not expressed interest in the opera. Nevertheless, she has maintained a positive view of the queer community throughout her career, belying the heteronormative and often bigoted behaviours that dominated the country music scene. She welcomed drag queens, underwent plastic surgery and embraced the disco scene at Studio 54 with her hit, *Baby I'm Burnin'* (1978). Tabloids were left red-faced when they attempted to expose the story of her sharing a Central Park apartment with her manager. She politely explained, 'He's not interested in any woman.'[83] Parton also embraced her Beverly Hills neighbours, stating, 'Mostly it's all gay up and down this street, and you know, they're just gentle, sweet, sensitive people. They never bother me. They want to protect me. They're honored that I'm here, and I am honored that they're here. It's a sweet feeling.'[84]

Heartbreak Express shines a spotlight on a rarely explored aspect of queerness – the unadulterated fanaticism of the gay icon in the extreme form of unhinged memorabilia collecting. There are more than a few young queers who have lip-synced the hits of their favoured diva and adorned their bedroom walls with their images. The shared enjoyment of celebrity creativity can provide a welcome escape, but the deep-rooted cause of resulting obsessions has yet to be fully understood, particularly when they frequently manifest prior to most individuals' understanding of their sexual orientation. To better understand queer identity, we can look to the female icons we so habitually idolize.

THREE WAY, ROBERT PATERSON

The suggestive title of Robert Patterson's 2016 opera *Three Way* is provocatively misleading. Rather than it portraying a sexual relationship involving three people, it refers to the structure of the work as it presents three distinct narratives. The innuendo that the opera is somehow related to explorations of taboo sexual practices is, however, absolutely pertinent. Paterson pointedly asserts that this is not a queer opera, which brings into question its inclusion in a book called *Queer Opera*. Unlike the cheeky *double entendre* of the title, in this case Paterson's point is poignant. Although there are representations of a wide variety of sexual proclivities, including some which could easily be categorized as queer, it is the notion of categorization itself that is being rejected. Paterson explains, 'We believe sexuality is a fluid and mysterious energy central to everyone's identity. Our characters search for greater authenticity, intensity and communion.'[85] The notion of assimilation is represented through characters who deny themselves sexual authenticity by internal and deeply embedded instincts to conform sexually.

Such thoughtful consideration to adopt a non-conforming stance on sexual categorization reflects the growing acceptance of sexual and gender fluidity as an established sociological theory. Michel Foucault posited in his book *The Archaeology of Knowledge* (1969) that knowledge is not universal, irrefutable and objective but rather forms out of a historically positioned set of codified thinking processes that defines a particular epoch. This shared, interdisciplinary thought processes allow for new knowledge to emerge as a result of the change in fundamental thinking of the era, which Foucault referred to as '*epistemes*'. The rules that govern these '*epistemes*' operate subconsciously but guide our thinking.[86] The multimodal composition of queerness and the possibility of reorienting our perceptions of gender and sexuality are defining characteristics of the postmodern age. We are able to reconsider the rigid characterizations of sexuality because of our ability to critique the big ideas of the modernist era.

The three one-act operas that form *Three Way* are entitled *The Companion*, *Safe Word* and *Masquerade*. In *The Companion*, a futuristic view of object sexuality is explored through Maya, who lives with her android lover named Joe. Joe has been programmed to interact as humanly as possible, but despite his pleasing aesthetics and impressive capabilities, Maya feels that something is missing, as Joe's consent or non-consent to sexual activity is assumed. She arranges for a technician to install new experimental software. The technician Dax is attracted to Maya, but Maya explains that she is only interested in the concept of a 'perfect man' which only an artificial companion can provide. Dax manipulates Joe to behave poorly, which upsets Maya. Dax explains that he is leaving Maya to have a relationship with another android who lives up the street but before leaving points out that Maya and Dax have indicated through their biochemical fluctuations that they are in love. Object sexuality was also explored in Kate Whitley's opera *Unknown Position* (2011).

For *Safe Word*, we enter the dungeon of a professional dominatrix. When Mistress Salome and the client first meet, it is because the regular Domme is sick. The client displays all of the typical characteristics of a privileged, cis-male businessman. He retreats to the changing room to adopt his fetish for dressing up as a young girl and reappears in the guise of 'Pollie Puddlepanties', who is spying on an opera diva. The Domme begins her session of degradation and punishment until the client expresses a need for something different. He wishes to subvert the role play and to dominate her instead. When she refuses, the ensuing argument turns physical, and with Mistress Salome strangling the client with a chain, he utters the safe word before collapsing. When he surprisingly sits up, refusing the tip that she left on his lifeless body, it becomes clear that it was *she* who paid for the session, to experience her fetish for being a dominatrix who murders a dangerous client. The traditional concepts of masculine and feminine behaviour, in particular power inequality, are subverted and then challenged and allow for a variety of readings depending on the epistemological position of the observer.

In the third opera, *Masquerade*, the action unfolds in a country mansion, where a dinner party and holiday celebration are taking place. The guests were invited to the gathering by 'Pleasure Pilgrims', who are an online community of sensualists and hedonists. Four couples attend this particular evening, masked and willing to explore the boundaries of erotic expression. Jillian and Bruce DeBridge are the hosts of 'Pleasure Pilgrims' and owners of the mansion. Marcus and Jessie are a married straight couple in their thirties, hoping to reinvigorate their waning sex lives, Connie and Larry are experienced swingers and Kyle and Tyler are a genderqueer couple who do not self-identify as transgender. Kyle and Tyler's arrival sparks tension with Larry amidst greetings and casual sexual innuendo, such as Larry's quip, 'I'm wild! *Rrrraoow!* But you can pet me.'[87] The guests go off to change and prepare for the evening and upon re-entering the scene sing of their hopes for the evening's outcomes. A group encounter is expressed musically with all characters offstage, suggestive of several climaxes. At the end of the evening, each character reflects on their encounters and departs satisfied and happy with the experience. The masquerade symbolizes the secret thoughts that each of us hide, and the anonymity that the mask brings provides opportunity for transformation.

Paterson and librettist, David Cote, set out to create postgendered, pansexual characters in Kyle and Tyler, in order to represent the modern world. Their treatment in the narrative allows them to participate sexually, in the same way that couples identifying as heterosexual do, free of judgement or mockery. The moments of tension that Kyle and Tyler experience provide instants of levity rather than any focused attention of moral issues and are resolved with Larry's consensual encounter with Kyle. There are apparent connections to

Shakespeare's *A Midsummer Night's Dream*, both in terms of the theme of transformation, albeit in this case an orgy rather than sleep, and in terms of characters. Larry's boisterousness matches the dim but harmless Bottom, and the androgyny that is so often manifest in Puck can be linked with Kyle. Jessie and Marcus could easily be Hermia and Demetrius, and Jillian and Bruce, the benign puppet masters who oversee the action, could be Titania and Oberon.[88]

Tyler sings, 'We're gender non-conforming',[89] followed by Kyle who explains, 'I'm biologically male but reject cis-male social codes.'[90] This prompts a discussion with Larry to help him understand that cis-male does not mean 'sissy'. As the explanation continues, including the epistemology of the term 'cis', Larry's ignorance creates space for the lesson in gender identity terminology. He clings to his understanding of binary labels by asking them, 'So, ya'll are gay?'[91] Although operatic traditions of gender bending are almost as old as opera itself, this is likely the first self-identification of gender fluidity and instruction on associative terminology in an operatic context. Tyler later sings, 'Some of us believe fences should come down',[92] supported by Kyle, 'Social attitudes have evolved. Gender barriers dissolved',[93] followed by Kyle once more, 'And the revolution happened in our beds.'[94] They then sing together, 'Male or female, it's all in flux: You are whatever you construct. Become the creature you imagine in your heads.'[95]

Kyle is alone and sings the aria 'Why so shy?'[96] In it, notions of sexual acts being natural physical expressions that have been subjugated into acts of shame through 'laws and lies'.[97] The message is transparently clear that the applications of labels with their associating moral judgements result in a loss of freedom. Kyle sings of a utopian view of a society that does not care who or how they love but is nevertheless unable to participate in the organized sexual activity and is frustrated. Equally frustrated is Larry, whose seeming inability to perform sexually, despite being with two attractive women, makes him despondent. His aria, 'Not my night'[98] is personal moment of sexual dysfunction but is also a commentary on the heteronormative society that he reflects. Earlier he sang, 'Call me old-fashioned, but I don't want any weird stuff tonight.'[99] His refusal to divert from the strict sexual codes that help him make sense of his world acts as a barrier to transformation and pleasure. The first text to be sung homophonically by the ensemble is the word 'Transform!',[100] immediately prior to the 'Shadowy orgy' interlude. Almost as a call to arms, the cast disappear into the safety of darkness and only emerge after successful sexual liaisons. In order for each person to achieve fulfilment, transformation needed to take place, and for each character, the transformation related to different behaviours.

Cote's satirical libretto utilizes a scheme of slightly clumsy rhyming couplets which contribute to the light-heartedness of the narrative. None of the characters throughout the three one-act operas takes themselves to a degree of seriousness where humour is absent. The lack of discernible villain in the narrative is a notable feature and a challenge for any creative team. Another common thread between the three stories is the notion of characters not being how they initially appear, forcing the observer to question assumptions and how they are made. Paterson's score is similarly insouciant and entertaining, clothed in comfortable diatonicism and utilizing pleasing, singable phrases. The arias are formed like discrete songs and the conversational, connecting recitatives are uncomplicated. There is a diversity of musical styles throughout the work, highlighting the humour in the text, and with sudden changes, just as the characters unexpectedly change.

Paterson and Cote have created a piece which contributes to the discourse of sexual and gender identity. None of the sexual practices are themselves modern. Whether the depictions of eroticism are offensive or not depends on the values of the observer and informed by the society in which they live. As Foucault attests, sex has not changed, but societal attitudes to it are in a constant state of flux. He noted the change of attitude in the late Victorian period:

> Sexuality was carefully confined; it moved into the home. The conjugal family took custody of it and absorbed it into the serious function of reproduction. On the subject of sex, silence became the rule. The legitimate and procreative couple laid down the law. The couple imposed itself as model, reinforced the norm, safeguarded the truth, and reserved the right to speak while retaining the principle of secrecy.[101]

Furthering such discourse in the form of an opera, with all of the associations of class, intellectualism and culture, helps us to examine the messages in a more subjective way than perhaps might be achieved through popular culture. Queerness in televised media can be derided immediately and vocally, whereas in the theatre, the audience is expected to wait quietly in their seat and voice opinions only at the designated time and in earshot of those who may disagree. Time for reflection is mandated through necessity, and rational, open-minded dialogue is encouraged. The likelihood is that even queer audience members can have much to learn about non-conforming, gender-fluid, pansexuality. There are many Larrys who still need things to be carefully explained so that they too can transform themselves and embrace freedom.

NOTES

1. Ruthann Robson, 'Assimilation, marriage, and lesbian liberation', *Temple Law Review* 75 (2002): 709.

2. Kenji Yoshino, 'Covering', *Yale Law Journal* 111, no. 4 (2001): 769.

3. Douglas C. Haldeman, 'Gay rights, patient rights: The implications of sexual orientation conversion therapy', *Professional Psychology: Research and Practice* 33, no. 3 (2002): 260.

4. Alberto Ginastera and Manuel Mujica Láinez, *Bomarzo Op. 34: Opera in 2 Acts and 15 Scenes* [full score] (Aldwych, London: Boosey & Hawkes, 1966–1967), 20.

5. Ginastera and Láinez, *Bomarzo*, 22.

6. Ginastera and Láinez, *Bomarzo*, 33.

7. Ginastera and Láinez, *Bomarzo*, 54.

8. Ginastera and Láinez, *Bomarzo*, 58.

9. Ginastera and Láinez, *Bomarzo*, 37.

10. Ginastera and Láinez, *Bomarzo*, 37.

11. Alberto Ginastera and Mujica Láinez, 'Origins of an Opera', joint lecture, reprinted in the *Central Opera Service Bulletin* 9, no. 5 (1967): 10–13.

12. The garden of sixteenth-century Duke Orsini, with its collection of stone monsters, can still be seen in the village of Bomarzo, north of Rome.

13. Ginastera and Láinez, *Bomarzo*, 49–51.

14. Ginastera and Láinez, *Bomarzo*, 53–54.

15. Pola Suarez Urtubey, 'Ginastera's "Bomarzo"', *Tempo* 84 (1968): 14–21.

16. Dario Prieto, '"Bomarzo": 50 years after the scandal', *Elmundo*, 12 April 2017, accessed 3 August 2021, https://www.elmundo.es/cultura/teatro/2017/04/12 /58ed6937ca4741494a8b45f9.html.

17. Ruth Sara Longobardi, 'Reading between the lines: An approach to the musical and sexual ambiguities of death in Venice', *Journal of Musicology* 22, no. 3 (2005): 327–364.

18. Benjamin Britten and Myfanwy Piper, *Death in Venice, An Opera in Two Acts, Op. 88* [full score] (London: Faber Music Limited, 1979), 11.

19. Britten and Piper, *Death in Venice*, 11–12.

20. Britten and Piper, *Death in Venice*, 12.

21. Britten and Piper, *Death in Venice*, 84.

22. Thomas Mann, *Death in Venice, Tonio Krőger, and Other Writings* (New York, NY: The Continuum Publishing Company, 2003), 130.

23. Britten and Piper, *Death in Venice*, 119–123.

24. Clifford Hindley, 'Contemplation and reality: A study in Britten's "death in Venice"', *Music & Letters* 71, no. 4 (1990): 511–523.

25. Britten and Piper, *Death in Venice*, 158.

26. Britten and Piper, *Death in Venice*, 177.

27. Britten and Piper, *Death in Venice*, 153.

28. Britten and Piper, *Death in Venice*, 172–173.

29. The exercise book (Envelope 1 in the Aldeburgh archive). The passage quoted is on page 17.

30. Sandra Corse and Larry Corse, 'Britten's "death in Venice": Literary and musical structures', *The Musical Quarterly* 73, no. 3 (1989): 344–363.

31. Donald Mitchell and Richard Wagner, eds., *Benjamin Britten: Death in Venice* (Cambridge: Cambridge University Press, 1987).

32. Christopher Chowrimootoo, 'Bourgeois opera: "Death in Venice" and the aesthetics of sublimation', *Cambridge Opera Journal* (2010): 175–216.

33. Brooke W. McKeever, 'Public relations and public health: The importance of leadership and other lessons learned from "Understanding AIDS" in the 1980s', *Public Relations Review* 47, no. 1 (2021): 102007.

34. Mari Yoshihara, 'A quiet place in a not-so-quiet nation', in *Leonard Bernstein and Washington, DC*, NED – New edition, eds. Daniel Abraham, Alicia Kopfstein-Penk, and Andrew H. Weaver (Woodbridge: Boydell & Brewer, University of Rochester Press, 2020), 267–294: 271. Quoted in 'Benton for Mayor' letter, n.d., box 804, folder 3, Amberson Business Papers, Leonard Bernstein Collection, Library of Congress.

35. Yoshihara, 'A quiet place in a not-so-quiet nation', 271.

36. Leonard Bernstein and Stephen Wadsworth, *A Quiet Place: An Opera in Three Acts* [Full score] (New York: Jalni Publications, Boosey & Hawkes, 1983), 122.

37. Bernstein and Wadsworth, *A Quiet Place*, 122.

38. Bernstein and Wadsworth, *A Quiet Place*, 123.

39. Bernstein and Wadsworth, *A Quiet Place*, 123.

40. Bernstein and Wadsworth, *A Quiet Place*, 400.

41. Bernstein and Wadsworth, *A Quiet Place*, 170.

42. Bernstein and Wadsworth, *A Quiet Place*, 412.

43. Bernstein and Wadsworth, *A Quiet Place*, 173–174.

44. Bernstein and Wadsworth, *A Quiet Place*, 172.

45. Bernstein and Wadsworth, *A Quiet Place*, 183.

46. Bernstein and Wadsworth, *A Quiet Place*, 495.

47. Bernstein and Wadsworth, *A Quiet Place*, 307–308.

48. Tuck Lon, 'The frenzy of "a quiet place"', *The Washington Post*, 1983, C1.

49. Paul R. Laird, 'Bernstein's monument to American Diversity', in *Leonard Bernstein and Washington, DC*, NED – New edition, eds. Daniel Abraham, Alicia Kopfstein-Penk, and Andrew H. Weaver (Woodbridge: Boydell & Brewer, University of Rochester Press, 2020), 209–231.

50. Petra L. Doan and Harrison Higgins, 'The demise of queer space? Resurgent gentrification and the assimilation of LGBT neighborhoods', *Journal of Planning Education and Research* 31, no. 1 (2011): 6–25.

51. Robson, 'Assimilation, marriage, and lesbian liberation', 709–820.

52. Daniel Harris, *The Rise and Fall of Gay Culture* (New York: Hyperion Books, 1997), 4.

53. Griffin Candey, Interview with Andrew Sutherland, 23 July 2021.

54. Hillary LaBonte, 'Analyzing gender inequality in contemporary opera' (PhD diss., Bowling Green State University, 2019).

55. Anke Charton, 'Voicing challenge: Trans* singers and the performance of vocal gender', in *Under Construction: Performing Critical Identity*, ed. Marie-Anne Kohl (Basel, Switzerland: MDPI, 2021), 107–126.

56. Candey, Interview with Andrew Sutherland.

57. Griffin Candey, *Sweets by Kate* [Piano/vocal score] (Unpublished, 2016), 141.

58. Candey, *Sweets by Kate*, 148.

59. Candey, Interview with Andrew Sutherland.

60. Candey, *Sweets by Kate*, 170.

61. Megan Ihnen, 'Talking "Sweets by Kate": "You don't need anyone's permission"', *Sybaritic Singer*, 12 July 2017, accessed 19 July 2021, https://sybariticsinger.com/2017/07/12/sweetsbykate/.

62. Georges-Claude Guilbert, *Gay Icons: The (Mostly) Female Entertainers Gay Men Love* (Jefferson, NC: McFarland, 2018).

63. Simon Gage, Lisa Richards, and Howard Wilmot, *Queer: The Ultimate User's Guide* (London: MQ Publications, 2002), 24.

64. Richard Goldstein, 'My country music problem—and yours', *Mademoiselle* 77, no. 2 (June 1973): 114.

65. Nadine Hubbs, '"Jolene," genre, and the everyday homoerotics of country music: Dolly Parton's loving address of the other woman', *Women and Music: A Journal of Gender and Culture* 19, no. 1 (2015): 71–76.

66. Gage et al., *Queer: The Ultimate User's Guide*, 24.

67. Deborah Evans Price, 'Dolly Parton Q&A: The country legend on Nashville and why she supports her gay fans', *Billboard 126*, no. 36, 1 November 2014, accessed 14 October 2021, Dolly Parton Talks Supporting Gay Fans | Billboard – Billboard.

68. Maxine L. Grossman, 'Jesus, mama, and the constraints of salvific love in contemporary country music', *Journal of the American Academy of Religion* 70, no. 1 (2002): 83–115.

69. George Lam and John Clum, *Heartbreak Express: Chamber Opera in One Act* [Full score] (Unpublished, 2015), 3.

70. Lam and Clum, *Heartbreak Express*, 20.

71. Lam and Clum, *Heartbreak Express*, 20.

72. Lam and Clum, *Heartbreak Express*, 47.

73. Lam and Clum, *Heartbreak Express*, 50–51.

74. Paul A. Witty and Harvey C. Lehman, 'Sex differences: Collecting interests', *Journal of Educational Psychology* 22, no. 3 (1931): 221.

75. Russell W. Belk and Melanie Wallendorf, 'Of mice and men: Gender identity in collecting', in *Interpreting Objects and Collections*, ed. Susan M. Pearce (Milton Park: Routledge, 2012), 252–265.

76. Lam and Clum, *Heartbreak Express*, 55.

77. Lam and Clum, *Heartbreak Express*, 56.

78. Lam and Clum, *Heartbreak Express*, 56.

79. Lam and Clum, *Heartbreak Express*, 57–59.

80. Lam and Clum, *Heartbreak Express*, 101–102.

81. Timotheus Vermeulen and Robin Van Den Akker, 'Notes on metamodernism', *Journal of Aesthetics & Culture* 2, no. 1 (2010): 5677: 2, 1–14.

82. Tawfiq Yousef, 'Modernism, postmodernism, and metamodernism: A critique', *International Journal of Language and Literature* 5, no. 1 (2017): 33–43.

83. Eric Weisbard, 'Duets with modernity: Dolly Parton and country', in *Top 40 Democracy: The Rival Mainstreams of American Music* (Chicago: University of Chicago Press, 2014), 70–111: 97.

84. Weisbard, 'Duets with Modernity', 108.

85. Robert Paterson and David Cote, 'Three way and the LGBTQ community', *Robert Paterson: Composer*, June 2020, accessed 12 December 2021, https://robert-paterson.com/three-way-and-the-lgbtq-community.

86. Michel Foucault, *Archaeology of Knowledge*, trans. A. M. Sheridan Smith (London & New York: Routledge, 2013).

87. Robert Paterson and David Cote, *Three Way: A Trio of One-Act Operas* [Piano/vocal score] (Brooklyn, NY: Bill Holab Music, 2014), 148.

88. Arlo McKinnon, 'Three way', *Opera News Magazine*, September 2017 – Vol. 82, no. 3.

89. Paterson and Cote, *Three Way*, 157.

90. Paterson and Cote, *Three Way*, 157.

91. Paterson and Cote, *Three Way*, 160.

92. Paterson and Cote, *Three Way*, 164.

93. Paterson and Cote, *Three Way*, 164.

94. Paterson and Cote, *Three Way*, 164.

95. Paterson and Cote, *Three Way*, 164–165.

96. Paterson and Cote, *Three Way*, 199.

97. Paterson and Cote, *Three Way*, 201.

98. Paterson and Cote, *Three Way*, 220.

99. Paterson and Cote, *Three Way*, 188.

100. Paterson and Cote, *Three Way*, 246.

101. Michel Foucault, *The History of Sexuality: 1: The Will to Knowledge*, trans. Robert Hurley (London: Penguin, 2019), i.

Chapter 6

Killing Queers

On the night of 12 June 2016, Pulse Nightclub in Orlando, Florida, was hosting a Latin night. Many of the 320 patrons were Latino and gay and ordering their last drinks at around 2:00 am. When twenty-nine-year-old Omar Mateen entered the club to begin a three-hour ordeal in which forty-nine people would be shot and killed directly or by ricochets, no one was aware of the assailant's struggles with his own same-sex desires.[1] The massacre prompted an international outpouring of grief for the victims and their families and the perfunctory 'thoughts and prayers' statements from the political arena. Mateen had perpetrated the atrocity inside a space which the queer community reasonably assumed was a safe space. Questions over the motivations of such horror allow an exploration into the underlining causation of queer homicides which have shown an increased trend in recent years. The Pulse massacre may be the single-most deadly event against the US queer community; however, the vigilante anti-queer perpetrators of homophobic violence have been terrorizing the queer population in far greater numbers for many years. In 2017, the National Coalition of Anti-Violence Programs (NCAVP) registered the greatest number of anti-queer homicides since official recording of the statistics began twenty years earlier.[2]

A comprehensive, international, statistical evaluation of trends in attacks against LGBTQ+ communities is currently impossible as official statistics in many countries are inadequate and rare. Even when satisfactory systems for monitoring, recording and reporting homophobic hate crimes are in place, victims are often hesitant to come forward, and motives for violence are not always properly understood by law enforcement officials. However, there has been extensive research in recent years, examining the phenomenon of homophobic hate crimes, which has allowed greater insight into the motivations for extreme violence. Gruenewald's 2012 study revealed that violence

189

against sexual minorities was often especially brutal, frequently consisted of bashings rather than firearms and served as a warning to other gender non-conformists that their difference is not tolerated.[3]

Various attempts to categorize homophobic homicides have been undertaken, and criminologists suggest that thrill-seeking, retaliation, the impulse to defend territory and the conviction that certain minority groups should be eliminated form the key groupings. Another categorization from Gruenewald and Kelly considered two broadly defined categories: predatory homicide and responsive homicide. The former consists of premeditated, orchestrated attacks prior to encountering the victim, which send an ominous warning to the wider queer community. Perpetrators either stalk their victims or lure them into a scenario in which the violent act can be carried out. Responsive homicide occurs in response to a perceived insult, an unwanted sexual advance or, in infrequent cases, instances of mistaken gender identity involving transgender individuals.[4]

In some societies, the murder of an LGBTQ+ person is labelled an honour killing, giving the perpetrator a moral obligation for the act and highlighting the potency of patriarchal structures. Ideologically motivated murders allow the offender to conserve a sense of dominance within the family and society.[5] Although in the West, legislation such as the Matthew Shepard Act (2009) provides a sense of protection, statistically, homophobic hate crimes tend to increase following any kind of progressive advance for the queer community. Societies which allow honour killings to maintain an agenda of patriarchal dominance and those that wish to protect its queer citizens both witness unusually brutal attacks levelled at those who represent minority sexual groups.

Operas in which murder forms an important part of the narrative are not rare and include *Don Giovanni* (Wolfgang Amadeus Mozart, 1787), *Lucrezia Borgia* (Gaetano Donizetti, 1833), *Carmen* (Bizet, 1875), *Lakmé* (Léo Delibes, 1883), *Madama Butterfly* (Giacomo Puccini, 1904), *Wozzeck* (Alban Berg, 1925) and *The Threepenny Opera* (Kurt Weill, 1928), among many others. However, presentation of the act of murder taking place on stage was only barely acceptable from the late nineteenth century. In Strauss' *Elektra*, the title character is symbolically murdered in the intense conclusion of the score following her murderous rampage of revenge on her father. In Berg's *Lulu*, the Countess Geschwitz is despatched by Jack the Ripper as he exits his crime scene. Nico Muhly explores a tragic real-life murder-suicide involving two young boys involved in a queer cyber relationship. The heartbreaking murder of Matthew Shepard and subsequent legislation attempts are given operatic treatment by Michael W. Ross in *Not in My Town*. In Kevin March's *Les Feluettes*, the perpetrator is forced to relive the events he put in motion that led up to the death of one man and the incarceration of his lover. George Benjamin gives an account of the deposition and murders of King Edward II and his lover, Piers Gaveston, in *Lessons in Love and Violence*. Another murdered political figure is that of Harvey Milk in Stewart Wallace's opera, and the final murder, although contended by some as suicide, is in Justine F. Chen's *The Life and Death(s) of Alan Turing*. These were not the only queer deaths in operas, and several others are discussed in other chapters, but they provide a variety of situations in which representations of queerness are brutally expunged.

ELEKTRA, RICHARD STRAUSS

One way to assess the degree to which a fictional work represents women is by use of the Bechdel Test. The test first appeared in 1985 in Alison Bechdel's comic strip, *Dykes to Watch Out For*. The strip was entitled 'The Rule' and sets out three provisions for satisfying requirements for gender representation:

1. The movie has to have at least two women in it,
2. who talk to each other,
3. about something other than a man.

A requirement that the two characters be named is sometimes included. Although this test lacks rigour by providing opportunity for anti-feminist work to be assessed positively, when applied to Strauss' opera, *Elektra* (1909), all requirements are unquestionably met. It is not until the second half of the one-act opera that a man's voice is heard, and even then, the opera remains dominated by female characters controlling the narrative. *Elektra* followed soon after *Salome* (see chapter 2), and the two works are often considered as companion pieces, owing to the many shared features, not least of which is the eroticization of the leading female character.

Elektra (or Electra) is represented in several plays by different authors, including Aeschylus, Sophocles and two separate plays by Euripides. In the version by Aeschylus, Orestes and Electra arranged for Orestes, with the help of his lover, Pylades, to enact revenge on Clytemnestra and Aegisthus for the murder of King Agamemnon. In Euripides' account, *Iphigenia in Taurus* (see chapter 1), Agamemnon had agreed to sacrifice his daughter, Iphigeneia, for safe passage of his ships to the Trojan war. Orestes murders Clytemnestra and is sent to Tauris as punishment for matricide. Iphigeneia was rescued at the last moment by the goddess Artemis and taken to Tauris on the Black Sea, and there she was reunited with Orestes and Pylades. The three manage to escape their own sacrifice and return to Mycenae, where Electra marries Pylades.

The version by playwright, novelist, essayist, librettist and poet Hugo von Hofmannsthal (1874–1929) came in the form of a drama, released in 1903.

He was then approached by his friend Richard Strauss to reconceive the text as a libretto for an opera. The text was modified with the introduction of new lines at two pivotal moments. Hofmannsthal re-read Sophocles' version of *Electra* in 1901, a period of intense interest in Greek mythology which saw a series of incomplete projects such as *Leda and the Swan, Zeus and Semele, Gyges and his ring* and *Pentheus and Dionysus*.[6]

Following the murder of her father, Elektra is driven by unquenchable rage and desire for revenge. She is the archetypal 'hysterical' woman, although Hofmannsthal rejected the term in preference for *Besessenheit* (obsession). He concurred with Freud that staging a hysterical attack was dramatically problematic. Both Hofmannsthal and Strauss would have been familiar with the recent development of psychoanalysis that accompanied the term 'hysteria', which was singularly applied to female behaviour, and a malady to which women were believed to be particularly susceptible. Dating back to a description of the term found in the Kahun Papyrus (1900 BC), it was then used by Plato in *Timaeus*, in which he wrote that when the uterus is not joined with the male, giving rise to new birth, the woman becomes depressed. This view was shared by Aristotle and Hippocrates. Hippocrates felt the best cure for hysteria was regular sex. Treatments in the Victorian era included bleeding, a course of ice-water injections into the rectum, insertion of ice into the vagina, leeching of the labia and cervix, circumcision and normal ovaritomy to trigger artificial menopause.[7] Freud subverted the prevailing thinking and considered hysteria to be the result of a lack of libidinal evolution, a repression of erotic impulses, which could result in failure to conceive.[8]

Feminism and hysteria were inexorably linked in discourse for around half a century. Popular theorists enjoyed dismissing feminists as 'hysterical hermaphrodites' and their male sympathizers as 'castrated collaborators in the genocide of the race'.[9] Hysterical behaviour manifests in several of the female characters in *Elektra*, in particular Elektra and Klytämnestra, and Hofmannsthal's attitudes towards women can be seen in his development of their characters. In Sophocles' version, Clytemnestra justifies Agamemnon's murder with the defence that he was prepared to sacrifice his daughter, Iphigenia. Hofmannsthal removes this point, and Klytämnestra is instead compelled by wanton lust.

Just as Salome had done, Elektra challenged civilized decorum with heightened sexual proclivity. She has abandoned the heteronormative expectations placed on a woman and redirected her impulses towards her sister and then later, her brother. Reviewers of the premiere season were quick to apply the term 'lesbian' to Elektra's scene with Iphigenia, and several observers noted her 'libidinal' fixation with her father. The contrivance that generated these charges of deviant behaviour was certainly calculated. The long, verbal seduction of her sister is a recruitment attempt for the act of matricide. The language is sexually charged and erotic, and her demeanour is quite changed compared to interactions with her mother and brother. When engaging with Klytämnestra, she is strong and incisive, with her brother, she is warm and soft, but with Chrysothemis, she uses every seductive weapon in her arsenal. Observers of Freud would connect the father fixation of Elektra with this displaced sexuality; her hysterical bloodlust obsession has expunged any healthy expression of sexuality, and so she attempts to corrupt her chaste sister and to satisfy her in more than one way.[10]

In Hofmannsthal's 1903 play script, Elektra's propositions to Chrysothemis are unwelcome, and she repeatedly pleads with her to let her go. As well as physically enfolding her, Elektra showers praise on her sister's beauty, which can only be interpreted as uncomfortable predation. The scene was so undeniable in its erotic intent that several critics acknowledged the '*lesbisches Verhältnis*' (lesbian relationship). Elektra begins her seduction:

Du! Du! Denn di bist stark!	You! You! Because you are strong!
Wie stark du bist!	How strong you are!
Dich haben die jungfräulichen Nächte stark gemacht.	The virgin nights made you strong.
Überall ist so viel Kraft in dir!	There is so much power in you everywhere!
Sehnen hast du wie ein Füllen,	You have sinews like a colt,
Schlank sind deine Füße.	Your feet are slim.
Wie schlank und biegsam –	How slim and flexible –
Leicht umschling ich sie, –	I easily embrace her, –
Deine Hüften sind!	Your hips are!
Du windest dich durch jeden Spalt,	You wind your way through every crack
du hebst dich durchs Fenster!	You'd get through the window!
Laß mich deine Arme Fühlen:	Let me feel your arms:
Wie kühl and stark sie sind!	How cool and strong they are!
Wie du mich abwehrst, fühl' ich, was das für Arme sind.	How you resist me, I feel what kind of arms they are.
Du könntest erdrücken, was du an dich ziehst.	You could overwhelm what you attract to yourself.
Du könntest mich, oder einem Mann in deinen Armen erstikken!	You could choke me or a man in your arms!
Überall ist so viel Kraft in dir!	There is so much power in you everywhere!
Sie strömt wie kühles, verhaltnes Wasser aus dem Fels.	It flows like cool, restrained water from the rock.
Sie flutet mit deinen Haaren auf die starken Schultern herab!	It floods down with your hair on your strong shoulders!
Ich spüre durch die Kühle deiner Haut das warme Blut hindurch, mit meiner Wange Spür' ich den Flaum auf deinen jungen Armen:	I feel the warm blood through the coolness of your skin with my cheek I feel the down on your young arms:
Du bist voller Kraft, du bist schön, du bist wie eine Frucht an der Reife Tag.[11]	You are full of strength, you are beautiful, you are like a fruit on the ripened day.

This text comes from the opening of Elektra's soliloquy. Following this section, there is even penetrative language as she continues hounding her sister, '*will ich mich rings um dich, versenken meine Wurzeln in dich und mit meinem Willen dir impfen das Blut!*'[12] (I want to be around you, sink my roots in you and with my strength of will, inoculate your blood!). As Chrysothemis attempts to free herself from Elektra's insistent embrace, she warns Elektra not to use such language in their familial home, but Elektra resumes with vigour, exclaiming that she will be 'more than a sister'[13] and that she will serve Chrysothemis '*wie deine Sklavin*'[14] (like her slave). The tradition of interpreting the scene as a seduction has remained the preferred reading of Hofmannsthal's text, and his implied reference to the incest narrative in Ovid suggests that a sexually charged encounter was anticipated.

Immediately following Elektra's sexually charged phrase, there is a triplet figure in the strings that boldly rises by an octave, providing a short fanfare motif. Strauss is indicating that the text is significant and a pivotal moment in the scene. The double meaning of the penetrative language adds to the sexualization of the aria and the forceful nature of Elektra's efforts. This is a highly erotic and purposeful moment, and the short, two-bar figure that soon follows foreshadows a positively triumphant motif to be used six years later in his *Eine Alpensinfonie* (1915). This may have been the final push to totally dominate Chrysothemis and bend her to her will.

The section in which Elektra states that she will be more than a sister, the music becomes noticeably sweeter. The harmonic underpinning remains in constant flux, but the orchestration is light and the texture sparser than in previous passages in the scene. The constantly changing mood of this scene gives a sense of Elektra trying every character trait she has to convince her sister to join her quest and satisfy her needs. The angularity of the phrase ending which rises a perfect fifth and then falls a major seventh amidst a rising, chromatic passage in the strings and lower woodwind suggests that being her sister's slave may not be something she welcomes. The phrase 'more than a sister' is resonant with a passage from Ovid's *Heroides II*, in which Canace, the daughter of Aeolus, gave birth to her brother's child. She asks, '*Cur umquam plus me, frater, quam frater amasti, et tibi, non debet quod soror esse fui?*' (Why, brother, did you love me as more than a brother, and why have I been to you what a sister ought not to be?) (Heroides XI.23f.).[15] Hofmannsthal was familiar with Ovid's play from his schooling at the *Akademisches Gymnasium* in Vienna, where Ovid was a favoured author.

Both *Salome* and *Elektra* were inspired by theatrical works by Wilde and Hofmannsthal, respectively, and Strauss had seen both during the 1902–1903 season at Berlin's *Kleines Theater*. The popularity of both plays is a reflection of shifting attitudes of the public. Nearly forty years prior to the premiere of Strauss' *Elektra*, Wagner had given theatrical rendering of incestuous relationships in *Die Walküre* (1870). The 1819 play, *The Cenci* by Percy Shelley (1792–1822), was not premiered until over a century later, in 1922, because of the incestuous content. Shelley's play mirrors the general plot of *Elektra* with several siblings conspiring to murder their father. Audiences of Sophocles would not have been shocked by stories of incest or lesbianism, but Strauss-Hofmannsthal seems to have arrived at the right time for modern audiences to find the elements palatable.

Representations of Hellenism had endured a period of sanitization. The Victorians were fascinated by the ancient Greeks, even referring to the eighteenth-century England as the 'Augustan Age', but the Grecian influence had unsanitary associations. Athenian culture was considered by many aristocratic leaders to be too immoral and given to pederasty. Hofmannsthal, however, highlighted elements of bloodlust and psychopathy with echoes of the frenzied violence in Euripides' *Bacchae* (405 BC). Critics may have found much to bemoan regarding the sexualization of the female protagonist, which inverts the prevailing Hellenic perspective, but *Elektra* contributed to a changing perspective of psychology and anthropology. The shocked audience reception of the scandalous connection between sexualized neurosis and determined matricide was not exclusive to the premiere and has persisted for many subsequent productions.

Elektra screams, '*Triff noch einmal!*' (meet once again),[16] after hearing her brother beginning his frenzied attack on Klytämnestra. Strauss struck again and again with his music, creating a score of such force as to reach a point of no return.[17] This was not a statement of contempt for society but of anger – a progressive opera of supreme tension, uncompromising focus and musical unity, with a shattering climax giving platform for the great dramatic divas in opera. Ultimately, Elektra dies following the murder of her father, and the opera concludes with the removal of the perpetrator of queerness. It is one thing to represent queerness in opera but quite another to allow it to live on after the curtain has fallen. Strauss-Hofmannsthal provided a fresh look at the meaning of feminism in a time of constant critical reflection, and their depiction of queerness would inspire many more operatic liaisons.

LULU, ALBAN BERG

Alban Berg's second opera, *Lulu*, joined the catalogue of incomplete works in 1935 when the composer died from blood poisoning brought about by an insect bite. He had completed Act I and II, but Act III existed only in short score with the exception of the first 236 bars and some interludes. Berg's wife, Helene, forbad the completion of the orchestration; however, a clandestine version was realized by fellow Austrian composer, Friedrich Cerha (b. 1926), and the completed opera premiered in Paris in 1979. The libretto was adapted by Berg from a cycle of two plays by Frank Wedekind (1864–1918): *Erdgeist* (Earth Spirit, 1895) and *Die Buchse der Pandora* (Pandora's Box, 1904).

The title character is introduced during the prologue by a circus animal tamer. He entices his audience by itemizing his list of exotic creatures for our viewing curiosity. Each animal is a representation of one of the major characters in the story, but he saves his *pièce de résistance* until last, when he reveals Lulu, likening her to a beast. He prepares us to meet a dangerous animal in the form of a woman before leaving the stage. His prophetic words do not take long to prove pertinent. To suggest that Lulu is a complex character is an understatement. She is adored for her beauty by almost the entire cast who seek to claim her for their own and who pay for their association with their lives.

It is unclear why Lulu is motivated to manufacture such a wave of death. She represents the archetypal *femme fatale*, whose sinister impulses are beyond her control. The male characters who seek to possess her, as one possesses a rare and beautiful object, do so misogynistically. Lulu is an erotic fantasy, epitomizing the idea that a *femme fatale* is 'not the subject of feminism but a symptom of male fears about feminism'.[18] Although Lulu has been seen by many as an unfortunate and weak woman who gives herself to the male patriarchy, more recent interpretations have emerged. She can be seen as having feminist agency, resisting the barrage of suitors and embracing her sexuality. The violence that radiates from her may be a response to a society which has abused her for her eroticism. She seeks something in each of her lovers, and this fruitless pursuit represents the damaging pattern of swathes of gay men, searching for intimacy in all the wrong places.

Just as Lulu symbolizes emancipation, so too does Countess Geschwitz. Appearing in '*in einem sehr männlich anmutenden Kostüm*'[19] (in a very mannish outfit), she makes little attempt to disguise her desire for Lulu. The suffragette movement in the Weimar Republic was born in 1918 and women voted in Germany's first democratic elections in January 1919. The law was, however, still open to interpretation, and with women's suffrage under restriction by the emerging Nazi Party, the underground suffrage movement in the Weimar Republic continued. Countess Geschwitz represents this movement both in her actions and motivations and her chosen attire.

Geschwitz first appears in Act I, scene ii. Her opening phrase is addressed to Lulu, '*Sie glauben nicht, wie ich mich darauf freue, Sie auf unserm Künstlerinnenball zu seh'n*'[20] (You don't believe how I look forward to seeing you at our artistic ball). She reserves such affections for Lulu only. Lulu is wearing the fragrance that Geschwitz had recently gifted her, and it is admired by

Dr Schön. Eliminating any doubt of Geschwitz's sexual proclivities, she tells Lulu, 'I hope that you will want to come dressed up in men's clothing', to which Lulu replies, 'Do you think that will suit my figure?' Perhaps not the unequivocal response that Geschwitz might have hoped for, but neither was it a rebuke. In fact, cross-dressing does not seem an objectionable activity for Lulu, who later exclaims, '*Also, Ich mich im Spiegel sah, hätte ich ein Mann sein wollen . . . Mein Mann! (Blich auf ihr Bild).*'[21] (Seeing myself in the mirror, I wished I were a man . . . a man married to me! (with a glance at her portrait)).

Geschwitz and Lulu's characters are intertwined throughout the opera. Their relationship contrasts with Lulu's relationships with men most distinctly by Geschwitz's self-sacrifice. Adopting a maternal role, the countess does not try to capture and dominate Lulu but attempts to protect her. In the scene in the hospital, following Lulu's arrest, Geschwitz demonstrates the ultimate act of love by allowing Lulu to go free. The two characters impersonate one another, by swapping underwear, and consequently, Geschwitz contracts cholera from Lulu. Her lust for Lulu does not drive her to murder, heart attack or suicide, unlike Dr Schön, Dr Goll and the Painter. Rather, Geschwitz remains a constant, willing to support her during her numerous conquests and showing no outward signs of jealousy or rage. Her infatuation and lust for Lulu is also constant, and in Act II, scene ii, she once again extols Lulu's beauty when thinking about her, singing, '*Sie ist herrlicher an zuschau'n als ich sie jegekannt habe*'[22] (She is more wonderful to watch than I have ever known her).

Despite the relative constancy, the relationship between Lulu and Geschwitz begins to unravel with the gravitational pull of the violent conclusion of Act III. Geschwitz eventually denunciates Lulu's pattern of taking advantage of her kindness. The substantial orchestra creates a noisy background to the accusation, and along with the racket of the partygoers, some of the dialogue can be difficult to distinguish. The exchange occurs during the chorus scene, as their collective horror over the collapse of the Jungfrau-Railway shares diverts attention away from the quarrelling couple. It is at this moment we learn of the mutual affection that took place in the hospital. Lulu explains the plan to Alwa in Act II, scene ii, whereby due to an outbreak of cholera, Geschwitz took a nursing course, travelled to Hamburg and put on the underwear of a recently deceased patient. She then visited Lulu in prison and swapped underwear with her.

Geschwitz later states, 'In everything, you have betrayed me. Have you forgotten those passionate vows you made when ailing in hospital, lying alone in our hospital prison? I was persuaded to wear your clothes, take your place in jail.'[23] The texture of the orchestration is particularly dense at this moment, exacerbated but the unison singing of eight characters, who are celebrating their stock market windfall.[24]

A surprising breakdown of their relationship takes place in the final scene. Geschwitz is listening to Jack the Ripper and Lulu arguing over the price of their exchange. Jack the Ripper notices Geschwitz in the room, protecting Lulu with physical gestures as is customary for her. He observes, 'That is not "just your sister." The woman is obsessed with you (*stroking Countess Geschwitz's hair as one strokes a dog*).'[25] As they leave the room to consummate the act, Geschwitz declares suddenly that she intends to finally separate herself from Lulu. She sings of returning to Germany, enrolling at university and fighting for the rights of women. The score is marked, 'spoken, as if in a dream', suggesting that the countess has suddenly awoken from her trance-like, obsessive crush. Sadly, with Jack the Ripper's frenzied attack, Geschwitz was unable to carry out her plan. As if some kind of apology, Geschwitz's final words declared, once again, her true love for Lulu. 'Lulu! My angel! Love me just one more time! I'm by your side! Always by your side, for evermore!'[26]

Berg's use of twelve-tone sets to create a set of 'tropes' rather than a 'series'. It is the pitch content of the segments of material, rather that the order of notes, that characterizes each trope. The Countess Geschwitz is represented by a trope that consists of a perfect fifth and two pentatonic modes (figure 6.1).

The notes within each segment can be heard in any order, as can the segments themselves. There is no possibility for a retrograde or retrograde inversion of the trope as the order of the material cannot be delineated. The segment of Countess Geschwitz's trope consisting of black key notes is a shared component of the Acrobat's trope. As the countess lies bleeding out alone on the stage, the music utilizes a variety of transpositions of Geschwitz's trope. The exquisite, ascending intervals in her dying phrases capture her desire for Lulu, which like the height in the phrase seems to know no limits. Underpinning her final phrase, in which she declares her love for Lulu, the trope returns to its home key, concluding the opera.[27]

One of Berg's students, Theodor Adorno, wrote several important publications regarding his teacher, including a monograph in 1968, '*Berg: Der Meister des kleinsten Übergangs*' (Berg: The master of the smallest transition). In it, Adorno approaches the topic of Berg's own sexuality. Although he explicitly states that Berg was not homosexual, he describes his attitude towards sexuality with something that approaches wistfulness. He opined that Berg had a 'friendly' attitude to all things sexual and approached every sexual union with a sense of pride in others and himself.[28]

Figure 6.1   Countess Geschwitz's Trope. Created by the author

Adorno's reflections suggest of Berg as somewhat polymorphous sexuality, without anything perspicuous regarding homosexual attraction. Adorno also noted that Berg believed fervently that every decent human being, himself included, possessed a female constituent.[29] This was a notion espoused by Austrian philosopher, Otto Weininger (1880–1903). In his 1903 book, *Geschlecht und Charakter* (*Sex and Character*), Weininger proposes that all people exhibit male and female components. The male component being active, productive, conscious, moral and logical, while the female component possesses polar opposite characteristics. He argues that liberation is only possible for women who display masculine attributes, such as lesbians, and that female attributes are expended with the sexual function – both with the act, as a prostitute, and the product, as a mother. Much can be understood about *Lulu* through Berg's fascination with Weininger.

Lulu has attracted admiration from a wide range of philosophers, psychologists and musicologists, as well as audiences. For a Serialist opera, albeit far less strict than those of Berg's teacher, Arnold Schönberg (1874–1951), to achieve the status of 'regularly performed' in opera houses globally is testament to its unique significance and originality. Although Countess Geschwitz is not the first openly gay character in opera, as many have suggested, her contribution in *Lulu* is significant. Not only does she not feel any compunction to hide her identity, but she is not diminished in stature. Her role in the story is pivotal and powerful, and although she is symbolically undone through her unyielding desire, she is a role model for feminists who can celebrate her agency, loyalty, courage and love.

TWO BOYS, NICO MUHLY

The history of queerness and the necessity for disguise have had a long, symbiotic relationship. In repressive societies throughout the world, queers have developed the requisite skill known as 'passing' to avoid judgement, prosecution and even death. 'Passing' requires the individual to outwardly express heteronormative character traits, physical mannerisms and dress, in order to convince those around them that they are 'normal'. If this is successful, then a carefully established set of lies and half-truths can hopefully deter suspicion. In opera, disguise and gender appropriation have had a synchronous history. From the early operas of Francesco Cavalli and his Venetian contemporaries up until the early part of the twentieth century, cross-dressing by means of disguise has been a regular component. Originally, men dressed as women in order to comply with strict guidelines forbidding females on stage, but in the latter part of the nineteenth century onwards, roles for females dressed as men re-emerged, such as the role of Milada in Bedřich Smetana's *Dalibor* (1868),

Richard Strauss' Octavian in *Der Rosenkavalier* (1911), the Composer in *Ariadne auf Naxos* (1912) and Zdenka/Zdenko in *Arabella* (1933). A more contemporary approach to 'passing' comes in the form of online identities formed behind the on-screen personas of internet chat rooms in *Two Boys* (2011).

When Nico Muhly (b. 1981) was approached by the Metropolitan Opera in 2007 with a commission for the Lincoln Center Theatre New Works Programme, he was twenty-six, the youngest composer to be commissioned by the Met. His choice of narrative was based on real events, involving two boys engaged in an internet chat room. The internet becomes a vehicle for a story of disguise, deceit, sex and murder – all ingredients for a seventeenth-century opera. Muhly noted the historical place of the plot for his opera, saying, 'I'm not sure of any opera that doesn't have gay content, and murder. Don't they all?'[30] Just as the conventions of traditional *commedia dell'arte, tragicommedia, opera regia* or *intermedi* involved identity play, *Two Boys* involves gender appropriation but behind the apparent safety of a computer screen.

The opera is based on disturbing events that took place in Manchester, England, in 2003, details of which were initially reported in *The Guardian* in May 2004 and then in a 2005 issue of *Vanity Fair*, the primary source material for Muhly and his librettist, Craig Lucas. The opera scenes oscillate between flashbacks of the online encounters and the investigation that followed. The flash forward scenes largely involve the interrogation of the central character, Brian, by Anne, a detective working the case. Anne does not own a computer, nor understand the world of online chat rooms, and as such, she represents a contrasting, old-world perspective – a generation of people who have struggled to keep up with the fast-changing pace of cyberspace. Chat rooms have long since become a memory of an earlier phase of internet usage, and *Two Boys* serves as a nostalgic look at a bygone era. Brian is sixteen, naïve and trusting, and his enthusiasm for online socializing is shared by the majority of the cast, including the chorus who appear illuminated behind glowing laptop screens. Brian becomes entangled in a carefully constructed series of discourse, presented by a variety of fake characters and created by a thirteen-year-old boy, Jake. Jake is thirteen years old, clever, manipulative and queer.

Jake's assortment of disguises, which take the form of created cyber avatars, provides a contemporary equivalent of the seventeenth-century operatic cross-dressing role. Jake uses gender appropriation to create the character of Rebecca. Brian imagines he is talking to an attractive girl of a similar age, whose thumbnail is 'mindful16'. When they met online in Act I, scene iv, the score indicates, 'mindful16's [Rebecca's] thumbnail photo appears; a beautiful, composed teenage girl. Brian's photo shows a muddy, sweaty, grinning boy in a football jersey.'[31] As the chat transpires, their text is projected onto the set, while their physical and vocal presence on stage matches the character represented in the cyber world. Rebecca appears and sounds as the invented character and as Brian imagines her to be. Their discourse quickly turns sexual, and Jake's series of sexualized grooming begins.

The minimalist accompaniment in this scene provides an incessant and unobtrusive pulse to underpin the vocal lines, creating a cyber soundscape, constant, endless and omnipresent. The two voices utilize syllabic, speech patterns which avoid any hint of a melodic phrase. Muhly's frequent use of minimalist techniques has closely aligned him to Philip Glass by many observers and in this case provides a contemporary feel to the scene without the use of electronic instruments; Muhly stated that he 'didn't want it to look or sound like TRON'.[32] The soundtrack to the original film *TRON* (1982) was composed by Wendy Carlos using a Moog synthesizer, and the subsequent instalment *Tron: Legacy* (2010) featured a soundtrack by French electro-pop duo, Daft Punk.

Disguised as Rebecca, Jake is able to establish Brian's sexuality and relationship status. The advent of the internet provided a claimed space by society's spatially and ideologically marginalized groups, providing convenient interaction for sexual minorities that can be viewed as 'deviant'.[33] With the sense of freedom that perceived anonymity provides, along with feelings of belonging, cyberchat allows the individual to engage in risky behaviour that would otherwise be avoided.[34] Two opposing views concerning internet identity emerged in the 1990s. One perspective considers the online persona as a 'second self', through which an individual can curate and manage their online identity, separate from their physical self. The opposing view argues that online identity becomes enmeshed with physical identity, and that people's online and offline actions and desires are intertwined. In addition to enmeshment and second-self theories, further research has adopted a utopic view of anonymity and identity factors and views them as empowering experiences, protected from physical or actual risk by the virtual nature of cyberspace.

In *Two Boys*, Brian's disembodied interactions with Rebecca begin a process in which he is left vulnerable to the deception, manipulation, uninhibited behaviour and sexual abuse that follows.[35] The sexual nature of their interactions intensifies in their following encounter when Rebecca persuades Brian to display his genitals via his camera. She calls him a 'sexpert'[36] and convinces him to masturbate for her via his webcam. Brian's behaviour exemplifies the 'online disinhibition effect', discussed by cyberpsychologists as a phenomenon of unusual, unrestrained behaviour that manifests as either benign or toxic disinhibition.[37] Jake's invention of Rebecca has created a strong, sexual connection for Brian, and Jake can destroy her just as quickly as she was created.

Prior to Rebecca's second scene, the second source of sexualized, deviant behaviour is presented by the chorus. Indicating the internet as a nucleus for deviant and taboo sexual discourse, scene xii involves the chorus singing repetitive, layered phrases in the minimalist tradition. The phrases are disturbing and reflect a world in which no topic is off-limits. The stage directions indicate, 'Brian searches through chatrooms, each one more lurid than the last.'[38] Over the top of the chorus emerge two voices: an American Congressman, aged forty-nine, and his Page, aged nineteen. Their sung text outlines the grooming practices of an older man and his subordinate. The minor characters do not actively form a part of the unfolding narrative but further contextualize cyberspace as a space for promoting toxic disinhibition. Just as homosexuality in all its forms has been represented as a threat to humanity in so many repressed societies, so too is the internet regarded as a moral vacuum to be feared. The Congressman and his Page sing to each other:

Congressman: How's my favourite young stud doing
Page: tired and sore
Congressman: that's good, you need a massage
Page: tomorrow I have the first day of lacrosse practice
Congressman: Love to watch that, those great legs running
Page: they aren't that great
Congressman: well don't ruin my mental picture
Page: sorry
Congressman: Nice, you'll be way hot then
Page: hopefully
Congressman: Did any girl give you a hand job this weekend?
Page: I'm single right now
Congressman: Did you spank it yourself this weekend?
Page: no.[39]

The two voices sing in a manner that reflects much of the cyberspace chat, and rarely do they begin or end phrases on the same note but rather displaced by one step. The Page is not enthusiastic about the direction of the conversation but does not protest the nature of his boss' interests. Eventually, after being asked to measure his penis once again, the Page disappears, as indicated by the underlying chorus parts and the cessation of the repetitive arpeggiated figure in the orchestra. As Brian falls deeper into Jake's deceptive world, these chorus moments, replete with typos and emoticons, become increasingly dark. Initially, fairly innocuous text, such as 'who is this', 'you there' and 'I thought I'd lost you', makes way for off-handed obscenities and vile insults, 'You should kill yourself', 'u suck u suck u suck', and degenerating further into shocking phrases, including 'Looking for a well built 18-30 year old 2 b slaughtered then consumed'.[40]

Jake removes Rebecca's online presence by telling Brian that she had been murdered. Amidst conspiracy theories designed to confuse the grieving Brian, blame is ascribed to 'Peter_69', a gardener whom Brian then believes is a continuing threat to both him and Jake. In an attempt to avert a real threat to his safety, Brian agrees once again to masturbate via webcam for Peter. The extract from Act II, scene iii, shows a more forceful insistence on Brian to satisfy Peter/Jake's sexual demands.

Brian: what do you want?
Peter: i'm a sick fuk, they tEll u?
turn on ur cam
take out ur junk
u gormless chum
give me a little graveee mmm
gob on it
mm just testing! mm just testing!
watch out 4 ur peter![41]

Jake's avatar which first appears in Act I, scene xiv, presents as 'idealised version of Jake', which is contrary to Rebecca's initial description of him. Rebecca's version more closely resembled the boy that Brian finally met in person. 'Real Jake' replaces the well-built baritone with a thirteen-year-old boy with an unbroken voice. Jake may have facilitated a fictional version of himself to Brian; however, he was nonetheless 'idealized' – Brian's ideal version of an older and more physically mature boy who could potentially dominate him socially and physically. The version presented to the audience onstage is Brian's fantasy or projection of an idealized 'other'. Their meeting includes a subtle musical cue indicating that Rebecca was a product of mere fiction. When Jake explains her murder, the boys are united in mutual grief, and in an attempt to comfort Brian, Jake sings, 'I loved her, too',[42] which is followed by a short, chromatically ascending oboe solo, and then the next phrase, 'I'm still here. Jake's here. And I'll stay.'[43] The solo oboe was previously heard in Act I, scene xi, when Brian asks Rebecca to meet in person.

Jake stays the night at Brian's house, to comfort him over the loss of Rebecca, and we learn in the following scene, Act II, scene iv, that the sleep over included a sex act, followed by Brian's clumsy rejection of Jake the next morning. Brian recalls the moment to Anne in a flashback:

Anne: Did you have sex?
Brian: No. Well, I mean, okay, we sort of . . . he sort of blew me, I, you know . . . just to be nice. I didn't really want it or anything. I felt . . . sorry for him. It wasn't real.[44]

Brian's reflection of the event suggested that the interaction between them in real life did not represent reality, unlike the events in cyberspace involving Rebecca, Peter and a slew of other characters. Jake tells Brian of his inoperable tumour and, through several other invented characters, persuades Brian to end his suffering through the act of a mercy killing. Brian meets Jake at the shopping centre and, as instructed, stabs him in the heart while whispering in his ear, 'I love you bro.'[45]

Anne begins to suspect that Brian wasn't responsible for the murder, but that someone else was behind it. She returns home, having left her elderly mother alone all night, and after admonishing herself for her negligence begins ruminating on her failures as a detective. She sings, 'People see what they need to see, Don't you know? It's all a masquerade.'[46] The great ruse of the opera is that the audience is led to believe that the fictional characters are real, as they are seen through Brian's metadiegesis. Her reflection of her own naïvety over the murder case is also true for the cyberspace experience and the surprising way in which rudimentary disguise can fool any observer. Just as the Victorians were able to assume that the two gentlemen living together were just good chums, so too could the participants in internet chatrooms fantasize any conceivable characteristic of their online acquaintances. Jake's treble voice and all of the traditional associations of innocence and purity were in stark variance to reality. The sophistication of his deceit, the fabricated personas, his emotionally manipulated sex act with Brian and the orchestration of his own murder revealed that he was neither innocent nor naïve.

NOT IN MY TOWN, MICHAEL W. ROSS

Matthew Shepard was twenty-one years old when he was approached by Aaron McKinney and Russell Henderson at the Fireside Lounge in Laramie. After driving to a remote area of the Wyoming countryside, the two men, also in their twenties, proceeded to rob, pistol-whip and torture Shepard before taking his shoes and leaving him tied to a barbed wire fence in sixteen-degree weather. Mistaking him initially for a scarecrow, a cyclist discovered Shepard eighteen hours later, alive, in a coma and covered in blood. He had suffered fractures to the back of his head, causing extreme brainstem damage and affecting his ability to regulate vital functions. He never regained consciousness and died six days later on 12 October 1998.[47]

To reduce Matthew's suffering to this single, tragic event does not accurately reflect the litany of anguish he experienced as a result of his homosexuality. Just as horrific is that even in death, the extreme forms of bigotry found in the members of the Westboro Baptist Church and their minister,

Fred Phelps, continued to antagonize Shepard's grieving family and friends. Picketing his funeral with homophobic signs that read, 'Matt in Hell' and 'God Hates Fags', the congregants drew shock from an international audience which followed the events as they unfolded on television. Matthew Shepard's story is one of shameful, homophobic torment, a shockingly violent death and a determined response by his parents, friends, supporters and legislators to pass laws in support of victims of hate crimes.

Michael W. Ross' homage to Shepard's story takes the form of a musical drama that borrows occasionally from operatic conventions but sits comfortably in the musical theatre vernacular. *Not in My Town* (2016) was premiered by the independent, Floridian group, Opera Fusion. It is a one-act work in thirteen scenes that traces the events leading up to Shepard's death and the responses surrounding his funeral and legislation that followed. Ross' personal connection to Shepard's story began when he took part in the march and candlelight vigil in New York as Shepard still lay in a comatose state in intensive care. He expressed his deeply felt horror at the senselessness of the attack and commented on the importance of the event in terms of LGBTQ+ history in America, 'It may have been one of the most important turning points in the gay movement since the 1969 Stonewall riots.'[48]

The opera opens with Romaine, a twenty-year-old lesbian, coming to the defence of some students being bullied. Her response to being called a 'Stupid Dyke'[49] is to thank the bully, suggesting that she enjoyed the compliment. Ross established the basis of the conflict within the opening lines. The bully is given text that is blatantly immature and senseless, whereas Romaine represents fortitude and honour in the face of bigotry. Romaine and Matthew bond instantly, and with the exchanged declaration of homosexual identity, Romaine describes Matthew's sexuality as 'awesome'.[50] His aria, 'The World Is Mine', which opens scene ii, includes a sanitized backstory, 'Growing up I always felt a little different – like I didn't fit in my town. People would constantly beat me up and throw me to the ground all the time.'[51] It reveals nothing of his rape, endured on a school trip to Morocco, or the withdrawal, panic attacks or depression that resulted from his ordeal. In scene iv, he mentions being 'roughed up'[52] in Saudi Arabia, which may be a reference to the rape incident, but it is unclear.

Similarly, in the following scene, a flashback in which Matthew's parents discuss his declared homosexuality, the libretto adopts an overtly supportive tone which borders on a moral guidebook on how parents should respond. Musically, the scene is tonally unambiguous, adopting accessible musical structures and unsurprising chord progressions; however, the vocal lines avoid repeated phrases or attributable themes that might be expected in music theatre. The following scene, in which Matthew attends his first gay rally, is given an oscillating chord structure of a suspended seventh chord followed by the flattened submediant in a pulsing vamp pattern, over which the avoidance of melodic themes is continued. The chorus sing of two recent political defeats, including the attempted appeal of the 'Don't ask, don't tell' legislation but celebrate the many recent victories, 'Equality. Marriage. Taxes. Adoption. Love. Freedom. Benefits. My spouse. Filing jointly. Insurance. Job security. Hospital visits. Inheritance. Privileged information. Discounts. Acceptance. Medical decisions. The gene. The choice. Alternative lifestyle. Acceptance, equality. Human Rights.'[53]

Scene vii, 'Fireside Lounge/Torture', depicts Matthew's murder and the action unfolds over orchestral underscore, finishing with the only vocal line in the scene when Matthew sings, 'Oh God, have you forgotten me? Oh God, have you forgotten me? Please, don't leave me here to die out here alone.'[54] The text has echoes of one of the final seven words of Christ on the cross, allowing observers to make connections with the homophobic culture for which the Christian church is known. The music begins with repetitive, compound time patterns that echo chase scenes from any number of adventure film scores, replete with accented beats with added percussion for carefully placed punches which culminate with a series of descending discords at the end of the violent episode. Ross explains his use of conventional material, 'A lot of composers think they have to throw in all these complicated things . . . to make [opera] elitist.' He further describes his approach:

> My whole goal was to write something that the audience is going to grab onto.
> I want the words to be important. I don't repeat words. It's a very through composition, and it's in English. We need to grab people with our own language.[55]

Following the announcement of Matthew's death, scene x, 'Not in my Town', shows the Reverend Fred Phelps and his followers who are staging an anti-gay rally. Phelps sings, 'We are headed for the end of the world. The eyes of the Lord are always upon you. We will not allow that sort of perversion to run rampant in our towns.'[56] With the aid of a bullhorn, Phelps and his congregants reference Genesis, Romans, Leviticus Corinthians and Timothy, in their damnation of Matthew, until they are disrupted by Romaine and her band of angels. They are dressed in white robes with wings that are seven feet wide, which effectively block the protesters from seeing into the funeral. Phelps responds with further vitriol, 'No more queers, not in my town. No more Jews, not in my town. No more foreigners, not in my town.'[57]

That the title for the opera is taken from text representing a section of American society dominated by religious conservativism, rather than from the central characters, underlines the emphasis of the opera's narrative.

Romaine Patterson's actions, in shielding Shepard's family and friends from the harassment of Phelps' followers, sparked a nationwide response, catapulting her into the spotlight as an activist for hate crimes. The year 1998 was also the year in which another horrifying murder occurred, this time an African American man by the name of James Byrd Jr. Three white suprema-cists in Jasper, Texas, chained Byrd to the back of a pickup truck, dragging him for three miles along an asphalt road. Remaining conscious for much of the ordeal, he eventually died when his body hit the edge of a culvert, severing his head and right arm. What remained of his body was dumped unceremoniously outside a black church before the perpetrators drove off to enjoy a barbecue.[58]

The gruesome murders of Byrd and Shepard in the same year thrust hate crime legislation to the forefront of national and international legislators. The Wyoming Legislature rejected a bill to define attacks based on sexual orienta-tion as a hate crime. Bill Clinton then renewed attempts to extend federal hate crime legislation in 1997, but it was not passed by both houses of Congress until 2000. In 2007, the Matthew Shepard and James Byrd Jr. Hate Crimes Prevention Act passed the House of Representatives in the presence of Shepa-rd's parents; however, George W. Bush indicated he would veto the bill. The Act was revived and finally signed into law after passing both houses in 2009 by Barack Obama. The opera finishes with Romaine, who has just agreed to exchange vows with her girlfriend, Olivia, addressing the Anti-Defamation League in Washington, DC. The address is mimed with underscore; however, as the score comes to a conclusion, surtitles above the stage show the follow-ing lines, in a manner similar to a film epilogue:

> Judy Shepard speaks in front of a Senate panel for a Hate Crimes Bill. Judy and Dennis create the Matthew Shepard Foundation.
> Romaine goes to work at the Gay & Lesbian Alliance Against Defamation (GLAAD) and her Angel Action takes on a life of its own wherever Rev. Phelps may protest.
> Because of their activism and help from groups like the Human Rights Cam-paign, the Anti-Defamation League, celebrities and countless others, we now have the Hate Crimes Prevention Act.
> It was signed into law by President Barack Obama in 2009. He noted that it was another step to 'help protect our citizens from violence based on what they look like, who they love, how they pray'.
> We thank all the brave and tireless efforts of everyone who attempts to make the world a better place.[59]

The two perpetrators of Shepard's death, Aaron McKinney and Russell Hen-derson, both received two consecutive life sentences. In their defence, they pleaded to experiencing 'gay panic', a sort of temporary insanity brought on by alleged sexual advances towards them by Shepard. This phenomenon is believed to have formed from the cultural climate in which the two men were immersed. The 'gay panic' defence is underpinned by the notion that homophobes are thoroughly rational until presented with notions of queerness, which produces overwrought, panicky and defensive behaviour. This reasoning also attempted to position the perpetrators as victims, whereby they were defending themselves against unwanted sexual advances, which lead to a suspension of rational thinking.[60] The 'gay panic' defence was rejected by the judge and was at odds with the statement made by McKinney's girlfriend who testified that the perpetrators pretended to be gay in order to lure Shepard into the truck and rob him.

Ross' *Not in My Town* adds to the body of work that commemorates the life of Matthew Shepard, allowing people who were not yet born when the atrocity occurred to understand the depth of hate towards queer people generated in the Westboro Baptist Church. Phelps severed ties with the Baptist denomination and has been denounced by the Baptist World Alliance, the Southern Baptist Convention and other mainstream Christian denominations. The widespread condemnation for the church, which consists largely of Phelps' extended family, has not extended to a gag order, and despite several high court cases against Phelps, freedom of speech laws allow them to continue picketing the funerals of a long list of targeted minority groups which includes deceased, serving military personnel.[61] The perpetual struggle in the United States for the protection of vulnerable minority and individuals deemed as 'other' against those who seek to harm them continues.

LES FELUETTES (LILIES), KEVIN MARCH

The period known as *La Belle Époche* was a glittering and vibrant time of prosperity in the decades between France's humiliating defeat in the Franco-Prussian War (1871) and the devastation of the Great War (1914–1918). Georges-Eugène Haussmann's remodelling of Paris was complete (1870), the Eiffel Tower (1889) surpassed the record height for manmade structures and electric streetlamps sparkled above the newly built marvel of the underground metro. Some well-known queer luminaries, such as dancer Vaslav Nijinsky and impresario Sergei Diaghilev; Gertrude Stein and Alice B. Toklas (see chapter 2); musical patroness, Princesse Edmond de Polignac (née Winnaretta Singer); novelist Marcel Proust; and writer and filmmaker Jean Cocteau, managed to enjoy amorous relations at a time when homosexuality was widely greeted with disgust and hostility. In 1912, the same year as the events retold in *Les Feluettes*, the Portland scandal in the United States, in which dozens of men and boys were arrested on charges relating to sodomy, led to state legislation allowing for the forced sterilization of 'sexual perverts'. It seems the *époche* was only *belle* for those fortunate to avoid the prevailing aggression towards queerness.

Although the opera *Les Feluettes* (2016) predominantly refers to events of 1912, it is told by means of a play-within-a-play, in a prison in 1952. The libretto was devised by Canadian author, Michel Marc Bouchard, an adaptation of his own play, *Les Feluettes ou la répétition d'un drame romantique* (1987). Within the narrative, students at Roberval College, a Catholic school in Roberval (around 250 kilometres north of Quebec City), rehearse the scandalous and sensual play, *Le Martyre de saint Sébastien* (The Martyrdom of St. Sebastian) by Gabriele D'Annunzio (1863–1938). The play involves the infamous scene of Saint Sebastien's first attempt at martyrdom. Sebastian, frequently depicted as a beautiful youth, leaning semi-naked against a tree, pierced with arrows, is frequently depicted in paintings by Botticelli, Rubens, El Greco, Titian, Dali and many others in physical poses that are often suggestive of sadomasochism. D'Annunzio exploits the homoeroticism of Sebastien, considered by many as a gay icon, by conflating him with the pagan figure, Adonis, and the Vatican included the play on its Index of Prohibited Books all of D'Annunzio's works. Parisian Catholics attending the production were threatened with excommunication, such was the scandalous nature of the play.

The entire cast of March's opera consists of male performers, based on the dual settings of a boy's school and a prison. There are three female characters, played by men, adding to the gender ambiguity that forms such a rich thread throughout operatic history. After several voice types were considered, March eventually ascribed the Comtesse Marie-Laure de Tilly to a baritone and cast Mademoiselle Lydie-Anne de Rozier as a countertenor. There is also a comic relief character in the student play who presents a young Syrian slave girl. The two protagonists, Simon Doucet and Count Vallier de Tilly, fall in love during the rehearsal of the play. Simon is a beautiful, young man with an impulsive nature and prone to pyromania. Vallier is a sensitive soul and was nicknamed '*Feluette*' (Lily) by the priest, Bilodeau, in reference to his thin physique and effeminate nature, although symbolically, Lilies represent fertility and purity. Lilies are also popular funeral flowers due to their connection with transience and death, a prophetic choice of association in this opera. They are also the flower of royalty, reflecting Vallier's station and an obsession for Oscar Wilde, who drew sexual imagery from them.

The prologue, set in the prison in 1954, establishes the premise that Simon has been unjustly incarcerated, and that the bishop who has come to give his last confession is Bilodeau, the person responsible for Simon's predicament. With the prisoners announcing that they will play the various roles in the story, including Bilodeau himself, the first scene then presents the rehearsals of *Le Martyre de saint Sébastien* in 1912. Simon is to play St Sebastian, while Vallier presents Sanaé. The opening lines of the scene are instantly homoerotic, 'Tie him to the trunk of the most beautiful of the laurel trees; then unleash your arrows upon his naked body until you empty your quivers, until his naked body looks like that of a wild hedgehog.'[62] Craving death so as to be reborn, Sebastian (Simon) flirtatiously invites Sanaé (Vallier) to kill him, 'If you ever loved me, may I know the measure of your love through the agony of your arrows.'[63] The term *la petite mort* (the little death), meaning a brief loss or weakening of consciousness, in modern usage references the sensation of post-orgasm which has been likened to a unique state of consciousness comparable to death.

With the temporary departure of the frustrated Father St Michael, the two boys are left on stage, and in the solitude, their romance blossoms; Vallier sings, 'So, I move slowly towards you, and, as if carried away with an ardour which, until now was unknown to me, and I embrace you.'[64] He then stops reading from the script, 'Tell me you love me, and then I'll kill you!'[65] Simon reciprocates his advance, admitting to Vallier, 'I've never felt this good with anyone else. I've never felt this good in my whole life.'[66] His only hesitation being to tell Vallier that he loves him establishes the nature of the beginning phase of their relationship. Despite being the '*Feluette*', with its connotation of feminine weakness, Vallier is the most assured of his feelings and most willing to honour them of the two.

Opera plots frequently deal with the theme of doomed love and invariably provide immovable forces outside of the relationship that place insurmountable obstacles on the romance. Such pressures often stem from a moral attitude underpinned by a supressed society that deems certain liaisons unacceptable on the grounds of religion, race, class, politics or in this case gender. Vallier and Simon barely have time to express their feelings before opposition to their union bares down on them with force. Monsignor Bolideau, who is watching the 1954 re-enactment from his temporary imprisonment of the confessional, becomes incensed when the two prisoners playing Vallier and Simon kiss, insisting that the scene be stopped on the basis of indecency. Bolideau warns Simon of the impending repercussions if their actions were discovered, 'And you, Simon, what if your father knew about all this? You are intimate with Vallier as if he were a girl! You caress him, you pet him as if he were a girl.'[67] When Simon's father learns of the passionate kiss that his son shared with Vallier, he punished him with lashes from his whip. In the score, the action which took place offstage was performed by the chorus, who, removing their belts, 'beat the ground twenty-two times with violence'.[68]

Villier composes Simon a love letter which concludes with the phrase, 'I compose you, I create you, let you live, I kill you, I bring you back to life.'[69] This becomes a literary and musical motif in the opera and connects the story of St Sebastian's martyrdom with the unfolding narrative. Villier's aria at the end of the first episode provides a visceral moment and an emotional climax in the middle of the first act and its final few bars, almost *a cappella* but for a few notes on the harp are intimate and heartfelt. It contrasts with the following scene, beginning with the chorus singing, '*Magnifique! Magnifique!*',[70] set to a seductively memorable waltz tune that becomes a recurring musical theme throughout the opera. The chorus are delighted with the spectacle of Mademoiselle Lydie-Anne de Rozier's hot-air balloon. With Simon's beating from his father, he resolves to denounce Vallier for fear of further reprisals, 'It's time for me to start considering girls. I have to start thinking about girls now.'[71] Simon becomes engaged to Lydie-Anne; however, Vallier appears, dressed as Caesar, and publicly and seductively praises his beauty. This abruptly ends the celebrations, but it raises doubt for Simon who has been struggling to show Lydie-Anne appropriate levels of intimacy.

It is at this point, during Simon's aria, that the silent presence of Bolideau reveals the true love triangle in the story. His hitherto unknown passions for Simon are exposed in his aria, during which he resolves to destroy the hot-air balloon and thereby ensuring Simon stays in Roberval. Monsignor Bolideau reacts with considerable denial upon this representation of him; however, the truth of his actions is revealed in his journal which serves as a confession. The beginning of the second act in which Vallier is taking a bath sees a rapprochement of the two men, as Simon confesses to the difficulty of a pretend marriage, 'I do not love her as she wants me to',[72] and his undeniable love for Simon which he finally declares. For much of this scene Vallier stands in the bathtub, naked and facing Simon, heightening the eroticism of the moment and also underlining Vallier's willingness to be vulnerable.

After spending the night together by the lake, Bilodeau appears, declaring his love for Simon and imploring him for a kiss, 'Kiss me. Like the Saint kisses his friend.'[73] Simon refuses and violently pushes him out of the room. With the doors closed, the two men recall earlier phrases from their play, 'But to be reborn, my archers, I have to die, I have to die. If you ever loved me, may I know the measure of your love through the agony of your arrows.'[74] Simon takes an oil lamp and smashes it on the ground. Holding Vallier tight, the two collapse while holding hands and choking on the enveloping smoke. This act of arson was prophesized by Bilodeau in the first act, 'He said it. When you set a fire somewhere, you do it out of love for him!'[75] The epilogue reveals that Bilodeau rescued Simon but left Vallier to die. The prisoners approach the bishop with knives poised to strike but in the last moments of the opera drop them on the ground, sentencing him to consider his actions. He picks up a knife contemplatively before the final blackout.

March's score encapsulates an eclectic set of musical influences that combine in a cohesive sound world which is part lyricism, part atonality and with use of motivic devices. Bouchard's stage directions indicate that the music of Debussy should be heard in the background during the rehearsal scene of *Le martyre de saint Sébastien*, and sections from Debussy's incidental music for *Le martyre de Saint Sébastien* can be heard, and his stimulus is a familiar presence throughout the opera.[76] During the dinner at the grand hotel, set at the end of the Edwardian era, the music references ragtime and Québécois folk music, a combination of influences from early Irish and French settlers. Ragtime was particularly popular around 1912, and March quotes Scott Joplin 'to give Lydie-Anne the feel of a sophisticated woman of the day'.[77] There is also French belle-époque-style cabaret, folk music for fiddle, accordion and wooden spoons and a nineteenth-century Napoleonic Anthem.

An important literary influence on March's musical structures comes from the subtitle of Bouchard's play, *La Répétition d'un drame romantique* (The Revival of a Romantic Drama). The notion of repetition has several symbolic meanings which include the idea of 'rehearsal' of the play and 'revival' of St Sebastian after his volley of arrows. The concept recurs with some frequency, especially in relation to the bathtub scene, where Simon's dramatic change of heart prompts his declaration of love for Vallier and in doing so is brought back into the loving relationship. The idea is even more literal when Simon is revived after the fire that claimed Vallier.

The themes of love, loss, desire, determination and obsession are not unique to the queer experience, and March seeks to clarify that the opera represents a universal experience. He stated, 'I would politely and gently disagree with the notion that the opera has a primarily gay theme.'[78] The notion of romances being thwarted by outside forces can be found in the epic romantic operas such as Puccini's *La Bohème* (1896) and *Tosca* (1899) and Gounod's *Romeo and Juliet* (1867). For members of the queer community, however, the force of pressure preventing meaningful same-sex relationships was constant and menacing. The year that Simon and his fellow inmates sought to educate Monsignor Bilodaeu of the damage that his closeted and unrequited passions caused saw the treatment of queers at a crossroads. In the United States, the pernicious McCarthy era (see chapter 2) and the associated 'lavender scare' forced thousands of queers to remain in the closet, while in the United Kingdom, the Wolfenden Commission sought to redress some of the homophobic laws that considered homosexual acts as immoral acts of deviancy. Homophobia may share common elements with other forms of oppression, each of which resonates within communities in their own way, but the long and painful story of queer subjugation has its own narrative. The doomed love story of Simon and Vallier now joins the discourse through the transformative medium of opera.

LESSONS IN LOVE AND VIOLENCE, GEORGE BENJAMIN

Of the seven British monarchs to have been allegedly queer, Edward II (1284–1322) was the first and arguably the best-known case given the manner in which it led to his untimely end. The disputed nature of his death, which many believe consisted of a red-hot poker being inserted into his fundament, adds a macabre fascination to his tumultuous time on the throne.[79] The binary question, 'Was he, or wasn't he?', which has dominated and divided historians, tells us more about the interpreter's political leanings, rather than informing a nuanced and scholarly discussion of gender identity and sexuality. The fourteenth century lacked the modern labels for homosexuals but certainly held firm the belief that sodomy was an abomination and that effeminacy was a marker for ineffective leadership. It is most likely that Edward II was murdered at Berkeley Castle following his deposition by his wife, Isabel, and the First Earl of March, Roger Mortimer; however, unsubstantiated and conflicting theories throw doubt on our collective understanding.

Sir George Benjamin's opera *Lessons in Love and Violence* (2018) explores the doomed relationship between Edward II, his lover, Piers Gaveston, his wife, Isabel, and Edward's nemesis, Roger Mortimer. The libretto by Martin Crimp is structured loosely on Christopher Marlowe's 1594 play, *Edward II*, and as well as avoiding the physical act of Edward's murder, he provides a tantalizing twist to the response of Edward III to his father's adversary. The seven-scene opera is given a neurotic, atonal treatment with a full orchestra replete with a battery of assorted percussion, cymbalom and celeste. The ambitious score reflects Benjamin's lessons with Messiaen, and the orchestra is used sparingly until the interludes between scenes, when explosions of rich, full-orchestral colour abound. Characters are given associated leitmotifs or instruments, such as Mortimer's connection with the cimbalom.[80]

The opera opens almost immediately with a bickering duet between the king and Mortimer. Mortimer lays out his objections to Gaveston, 'It's nothing to do with loving a man. It's love full stop that is poison. The whole human body. And the money you spend with Gaveston while people starve is unacceptable.'[81] The king's interjections fall on deaf ears as the two sing concurrently. The King and Gaveston are both played by baritones, in contrast to Mortimer's tenor. Gaveston's character is revealed to be the cause of misery through the introduction of two witnesses sought out by Mortimer and Isabel. The two witnesses are women who have survived atrocities attributed to Gaveston. Their villages have been burned to the ground, and they explain that their lands were confiscated and gifted to Gaveston by the king. As Mortimer and Isabel plan to destroy Gaveston, Isabel's two children observe their nefarious exchange, which will prove to be a crucial point in the narrative when Prince Edward (Edward III), played by a tenor, assumes the throne.

The king's relationship with Gaveston is not uniformly one of romance and affection as is made clear when the king questions Gaveston about whether he has hurt him, 'Not when you grip my neck. Not when you hold my right hand deliberately over a flame. Not even when you forced me to swim in winter under the dull grey ice till my lungs are beginning to split.'[82] These rather shocking incidents have not dulled Gaveston's love for the king, despite the patent power play and masochistic nature of their relationship. In a display for Mortimer's benefit, Gaveston places his hand around the king's neck, a gesture that suggests both violence and intimacy; the reaction of disgust from Mortimer confirms his attitude. In scene iii, set in a theatre, the underlying violence that seems to be an ever-present characteristic of their relationship surfaces again; the king sings, 'How can I love you? A man with the steel hand and sleepy smile of an assassin.'[83] Gaveston's response is surprising, 'Yes I'm a human razor: take care or I'll cut your throat.'[84] He explains his violent outbursts as a result of their relationship, 'Love is a prison: I wanted to see daylight.'[85] He declares his indisputable loyalty and bond he has with the king, 'You know where I am; inside your life. I've no life out of it. I live where you are looking: in the hard palm of your hand.'[86]

The entertainment begins after Isabel asks everyone to take their seats. She tells Gaveston that the musical entertainment, performed by two women, involves the Old Testament story of the killing of Saul and his son, Jonathan, followed by David's lament of his dying lover. The drama continues as Isabel and Gaveston engage in pointed discussion about him wearing Mortimer's ring. Mortimer then enters the scene and the multilayered, counterpointed ensemble swells to include the king as the pivotal moment of the narrative reaches its climax. On a high E, he demands that the entertainment stop, and that Mortimer be arrested. There is no reaction from the attending audience, and while urging everyone to listen to their king, it dawns on him that he has become an impotent ruler, unable to defend his lover who is dragged away to meet his fate.

In the following scene, the king reads from the recount of Gaveston's murder, 'And one man drove a sword through his body and another beheaded him in a ditch.'[87] As the king mourns the loss of his lover, Isabel demonstrates her inability to understand the idea of love between two men, urging him to kiss her as he grieves, then asking how it is that he could love Gaveston. He responds, 'Because he loved me more than all the world.'[88] Hinting at his knowledge of her secret liaisons with Mortimer, he questions her secrecy, 'Why have you turned away? Turned to the dark.'[89] Isabel responds with all the rage of a jilted lover having to endure her adulterous lover, 'Here – look are my tears. What have I ever hidden? No part of this body. No part of this mind – not my opinions.'[90]

In scene v, Isabel has taken the two children to Mortimer's house, and they begin by playfully offering gifts of pets to the young prince (the future Edward III) in order to begin control over him. Testing his leadership instincts, they present him with a madman who claims to be king. Despite the boy's pleas to be merciful, Mortimer strangles the man in front of him, singing, 'Understand that when you are king – there will be no room for one man's love for another – no room for madness – or for disorder inside the machinery of the regulated world.'[91] This phrase underscores Mortimer's medieval way of observing sexuality. From his perspective, the manifestation of homosexual desire in Edward II directly affected his ability to rule. His subversion of sexual norms represented chaos, and Mortimer clearly felt that the young prince could simply be taught to avoid the temptations of sexual deviancy when he became king. The scene concludes with Mortimer finally allowing Isabel to seduce him, thereby tacitly and symbolically consenting to committing regicide.[92] Ironically, such an act of seduction of the king's wife would end with the beheading of another queen in 1536, but Henry VIII was not hindered by rumours of queerness and, with a secure throne, could act with impunity.

Mortimer accuses the king of such moral degeneracy, that he has lost his mental faculties, 'that lechery – that sodomy – have decayed his mind'.[93] He dictates what is to be written in the account of his show trial, 'Write that instead of a man, this man has chosen to be nothing.'[94] He relinquishes the crown to Mortimer, and the two witnesses from scene ii appear to announce that he has a visitor. The king is convinced the Stranger is a manifestation of Gaveston. The Stranger insists that he is not, and in an echo of the scene in the Theatre in which Gaveston read the king's future by looking at his hand, the Stranger provides a lurid summation of his life and then whispers that he is already dead. Tormented by the hurt he inflicted on Gaveston, he begs the Stranger to bring him back to life, 'Hold my body over the fire, Gaveston. Make me alive. Bind me to a metal rack. Burn me. Make me alive. Love me.'[95]

In the final scene, the young prince exacts revenge on the man who arranged his father's death. In a departure from historical accuracy, in which Mortimer was ultimately hung at Tyburn gallows without trial, and displayed for two days and nights, Crimp's libretto provides a delicious alternative. The theatre from scene iii reappears, and the Young King awaits a performance with his mother. The Young King explains to Isabel that he has forbidden music but instead has arranged an 'entertainment'. With growing tension, an increasingly horrified Isabel gradually begins to understand that her son is no longer the political puppet she and Mortimer had hitherto controlled. The Young King explains the context to the entertainment, which outlines in detail the story of her conspiracy with Mortimer to depose, then murder his father, and the audiences silently take their seats to watch the ensuing scene, 'of a human being broken and broken by the rational application of human justice'.[96] Isabel's growing horror as the realization that her partner in crime is about to be tortured on stage as she is forced to watch is all the more satisfying for the notion of expunged queerness being avenged. Benjamin concludes the score with a menacing postlude of wandering demi-semi quavers over a held semi-tone that echoes the dying moments of Berg's *Wozzeck* (1922).

Historical Prince Edward was aged fourteen at the time of his father's removal from the throne. He journeyed to France where his mother and Mortimer planned the usurpation. His revenge for the murder of his father, and by association, Gaveston, saw an end to the deplorable homophobia inflicted on a ruling British monarch not seen since William Rufus (1060–1100). The lives of queer individuals are defined by their inhabited time and space. Edward II ruled England at a time when there was little understanding of homosexuality, other than the biblical opposition to sodomy. At a time of prevailing superstition, Edward's affair with Gaveston was lambasted, not just from a puritanical, spiritual perspective but because notions of effeminacy and subversive sexual practices attributed to the monarch were somehow responsible for the hardships of the time. This may be simplistic; Gaveston was widely disliked for his magnificent arrogance and the acerbic nicknames he afforded the earls and barons of the realm. Mortimer was certainly not alone in his grievances, and yet it is difficult to divorce the ultimate demise of the doomed lovers, with the astonishing bigotry that abounded in the dark ages.

Benjamin and Crimp's treatment of Henry and Gaveston's cruel, twisted and masochistic relationship gives added dimension to these much-maligned historical figures. Gaveston's deep loyalty to his king, to the extent that he would gladly suffer any tortuous treatment Henry dreamt up simply to please him, provides an alternative perspective to a man widely hated by his fellow countrymen. Depicting Henry as a man who enjoys deploying such acts of sadism to the man he loved adds to the image of a ruler who failed to fully grasp the worth of what was in front of him. Regardless of historical accuracy, the characters presented in *Lessons in Love and Violence* provide a varied and more nuanced view of queerness. As opera continues to openly explore queer themes, the dichotomy of good and evil, whereby queer is good and the bigoted society is evil, may ultimately wear thin. In order to be taken seriously, queer characters are occasionally going to need to be given a darker side, whereby queers can be perpetrators of as well as victims of evil through character flaws that follow no sexual assignation.

HARVEY MILK, STEWART WALLACE

Harvey Milk's political career occurred during a period of unimagined social progress for queer activists. In the same year Milk ran for a position with the San Francisco Board of Supervisors, the dehumanizing and irrationally homophobic policies of the McCarthy era were finally overturned when in 1973, a federal judge ruled that termination from federal employment could not occur if based exclusively on their sexual orientation. San Francisco had become a magnet for queers during the 1950s, and queer activism had become increasingly active with groups such as the Mattachine Society and the Daughters of Bilitis.[97] Bilitis was a female character romantically associated with Sappho. Milk's motivation for a political career began with wanting to redress the social and financial disparity that existed in the rapidly changing San Franciscan demographic. When he ran again in 1975, his focus was increasingly on queer issues, and he became a public face of the emboldened queer rights movement in the years following the Stonewall Uprising.

Two years after leaving his job as a broker on Wall Street, Milk moved with his lover, Scott Smith, into a San Francisco neighbourhood known as The Castro. The Castro remains the epicentre of the gay village for the city and was one of the first 'gaybourhoods' in the United States. Milk earned his nickname as the Mayor of Castro Street after standing on a crate with the word 'soap' and launching his candidacy.[98] This followed a dispute with a local business leader who endorsed a special tax for small business owners. Milk was in tune with the shifting demographics of San Francisco, which had morphed from a predominantly white, working-class population to one that comprised a range of ethnic minority groups, young and childless couples, queers, singles and a growing community of elderly. Milk's platform existed on the basis of providing a voice for these groups.

As is often the case with aspiring leaders who challenge the status quo, particularly from the position of 'other' within a broad context, the detractors, threatened by a changing world they do not understand, were ready to undermine Milk's agenda. Initially, Daniel White, also an elected member of the Board of Supervisors, worked well with Milk, agreeing on several areas of governance. However, following a disagreement regarding the opening of a facility for juvenile offenders, an irreconcilable rift emerged. In 1987, White resigned his seat as supervisor, and later, when he sought to reverse his decision, he was denied by the Mayor at Milk's request. He later entered the offices of Moscone and Milk, fatally shooting them both. During White's trial for the murder of Mayor George Moscone and Harvey Milk, he claimed diminished responsibility resulting from depression, coining the term 'twinkie defence' owing to his change in dietary habits. In 1984, he was paroled but allegedly confessed to intentionally killing Moscone and Milk in addition to intending to murder two other people in City Hall. Two years following his premature release, which angered the queer community, his marriage had fallen apart and he committed suicide.

Stewart Wallace's opera, *Harvey Milk Reimagined*, is a reworking of the original 1995 version, set to a libretto by Michael Korie and completed in 2019. In it, White's character is given a particularly sinister reading which hints at a much longer premeditation of bigoted attacks on members of the queer community. With the proliferation of queer characters and their allies in the opera, White casts a lonely shadow, isolated in his homophobia. The notion of 'other' is thereby subverted, and White's desperate and intolerant actions are magnified in their divergence from the prevailing theme of social progress. Korie's libretto mainstreams queerness, and moments of passion, tenderness, humour and determination abound. White, by contrast is out of step, given little in the way of a backstory which allows for a degree of empathy, and his musical material is less mellifluous at best and often unabashedly sinister. Whereas many other queer-themed operas construct narratives pertaining to a certain hero character and their supporters, *Harvey Milk Reimagined* is a raw and merciless depiction of a conflict of ideals. The white, heterosexual and patriarchal society, confused by an emerging world they do not understand and the racially diverse, queer community with their burgeoning political activism seeking an end to heteronormative hegemony, is channelled into the two equally binary protagonists.

The libretto makes frequent use of linguistic markers that would be instantly recognizable by a queer audience. The gendered humour that subverts stereotypes, attributing feminine terms to men and masculine terms to women, forms an important part of the shared humour. In Act I, part iii, set in Harvey's Walk-In Closet in the 1960s, we are introduced to a group of friends, known as Closet Lovers. Closet Lover Scott comments on the poor ventilation, 'A girl could suffocate.' Anne the Beard responds, 'Half the queens in town would scream for a walk-in closet!'[99] Such phrases celebrate queer identity and repudiate the use of derogatory language by claiming ownership of it. Scott enjoys using additional phrases claiming queer identity, stating to Harvey, 'You don't have to stand there and take that from her, a big butch number like you.'[100] In referencing Dan White as 'her', Scott ironically positions White as a member of the group. By applying the feminine pronoun, White shares the group identity; however, the irony becomes an insult to his heterosexual identity. Harvey cautions Scott's language by reminding him that they could be arrested.

White's character expresses his homophobia in Act I, scene i, following the prologue. White appears when the sensual, ritualistic and delicate orchestral texture is abruptly interrupted by his aggressive outburst, 'FAG-GOT-T!',[101] accompanied with tremolos in the horns and sudden and loud glissandi from the strings. His choice of terms such as 'Faggot!' and 'Dyke' contextualize him as a villain. His concise vilification of the queer community is in stark contrast to the relative celebratory nature of his targets. He is represented as a somewhat one-dimensional character, who favours short, sharp hate speech with ineloquent phrases such as 'Shut up, faggots! Move it along.'[102] His aggressive and callous character is reflected in Wallace's orchestration by contrasting his material with the previous passage which conveys an erotic and ethereal atmosphere. Wallace utilizes a loud buzzer, crash cymbals, tom-toms and temple blocks to break the playful atmosphere in the closet scene, whereas White's material consists of rhythmically rigid accentuated textures, combined with brash dynamics highlighted by shrill bursts in the woodwinds.

White's overt homophobia adopts a less violent tone in Act II, when he is seen in the formal, City Hall setting, 'What we have here is not what it seems. We have people flaunting preferences the vast majority of us do not approve of.'[103] In an attempt to shame Diane Feinstein, by singing, 'You hosted a Lesbian wedding in your backyard. Isn't that so, Dianne?',[104] it becomes clear that he has misjudged his audience and further isolates himself. Feinstein returns the discussion to the establishment of a half-way house for children, to which White responds, 'What do gays care about children?'[105] This phrase further diminishes White, whose lack of interest in child welfare contrasts him with the efforts of Feinstein and Harvey. Despite his propensity for bullying, White is not cast as the victor in his verbal sparring. When he retorts, 'I don't put my mouth where it don't belong, and I don't swallow',[106] Harvey replies, 'Don't knock it till you've tried it.'[107] Humour is attributed to several of the queer characters throughout the libretto, but never to White, who is by contrast shown to be hopelessly outwitted.

Act I, part iii is set in the aftermath of the Stonewall Uprising, and the Stonewall Girls appear singing and executing a kick line. The score indicates it is 'Party time!', during which the rhythmical unison material with accentuated beats change into playful, syncopated melodies for the chorus. The use of drum kit, snare drum and 'wah' on brass instruments with a nod to popular music underscores the change of mood. Later in this scene, when Scott kisses Harvey, it is marked by a hit on drum kit and a bass drum. The celebration of the Stonewall Girls continues, as well as the syncopated, jazz-inspired orchestral accompaniment, throughout the opera. A further example of syncopated rhythms and popular music references representing queer identity of this is in Act I, part iv, when the 'Milk Train' supporters, led by Anne, celebrate the progress of Milk's campaign. Harmon mutes in the brass, brushes on the snare drum and tempo indications, such as 'Lay Back', all provide musical association with a festive, queer community.

Scott is an instigator during the riots singing, 'Christopher Street. It's brick-throwing time, Harvey Milk, Midnight at The Stonewall Bar. This time, let's go to jail for us. Is it a date?' Harvey is reluctant, noting that he could lose his job on Wall Street. In an indication that he is being persuaded to participate in the resistance, he reflects, 'I stand up for myself as a Jew. Why not as a man who loves men?'[108] Soon after, the stage directions indicate the symbolic change in Harvey's position, 'Harvey lifts his hands over his head and snaps his handcuffs apart.'[109] This moment of renewed sense of purpose and identity is accompanied by the sounds of shattering glass routed through speakers. Harvey remembers his name and the history of his people, both Jewish and queer.

The dialogue from various characters encapsulates the unfolding action, while Wallace utilizes rhythmically accentuated *ostinati* with the full orchestra, highlighting the action with specific percussion instruments such as bullhorn, wood blocks, police whistle and bass drum. Accents once again fall on the beat, simulating marching and Anne's shout of 'GAY POWER!',[110] with only approximate indication of pitch is an arresting effect and a demand for society to listen. Scott then sings, 'You think homosexuals are revolting? Bet your sweet ass we are!'[111] A chorus of rioters then chime, 'Christopher Street belongs to the queers!'[112] The busy scene finishes with one last chant from the chorus of rioters as they leave the stage, 'Out of the closets and into the streets! Out of the closets and into the streets!',[113] sung a capella by the tenors and basses of the chorus.

Korie makes concerted effort to present Milk's dual identity of queer and Jew, and these are explored at several moments during the narrative. The existence of multiple, concurrent identities has been widely researched,[114] and the intersection of identity produces important drivers for social activism. Harvey references the use of colour-coded stars for Jewish prisoners in Nazi Germany, singing, 'My star is a pair of triangles: one pink, one yellow. They overlap as I do.'[115] Henrietta Wong provides another example; she exclaims, 'I am Henrietta Wong of Asians for Affirmative Action. With Gays moving in and whites moving out, now is our chance to build bridges.'[116] Her dichotomous labels of 'gays' and 'whites' suggest a view of minority groups having a shared opposition to a white, male patriarchy. Ironically, her separation of people into ideologically opposed groups does anything but build bridges. She later sings, 'I liked what he did, and not just for gays',[117] indicating that Harvey represented minority groups other than the queer community. Harvey later questions, 'Do you think they want their government run by Blacks, women, Asians, Latinos and gays?',[118] confirming his sense of minority groups being under-represented in government.

Harvey and Scott's relationship is provided numerous expressions of eroticism and intimacy. In Act I, a moment of erotic excitement is juxtaposed with sudden silence, followed by a rhythmical duet between the timpani and vibraphone, representing a kind of sensual ritualism. The words 'homo' and 'God' are given special importance from Wallace's use of dramatic silence. Later, in Act I, part iii, while Harvey and Scott embrace, gradually thickening textures ascend from the orchestra. This simultaneously communicates the exhilaration of the marching crowds and the euphoria of Harvey and Scott. Towards the end of the opera, Harvey states to his mother, 'Mama, I've slept with over a thousand men. If you don't know by now . . . I'm gay. Queer. Feigelah.'[119] This is part confession and part affirmation of his dual queer and

Jewish identities. Harvey constantly seeks approval from his mother, another familiar queer experience.

Harvey Milk Reimagined consists of polarities: whereas the queer community is presented as the normality, with an abundance of love, freedom and joy, heterosexual society represents the 'other', which is characterized by meanness, restriction and anger. White's villainous character is the ultimate symbol of the 'otherness', as his phrase 'We are the people who pay their taxes, go to church faithfully ev'ry Sunday'[120] implicates, by suggesting he does not only represent himself but also the customs and values of the dominant, heteronormative society. In contrast, Harvey's Mama appears as a gentle, idealized dream figure: she does not seem real and only appears occasionally as a concerned, symbolic guardian angel for Harvey. Whereas White's appearance on stage is usually accompanied with loud and dissonant textures with upwards glissandi, Mama's lines are mellifluous and gentle. Both roles are archetypical; White represents a toxic and brutal father figure, and Mama's appearances only radiate innocence, purity and passivity. As with the myth of Oedipus, anger and tension build between the 'father' (White) and the 'son' (Harvey), until a fatal conflict transpires. As de Kuyper argues, homosexuality is also a fundamental part of heterosexuality, 'The other is in himself and around him.'[121] Homophobia stems from the frustration of not being able to be 'at the same time the other gender and being "total"'.[122]

As with many art works that deal with the oppressive society that victimizes queerness, this opera provides a transparent juxtaposition between the righteous queers and the villainous straight, white man. The message does not promote the heroism of Milk, so much as demonize the hegemony of the heterosocial hierarchy. Although White's premature release from prison after only five years in Soledad State Prison greatly angered the queer community, still horrified by the violent attack, his subsequent demise is in opposition to the veneration of Milk's legacy in a multiplicity of art forms. Queer activism cannot eliminate hate crimes, but the energy generated can ensure that history records the barbaric events with the appropriate tone.

THE LIFE AND DEATH(S) OF ALAN TURING, JUSTINE F. CHEN

Until 2009, the man voted in a 2019 BBC series as the greatest person of the twentieth century was a relatively obscure figure. British prime minister Gordon Brown addressed the government, making an official, public apology for the appalling way he was treated. This was followed in 2013 by a posthumous pardon by HM Queen Elizabeth II, which allowed the introduction of a new law known as the 'Alan Turing Law'. This law retroactively pardoned 49,000 men who had been cautioned or convicted under archaic legislation outlawing homosexual acts. Turing (1912–1954) now features on the Bank of England £50 note and is commemorated by numerous statues. Public interest in Turing was initially sparked in 1983, with the publication of Andrew Hodges' biography, *The Enigma of Intelligence*, and a proliferation of material followed, including David Leavitt's biography, *The Man Who Knew Too Much: Alan Turing and the Invention of the Computer* (2006), and others by Gottfried (1996) and Copeland (2012), as well as several documentaries and a Hollywood biopic *The Imitation Game* (2014) directed by Morten Tyldum.[123]

To state that Turing saved England from the Nazi threat in World War II may not be overstating the significance of his contribution to the war effort. Official war historian Harry Hinsley estimated that thanks to Turing's groundbreaking work at the codebreaking centre at Bletchley Park, the war was shortened by two years and saved around fourteen million lives. The Government Code and Cypher School (GC&CS) included a section known as Hut 8, which focused on cryptanalysis of the German navy's infamous Enigma machine. Believing that the Enigma machine provided undecipherable codes, the Nazi regime communicated much of their military strategy through it, giving them a distinct advantage.

Following the end of the war, Turing continued his work on creating a 'universal computing machine' at the National Physical Laboratory, where he designed the Automatic Computing Engine, one of the earliest blueprints of a stored-program computer. His accomplishments were never fully recognized in England during his lifetime, as much of his work was protected through the Official Secrets Act. In 1952, Turing was prosecuted under the Labouchere Amendments of 1885, which listed 'gross indecency', including homosexual acts, as a criminal offence and remained in force until 1967. Presented with the option of chemical castration treatment and imprisonment, he chose the former. The treatment involved changes in hormone levels designed to reduce his libido, known then as stilboestrol, and now as diethylstilbesterol, a synthetic oestrogen which 'feminized' his body with impotency and the formation of breast tissue. He was also barred from his consultancy work for the Government Communications Headquarters.

Had Turing not been burgled, and had he not reported it to the police, in the process acknowledging his relationship with the perpetrator, nineteen-year-old Arnold Murray, his important work as the 'father of the computer' could have continued. The libretto condenses and distorts the timeline of Turing's burglary and arrest. In actuality, the burglary that Alan reported occurred weeks later; he and Arnold saw each other for a few weeks on and off, and Arnold was bragging to a low-life acquaintance at the bar, who then broke into Alan's house. Arnold was culpable in the actual event as an accessory but was tried for gross indecency along with Turing. Turing's solicitor provided no defence during his trial, and Murray's charges were dismissed. Turing's body was found by his housekeeper, next to which was a half-eaten apple which is speculated to have been injected with cyanide. An inquest determined that he had committed suicide, and a popular theory espoused by two biographers is that he was inspired by the scene from Walt Disney's film, *Snow White and the Seven Dwarfs* (1937), in which the Wicked Queen submerges her apple in poison; it was Turing's favourite movie. He was fascinated by the scene in which the queen transforms into the hag, a representation of transhumanism and process of soul transference.

Acknowledgement of Turing's contributions was late in coming, and more recently, he was further immortalized in operatic form by composer Justine Chen and librettist David Simpatico. Commissioned in 2012 as part of their Composer Librettist Development Program, the two-act opera is currently in development at American Lyric Theater, having undergone a series of workshops and concert performances. Part One is entitled 'The Rise of Alan Turing', followed by Part Two, 'The Fall of Alan Turing'. The meaning behind the bracketed plural in the work's title is revealed in scene viii of Part Two. Death One explores the most widely accepted version of events – that Turing committed suicide. Death Two and Three discuss the two divergent theories belonging to Turing's mother and close friend as well as former fiancée, Joan Clark. His mother believed that he had poisoned himself by accident, while Joan was convinced that he was murdered as part of a government conspiracy. Death four is entitled 'Transfiguration', symbolizing Turing's final experiment in which he uploads his soul to the digital universe.

In the first scene that follows a short prologue, Alan is with his close friend, Christopher Morcom, in a Cave of Wonders. The two young men, seventeen and eighteen, respectively, have been running, and their conversation is interrupted with the appearance, by means of a flashback, of a group of boys from Sherborne School, 'a tumble of raging hormones and in-borne privilege'.[124] The older boys have adopted the term 'Masters', while the underclassmen which include Alan and Chris are endeared as 'Fags'. The 'Fag-masters' instruct their servants to undertake a series of what can be considered as repressed, homoerotic duties, such as boot cleaning and wrestling matches. 'Fagging', a time-honoured practice in British boarding schools whereby younger boys were made to act as personal servants to older boys, first appeared in accounts going back to the seventeenth century but likely existed even earlier. The boys eventually exit the scene, leaving Alan terrified and crying. It is in the moments that follow, as Chris comforts Alan, that the loving relationship they share is revealed (figure 6.2).

At this moment of the scene, the chorus have moved offstage and echo chosen parts of the text homophonically. In doing so, they provide a dream-like

Figure 6.2 Chris and Alan's Love Scene, Part I, Scene i. Justine F. Chen and David Simpatico, *The Life and Death(s) of Alan Turing*, pp. 48–49 [piano/vocal score], Unpublished, 2019.

atmosphere – rhythmically unobtrusive and uncomplicated and underpinned by static strings, replete with harmonics. Chen allows the disturbance of the school boys to melt away, but the intimacy and eroticism of the moment ends with Chris' departure, followed by whisperings from the chorus that reveal his untimely death from consumption. The chorus occupies three distinct roles within the space of a few minutes in this scene, contributors to onstage, sonic effect and Greek chorus. In real life, Alan acknowledged Chris, an outstanding student and science enthusiast, as the inspiration for much of his accomplishments; however, Chris was uncomfortable with outward displays of affection, and Alan did not reveal his true feelings towards his friend.[125]

The chorus functions as a mechanism by which the chronology of Turing's life is suddenly advanced. Through contrapuntal whisperings, spoken word and sung text, carefully selected phrases signpost new characteristics of the period ahead of the following scene. The whisperings and occasional use of *Sprechstimme* also offer a sense of secrecy, symbolic of Turing's own personal, sexual secrets, as well as the Official Secrets Act which would soon shroud all of his work and the 'chatter of a thousand clicking, code-breaking needles'. In the following scene, Alan is with Fred Clayton, a fellow with Alan at Cambridge, and although about to be married expresses a bi-curious nature as the two grapple shirtless with a boat they are dragging through the sand. Fred provokes Alan with repeated sexual innuendo, and their language increases in eroticism until Alan kisses Fred. Fred cruelly rejects the physical gesture, admonishing Alan, and hints at the dangers of being caught while reminding him of his impending marriage.

In the following scene, 'The Code-breaker', Alan's flirting with Steve Todd, his handsome assistant, alarms some of his co-workers. Explaining that he is speaking in code, he sings cheekily, 'So hot, one might have to blow on it, sir.'[126] The use of codified queer language is a familiar trope in sexually oppressive societies, but here, Simpatico reveals its use to the audience. Alan is cautioned by Don Bayley, 'Your behavior is arrogant, foolish and reckless! What if some handsome spy seduces you?'[127] Bayley's character is played by the same baritone that sings the role of the Bobby and the Prosecutor, and all three represent the institutional homophobia of post-war Britain. Bayley's exasperation is matched by Alan's mother in the following scene, who pleads with him, 'Can't you try at least to blend to pass, to do as you should?'[128] Alan rejects her position on a need for a loveless social contract in the form of a marriage. He explains his decision to Joan, 'You see, I have certain homosexual ah tendencies', which Joan considers 'A glitch'.[129] Joan is willing to enter into a common arrangement in Britain whereby 'an acceptable cover for men and their wives. With room on the side for a friend, or a lover'[130] can offer safe harbour from a gossiping society and homophobic justice system.

In scene v, when Alan encounters the flirtatious Arnold Murray, Chris appears in the form of a ghost. He echoes the warning of the Bobby, 'Go, before you catch your death',[131] a premonition of the fate of his dalliance with the nineteen-year-old thief. Part Two begins the morning after Alan and Arnold have slept together, and as the conversation regarding the money Arnold has stolen from Alan's wallet escalates, Arnold's denial extends to his sexuality when he shouts, 'You know what else? I like girls! I like girls, I'm not some bloody pervert!'[132] The last phrase is vocalized using *Sprechstimme*. It is not the missing money that riles Alan but the deceit and accusation of perversion which provokes him to call the police.

The trial that follows presents Alan in a defiant role reminiscent of Oscar Wilde's acerbic response to a courtroom half a century earlier and is an invented fantasy from Simpatico intended to depict what Turing may have imagined as a gallant defence. In it, Alan subverts the prosecution process by requesting a definition for 'gross indecency',[133] which the bumbling prosecutor struggles to adequately provide. Following the verdict in which the options of hard labour or chemical castration are tabled, Alan retorts, 'Your Honor, no matter what manner of poison you throw our way, people like me, we will survive.'[134] This visceral moment forms part of the social phenomenon known as collective memory, a dimension that represents a shared memory within a cultural group.[135] For queers, the spaces represented in this opera evoke an experience of the past which is tactile and intuitive, a collective memory of a well-established political identity, that of a prejudiced society denying the possibility of a dignified and satisfying life.[136]

The Life and Death(s) of Alan Turing joins a growing list of operatic tributes to important historical queer figures such as King Edward II in George Benjamin's *Lessons in Love and Violence*, Gertrude Stein in Ricky

Gordon's *27,* Oscar Wilde in Theodore Morrison's *Oscar,* Eleanor Roosevelt in Daniel Davis' *The Impossible She* and Harvey Milk in Stewart Wallace's *Harvey Milk Reimagined.* This resource has only just begun to be tapped for operatic material, and the seemingly limitless possibilities of other historical figures being added to the repertoire of operatic accounts are tantalizing. Chen and Simpatico have created a recounting of Turing's life that celebrates his genius and recognizes the senselessness of bigotry and homophobia that is England's shame. The personification of the sexual oppression that characterized this dark period of Britain's history comes in the form of several minor characters but is most effectively conveyed by a clever use of the chorus. Often split between onstage and offstage choirs, the complexity of their material, combined with their omnipresence throughout the opera, with a minimum requirement of twenty-four voices, is suggestive of a medium to large, professional company needed to stage it effectively.

Alan Turing is rightly acknowledged in British culture following the decades of disregard. His contribution to the war effort and his unfinished work on conceptualizing what might have been the world's first computer make him a towering intellectual figure. His humiliation that led to his untimely death based on a consensual gay sexual encounter in which he was the victim of a crime reflects a low point for the British judicial system. Just as with Oscar Wilde, another fiercely queer intellect, Turing's heroism comes not in the form of outsmarting the Enigma machine but in his refusal to play the game that so many other men so willingly engaged in. Refusing the kind offer of Joan's to a non-sexual marriage may not have been a street-smart move, but it reflects a man unwilling to betray his principles. Such marriages of convenience were relatively common and were known colloquially as a 'Lavender Marriage' or 'Marriage Blanc'. At every point following his encounter with Murray, he made a series of stupid decisions or gallant resolutions, depending on the perspective of the observer. Throughout history, legislators have compromised the ability of their citizens to fulfil their creative potential through fear of behaviours and identities that, although posing no discernible threat to society, are deemed as some form of danger to society at large. Such legislation is not merely a temporal anomaly belonging to a forgotten generation but continues unabated and with populist support in regions throughout the world today.

NOTES

1. E. Cram, 'Pulse: The matter of movement', *QED: A Journal in GLBTQ Worldmaking* 3, no. 3 (2016): 147–150.

2. Emily Waters, 'Lesbian, gay, bisexual, transgender, queer, and HIV-affected hate violence in 2009: A 20th anniversary report from the national coalition of anti-violence programs' (New York, NY: National Coalition of Anti-Violence Programs (NCAVP), 2017), accessed 4 March 2022, https://ncvc.dspacedirect.org/handle/20 .500.11990/257.

3. Jeff Gruenewald, 'Are anti-LGBT homicides in the United States unique?' *Journal of Interpersonal Violence* 27, no. 18 (2012): 3601–3623.

4. Jeff Gruenewald and Kristin Kelley, 'Exploring anti-LGBT homicide by mode of victim selection', *Criminal Justice and Behavior* 41, no. 9 (2014): 1130–1152.

5. Tri Keah Henry, Brittany E. Hayes, Joshua D. Freilich, and Steven Chermak, 'Comparison of honor killings to anti-LGBTQ homicides', *Journal of Aggression, Conflict and Peace Research* 10, no. 4 (2018): 272–282.

6. Philip Marshall Ward, 'Hofmannsthal, Elektra and the representation of women's behaviour through myth', *German Life and Letters* 53, no. 1 (2000): 37–55.

7. Andrew Scull, *Hysteria: The Biography* (Oxford: Oxford University Press, 2009).

8. Kurt Borg, 'Narrating trauma: Michel Foucault, Judith Butler and the political ethics of self-narration' (PhD diss., Staffordshire University, 2019).

9. Quoted in translation in Harriet Anderson, *Utopian Feminism: Women's Movements in Fin-de-Siecle Vienna* (New Haven, CN: Yale University Press, 1992), 231–232.

10. Peter Gahan, 'Jitta's atonement: The birth of psychoanalysis and "the fetters of the feminine psyche"', *SHAW: The Annual of Bernard Shaw Studies* 24, no. 1 (2004): 128–165.

11. Richard Strauss and Hugo von Hofmannsthal, *Elektra, Op. 58* [full score] (Berlin: Adolph Fürstner, 1916), 208–211.

12. Strauss and von Hofmannsthal, *Elektra*, 219–220.

13. Strauss and von Hofmannsthal, *Elektra*, 223. *Von jetz an will ich deine Schwester sein, so wie ich niemals deiner Schwester war!* (From now on, I want to be your sister, just as I never was your sister!).

14. Strauss and von Hofmannsthal, *Elektra*, 227.

15. Peter Olive, 'Reinventing the barbarian: Electra, sibling incest, and twentieth-century Hellenism', *Classical Receptions Journal* 11, no. 4 (2019): 407–426.

16. Strauss and von Hofmannsthal, *Elektra*, 305.

17. Martin Bernheimer, 'BLOOD SISTERS (the Works and Career of Richard Strauss Is Discussed, in Particular the Two Characters Salome and Elektra)', *Opera News* 64, no. 2 (1999): 10–14.

18. Mary Ann Doane, *Femmes Fatales* (Milton Park: Routledge, 2013), 2–3.

19. Alban Berg, arr. Erwin Stein, *Lulu* [piano reduction] (Vienna: Universal Edition, 1936), 166.

20. Berg, *Lulu*, 166.

21. Berg, *Lulu*, 168.

22. Berg, *Lulu*, 264–265.

23. Berg, *Lulu*, 181.

24. Clara Hunter Latham, 'How many voices can she have? Destabilizing desire and identification in American Lulu', *The Opera Quarterly* 33, no. 3–4 (2017): 303–318.

25. Berg, *Lulu*, 201.

26. Berg, *Lulu*, 203.

27. George Perle, 'The music of "lulu": A new analysis', *Journal of the American Musicological Society* 12, no. 2/3 (1959): 185–200, accessed 26 May 2021, doi:10.2307/829540.

28. Kevin S. Amidon, 'What happens to countess Geschwitz? Revisiting homosexuality in Horkheimer and Adorno', *New York Journal of Sociology* 1 (2008): 1.

29. Richard Leppert, 'Music "pushed to the edge of existence" (Adorno, listening, and the question of hope)', *Cultural Critique*, no. 60 (2005): 92–133.

30. Michael McDonagh, 'Composer Nico Muhly on his "gay opera"', *Bay Area Reporter*, 10 January 2013, 13, accessed 13 August 2021, https://issuu.com/bayareareporter/docs/january_10_2013.

31. Nico Muhly and Craig Lucas, *Two Boys: An Opera in Two Acts* [Full score] (New York, NY: St. Rose Music Publishing Co., 2013), 38.

32. Mary H. K. Choi, 'thefader.com', *The Fader*, 18 October 2003, accessed 3 October 2021, http://www.thefader.com/2013/10/18/interview-nico-muhly.

33. Chris Ashford, 'Queer theory, cyber-ethnographies and researching online sex environments', *Information & Communications Technology Law* 18, no. 3 (2009): 297–314.

34. Margaret Gratian, Sruthi Bandi, Michel Cukier, Josiah Dykstra, and Amy Ginther, 'Correlating human traits and cyber security behavior intentions', *Computers & Security* 73 (2018): 345–358.

35. Naomi Barrettara, 'Cyber-narrative in opera: Three case studies' (PhD diss., City University of New York, 2019).

36. Muhly and Lucas, *Two Boys*, 65.

37. John Suler, 'The online disinhibition effect', *CyberPsychology & Behavior* 7, no. 3 (2004): 321–326.

38. Muhly and Lucas, *Two Boys*, 112.

39. Muhly and Lucas, *Two Boys*, 149–157.

40. Marianna Ritchey, 'Nico Muhly, two boys. Nonesuch Records 7559795602, 2014, 2 CDs', *Journal of the Society for American Music* 9, no. 2 (2015): 252–255.

41. Muhly and Lucas, *Two Boys*, 204–210.

42. Muhly and Lucas, *Two Boys*, 218.

43. Muhly and Lucas, *Two Boys*, 219.

44. Muhly and Lucas, *Two Boys*, 264–265.

45. Muhly and Lucas, *Two Boys*, 280.

46. Muhly and Lucas, *Two Boys*, 282–283.

47. Cameron Muir, 'Misunderstood: The Matthew Shepard hate crime and its intercultural implications', *Proceedings of the New York State Communication Association* 2011, no. 1 (2012): 6.

48. Town-Crier Editor, 'April 4 Fundraiser in Wellington to aid opera fusion project', *Town-Crier*, 25 March 2016, accessed 27 January 2021, https://gotowncrier.com/2016/03/april-4-fundraiser-in-wellington-to-aid-opera-fusion-project/.

49. Michael Ross, *Not in My Town* [Piano/vocal score] (Unpublished, 2016), 6.

50. Ross, *Not in My Town*, 8.

51. Ross, *Not in My Town*, 10.

52. Ross, *Not in My Town*, 33.

53. Ross, *Not in My Town*, 3.

54. Ross, *Not in My Town*, 59.

55. Rod Stafford Hagwood, '"Not in my town" revisits Matthew Shepard story', *South Florida Sun Sentinel*, 1 June 2016, accessed 28 January 2022, https://www.sun -sentinel.com/entertainment/theater-and-arts/sf-lauderdale-opera-matthew-shepard -advance-20160601-story.html.

56. Ross, *Not in My Town*, 77–78.

57. Ross, *Not in My Town*, 87–88.

58. Konor Cormier, 'Increase the peace means increase the penalty: The impact of the James Byrd, Jr. hate crimes act in Texas', *Texas Tech Law Review* 34 (2002): 343.

59. Ross, *Not in My Town*, 10.

60. Muir, 'Misunderstood', 6.

61. Joseph O. Baker, Christopher D. Bader, and Kittye Hirsch, 'Desecration, moral boundaries, and the movement of law: The case of Westboro Baptist Church', *Deviant Behavior* 36, no. 1 (2015): 42–67.

62. Miche Marc Bouchard, *Les Felluetes* (Unpublished libretto, 2015), 7.

63. Bouchard, *Les Felluetes*, 8.

64. Bouchard, *Les Felluetes*, 9.

65. Bouchard, *Les Felluetes*, 9.

66. Bouchard, *Les Felluetes*, 9.

67. Bouchard, *Les Felluetes*, 11.

68. Bouchard, *Les Felluetes*, 15.

69. Bouchard, *Les Felluetes*, 15.

70. Bouchard, *Les Felluetes*, 16.

71. Bouchard, *Les Felluetes*, 20.

72. Bouchard, *Les Felluetes*, 39.

73. Bouchard, *Les Felluetes*, 44.

74. Bouchard, *Les Felluetes*, 46.

75. Bouchard, *Les Felluetes*, 12.

76. Réjean Beaucage, 'Kevin March and Les Feluettes: An American inspired by France', *La Scene Musicale*, 1 April 2016, accessed 14 January 2022, scena.org/lsm/ sm21-6/sm21-6_march_en.html.

77. Arthur Kaptainis, 'Composer Kevin March says Les Feluettes was an opera all along', *Montreal Gazette*, 3 June 2020, accessed 5 May 2022, https://montrealga- zette.com/entertainment/composer-kevin-march-says-les-feluettes-was-an-opera-all -along.

78. Kaptainis, 'Les Feluettes was an opera all along'.

79. This story emerges around sixty years after Edward's murder. In all like- lihood, he died from suffocation, having being held down and smothered with a pillow, but the poker story that has become popular with the idea of a humiliated,

emasculated King being sodomized to death is too tantalizing a story to be troubled by the truth.

80. Fiona Maddocks, 'Lessons in love and violence review – a bolder, angrier, more tender George Benjamin', *The Guardian*, 20 May 2018, accessed 15 December 2021, https://www.theguardian.com/music/2018/may/19/lessons-in-love-and-violence-review-george-benjamin-royal-opera.

81. George Benjamin and Martin Crimp, *Lessons in Love and Violence: Opera in Two Acts* [Full score] (London: Faber Music, 2017), 1.

82. Benjamin and Crimp, *Lessons in Love and Violence*, 14–15.

83. Benjamin and Crimp, *Lessons in Love and Violence*, 59.

84. Benjamin and Crimp, *Lessons in Love and Violence*, 60.

85. Benjamin and Crimp, *Lessons in Love and Violence*, 61.

86. Benjamin and Crimp, *Lessons in Love and Violence*, 73.

87. Benjamin and Crimp, *Lessons in Love and Violence*, 94–95.

88. Benjamin and Crimp, *Lessons in Love and Violence*, 98.

89. Benjamin and Crimp, *Lessons in Love and Violence*, 99.

90. Benjamin and Crimp, *Lessons in Love and Violence*, 100–101.

91. Benjamin and Crimp, *Lessons in Love and Violence*, 126–127.

92. Edward was murdered around four months after his deposition, therefore technically not an act of regicide.

93. Benjamin and Crimp, *Lessons in Love and Violence*, 143–144.

94. Benjamin and Crimp, *Lessons in Love and Violence*, 146.

95. Benjamin and Crimp, *Lessons in Love and Violence*, 166.

96. Benjamin and Crimp, *Lessons in Love and Violence*, 180–181.

97. Jason Edward Black and Charles E. Morris III, 'Harvey Milk and the hope speech', *Voices of Democracy Journal* 6 (2012): 63–76.

98. Harvey Milk, *An Archive of Hope: Harvey Milk's Speeches and Writings* (CA: University of California Press, 2013).

99. Stewart Wallace and Michael Korie, *Harvey Milk Reimagined* [Full score] (New York: Sidmar Music, 2019), 77–80.

100. Wallace and Korie, *Harvey Milk Reimagined*, 90–100.

101. Wallace and Korie, *Harvey Milk Reimagined*, 65.

102. Wallace and Korie, *Harvey Milk Reimagined*, 97.

103. Wallace and Korie, *Harvey Milk Reimagined*, 306.

104. Wallace and Korie, *Harvey Milk Reimagined*, 388.

105. Wallace and Korie, *Harvey Milk Reimagined*, 400–401.

106. Wallace and Korie, *Harvey Milk Reimagined*, 407–408.

107. Wallace and Korie, *Harvey Milk Reimagined*, 409.

108. Wallace and Korie, *Harvey Milk Reimagined*, 130–131.

109. Wallace and Korie, *Harvey Milk Reimagined*, 149.

110. Wallace and Korie, *Harvey Milk Reimagined*, 159.

111. Wallace and Korie, *Harvey Milk Reimagined*, 167–168.

112. Wallace and Korie, *Harvey Milk Reimagined*, 169.

113. Wallace and Korie, *Harvey Milk Reimagined*, 181.

114. Hector Y. Adames, Nayeli Y. Chavez-Dueñas, Shweta Sharma, and Martin J. La Roche, 'Intersectionality in psychotherapy: The experiences of an AfroLatinx queer immigrant', *Psychotherapy* 55, no. 1 (2018): 73.

115. Wallace and Korie, *Harvey Milk Reimagined*, 138–139.

116. Wallace and Korie, *Harvey Milk Reimagined*, 238–240.

117. Wallace and Korie, *Harvey Milk Reimagined*, 247.

118. Wallace and Korie, *Harvey Milk Reimagined*, 323–324.

119. Wallace and Korie, *Harvey Milk Reimagined*, 510–512.

120. Wallace and Korie, *Harvey Milk Reimagined*, 320–321.

121. Kenneth Lewes, 'A special oedipal mechanism in the development of male homosexuality', *Psychoanalytic Psychology* 15, no. 3 (1998): 341.

122. Eric De Kuyper, 'The Freudian construction of sexuality: The gay foundations of heterosexuality and straight homophobia', *Journal of Homosexuality* 24, no. 3–4 (1993): 137–144: 142.

123. Laura Doan, 'Queer history queer memory: The case of Alan Turing', *GLQ: A Journal of Lesbian and Gay Studies* 23, no. 1 (2017): 113–136.

124. Justine F. Chen and David Simpatico, *The Life and Death(s) of Alan Turing* [Full score] (Unpublished score, 2019), 21.

125. Georgina S. Voss, '"It is a beautiful experiment": Queer(y)ing the work of Alan Turing', *AI & Society* 28, no. 4 (2013): 567–573.

126. Chen and Simpatico, *The Life and Death(s) of Alan Turing*, 86.

127. Chen and Simpatico, *The Life and Death(s) of Alan Turing*, 114.

128. Chen and Simpatico, *The Life and Death(s) of Alan Turing*, 132–133.

129. Chen and Simpatico, *The Life and Death(s) of Alan Turing*, 138.

130. Chen and Simpatico, *The Life and Death(s) of Alan Turing*, 139–140.

131. Chen and Simpatico, *The Life and Death(s) of Alan Turing*, 156.

132. Chen and Simpatico, *The Life and Death(s) of Alan Turing*, 181.

133. Chen and Simpatico, *The Life and Death(s) of Alan Turing*, 191.

134. Chen and Simpatico, *The Life and Death(s) of Alan Turing*, 205.

135. Maurice Halbwachs, *On Collective Memory* (Chicago: University of Chicago Press, 2020).

136. Doan, 'Queer history queer memory', 113–136.

Chapter 7

Homoerotic Awakening

With the onset of puberty comes the transformative process into adulthood when sexual urges usually begin to manifest. For many, this is a time of self-discovery, curiosity and pleasure. For queers, this journey into erotic adventures is often complicated by aggressive, conscious repression for fear of natural, sexual urges revealing an identity that is rejected internally and by others. For many of the adult characters in the operas discussed in this chapter, such forceful denial of natural processes results in a latency, whereby the need to recognize sexual impulses surfaces as forcefully and problematic as the repression. We turn once again to Freud for an explanation of the phenomenon of latent homosexuality.

The inverse form of Freud's Oedipal complex, in which the child forms an unconscious erotic attachment to the parent of the same gender and rivalry with the parent of opposite gender, fosters latent erotic, homosexual urges for adults. Freud's negative Oedipal etiological explanation views homosexuality as a regression away from heterosexuality. According to Freud, when internal reticence compounded by external frustration become an inhibitor of heterosexual development, regression draws the person back to earlier psychosexual moments of fixation. These fixation points can include a constitutional predisposition or traumatic overstimulation.[1]

Richard Isay supports the notion that homosexuality is not a failed version of heterosexuality on the basis of the denial of reproduction. He proposes that manifest homosexuality emerges from an alternative constitutional and psychosexual framework than latent homosexuality. His research asserted that homoerotic fantasies are often present from the ages of four or five years, a period which is analogous to the Oedipal stage shared by heterosexual boys. The point of difference being that the primary sexual object for homosexual boys is their fathers.[2] In this paradigm, the boy is inclined towards romance

233

with the father and an envious and competitive relationship with the mother, while the father provides a concomitant withdrawal. Latent homosexuality is fostered in part by Oedipal disappointment, whereby homoerotic urges are attacked and criticized, often labelled as taboo. Reinforced powerfully by the need for social conformity, the suppressed impulses impact personality development, a dormant force waiting with expectation for eventual release.[3]

The five characters in this chapter each express a homoerotic awakening in very different ways. In Szymanowski's *Król Roger*, the title character's suppressed homoerotic urges are awakened with the arrival of a beautiful, young shepherd boy, forcing him to question his conservative ideals of moral order. Tippett explores latent homosexuality in his opera *The Knot Garden* through Faber's sexual advances towards Dov in a milieu of heightened sexual tension. Kimper's title characters Patience and Sarah both explore their new-found erotic urges quickly after first meeting in a narrative which plays with gender identities and female independence. With a sudden and unexpected attraction towards a beautiful, young model, Petra von Kant teeters on the edge of insanity with her insatiable need to control the object of her lust in Barry's astoundingly unique score, *The Bitter Tears of Petra von Kant*. The final opera in this chapter is from Daniel Thomas. By stark contrast to Barry's drama, Davis explores the lesbian love affair of Eleanor Roosevelt and Lorena Hickok in *The Impossible She* in an opera imbued by beautiful poetry and quiet sensuality. With the exception of *Patience and Sarah*, each of these operas involves bisexual characters who, for a variety of reasons, give in to the underlying homoerotic urges that have hitherto remained dormant but are now awakened.

KRÓL ROGER (KING ROGER), KAROL SZYMANOWSKI

Travelling through southern Europe in 1914, Karol Szymanowski (1882–1937) was in the company of a young heir to a chemical fortune, Stefan Spiess. The two travelled regularly together, drinking in the heady delights of the Mediterranean, where the concept of homosexuality was tolerated and accepted to a greater degree than his conservative homeland, Poland. Szymanowski confessed to Arthur Rubinstein (1887–1982) of his delight with the trip, 'I saw a few young men bathing who could be models for Antinous. I couldn't take my eyes off them.'[4] These trips must have had a liberating effect on the composer, who invoked the twelfth-century Sicilian King Roger II (1095–1154) in his next opera. Szymanowski's middle period is characterized by his interest in orientalism, inspired by frequent visits to Italy and Sicily, Algiers and Tunis, where he enjoyed the cultural melting pot of the Mediterranean and Arabic worlds. This is exemplified in his Third Symphony

(1916), with the homoerotic overtones of thirteenth century from Arab mystic Jalal' al'Din Rumi's poem, *Song of the Night*.

Szymanowski's visits to Italy were also recalled in his novel, titled *Efebos*, written between 1917 and 1919. The novel was never published as it included erotic recollections of homosexual liaisons of the central character, Prince Ali Lowicki.[5] Thought to be lost in World War II along with many of the composer's early works when the Szymanowski estate at Tymoszówka was destroyed during peasant riots, a small portion survived. The book was blatantly semi-autobiographical, and an account of the plot was published by Szymanowski's cousin and collaborator on *Król Roger*, Jaroslav Iwasz-kiewicz (1894–1980). Also known under his literary pseudonym, Eleuter, Iwaszkiewicz was also homosexual and the two spent much time travelling around Italy, although always returning to Poland. It was in the summer of 1918 that the two cousins conceived of the project.

Also referred to by Szymanowski as the 'Sicilian drama', the opera was first entitled 'The Shepherd' and, beginning in 1918, took six years to complete. Although Iwaszkiewicz was tasked with setting the libretto, Szymanowski made numerous amendments before the completion of the first draft in 1920. During the embryonic stage of the opera, the composer met a young, Russian refugee, Boris Kochno (1904–1991). He told Rubenstein of this youthful man of extraordinary beauty, and the two enjoyed a brief affair which inspired Szymanowski who claimed that it was only thanks to their love that he could write so much music. He lost contact with the young man when the composer helped him to escape Warsaw. Later, in a trip to Paris, Szymanowski met with ballet impresario, Sergei Diaghilev (1872–1929), and learned, to his bitter disappointment, that Kochno had become his secretary and lover.

The fin de siècle period was an artistic period, dominated by the musical concepts of Wagner and, philosophically, by the thinking of Arthur Schopenhauer (1788–1860) and Friedrich Nietzsche (1844–1900). Schopenhauer's characteristic pessimism connected erotic ecstasy with death, while Nietzsche, by contrast, espoused the invigorating properties of Dionysian fervencies.[6] Szymanowski drew inspiration from all of these sources, and *Król Roger* is also a product of his attempt to explore erotically charged elements found in Wagner's *Tristan und Isolde* (1865). The narrative of *Król Roger* persistently suggests psychoanalytical aspects of eroticism. As well the Shepherd's narcissistic tendencies, Roxana's attempts to seduce Roger have overtones of maternal instincts that evoke Oedipal conflicts.

Król Roger is set in three acts and explores the themes of 'duality' and 'transformation'. As with Britten's *Death in Venice* (see chapter 5), the narrative interprets Friedrich Nietzsche's Apollonian and Dionysian conflict as established in his 1872 book, *The Birth of Tragedy from the Spirit of Music*. Apollo is embodied by the religiously conservative King Roger, whose control over his Christian orthodox kingdom is turned upside down by a beautiful, young shepherd. The shepherd introduces the royal court to the delights of Bacchanalian, erotic seduction. The King's wife Roxana is quickly seduced by the pagan abandonment of the bewitching youth, but the King, steadfast in his sense of duty and public persona, is a tougher nut to crack. Roxana's conversion represents a bitter blow for the King; however, one reading of her motivation is that rather than wanting to run away with the beguiling young shepherd, Roxana simply wanted to rekindle her sexual relationship with her husband. Roger's turmoil may reflect Szymanowski's personal, internal conflicts as an openly practising homosexual functioning in an unaccepting, conservative society.

The king's character is based on the Norman King Roger II (1095–1154), a member of the Hauteville dynasty. He was responsible for uniting all of the Norman conquests of Italy into a single kingdom with centralized government. During his reign, a period of enlightenment in which religious and academic tolerance stems from a pluralistic, cultural society thrived. During his travels, Szymanowski admired the fusion of various Mediterranean, African and Middle Eastern backgrounds that made up the Sicilian population, and it is reflected in the 'exoticism' of Edrisi's character. Other than these basic points, there is little basis of historical fact to *Król Roger*.

This highly sexualized opera involves no overtly queer characters or same-sex relationships; however, the Dionysian allegory of the beautiful, young shepherd, seductively tempting the king and his courtiers, provides a foundation for a homoerotic struggle that challenges sexual identity as much as any sense of morality. Alone and abandoned by his followers, Roger sings a hymn to the sun, which provides opportunity for several interpretations. Roger has perhaps awakened from a dream and rejected the wicked ideals of pleasure presented by the Shepherd. Alternatively, he accepts the prevailing ecstatic vision of a Bacchanalian freedom. It is also possible that Roger has found harmony in the idea of a concurrent ideology, where Apollo and Dionysus are both free to exert influence. Ultimately, it is clear that Roger has experienced a transformative moment. Certainly, *Król Roger* exhibits none of the gory bloodletting of Euripides' original ending, a decision seemingly at odds with many of his predecessors such as Strauss (*Salome*), Puccini (*Madame Butterfly, Tosca*), Poulenc (*Dialogues des Carmélites*), Massenet (*Cléopâtre*) and Halévy (*La Juive*).

Just as a dichotomous philosophical conflict unfolds in the libretto, so too does Szymanowski's score. Alternating between Wagnerian use of leitmotiv and an impressionistic aesthetic, the score illustrates a tension between two divergent musical styles. Each of the three acts demonstrates symbolic stylistic transformations that relate to the evolving narrative. Act I, known as the 'Byzantine act', begins with the mixed chorus and a chorus of children, chanting from the depths of a large cathedral, in oscillating psalmody. Medieval modes form the basis of the harmonic material, and an ecclesiastical atmosphere dominates the textures. Act II, the 'Oriental act', opens with chromatic lines that verge on atonality.[7] Set in the royal palace, architecturally influenced by a mixture of Oriental and European styles, the music utilizes Arabic augmented seconds and mordents, and there are distinct references to Moroccan oboe melodies. Complex rhythms that inform the character of the religious dance begin in 7/8 (4+3), and a hypnotic ostinato underpins an Indian-inspired melody that represents the Shepherd. Act III, the 'Greco-Roman act', has a mystical quality and is less dramatic than the second act but involves the shepherd disguised as Dionysus, converting Roger among the ruins of a Greek theatre. Roxane, in the form of a maenad, is given a final dance before disappearing and then the opera is completed with the king's final hymn to Apollo.

Szymanowski's dualism extends to his use of major and minor triads to reflect the male/female, attraction/repulsion dichotomies.[8] The choral opening set in a Byzantine church in Palermo consists entirely of triads, until King Roger and his court enter. At this point, the music becomes chromatic to the point of tonal ambiguity and the passage includes much of the important melodic and harmonic material on which the opera is based such as some of the 'oriental' material to appear in Act II.

The harmony is densely packed with associative material, echoing Wagner. There are two unresolved augmented chords in the midst of oscillating major and minor chords, underpinned by a winding chromatic melody. All of the sound worlds are present in this thickly textured orchestral material. Edrisi, who reports the appearance of the shepherd, is given an 'oriental' four-note, descending motif, and ariations of this motif highlight the oscillating major/minor trait.

The appearance of the Shepherd interrupts the chanting chorus, and suddenly the religious fervour is invaded by a bold declaration of reverence to aesthetic beauty. The king exclaims that he is destroying his people by his mere presence, to which the Shepherd replies, '*Mój Bóg jest pie-kny jako ja*'[9] (My God is beautiful like me). The melody is given a whole-tone treatment, while the chords that follow begin their descent from adjacent major sixth chords to a disintegration into chromatic dissonance. The orchestral response to the Shepherd's line prophesies his arrival, bringing discord to the kingdom. Later in the act, the Shepherd's smile represents an important symbolic moment in the opera and is mentioned no less than thirteen times. It comes in response to the king's statement that the Shepherd has total freedom in his kingdom. His smile receives a variety of descriptions, including 'wonderful' or 'miraculous' (*cudowny*)[10] or as full of 'mystery' or 'secrecy' (*tajemnicy*).[11] Suspicious of the foreigner in his midst, Roger perceives malice and deception in the youth's eyes; however, the Shepherd notes the king's appreciation for '*mitują uśmiech mój,i mój taneczny śpiew*'[12] (my smile and my dancing singing). In Act III, Roger recognizes the same smile on Roxana, who has been utterly seduced by the smile. This provides a shared erotic link between the Queen and the Shepherd, and the androgyny of the boy seems to lean to the feminine.

The moment of the Shepherd's seductive smile is also bathed in whole-tone constructs – the Dionysian expression of beauty. According to Plato's *Symposium* (c. 385–370 BC), the 'ladder of love' represents the ascent of a lover from a purely physical attraction to something beautiful, such as a beautiful body, to actual contemplation of the Form of Beauty itself. It is on the highest rung of the ladder that the very essence of beauty is found. The ladder is presented by Diotima at a men's banquet, involving impromptu philosophical speeches in praise of Eros, the Greek god of love and sexual desire. Roger sees in the shepherd a reflection of his own femininity, and he finds the eroticism of the youth disturbing. The central characters in the opera are personifications of Roger's psyche; Edrisi represents his conscious and rational qualities, while the shepherd embodies the unconscious and rational part. In Act II, with Roger's denial of Eros, he finds himself isolated, with only Edrisi onstage following the oriental dance and call to follow the shepherd. Musically, Szymanowski treats Roger's loneliness with bare fifth chords, the absence of either major or minor tonality signifying the denial of Eros. The main tenant of Szymanowski's book *Efebos* was the idea of freedom gained from the work of Eros.

During Act II, as the seductive presence of the Shepherd invades the imagination of the king and his court, threatening the peace and order in the kingdom, the dialogue is laden with symbolic omens. King Roger sings, 'In the eyes of the shepherd a fire flared up which will scorch my heart to ashes.'[13] Queen Roxana, however, dispels any omens of danger, interceding in support of the shepherd. She sings, 'Tonight the eagle will not hunt even the smallest bird; the serpents sleep around lily stalks; goodness flows down to us from the white flame of the planets. Ah!'[14] Her remarks only serve to heighten the tension but more importantly illustrates her endorsement of the shepherd and his ideals.

The representation of androgyny throughout the opera is not accidental. Iwaszkiewicz and Szymanowski explored numerous religious and sexual taboos in their projects, and they frequently made use of the process of aesthetic sublimation. Aesthetic sublimation presents the normative claim for fulfilment while concurrently revealing that such a claim cannot and ought not be satisfied. In a 2009 production at the Gran Teatre del Liceu in Barcelona, the shepherd was dressed in drag for certain scenes.[15] To understand the implications of androgyny in *Król Roger*, we must explore the dual parts of the ego, which develops from the manifestation of sexual identity into sexual practice. Tadeusz and Maj (2020) argue that transference of one's sexual ego to a male ego requires confrontation with the fatherly ego, and such a confrontation between 'father' (King Roger) and 'son' (the shepherd) ends in either verbal or physical conflict. If the process involves autosexual or homosexual identity, the negative effects of the Oedipus complex can be mitigated. Therefore, the Shepherd's Oedipal and non-Oedipal sexual practices are not irrational. Through the process of the king's initiation into the Dionysian ideals, the Oedipal ego becomes androgynous, attaining the level of the self.[16] During the individual development of self, the Oedipal ego is neutralized by an alternative, erotic behaviour, and it can therefore attain self-realization as a meta-sexual androgynous ego.

Szymanowski suffered from the effects of childhood tuberculosis, which was exacerbated by financial stress. In 1927, he was forced to accept the position of chief of the Fryderyk Chopin Music Academy in Warsaw to alleviate his deepening fiscal problems. When Rubenstein met up with the ageing composer, he noted his developing hypersensitivity to noise and agoraphobia. Szymanowski died in a sanitorium in Lausanne at the age of fifty-four, the same year the pink triangle began to be used in German concentration camps to identify sodomites.

THE KNOT GARDEN, MICHAEL TIPPETT

Michael Tippett's third opera *The Knot Garden* (1966–1970), which presents changing British attitudes to gender identity, war, violence, sex, homoeroticism and social alienation, coincided with the introduction of the Sexual Offences Act in 1967, decriminalizing homosexual acts in England and Wales between two men over the age of twenty-one in private. It would be another three years before Britten's *Death in Venice* and another eight years until Peter Maxwell Davies made public his homosexuality, making Tippett a pioneering queer opera composer in Britain, matched by Lou Harrison across the Atlantic with his opera, *Young Caesar* (see chapter 1). Gay liberation in the late 1960s and early 1970s shared many characteristics of other prevailing protest movements from the period, but most importantly that it was a genuine revolution which encountered violent police repression and a mixture of thinly veiled tolerance and measured judgement from liberal humanists.

The three-act opera involves seven characters: Faber, a civil engineer; Thea, his wife, a gardener; Flora, their ward, an adolescent girl; Denise, Thea's sister, a freedom fighter; Mel, a black writer; Dov, his white lover, a musician; and Mangus, a psychoanalyst. Mangus' function in the opera is that of a voyeur, and his motivation is ambiguous such that the audience is left

to consider possible erotic interest in either Flora, Dov or Thea. Underlying
sexual tension between various characters is evident immediately when Flora
rushes hysterically and tearfully onto the stage, prompting Thea to accuse
Faber of being lecherous. The breakdown of the marriage between Thea and
Faber forms a central tenet of the opera, but Mel and Dov, a gay couple, are
experiencing similar tensions in their relationship which they play out when
presenting Shakespeare's *The Tempest* (c. 1610–1611) in a 'play-within-a-
play' structure. Tippett created his own libretto for *The Knot Garden*, which
comprises a highly fragmented series of short scenes that present as a mosaic
of rhetorical dramas. The drama does not unfold in a conventional form, but
the nature of each relationship unravels through a string of brief and unresolved exchanges. Tippet's use of discontinuous narrative serves to heighten
the dramatic tension of each exchange, and this is supported by unpredictable
juxtapositions of musical ideas.[17]

Faber and Thea's dysfunctional marriage provides a symbolic representation of the decline of traditional, heteronormative concepts of Christian
morality as described by Jung in a 1929 letter to Walter Corti:

> We live in the age of the decline of Christianity, when the metaphysical prem-
> ises of morality are collapsing . . . That's why the young are experimenting like
> young dogs. They want to live experimentally, with no historical premises. That
> causes reactions in the unconscious, restlessness, and longing for the fulfilment
> of the times.[18]

Bernstein would approach the same topic in *A Quiet Place* (see chapter
5), in which characters clinging to archaic notions of a nuclear family are
increasingly marginalized by changing societal values that more willingly
accept diversity. With the abolition of the theatre censorship law in 1967, the
requirement of plays to be presented to Lord Chamberlain's office for exami-
nation and licensing ceased. The former custodian of moral standards, based
on conservative, Christian and pro-establishment values, would restrict any
form of offensive, indecent or blasphemous material, and overtly homosexual
themes were particularly targeted.

The Knot Garden is imbued with symbols to such an extent that they tend
to obfuscate a sense of recognizable reality. A knot garden is a formal box
hedge and low shrub formation, popular in Elizabethan England, and reflecting the architecture of the respective property. Knot gardens were sometimes
considered as a maze and is of special importance symbolically in the second
act with characters being 'sucked in' and ejected from its labyrinth for each
exchange. Tippett suggests in the score that the scene may be controlled by
Mangus like a 'huge puppet show'.[19] Tippett's interest in Jungian psychology is reflected in his use of the knot garden as a metaphor for the Jungian
Collective Unconscious, which Tippett felt could provide truth, empathy and

togetherness as an anecdote to feelings of isolation and disorientation in a violent and 'godless' world.[20]

It is perhaps with Dov that Tippett connected especially, as he explained, 'The question is often posed to me: with which of your operatic characters do you most identify? The assumed answer is usually Mangus [. . . but] for me, an identification with Dov, the singer, the musician who expresses heartbreak, has always seemed close.'[21] Despite this, there is a discernible lack of detail underpinning the motivation of Dov's character, and it is perhaps this semi-formed state that prompted Tippett to compose further material for him outside of the opera. Dov and Mel's broken-down relationship is instantly apparent, as they portray Arial and Caliban from *The Tempest*, which seems to be an effort to avoid dealing with their fragile connection. When Thea seduces Mel with little effort, Dov is left 'howling like Ariel's dog',[22] just as the one Arial impersonates in the play. At the time of writing this opera, Tippett's own turbulent relationship with Karl Hawker was reflected in Mel, who was questioning his own sexuality. His relationship with Hawker ended as a result of Tippett's burgeoning affair with music writer, Meirion Bowen.

Tippett's autobiographical link with Dov and his painful howling over Mel's betrayal is most likely linked with the suffering that the composer experienced when his relationship with Wilfred Franks ended. Their relationship represented the deepest feelings of love Tippett had ever known, and when Franks left Tippett to get married, communication ended abruptly. It was at this emotional nadir that the composer sought help from Jungian psychologist, John Layard, and the invention of Dov may signify a cathartic release of the psychological misery that he had endured. Dov's alignment with Arial throughout the opera emphasizes his queerness and musicality. Arial is a fairy sprite and has a long tradition of being depicted with asexual and androgynous characteristics. He is male, yet all of the roles he plays at the command of Prospero are female; sea nymph, harpy, Ceres and productions of *The Tempest* routinely explore the ambiguity of his gender.

Gender ambiguity was a concept at odds with the prevailing view in 1960s Britain, that gender and sexuality were inextricably linked. Tippett constantly wrestled with the widely held societal belief that homosexuality was both a symptom and a cause of effeminacy. Karl Ulrich (1825–1895) proposed that homosexuality was neither a sin nor an illness and considered the possibility of a 'third gender', whereby a feminine soul was enclosed in a male body.[23] Similarly, Michel Foucault (1926–1984) considered the idea that homosexuality represented an 'interior androgyny' or 'hermaphrodism of the soul'.[24] The popular stereotype in the early part of the twentieth century of gay men and musicians as perpetuators of effeminacy and sexual abnormality was something of which Tippett was conscious, and he frequently explored the concept of masculinity and femininity being a singular union. He complained that as a student, he felt that composers and musicians were considered in terms of a feminine sensibility but not in terms of masculine intellect, whereas artists involved in literature or drama were given permission to use their intellectual faculties to explore their created worlds. By creating Dov as musician and Mel as a wordsmith, they symbolize opposing gender identities as do so many of their other characteristics explored throughout the opera. His treatment of Dov as an androgynous Ariel can be considered as an embodiment of his ideals of gender identity.

With Faber's crumbling relationship with Thea, he seeks alternative ways to explore his sexuality, and in Act II, his curiosity manifests in an erotic flirtation with Dov. He sings, 'Dov, what if I want you: have power to tempt, to force? Come. I never kissed a man before.'[25] Faber's curiosity regarding his dormant homosexual impulses suggests that long-held desires surface when opportunity is presented. His marriage no longer provides the barrier for him to act on his instincts, and subconscious impulses become conscious action. Jung wrote extensively on human instincts and asserted that no instinct rivals the spirit as strongly as the sexual instinct. He also explained that pressures to conform or to deny natural instincts create psychological splits between inner needs and outer demands.[26] Tippett encountered several instances where lovers suppressed their sexual instincts in order to conform to the conservative demands of society, and through Faber, he is able to allow it to rise to the surface and breathe.

Faber is 'whirled away' as Mel is 'whirled off' and the scene merges into a song and dance number with and obligato clarinet arpeggiating over a texture characterized by muted brass, Jazz guitar and drum kit. Mel accuses Dov of loving 'the manhood, not the man you make your god'.[27] He then challenges him to 'Strip off the sham!'[28] Dov simply responds to Mel's denunciation with the phrase, 'I love you.'[29] It is moments such as these where Tippett's score seemingly preferences symbolism and meaning over visceral music evocative of some form of humanizing emotion. His reference to Jungian psychology, frequent use of literary references and allusions, such as *Alice in Wonderland* and *All's Well That Ends Well*, coupled with his interest in the surrealist world of Dadaism, govern his eclectic approach to his music such that the audience can be left somewhat bewildered and unsure of how they should react.

Tippett's initial concept of *The Knot Garden* was not to avoid the use of a central character or characters but to present a number of contemporary figures, through which to explore relationships through the lens of a psychoanalyst. Denise is the final character to arrive in the narrative, and she symbolizes the flourishing women's liberation movement of the day. Gay liberation owes much of its momentum to the pioneering feminist movement and the promotion of civil rights for social minorities. Her commanding entrance puts her strength of conviction on full display and her half-majestic, half-sinister appearance is compounded by the effects of torture that have left her 'twisted or otherwise disfigured'. She sings, 'I want no pity. This distortion is my pride. I want no medal. The lust of violence has bred contamination in my blood. I cannot forget.'[30] Her ambition is to achieve equal respect in the eyes of a patriarchal system, and by rejecting sympathy, she embraces sexual equality.[31]

Tippett created the libretto and the score for *The Knot Garden*, and his musical eclecticism matches the complexity of his literary framework. The opera begins with a clear statement of a twelve-tone row: B, F, C sharp, D, G, G sharp, B flat, A, C, E flat, E, F sharp, and there is strong chromaticism throughout, although the final moments comprise several ascending whole-tone scales. In addition to the angular vocal declamations, there is frequent use of extend vocal techniques such as the anthropomorphized manifestations of Arial's bird and dog, Caliban's grunts, Flora's wordless whimpering and several instances of whistling. Denis and Flora both have extended coloratura moments, and there is even use of the technique known as the *trillo* from the Italian renaissance. Any sense of melodic familiarity is contained discreetly within a short scene, rather than developing as a *leitmotiv* for any of the characters. Moments of diegetic music in the form of the cathartic blues ensemble at the end of Act I, and the Schubert lied in Act II disrupt the action. The Blues references, as well as the phrase in which Dov explains his place of origin, 'I was born in a big town . . , where the buildings grew so mighty high',[32] and the general informality of the text, reflect Tippett's recent discovery of America, which had enormous impact on his creativity.[33]

The final act involves the staging of *The Tempest*. Mangus declares the beginning of the play by explaining that the garden has now become an island for the benefit of the audience and fellow thespians alike. Through the process of the performance in which each of the players represents the roles assigned by Magnus, the fate of each of the relationships unfolds. Mangus reveals that Prospero is fake and confesses that he is 'but a foolish, fond old man, just like the rest of you; whistling to keep my pecker up; whistling to a music compounded of our groans and shrieks'.[34] Thea and Denise, who remained in their own characters, had been critical of Mangus as the voyeuristic impresario, witness Mangus' disenchantment, having been tricked by Eros 'in his masks of love'.[35] The ensemble concludes by espousing the Jungian ideals of individuality and the natural expression of sexual instinct by singing, 'If for a timid moment we submit to love, Exit from the inner cage, turn each to all.'[36] Led by Dov, they call on the audience to embrace these ideals in the moment before exiting. Finally, Thea and Faber are resolved to reconciliation; the process of change, sexual discovery and understanding achieved through the theatricality created by the psychoanalyst has ultimately healed the wounds.

PATIENCE AND SARAH, PAULA M. KIMPER

In historical dramas involving queer characters, the external pressures exerted at budding homosexual relationships are seemingly endless. In 1816 Connecticut, known as the 'Year Without a Summer' because of severe climate abnormalities causing a dramatic drop in temperatures, conventional attitudes towards queerness were equally frosty. The opening lines of the preamble to Connecticut's Laws of 1672 included the first American 'code', a list of 'Capitall offences lyable to death',[37] written in Plymouth Colony in 1636 and including treason, murder, witchcraft, arson, sodomy, rape, buggery (referring here to bestiality) and adultery. Not quite the unreserved haven for minorities fleeing persecution in search of a country free from religious and political oppression.

Adding to the political hegemony was the omnipresent views of the conservative church, which asserted its values into the heart of the community and its behaviours. The Puritans of the New England colonies functioned under the belief that their new home would suffer the same consequences as the Jews in Palestine should any sexual 'abominations' be tolerated. Sodomy was subsequently considered a 'fearful' sin. The early Quakers in Pennsylvania viewed homosexual acts with shared abhorrence; however, adopting a less vengeful approach introduced a penalty of six months imprisonment:

> If any person shall be Legally Convicted of the unnatural sin of Sodomy or joining with beasts, Such persons shall be whipt, and forfeit one third of his or her estate, and work six months in the house of Correction, at hard labour, and for the Second offence, imprisonment as aforesaid, during life.[38]

Such a punishment was positively humane in comparison to the death penalty and remained the most progressive penalty in any American state until 1961.

Paula Kimper's opera *Patience and Sarah* (1998) marked the end of a relatively lengthy quiet period for queer opera. The work is based on the novel of the same name, penned by Alma Routsong under the pseudonym, Isabel Miller. The libretto was created by Wende Persons, a college friend of Kimper, with whom she developed a relationship following a commitment ceremony for mutual friends they both attended in 1990. Person's libretto was completed within three weeks as a response to a lesbian opera singer to whom Persons was attracted, who explained her difficulty with identifying with the straight characters she was constantly asked to play. Following a search for suitable literature, she was interested in the happy ending found in Miller's story. Miller signed over the rights to her story just prior to her death after hearing excerpts of Kimper's score.

Patience and Sarah was commissioned by American Opera Projects and it premiered in 1998 at the Lincoln Center Festival in New York. The opera deals with universal themes of gender ambiguity, sexuality, eroticism and heteronormative hegemony from a specific time and place. Kimper explained, 'It is a positive story, inspired by real-life early 19th-century lesbians. Patience and Sarah deals with the universal themes common to all relationships of shame and guilt, of passion and commitment, and of honesty with one's families.'[39] In addition to the two title characters, there is a role for a bisexual man whose homosexual interests manifest through a mistaken identity plot twist – a narrative device with an extensive history in opera.

The two protagonists present as stark opposites in the narrative, and Kimper further contrasts their characteristics through their vocal material. Patience comes from a well-to-do family, she has a strong interest in painting and is imbued with thoroughly feminine qualities. She is written as a lyric soprano with mellifluous phrases frequently in the high register. In scene iii, Patience becomes jealous and sings, 'Who's Rachel?',[40] beginning on fortissimo, accented high B, then repeated in a much lower register as she realizes her overreaction given that Rachel is Sarah's sister. By contrast, Sarah comes from a hard-working family in which all children are female and, consequently, is expected to adopt the role of a boy – dressing as such and working physically to help her family make ends meet. Sarah is a mezzo-soprano, and her melody lines are simpler and occupy the lower parts of the female vocal tessitura. The juxtaposition of these characteristics provides a space in which gender roles are explored as utilitarian as well as the basis for eroticism.

In the opening scene, Sarah articulates the reason for her boyish ways to Sarah whom she has just met, 'I'm Pa's boy. He couldn't get one the regular way, just got girls, so he picked me out to be a boy.'[41] Patience, who is instantly curious about her new friend, asks, 'Do you like it?' Sarah responds to her, 'Being a boy? It's best, I expect, Anyhow, it seems natural now.'[42] The word 'natural' to describe a form of gender fluidity stretches forward in time with heightened awareness of modern relevance. The term 'natural' reappears in a later scene when Patience attempts a reproachment with her sister-in-law. She reflects, 'You used to come here to see me, but then you saw Edward and you liked him better',[43] to which Martha responds, 'Well, it's only nat'ral.'[44] The same term is used for the compelling force of physical attraction, occurring naturally in both homosexual and heterosexual instances. In an earlier scene, Patience muses over her initial meeting with the captivating Sarah, 'Who is this brave and outrageous young woman? . . . Standing there in her boots and breeches, wearing that smile and telling her dreams?'[45]

In scene ii, Patience learns of Sarah's desire to leave her family farm and go 'pioneering' in an attempt to buy land and create a life for herself. Patience asks, 'Do you think anyone would let a woman alone with no money buy land?'[46] and Sarah responds, 'They don't have to know I'm a woman.'[47] The basis of the opera rests on the frustrated attempts to achieve the goal of independence, and following their meeting, the two women set about achieving it together. The real-life figures, Mary Ann Willson (Patience) and Miss Brundage (Sarah) who managed to live and farm together on Red Mill Road, Greenville Town, Greene County, New York State, for many years, were well aware of the legislation that made such an exercise virtually impossible.

The American colonies adopted the same laws as the various mother countries which generally dictated that husbands would control women's property. The nineteenth-century common law of coverture vested all legal rights to the husband, and married women were prohibited from entering into any contract without consent of their husbands. Single women were a rarity at this time, and as legislators were uniformly men, any need for reform took many years to be considered.[48] In New York, legislation was passed giving women some say in how their husband dealt with their assets, requiring married men to include their wife's signature on all property deeds which they intended to sell or transfer. Additionally, a judge was required to meet privately with the wife to receive confirmation of her approval. Although women in Connecticut maintained a complete lack of agency, an 1809 law was introduced which permitted married women to execute wills. This allowed a man other than the husband to manage their assets in a trust. These and other laws which took small steps towards acknowledging women did so only on the provision that they followed the heteronormative practice of marriage.

The blossoming romance between Patience and Sarah is discovered, and Patience's sister-in-law Martha voices her disapproval, 'There's fit ways, and there's unfit ways!'[49] She cannot quite bring herself to articulate the precise form of her objections. The music involving characters from the two families takes on a gloomier quality, which gives way to a sunnier style when they are left alone. This is particularly evident in Act I, scene iii, when they declare their feelings for one another. Sarah sings, 'There's something else. There's how I feel. You might not like it, I care for you', and Patience responds, 'I want you to, I care for you, too, I don't want you to stop.'[50] Soon after this, they kiss and then embrace. The music characterizes the heightened anticipation in the lead-up to physical intimacy and is generally given a romantic tonal quality with frequent use of a series of unresolved suspensions. Sarah asks, 'Was that a feeling I felt in you?'[51] and they sing together a recurring phrase, 'That's something powerful.'[52] They sing separately initially but then homophonic and in thirds when singing together. Another kiss follows.

In Act I, scene iv, Sarah explains to her sister Rachel of the nature of her feelings for Patience, singing, 'I found my mate.'[53] Rachel does not immediately understand and is jealous of her sister's diverted attention, 'I hate her. She's rich and that's why';[54] however, Sarah elucidates, 'It's different, She kissed me. I never felt such a feeling.'[55] In an attempt to understand the situation, Rachel reaches for Sarah's adopted gender role, 'I used to worry no man would have you. I never thought to worry you'd think you was a man',[56] but Sarah corrects her, 'I'm not. I'm a woman that's found my mate.'[57] Sarah is quick to embrace her new relationship with Patience and makes no attempt to conceal it, choosing to announce it to her shocked and outraged family. When Patience's brother Edward confronts her, singing, 'Sarah Dowling is making it her brag that you're her mate . . . Something like wife she means . . . She says the two of you are like man and woman',[58] Patience is terrified, turning pale, and repudiates the allegation. Pa confirms the patriarchal approach to women who refuse to conform, roughing Sarah up and pushing her to the ground, 'That's to show if you don't know enough to do right, I can still make you.'[59]

In Act II, scene i, Sarah is forced to retreat to her imagination when she departs alone to go 'pioneering'. Imagining a letter she would write, she sings, 'Oh, Patience, I wish I could write to you, I wish I could tell you how hard it is out here alone. Patience, my love.'[60] The farmers out West believe her to be a boy, and Sarah adopts the name Sam to maintain her disguise. One farmer's daughter woke her early, urging her to be on her way as her father was planning to turn her in for a reward. She professed, 'Sam, you're sweet'[61] and kissed her. Sarah explained to Patience in her imaginary letter, 'But it wasn't like your kisses, nothing to feel real deep.'[62] This *en travesti* role adds to the long tradition of operatic breeches roles such as Leonore's alias, Fidelio, in Beethoven's opera of the same name (1805) and Strauss' roles of the Composer in *Ariadne auf Naxos* (1912) and Octavian in *Der Rosenkavalier* (1911).

When Sarah stumbles across the path of Parson Peel in Act II, the two become unlikely travel partners. As with the farmer's daughter, Peel, a young travelling bookseller, believes Sarah to be a boy named Sam. As the Parson is teaching Sam (Sarah) to read, he (she) makes occasional errors, which he corrects. One of the errors involves misreading 'meat' for 'mate', an echo of the term used to describe her relationship with Patience in Act I and a reminder that she has not been forgotten. The Parson and Sarah discuss astrology and Sarah searches for meaning from hers and Patience's star signs. This is followed by the Parson singing a lullaby to 'Sam' in which he sings of love, 'Let me kiss you one more time, and let me hold your hand.'[63] With the Parson's belief that he is singing to a young man, the scene has homoerotic undertones supported by subtle stage directions, 'He resists an urge to touch her by sitting on his hands.'[64] The parson reveals that he is married, but when questioned by Sarah about his way of life, he responds ambiguously, 'I love my wife, and I love the open road, it's just the way I am. You have to be yourself, Sam, and live your dreams.'[65]

In Act II, scene iii, Patience and Sarah, although separated by distance, sing a duet in which they articulate their romantic desire for one another. The moment is abruptly interrupted with the Parson declaring his erotic desires for 'Sam', singing with his arm around him, 'I suppose you think men don't do this. I assure you that men have loved and embraced each other since the beginning of time.'[66] To the Parson's surprise, Sarah reveals her correct name and gender. Their parting at the end of Act II is on friendly terms.

Sarah returns home and notices that one of her sisters is dressed as a boy in Act III, scene i. After hearing of some of her sister's adventures, Rachel misreads the relationship Sarah had with the Parson, 'You was trapped in your lie of being a boy.'[67] This is followed by an awkward reunion between Patience and Sarah, which is overseen by Edward and Martha, neither of whom trusts the two women alone together. Later, Patience visits Sarah during an ice storm to give her a reading lesson and they rekindle their shared desire to go pioneering to Genesee. The reading lessons continue and on one occasion, Sarah arrives at the White household to find that Patience's family is out, allowing them time alone. With their momentary solitude, Sarah sings, 'When I first came back, I couldn't believe I'd ever kissed you or ever would again.'[68] They quickly begin imagining growing old together in blissful union; Patience sings to Sarah while caressing her and kissing her neck, 'Shall I tell you what our house looks like? Or what happens there?'[69] As they begin undressing and kissing passionately, Martha enters, observing them in quiet shock before exploding, 'What are you doing?'[70] Edward quizzes her about the efficacy of her prayers, to which Patience responds, 'I found I didn't wish to be free of it.'[71] After an uncomfortable wrangle over the disapproved relationship, Sarah leaves and Patience rebukes Martha's judgement of her by singing, 'Sarah's my family now.'[72]

In a surprising change of heart, Edward gives his blessing to the couple who leave together to start a life in Albany. As the boat leaves, the two women realize they are completely alone together and become increasingly exhilarated as they discuss their future together in short, segmented, interjecting phrases. The picture is idyllic, and as they sing of their love for each other the phrases climb higher, finishing on an interval of a perfect fifth with Patience on a high B flat.

Kimper was initially concerned about writing an opera with overtly lesbian characters. As well as being daunted by the prospect of writing an opera, she did not want to embrace being pigeon-holed as a queer composer because of the negative baggage that she felt would come with it. She noted that although the *en travesti* roles offered an unspoken acceptance of alternative expressions of gender, the rare depictions of lesbian characters were unsatisfying, stating, 'There are sometimes lesbian characters, but they're not happy people.'[73] *Patience and Sarah* was not the first opera to include self-identifying lesbians, but given that they are the title characters and central protagonists, this opera breaks new ground. The blossoming romance and eroticism between the two women are carefully balanced with the tension provided by the wider family members. The addition of the Parson is important in the way that his queerness is presented positively; he is friendly, helpful and honourable, helping to break the mould of homosexuality representing something sinister, damaged or untrustworthy. His arrival in the second act signifies queerness as a symbol of love and acceptance in contrast with the disapproval and constant hinderance of the heteronormative world. He is also a fascinating part of the narrative by representing organized religion in a positive way within a queer context – an unlikely prospect in 1816.

The sudden change of heart by Patience's family to allow her to follow her dreams and leave with Sarah goes largely unexplained; however, it provides the happy ending that Kimper was looking for in a libretto. She sets the final act in a neo-romantic style reminiscent of Poulenc and full of sunny optimism. The Lincoln Center Festival premiere was supported by the American Opera Project (AOP) and received praise from critics. AOP aims to tell American stories that provide voices for diverse parts of the community, and *Patience and Sarah* is one of three LGBTQ+ initiatives along with *Paul's Case* (2015) by Gregory Spears, based on a short story by Willa Cather, and Laura Kaminsky's *As One* (see chapter 5).

Mary Ann Willson, the historical figure behind Patience, has taken her place as one of several important American lesbian artists. She is considered to be one of the first American watercolourists, with pigments made from berry juice, brick dust and vegetable dyes. Her diverse subjects ranged from a primitive folk-art portrait, *The Two Sisters* (c. 1820), a portrait of George Washington astride his horse, a fanciful *Marimaid* (Mermaid, c. 1815) and *Pelican with Young* (c. 1815). It is believed that she stopped painting with the death of Miss Brundage, and her work enjoyed a rediscovery in 1943 with her watercolour series, *Prodigal Son*, now in a collection with the National Gallery of Art.[74] Despite all of the external pressures on their relationship, Willson and Brundage defied the odds and lived their idyllic life together on their little farm on Red Mill Road, Greenville Town, Greene County, New York.

THE BITTER TEARS OF PETRA VON KANT, GERALD BARRY

Unrequited love is a familiar theme throughout the range of dramatic platforms and opera has depicted its fair share, such as in Puccini's *Madama Butterfly*, Mozart's *Don Giovanni*, Donizetti's *Lucia di Lammermoor* and Tchaikovsky's *Eugene Onegin*. These are just a few of the many operas that feature characters thwarted by a desire for another that is unreturned. These are all examples of heterosexual desire; however, Gerald Barry's opera, *The Bitter Tears of Petra von Kant* (2005), based on Rainer Werner Fassbinder's screenplay for the film by the same name, offers a lesbian perspective. The film and the opera differ in terms of the pace of delivery; where Fassbinder sets a slow, deliberate and languorous tone, Barry presents a fast-paced, relentless thrust, characterized by repetitive rhythms, bold interjections from brass and percussion and a general frenzy.[75] The arresting opening moments of the overture introduce an angular, jaunty theme from unison horns, distinctive with its driving rhythm and conspicuously absent harmonic underpinning until the entry of the remaining instruments with an inverted form of the material. With the entry of Petra's opening lines, the music is structured with frenetic and acrobatic vocal lines interspersed with loud and equally frenzied punctuations from the orchestra. The effect presents the title character with a feverish nervousness, as she chats incessantly with the other characters.

Petra, a successful but arrogant fashion designer in her mid-thirties, reveals to her friend, Sidonie,[76] the details of her recent disastrous marriage. The extreme intervallic leaps in her vocal line suggest there is something unhinged about Petra. The explanation recounts aspects of the doomed relationship that do not satisfactorily explain the real cause of the problems, other than the suggestion that there were complex reactions to a power play between the two. She describes their sexual inelegance in the final period before the separation, 'He tried to hang on to me, at least in bed. But the disgust came with that part. He tried technique, then force. I let him mount me. Endured it. But . . . he seemed so filthy to me. He stank. He smelt like a man. Just the way men stink.'[77] Petra's revulsion for her ex-husband gathers intensity as she recalls feeling like, 'He had me the way a bull takes his cow.'[78]

Sidonie introduces Petra to Karin, a 'charming young lady'[79] she met on a ship from Sydney to Southampton, who wants to make a life for herself in Germany. Karin is impressed with Petra's relative youth, given her accomplishments, 'Success and fame. I don't know . . . it somehow goes with age.'[80] Petra responds by complimenting Karin on her figure. Karen's material is distinctly less frenzied than Petra's, and this contrast foreshadows the position of power that will emerge between the two.[81] In Act II, which continues on ceaselessly from Act I, Petra is characteristically nervous and preparing herself for Karin's visit, and during their conversation, it transpires that Karin is married and that her husband has remained in Australia. The scene concludes with Petra's reaction to Karin's story of her father killing her mother and then hanging himself. Petra is naturally shocked and evidently overcome with nurturing instincts which quickly escalate into desires for physical closeness. Petra invites Karin to live with her, a logical arrangement but one that provides proximity and possibilities of romance. She sings, 'I love you. I love you, Karin. I love you. Together, we can conquer the world. I'm confused. I want to touch you, and kiss you.'[82] Karin reciprocates partially but explains that she needs more time and uses the word 'like' in place of Petra's 'love'.

The disparity of levels of affection between the two women becomes more apparent as the relationship develops. The ongoing low-level bickering and squabbling reveals that Karin has been out all night, dancing with a 'big black man with a big black cock'.[83] Despite the promises of a relationship that embraced freedom, without the shackles of obligation, Petra is upset. Karin accuses her of being hysterical, which is reflected in the vocal material of both sopranos. This callous use of the term feeds into the nineteenth-century discourse on hysteria, considered to be a psychological disease found predominantly in women which today might be diagnosed as neurasthenia, hypochondriasis, depression, conversion reaction or ambulatory schizophrenia. Freud rose to international fame by redefining it and forming the basis of psychanalysis.[84] Karin's casual use of the word is loaded with meaning and positions her in the world of heteronormative hegemony, and to subjugate Petra's sexual identity, creating a power imbalance in Karin's favour.

Petra furthers the imbalance with desperate proclamations of adoration, 'You're beautiful. I love you so . . . I love you so badly it hurts.'[85] With the unexpected phone call from Karin's husband who has just arrived in Europe, she excitedly makes arrangements to fly and see him. This predictably sets off Petra's jealousy once again and this time, her reaction inspires her to call Karin a 'stinking little whore'[86] and spit in her face. Act IV begins with Petra, alone and drunk, vowing retribution and hurling abuse, while simultaneously declaring her deep, unrequited love. Her mother, daughter and friend, Sidonie, arrive to celebrate her birthday, which ends with another of Petra's extreme outbursts. As she abuses everyone in the room, she readily accepts that the cause is her disastrous relationship with Karin, which effectively outs her to her mother. The act ends with Petra's emotional statement of her wish for suicide, 'It just takes a few pills, mama. You wash them down with water and you sleep.'[87]

In the final act, the dramatic climax quickly subsides as Petra atones for her outburst to her sympathetic mother. Just as the conversation relaxes into a mode of acceptance and comfort, Petra articulates her epiphany regarding her relationship with Karin. She sings:

> It wasn't love I felt for her. I just wanted to possess her. Only now, that it's all over, am I beginning to experience love. This has taught me a lot, mother, and caused me a great deal of suffering. I had to learn, but should it have to hurt so much?[88]

The profound self-reflection has only just occurred, when the phone rings. It is Karin, and the two women agree to meet in what seems like an amicable *rapprochement*. The opera ends with an unexpected change in Petra's behaviour. Throughout the drama, the voiceless character of Petra's assistant, Marlene, has been a constant presence. Bossed around by Petra and treated with contempt, Marlene brings an endless supply of refreshments into each scene for the other characters. Her daughter expresses her disapproval at Petra's boorish mistreatment of Marlene, 'Why do you treat her so badly mother?'[89] Petra responds, 'Because she doesn't deserve any better, and she doesn't want it any differently anyway. It makes her happy, can't you tell?'[90] This phrase suggests Marlene's demure demeanour may hide her besotted passion for Petra, which compels her to endure a tormented masochistic existence.

Whenever mentioned, the orchestral interjection that defines Marlene's activity is characterized by especially enraged musical passages. In the final pages of the opera, Petra attempts to redress her horrible treatment of her loyal assistant, 'I need to atone, Marlene. For all I've done to you. In the days to come, we'll work together – really together – and you can enjoy yourself, just as you deserve.'[91] Marlene than approaches Petra and kneels before her in an act of subservient supplication, to which Petra responds, 'No, not like that. Let's sit down together . . . Tell me about your life.'[92] Barry discussed his love for Marlene's character, saying, 'The music is full of her. Often the orchestra goes mad when she is around. I am not sure what it is saying, but it is very dark and murky.'[93] The opera's narrative does not include Marlene's rebuke of Petra's change in attitude by packing her things and leaving, which occurred in Fassbinder's play.

By providing an all-female cast, men are relegated in this narrative to voiceless and formless entities, described and discussed from the female perspective. The seven men include Petra's ex-husband and father, Sidonie's ex-husband, Karin's husband, father and dalliance. It is only the insatiable black man who escapes a negative assessment from the respective female characters. Although the opera well and truly passes the Bechdel test, the importance of Petra's ex-husband in the themes of the drama is fundamental. Frank is afforded a withering commentary when Petra describes him to Sidonie; however, it is in the seemingly throw-away line, 'He wanted me kept. And so, in this roundabout way and all on its own, oppression made itself felt',[94] that we understand the cycle of narcissistic and masochistic behaviour that manifests in Petra. The disgust which Petra experienced made a profound impact, but Petra then passed on that mode of conduct to her treatment of Marlene. As Karin's dominance in her relationship with Petra asserted itself, she then applied the same form of masochism to Petra; however, the negative reaction in this instance was explosive.

The forms of oppression that exist in *The Bitter Tears of Petra von Kant* are derived from the internal relationship paradigms of the characters, rather than an oppressive external force that disapproves of anything that operates outside of a strict, binary gender system. The forces that directly oppress Marlene and Petra emerge and manifest within the emotional dynamics of relationships that are both queer and heteronormative. Fassbinder, himself a queer man, thereby establishes the notion of queerness as a universal experience, and the story's two protagonists are assigned bisexual identities rather than anything strictly lesbian. There is much to be learned from this opera from its themes of unrequited love, dominance, gender roles, abuse and control through manipulation, particularly when we discover that it is the long-suffering Marlene who has wielded the most control over her relationship with Petra than any other character.

THE IMPOSSIBLE SHE, DANIEL THOMAS DAVIS

Eleanor Roosevelt (1884–1962) was a controversial but popular figure during her lifetime, and the celebration of her achievements has only solidified her status. Her public persona was carefully crafted around her marriage to the thirty-second president of the United States, Franklin D. Roosevelt (FDR, 1882–1945), as the First Lady and mother of five. All of these heteronormative facets of her life formed a part of her identity but not all of it. Eleanor's bisexuality may have been erased through the carefully edited, public perception of heteronormativity, but in reality, her queerness was an omnipresence in her life. One of Eleanor's lesbian relationships began in 1932 when Lorena Hickok, known by many as 'Hick', was assigned to cover FDR during his first presidential campaign by the Associate Press. It was a relationship that would positively impact both women who, in many ways, were polar opposites. Lorena came from an impoverished background, was beaten by her father and left home at thirteen to become an independent, self-made woman. She was the first woman to be published under her own byline in *The New York Times*, and she was overtly lesbian. Eleanor came from a wealthy family of prominent New York socialites and on her wedding day was given away by the president of the United States at the time, Theodore Roosevelt (1858–1919).

There can be no doubt of the veracity of Eleanor and Leonora's relationship. Their daily correspondence articulates their deep affection, they frequently travelled together and Leonora eventually worked for the FDR administration as her relationship with Eleanor compromised her journalistic integrity. Historians do not doubt that the two women were completely in love but disagree over the extent to which their love manifested physically.[95]

Leonora's influence over Eleanor can be seen in sharpest focus with her suggestion that Eleanor hold her own press conferences and to restrict attendance to female reporters. This had a direct impact on the employment prospects for women in major papers. Leonora also suggested that Eleanor publish a daily column that outlined her experiences as First Lady, called 'My Day', as well as regular publications in magazines, all of which benefited from Leonora's editing expertise.[96] They became the first queer female power couple that Americans never knew they had.

Eleanor and Leonora operated in a gendered world that deemed their minds and bodies to have little value. The 'Present Voice' is personified in Davis' opera, *The Impossible She* (2019), by a saxophonist – symbolically genderless, wordless and yet an ever-present commentator on proceedings. Present Voice interacts with the voiced characters both musically and physically. Presenting voiceless characters through a specific instrument has been used increasingly as a technique in opera, such as Benjamin Britten's apprentice in *Peter Grimes* (1945), Nico Muhly's 'ghost Marnies' in *Marnie* (2017) and the 'Sodbuster' in Missy Massoli's *Proving Up* (2018); however, the frequency and manner of Davis' 'Present Voice' is considerably more intrusive in the action than with these other examples. In certain moments during the interludes, the saxophone plays concurrently with multiple layers of prerecorded saxophone material, allowing for a large saxophone ensemble.

The tensions that arise from Roosevelt's love for Leonora and the public pressures that accompany both of their positions are borne out amidst the misery of the Great Depression and the New Deal (1933–1939) that followed. The narrative is focused on events between 1932 and 1934, as Eleanor's role as wife of the Governor of the State of New York changed to First Lady of the United States. This period was particularly transformative for Eleanor, not only politically but also personally.

The title of the opera derives from a 1646 poem, 'Wishes to His Supposed Mistress', by Richard Crashaw (c. 1613–1649). The poem comprises forty-two rhyming tercets, in which Crashaw fuses female eroticism with maternal affections. It begins,

Who e'er she be
That not impossible she
That shall command my heart and me;[97]

The two characters sing the contents of the poem together in scene iv, during which they undress in what the libretto describes as a 'gently unfolding sex scene'. During one of many car journeys, or while enjoying a picnic, or unwinding after writing another speech together, Eleanor and Leonora would read poems from *The Oxford Book of English Verse* together. It represents an escape from the 'outside world'. Davis' libretto abounds with literature references such as metaphysical poetry, fragments of newspaper articles, intimate love letters and lyrics from Depression-era ballads. The 'Outside World' is embodied by the only male vocalist in the cast, a character loved by both women but whose nature is to suppress their forbidden romance. Davis explains Outside World as 'a shape-shifting figure who intrudes on, yet also fuels the two women's relationship'.[98] Outside World presents as a man, down on his luck and struggling with the pressures of the Great Depression and clinging to the hope that FDR's New Deal offered, and in another guise, a journalist who comments satirically on Leonora's trajectory.

The Impossible She is structured with five scenes that are separated by 'Radio Interludes'. The interludes express a range of characteristics of the Outside World, and the era is educed through the use of broadcasted, pre-recorded arrangements of Depression-era songs, such as Woody Guthrie's 'I Ain't Got No Home' and Bernard 'Slim' Smith's 'Breadline Blues' over a vintage radio. Outside World sings to the accompaniment of the radio and chamber orchestra, as well as the Present Voice, played live on stage with use of four sizes of saxophone. The eclecticism of the score also includes a post-minimalist use of repeated and fractured phrases and words, and short musical cells are repeated in hypnotic *ostinati* in long cycles that characterize each scene.

In the first scene, Outside World describes Eleanor as 'one of us boys',[99] followed by a list of criticisms of her physical appearance. His suggestion of androgyny owing to 'Physical attraction, she is without'[100] provides the patriarchal platform that has shaped her view of the world. The phrases are short, syllabic and given angular melodic shapes, whereas by contrast, when Eleanor sings to Leonora, she quotes Frances Greville's (c. 1724–1789) 'Prayer for Indifference':

I ask no kind return of love,
No tempting charms to please;
Far from the hearts those gifts remove,
That sighs for peace and ease.[101]

Minimalism techniques make way for a simple, sombre and sincere tune that rarely ventures beyond the three-note material. The strings accompany with alternating *arco/pizzicato* cells and static harmonics, creating a dream-like state during which Present Voice is but a silent observer. Leonora is treated to the same physical critique from Outside World in the Radio Interlude that precedes scene v, 'She is a rotund lady with a husky voice, a peremptory manner, and baggy clothes.'[102] This base form of unsophisticated criticism is designed to reinforce a patriarchal hegemony by limiting the purpose of females to something upon which to look and always from the perspective of the male observer.

Scene iii is set in Rock Creek Park, Washington, DC, and the two women have embarked on their relationship with caution. They are enjoying the seclusion of the gardens near Augustus Saint-Gaudens' sculpture and Eleanor reads from the poem, 'To One Persuading a Lady to Marriage,' by Katherine Philips (1631–1664).

Forbear, bold youth; all's heaven here,
And what you do aver
To others courtship may appear,
'Tis sacrilege to her.
She is a public deity;
And were't not very very odd
Should she herself dispose?
Should she her SELF dispose?
Dispose to be a petty household god?[103]

Interspersed between lines of the poem, Leonora contemplates the issues that face them, particularly the need for her to gradually fit into Eleanor's past. The choice of Philips' poem not only matches the narrative but is also fitting given the frequent suggestions of female intimacy and eroticism that is found in her work. Philips attracted speculation over her own sexuality, compounded by the many poems she penned for fellow members of the Society of Friendship, namely Anne Owen and Mary Aubrey, who went by the names of Lucasia and Rosania, respectively. In this choice of poem, Davis emphasizes Eleanor's exulted, public position and explains to the youth that although flirtation may seem innocent, to a woman it represents a decision of great magnitude and one in which she stands to lose much; essentially women should not marry and fall under the control of men.

The reading of Philips' poem continues soon after with the second stanza following the inauguration ceremony of FDR. The music matches the general style of the other poetry readings and contrasts with the musical manifestations of the hundreds of thousands of people, marching in the parade. Eleanor sings:

First make the sun in private shine
And bid the world adieu
That so he may his beams confine
In compliment to you:
But if of that you do despair,
Think how you did amiss
To strive to fix her beams which
More bright and large than his.[104]

Here, Philips continues with her feminist musings, reiterating that women have a greater purpose beyond following the orders of men. This time the roles have reversed and it is now Leonora who reads the poetry, encouraging Eleanor to take a more active public role in the future. Eleanor adopts the role, articulating her contemplations in the moments in between each line of the poem, singing, 'Love is a queer thing, it hurts one yet gives one more.'[105] These poetic scenes are romantic and emotionally revealing moments between the women, in which the absence of the Outside World brings a tranquillity and intimacy.

Scene v begins in the somewhat nondescript location of 'Ten Miles from Nowhere and Washington, DC'.[106] The vocal material comprises extracts from intimate letters the two women exchanged while separated by work schedules. This moment indicates the change in role for Leonora, who has stopped working as an independent journalist to observe the activities at unemployment camps across the United States on behalf of Eleanor and the administration. They sing:

ER: I only wished it was you in this bed. Darling, I'm beginning to be so impatient.
LH: Darling, only eighteen more days. Eighteen more days.
ER: Darling, I know they bother you to death because you are my friend. But someday, I'll be back in obscurity again and then no one will care but ourselves.[107]

Davis clarifies his position on the question of physical relations between the protagonists with his unobscured libretto. The text also hints at the notion of relationship longevity as Eleanor considers life out of the public spotlight. The opera concludes with further declarations of love interspersed with observations of the suffering of the unemployed. Historically, the relationship ended when Eleanor travelled to Geneva to work in a draft of the Universal Declaration of Human Rights in 1948, three years after the death of FDR. It was at this point that she met Swiss physician, David Gurewitsch. Gurewitsch was eighteen years her junior and became a constant companion and confidante to Eleanor. When Gurewitsch married Edna, it was clear that the three were going to create a life together. The three purchased a house together in New York and Eleanor lived out her days with them.

Eleanor's queerness has only relatively recently been understood with the advent of queer theorists who have been able to look through the layers of heteronormative sanitizing to which public figures are so often subjected. Her version of queerness or feminism divergence was paradoxical, as were so many facets of her life. She emerged as a powerful, female public figure but did not achieve this by adhering to established gender norms and heteronormativity. She is more than deserving of acknowledgement from feminist scholars for her achievements in providing women with a voice, representation and agency, both in the United States and internationally. With *The Impossible She*, another queer hero is celebrated in operatic form with freedom to be a more sexually authentic figure, regardless of the persona expressed to the outside world.

NOTES

1. Sidney H. Phillips, 'Homosexuality: Coming out of the confusion', *The International Journal of Psychoanalysis* 84, no. 6 (2003): 1431–1450.

2. Richard A. Isay, 'Heterosexually married homosexual men: Clinical and developmental issues', *American Journal of Orthopsychiatry* 68, no. 3 (1998): 424–432.

3. Leon Salzman, 'The concept of latent homosexuality', *The American Journal of Psychoanalysis* 17, no. 2 (1957): 161–169.

4. Arthur Rubinstein, *My Many Years* (London: Hamilton, 1987), 103.

5. Graeme Skinner, 'Szymanowski, Karol (1882 – 1937)', in *Who's Who in Gay and Lesbian History*, eds. Robert Aldrich and Garry Wotherspoon (Milton Park: Routledge, 2002), 430–431.

6. Paul Cadrin, ed., 'Education and musical culture in Szymanowski's writings', in *The Szymanowski Companion* (Milton Park: Routledge, 2016), 93–96.

7. Hans Heinz Stuckenschmidt, 'Karol Szymanowski', *Music & Letters* 19, no. 1 (1938): 36–47.

8. Stephen Downes, 'Themes of duality and transformation in Szymanowski's "King Roger"', *Music Analysis* 14, no. 2/3 (1995): 257–291.

9. Karol Symanowski, arr. Arthur Willner, *Król Roger: Opera in Three Acts* [Piano/vocal score] (Vienna: Universal Edition, 1925), 29.

10. Symanowski, *Król Roger*, 60.

11. Symanowski, *Król Roger*, 21.

12. Symanowski, *Król Roger*, 109.

13. Symanowski, *Król Roger*, 76–77.

14. Anna Corral and Ramon Lladó, 'Opera multimodal translation: Audio describing Karol Szymanowski's Król Roger for the Liceu Theatre, Barcelona', *The Journal of Specialised Translation* 15 (2011): 163–179.

15. Corral and Ramon, 'Opera multimodal translation', 163–179.

16. Tadeusz Kobierzycki and Filip Maj, 'Karol Szymanowskis opera King Roger–individuation, erotic transgression and musical aesthetics', *Scientific Yearbook of the University of Kuyavian-Pomeranian in Bydgoszcz*, no. 14 (2020): 7–21.

17. Edward Venn, 'Negotiating the labyrinth: Act II of Sir Michael Tippett's "the knot garden"', in *Second International Conference on Music and Gesture* (Unpublished, 2006).

18. Carl Gustav Jung, ed. Gerhard Adler, *Letters of C. G. Jung: Volume I, 1906–1950* (London & New York: Routledge, 2015), 69.

19. Michael Tippett, *The Knot Garden: An Opera in Three Acts* [vocal score] (London: Schott, 1970), 123.

20. Michael Graham, 'Shakespeare and Modern British Opera: Into "The Knot Garden"' (PhD diss., Royal Holloway, University of London, 2017).

21. Michael Tippett, 'Dreams of power, dreams of love', in *Tippett on Music*, ed. Meirion Bowen (Oxford: Clarendon Press, 1995), 221, 220–227.

22. Tippett, *The Knot Garden*, 60.

23. Diederik F. Janssen, 'Karl Heinrich Ulrichs: First theorist of erotic age orientation', *Journal of Homosexuality* 64, no. 13 (2017): 1850–1871.

24. Tamsin Spargo, *Foucault and Queer Theory* (Cambridge: Icon Books, 1999).

25. Tippett, *The Knot Garden*, 154–155.

26. Carl G. Jung, 'II. The Eros theory', in *Collected Works of CG Jung 7* (Princeton, NJ: Princeton University Press, 2014), 19–29.

27. Tippett, *The Knot Garden*, 158–159.

28. Tippett, *The Knot Garden*, 159.

29. Tippett, *The Knot Garden*, 160.

30. Tippett, *The Knot Garden*, 86–88.

31. Mai, Chih-Yuan, 'The Knot garden: A mirror of "love" and "relationships" in the swinging 60's Britain', *International Journal of Languages, Literature and Linguistics* 4, no. 4 (December 2018): 298–302.

32. Tippett, *The Knot Garden*, 192–193.

33. George T. King, 'A living tradition: Michael Tippett reaches 85 years', *Muziki* 22, no. 1 (1990): 64–73.

34. Tippett, *The Knot Garden*, 285–287.

35. Tippett, *The Knot Garden*, 289–290.

36. Tippett, *The Knot Garden*, 291–293.

37. Louis Crompton, 'Homosexuals and the death penalty in colonial America', *Journal of Homosexuality* 1, no. 3 (1976): 277–293: 278.

38. George Staughton, Benjamin Nead, and Thomas McCamant, '*Charter to William Penn, and Laws of the Province of Pennsylvania, Passed between the Years 1682 and 1700*' (Farmington Hills, MI: Gale, 1879), 110.

39. Sally Parker, Helene Snihur, and Jan Waxman, 'The story of the opera', *Rochester Review*, accessed 23 January 2022, https://web.archive.org/web/20100624 033107/http://www.patienceandsarah.com/URstory.html.

40. Paula Kimper and Wende Persons, *Patience and Sarah: A Pioneering Love Story* [Piano/vocal score] (Brooklyn, NY: Once in a Blue Moon Publishing Co., 1998), 40.

41. Kimper and Persons, *Patience and Sarah*, 16.

42. Kimper and Persons, *Patience and Sarah*, 17.

43. Kimper and Persons, *Patience and Sarah*, 66.

44. Kimper and Persons, *Patience and Sarah*, 66.

45. Kimper and Persons, *Patience and Sarah*, 22.

46. Kimper and Persons, *Patience and Sarah*, 27–28.

47. Kimper and Persons, *Patience and Sarah*, 28.

48. B. Zorina Khan, 'Married women's property laws and female commercial activity: Evidence from United States patent records, 1790–1895', *The Journal of Economic History* 56, no. 2 (1996): 356–388.

49. Kimper and Persons, *Patience and Sarah*, 35.

50. Kimper and Persons, *Patience and Sarah*, 43.

51. Kimper and Persons, *Patience and Sarah*, 47.

52. Kimper and Persons, *Patience and Sarah*, 48.

53. Kimper and Persons, *Patience and Sarah*, 57.

54. Kimper and Persons, *Patience and Sarah*, 58.

55. Kimper and Persons, *Patience and Sarah*, 60.

56. Kimper and Persons, *Patience and Sarah*, 62.

57. Kimper and Persons, *Patience and Sarah*, 62.

58. Kimper and Persons, *Patience and Sarah*, 67.

59. Kimper and Persons, *Patience and Sarah*, 74–75.

60. Kimper and Persons, *Patience and Sarah*, 97.

61. Kimper and Persons, *Patience and Sarah*, 100.

62. Kimper and Persons, *Patience and Sarah*, 100.

63. Kimper and Persons, *Patience and Sarah*, 127.

64. Kimper and Persons, *Patience and Sarah*, 130.

65. Kimper and Persons, *Patience and Sarah*, 129.

66. Kimper and Persons, *Patience and Sarah*, 139–140.

67. Kimper and Persons, *Patience and Sarah*, 161.

68. Kimper and Persons, *Patience and Sarah*, 190.

69. Kimper and Persons, *Patience and Sarah*, 194.

70. Kimper and Persons, *Patience and Sarah*, 195.

71. Kimper and Persons, *Patience and Sarah*, 197.

72. Kimper and Persons, *Patience and Sarah*, 207.

73. Stephen Raskauskas, '7 American operas that put LGBTQ issues center stage', *WFMT*, 20 June 2017, accessed 25 October 2021, https://www.wfmt.com /2027/06/20/7-american-operas-put-lgbtq-issues-center-stage/.

74. Carla Williams, 'American art: Lesbian, nineteenth century', *GLBTQ Online Archive*, 2002, accessed 26 October 2021, http://www.glbtqarchive.com/arts/am_art _lesbian_19c_A.pdf.

75. Anna Picard, 'The bitter tears of Petra von Kant, English national opera, London', *The Independent*, 25 September 2005, accessed 29 October 2022, https:// www.independent.co.uk/arts-entertainment/music/reviews/the-bitter-tears-of-petra -von-kant-english-national-opera-london-314718.html.

76. In the play, Sidonie is Petra's cousin.

77. Gerald Barry and Werner Fassbinder, *The Bitter Tears of Petra von Kant: Opera in Five Acts* [Full score] (London: Schott, 2004), 111.

78. Barry and Fassbinder, *Bitter Tears of Petra von Kant*, 113.

79. Barry and Fassbinder, *Bitter Tears of Petra von Kant*, 125.

80. Barry and Fassbinder, *Bitter Tears of Petra von Kant*, 129.

81. Conor Kostick, 'Live reviews: The bitter tears of Petra von Kant', *The Journal of Music*, 1 November 2002, accessed 4 November 2021, https://journalofmusic .com/criticism/live-reviews-bitter-tears-petra-von-kant.

82. Barry and Fassbinder, *Bitter Tears of Petra von Kant*, 268.

83. Barry and Fassbinder, *Bitter Tears of Petra von Kant*, 310.

84. Carroll Smith-Rosenberg, 'The hysterical woman: Sex roles and role conflict in 19th-century America', *Social Research* 39, no. 4 (1972): 652–678.

85. Barry and Fassbinder, *Bitter Tears of Petra von Kant*, 329.

86. Barry and Fassbinder, *Bitter Tears of Petra von Kant*, 360.

87. Barry and Fassbinder, *Bitter Tears of Petra von Kant*, 498.

88. Barry and Fassbinder, *Bitter Tears of Petra von Kant*, 524–526.

89. Barry and Fassbinder, *Bitter Tears of Petra von Kant*, 421.

90. Barry and Fassbinder, *Bitter Tears of Petra von Kant*, 421–422.

91. Barry and Fassbinder, *Bitter Tears of Petra von Kant*, 535–537.

92. Barry and Fassbinder, *Bitter Tears of Petra von Kant*, 539–540.

93. Higgins, Charlotte, 'It's like being attacked by knives', *The Guardian*, 9 September 2005.

94. Barry and Fassbinder, *Bitter Tears of Petra von Kant*, 95–96.

95. Rick Perdian, 'Rhymes with opera explores loneliness and love in two world premieres', *Seen and Heard International*, 20 May 2019, accessed 12 September 2021, https://seenandheard-international.com/2019/05/rhymes-with-opera-explores -loneliness-and-love-in-two-world-premieres/.

96. Jennifer Reed, 'Queering Eleanor Roosevelt', *The Journal of American Culture* 39, no. 1 (2016): 9.

97. Richard Crashaw, *Poems of Richard Crashaw* (Milton Park: Routledge, 1887), 56–60.

98. Anne E. Johnson, '"The impossible she": Lesbian Romance tells moving story', *Classical Voice North America*, 13 May 2019, accessed 7 November 2021, https://classicalvoiceamerica.org/author/anne-e-johnson/.

99. Daniel Thomas Davis, *The Impossible She: Opera in Five Acts* [Full score] (Unpublished, 2019), 9.

100. Davis, *The Impossible She*, 10.

101. Davis, *The Impossible She*, 31.

102. Davis, *The Impossible She*, 186.

103. Davis, *The Impossible She*, 107–111.

104. Davis, *The Impossible She*, 126–132.

105. Davis, *The Impossible She*, 132.

106. Davis, *The Impossible She*, 188.

107. Davis, *The Impossible She*, 188–190.

Conclusion

I have set out to explore the many different ways that queerness has been represented in operatic form. The historical narrative which continues to unfold includes some fascinating characters who have, in various ways, advanced the social and political agenda for queer people. The operas have also revealed much about the complex psychological corollaries that come with the queer experience. Ultimately, queerness as an embodied, sexual act has changed very little since antiquity. What continues to evolve are the attitudes of the society in which queers experience judgement, oppression and violence. Homophobic attacks of queer people did not vanish with the advent of post-Stonewall legislation in the United States, and although advances in avenues for legal recompense have become more prevalent in much of the modern world, the experience on the street recounts a familiar story.

Homophobia, misogyny and racism have many shared ideals including subjugation, marginalization, depreciation and disempowerment; however, queerness differs in one important way. Queers can attempt to hide their queerness. The closet, a place of darkness and confinement, is also a perceived place of safety. Each queer individual, upon discovery of their 'otherness', is faced with a choice so difficult that for many, suicide is preferable. All queer people must decide whether to remain hidden or to come out. The closet is, of course, a metaphorical construct, but why was it constructed? The notion of the closet would baffle the ancient Greeks, whereas for the Victorians, it was mandatory but for the fearless. Harvey Milk stated, 'I would like to see every gay lawyer, every gay architect come out, stand up and let the world know. That would do more to end prejudice overnight than anybody could imagine.'[1] 'Coming out of the closet' is a twentieth-century metaphor, borrowed from the world of upper-class, young debutantes being introduced to society and its eligible bachelors. It was then adopted by an elite group of gay men prior to World War II, who 'came out' at underground drag balls.[2] It has since been applied to a multiplicity of contexts, but its meaning for queers is unique and deeply understood from a phenomenological perspective.

In the world of opera, queer characters have often had to remain hidden in plain sight despite the prevalence of gender-bending narratives, cross-dressing, castrati and the prevalence of homosocial settings that abound within the art form. With the fast-emerging queer repertoire being introduced to opera houses around much of the world, composers and librettists can directly engage with queerness without subterfuge or metaphor. With the rise of operas that explore queerness, the question of classification emerges. Should we be calling them 'gay operas'? If we do, we are creating categories that separate, isolate and marginalize the works; if we do not, we are not acknowledging or promoting with accuracy the meaning the operas have for queer people. By referencing them simply as 'operas' we risk the queerness of these operas being kept quiet, lingering in the shadows to avoid causing offence. Bernstein certainly understood the backlash of a conservative society against queerness being depicted in operatic form, and yet, without the groundbreaking operas of the post-Stonewall era, we may not have the works we have enjoyed in recent decades.

In a time of relative sexual liberation for many large, urban areas throughout the world, the need for queer opera may be questioned. Homosexuality is enjoying greater public acceptance, gay communities are becoming more visible, dating aps for queer and heterosexual people intermingle, promoting sexual and gender fluidity, so the arts may not be needed to serve the same function as it did before queer liberation. Queer opera may also be preaching to the converted, given the propensity for cultured, educated and open-minded audiences to largely patronize the theatre.[3] And yet, the need to represent queer culture and give voice to queer artists will always be there. There will be no end game in terms of portraying the uniquely queer stories as part of the evolution of the human condition. The glass ceiling has been cracked, badly damaged by numerous outstanding composers and librettists, but parts of it remain perfectly intact. There are many opera houses across the globe, yet to stage any of the works explored in this book, in particular those written in the since the turn of the twenty-first century, and far too few companies commissioning operas that focus on queerness.

WHY LGBTQI+?

The ever-expanding acronym for the multiplicity of terms that define the all-embracing queer community represents a constantly evolving view of minority gender and sexuality forms. The term 'queer', which I have adopted as an expedient umbrella term, has a fascinating linguistic history. With the dramatically changing definition of queerness over several centuries, the process of categorizing to whom the label can apply has been a moveable feast, impacting our interaction with queer-coded texts. Queers have always been here, but we have not always considered ourselves through use of the same language. The Enlightenment saw a shift from an emphasis of labelling sex acts such as sodomy and applying them to individuals – *sodomite* – and sexuality began a process of organization and compartmentalization of sexual orientation.

In 1869, sexologist Karl Westphal (1833–1890) considered the idea of homosexuality as a psychiatric disorder in his paper on 'contrary sexual feeling', allowing the term to be applied as a noun. At the turn of the twentieth century, terms such as 'lesbian' and 'tribad' and 'invert' and 'sapphist' were being used concurrently in texts with lesbian and sodomite being perceived negatively in legislative contexts.[4] Richard von Krafft-Ebing (1840–1902) provided the earliest systematic discussions of queer terms in his book *Psychopathia Sexualis* (1886), including a taxonomy of twenty psychosexual disturbances. He discusses concepts such as 'inverts' and '*antipathetic sexualis paranoica*' to describe what is now regarded as homosexuality. He used the term '*metamorphosis sexualis paranoica*' in place of 'gender dysphoria' and referred to terms such as 'androgyny' and 'gynandry'.[5] These terms enabled such categories to be regarded in medical terms, as a way of diagnosing abnormality, and also in legal terms so that their irregular sexual acts could be punished.

Throughout the 1940s through to the 1960s, the term 'queer' was generally considered a casual, derogatory term synonymous with pervert, sinner and deviant in the way that 'faggot' and 'dyke' are in modern vernacular. Beginning with the term 'gay', such terms began to be acculturated by the queer community, positively subverting their use in self-identity and eventually minimizing their negative impact as a slur. It was not until the 1960s that 'gay' became the preferred moniker for the heteronormative world at large.[6]

The acronym GLBT took shape with the differentiation of bisexuality in the early 1980s and transgender soon after in the following decade. With the AIDS crisis came a wave of activism in which the conflation of victims of the disease and homosexuality was repudiated, and organizations such as ACT UP, Queer Nation and the Pink Triangle sought to adopt the term 'queer' in recognition of all non-normative sexualities. Founded in 1985, the Gay, Lesbian, Bisexual, Transgender Historical Society (GLBTHS) debated the use of various terms and was polarized with divergent views on the word 'queer'. Senior members with vivid memories of the stinging homophobia associated with the term struggled to reconcile its adoption into approved linguistics;

however, younger activists considered the nexus of gender and sexuality to be well served by such a useful umbrella term.

With the evolution of queer studies, the term 'queer' has come to signify numerous ways of being beyond sexual practice. The term 'cisgender', often abbreviated to 'cis', was coined in 1994 and derives from Latin meaning 'on this side of'. It has the opposite meaning to transgender and, with common usage in dictionaries in 2015, reflects a revolution in the way that people consider gender through linguistic meaning.[7] The full acronym reflecting the rainbow of minority gender and sexuality has grown to include 'LGBTQQIP-2SAA', standing for lesbian, gay, bisexual, transgender, queer, questioning, intersex, pansexual, two-spirit, asexual and ally. Each of these is a hard-won recognition of identity and inclusion.

MORE QUEERS AND OPERAS

Books such as this can never claim to have included everything, and although I have attempted to be as comprehensive as possible, I acknowledge the limits of what I have covered by mentioning some more of the important composers and works here. Some queer composers who have contributed to the operatic repertoire but who have not (yet in some cases) written for queer characters include Jean-Baptiste Lully, Camille Saint-Saëns, Pyotr Ilyich Tchaikovsky, Francis Poulenc, Gian Carlo Menotti, Samuel Barber, Aaron Copland, Peter Maxwell Davies and, more recently, Jennifer Higdon, Claude Vivier, David Del Tredici, John Corigliano, Philip Venables, Thomas Adès, Jake Heggie and Tobias Picker.

Representing queerness in opera has changed greatly since the early part of the seventeenth century. The operas of Francesco Cavalli (1602–1676) could be quite licentious in the relatively liberal Venetian society. Innuendo and *double entendre* were so thinly veiled in works such as *Giasone* (1649) that any reading of the drama will acknowledge the comedic treatment of gender fluidity. Cavalli routinely employed a tenor to play the stock character role of the older woman lusting after a younger man. The plots were cheeky and involved plenty of gender disguise such as *La Calisto* (1651), in which Giove, a bass, disguises himself as Diana, a soprano, to seduce Calisto, a soprano. Although a liberal portrayal of gender and sexuality was a feature of Cavalli's work, his use of the misogynist aria as a device reminds us that Venice was not a bastion of social awareness of minority groups but rather gender and queerness were simply another opportunity to get a laugh.

At age eleven, Mozart's *Apollo and Hyacinth* premiered at Salzburg University, a Catholic school, with an all-male cast. Surprisingly, the homoerotic love triangle between Apollo, Hyacinth and Zephyrus formed the basis of

Rufinus Widl's libretto for a conservative environment in a conservative age. Until this work, homoeroticism was seldom featured on the stage but for the tradition of cross-dressing in Italian opera and *haute-contres* who performed *en travesti* for comedic effect in France. Hyacinthus was along with Ganemede, known for his homosexuality, and in this story offers affection for both Apollo and Zephyrus. Zephyrus returns his affections, *'O care! Quam libenter offerrem ilia pectusque, si tu Apollo mihi meus fores!'*[8] (My dear, how gladly would I offer my heart and body if you were my Apollo!). Widl used the mythical story not to promote homosexual behaviour but to warn against the sins connected with taking homosocial relationships too far. He would have been all too aware of the fertile ground for queer encounters in the close lodgings of pubescent boarding school, which 'were notorious for such sexual mischief'.[9] Apollo rejects their sacrifice, not out of jealousy as in the myth but out of anger that the erotic nature of Hyacinthus and Zephyrus' relationship has approached physical consummation. Zephyrus' jealousy of the friendship between Apollo and Zephyrus ultimately leads to him killing Zephyrus with a discus. Widl further limits the homoerotic content by the introduction of Melia, the object of Apollo's subsequent affections. The opera was well received by the 1767 audience because of the moral teaching tool provided for the boy's graduation, that homoerotic attachments are acceptable, provided they manifest within the boundaries of socially appropriate behaviour and do not interfere with the love of God.[10]

One particularly noteworthy queer composer is Ethel Smyth (1858–1944). Smyth was an ardent suffragette and openly lesbian. She composed six operas, which were largely comic operas and attracted predictable criticism as a female composer in the last two decades of the nineteenth century. Prior to this period, women had three avenues of opportunity to access theoretical instruction in music: daughters of noble or wealthy families, nuns or those fortunate to come from musical families. With the reluctant acceptance of women into the large, European conservatories, a change in gender disparity was finally becoming possible. Fearing the feminization of music that would inevitably occur, fin de siècle critics developed gendered criteria for the critical evaluation of women's music. The expectation was that women's music should be delicate, graceful, sensitive, melodic and for intimate-sized ensembles.[11] Virginia Wolf wrote to Smyth, 'Now why shouldnt [*sic*] you be not only the first woman to write an opera, but equally the first to tell the truths about herself? Isnt [*sic*] the great artist the only person to tell the truth? I should like an analysis of your sex life.'[12] She was the first female composer to be rewarded with a Damehood.

Kurt Weill (1900–1950) wrote numerous works for the stage, including several operas, but it was his music for Georg Kaiser's play[13] *Der Silbersee: ein Wintermärchen* (The Silver Lake: a Winter's Fairy Tale, 1933) that involved possible queerness. Olim, a policeman who has just enjoyed a win with the lottery, and Severin, a vagrant, develop a relationship when Olim shoots Severin and, struggling with his guilt, attempts to make amends. Their relationship is essentially homosocial, although in the final moments, they set off together over the frozen lake and into the unknown, allowing the audience to contemplate the nature of their connection. The work was banned by the Nazis after a run of sixteen performances.

Nineteenth-century grand opera is an unlikely setting for queer characters; however, there are works that have raised eyebrows among those who are keen to pick up on queer coding. Giuseppe Verdi's *Don Carlos* (1867) is based on the son of Phillip II of Spain. His friendship with Rodrigue, Marquis de Posa, an unmarried man, was given treatment by librettists, Joseph Mery and Camille du Locle, that suggests it may have been more than platonic. Certainly, Rodrigue's death scene is afforded an intensity by Verdi that might be reserved for the loss of a lover, and their duet in the opening of the drama is a highlight of the score. Rodrigue also distracts a lady in waiting of Carlos' stepmother by taking her aside to discuss the latest Parisian fashions. The love between two men or two women was curious marker in other operas from this period, such as Bellini's *Norma* (1831), Georges Bizet's *Les Pêcheurs de Perles* (1863) and Richard Wagner's *Tannhäuser* (1845) and *Parsifal* (1882).

Wagner's *Parsifal* deserves special mention for its homosexual undertones. Parsifal is an innocent fool, tasked with restoring the sacred male society that is in charge of protecting the Holy Grail. The Brotherhood has suffered a regression with the loss of the spear that pierced Christ's side. Consequently, Grail King Amfortas suffers an illness, and the cause of the disaster was the sexual relations he had with the witch, Kundry. Queer theorists point to the intercourse with a woman as representing sin, a fall from grace that is considered a crime by the knights. Parsifal refuses the physical temptations of the flower maidens and reaffirms his loyalty to the all-male order when repudiating Kundry's attempted kiss, thereby regaining the sacred spear and healing Amfortas. Nietzsche felt strongly about Wagner's protagonist refusing the temptations of a woman, 'Was this Parsifal meant seriously? For one might be tempted to suppose the reverse, even to desire that the Wagnerian Parsifal was intended as a joke.'[14] For Nietzsche, a man who rebuffs his natural urges to succumb to a woman's seduction must be a social deviant, which we may take to mean a homosexual.

Sadly, the work of queer opera composer Claude Vivier (1948–1983) was cut short when he was murdered at the age of thirty-five. Vivier was an openly gay composer, ejected from preparations for priesthood with the Marist Brothers for inappropriate behaviour and beginning his earliest works at the age of eighteen. His extant opera *Kopernikus: Rituel de la mort* (1979) has been revived in festivals celebrating Vivier's work, but it is his final, incomplete work *Glaubst du an die Unsterblichkeit der Seele?* (Do You Believe in the Immortality of the Soul?) that provides a shocking coda to the life of a queer composer. Vivier had been working on the opera, based on the death of Tchaikovsky in Paris. In a disturbing case of life-imitating art, he was working on a passage in which during a journey on the metro, he becomes attracted to a young man. The music breaks off abruptly with the phrase, 'Then he removed a dagger from his jacket and stabbed me through the heart.'[15] Vivier was stabbed to death in his apartment by a young Parisian man, Pascal Dolzan, a homeless nineteen-year-old who he had met that evening at a bar.[16]

In addition to his opera *Fellow Travelers*, Gregory Spears set another existing text with queer themes. *Paul's Case* (2013) is based on Willa Cather's 1905 short story by the same name. Paul is not directly revealed as homosexual but is described as a 'dandy'. The story is a coming-of-age tale about an insufferable brat who despises his instructors and their homilies. He steals some money and decides to live it up at the Waldorf-Astoria Hotel, becoming the picture of a 'dandy' he always fantasized about. During his short hotel stay, he meets up with a wild San Francisco boy, who is a freshman at Yale, and the two explore New York's lively night life. The relationship is not articulated as being sexual, but most readings of it suggest that it is at least homosocial. Ultimately Paul's escapade comes to an abrupt halt when he reads of his theft in the papers and shortly after commits suicide. In this tragic story, Paul's teachers are unable to articulate what it is about him that is different or objectionable, and themes of bullying and teenage suicide are as relevant now as they were when Cather wrote it.

The repertoire exploring queerness is constantly expanding, and one composer currently creating material that includes broad issues relating to gay sex is Philip Venables. He considers his exploratory work *Unleashed* to be a turning point in his work. It is a work created in collaboration with Nick Blackburn that explores a range of themes pertaining to gay sex. The libretto utilizes a deconstruction of verbatim interview fragments in which participants discuss their sex lives, organized around the legal transcript for the 1997 Laskey, Jaggard, Brown case in which the participants of consensual violent sex were prosecuted and imprisoned in the United Kingdom.

The final work to be mentioned is in the early stages of production at the time of writing. The genesis of *Glitter Balls* came from the collaborative efforts of Jorge Balça, librettist and director; Alannah Marie Halay, composer; and Rachel Hann, designer. The work has been entered with the European Network of Opera Academies (ENOA), which supports the creation of new works as part of the Opera Creation Journeys. This particular project called 'Queering Opera' specifically aims to tell queer stories queerly and also to reinvent operatic conventions. *Glitter Balls* is the story of Jo, assigned male gender at birth and who explores sexuality and gender in an underground scene. Beaten up and sexuality assaulted but saved by two drag queens, Jo goes home and their parents send them to conversion therapy. As the family are waiting, the doorbell rings, and the drag queens and friends arrive to rescue him and take him into their queer world. In the second Act, Jo encounters a range of queer individuals, and they will go through a process of self-discovery by meeting a rainbow of different identities. The stories are based on ethnographic research and became fictionalized. Using one-sided headphones (left or right), the audience can choose to tune into the inner thoughts of the protagonist – one score with additional material (with or without the added layer). The additional material heard through the headphones uncovers the deeper experience of queerness, beyond the superficial, and provides the audience with an overt choice of how to read the narrative. Jo is intended to be played by a non-binary, agendered or androgenous mezzo and one drag queen will be a trans woman, providing fresh opportunity to explore the potential and possibilities of trans voices.

CODA

Arguably the most interesting trend to be explored in this book is the dramatic growth of the independent opera scene in the United States. Unfettered from the need to secure large-scale commercial profit margins, small companies throughout the country have risen and fallen on the strength of groups of artists wanting to express themselves. Frustrated at the slow response of many of the larger companies to provide opportunities for contemporary works to be created in which diversity is acknowledged if not celebrated, the grassroots companies have responded and have an impressive repertoire to show for it. Such a phenomenon is not exclusive to the United States, nor are independent chamber opera companies a new innovation. In a review of the state of opera in Australia in 2016, one important point indicated, 'Artforms and companies where innovation has increasingly occurred have demonstrated the power of such vibrancy in attracting audiences and reducing financial pressures.'[17] However, if the financial risk of promoting sexual diversity is too great for the major houses, then the opportunity must be taken by autonomous, regional players.

Commentators have been discussing the issues facing the fiscal concerns of the opera industry for many decades. One of the recurring options to help solve a declining ticket revenue is to move towards the realm of music theatre. This seems to be a self-defeating proposition, whereby the problem with opera is to partially replace it with something else. Other solutions, such as providing experiences that are fresh and relevant, seem obvious but are at odds with the prevailing desire by companies to perform the Eurocentric canon of grand opera standards. If the aim is to make opera more meaningful, Midgette argues that companies should not simply introduce new works to unsuspecting audiences but create operas that can endure by considering aesthetic principles above utilitarian ones.[18] Some companies are yet to consider an inclusive environment for their audience and the value in allowing the queer community to feel at home once again in their houses.

I expect that there are many operatic works that explore queerness either overtly or through hidden coding that I have yet to discover. My interest was in the exploration of how opera has allowed the queer community to understand and develop its ongoing narrative. The privilege of getting to know these operas has been immense, and many of the characters with their associated musical embodiments have gotten very much under my skin throughout the writing of this book. I hope that my research will add to the growing body of work on queerness in all of its contexts and encourage those composers and librettists working on operas to continue giving voice to our community. As American activist Barbara Gittings stated, 'Gay rights means much more than getting good laws and rules, and changing bad ones, though that is a key step . . . The struggle for equal treatment has to be won in people's hearts and minds where it counts.'[19] Opera must continue to challenge queer stereotypes and to give pause to those mired in conservatism to allow their homophobia to be questioned for its irrationality.

NOTES

1. Cited in Patrick Corrigan and Alicia Matthews, 'Stigma and disclosure: Implications for coming out of the closet', *Journal of Mental Health* 12, no. 3 (2003): 235–248: 235.

2. George Chauncey, *Gay New York: Gender, Urban Culture, and the Making of the Gay Male World, 1890–1940* (Hachette UK, 2008).

3. Michael Bronski, *Culture Clash: The Making of Gay Sensibility* (Boston: South End Press, 1984).

4. Carl Westphal, 'Die conträre Sexualempfindung, Symptom eines neuropathischen (psychopathischen) Zustandes', *Archiv für Psychiatrie und Nervenkrankheiten* 2, no. 1 (1870): 73–108.

5. Richard von Krafft-Ebing, 'Über gewisse Anomalien des Geschlechtstriebes', *Archiv für Psychiatrie und Nervenkrankheiten* (1877): 291–312.

6. Paul Gabriel, 'Embracing our erotic intelligence', *Museums & Social Issues* 3, no. 1 (2008): 53–66.

7. Devath Suresh, 'Transgenders problems and administrative response', Society for Public Welfare and Initiatives, Available at SSRN 3768221 (2016), http://dx.doi.org/10.2139/ssrn.3768221.

8. Wolfgang Amadeus Mozart, *Apollo et Hyacinthus: Lateinische Comoedie in I Acte*, Mozart's Werke, Serie V: Opern, Bd.1, No.2 (Leipzig: Breitkopf & Härtel, 1879), 5.

9. Michael Sibalis, 'Male homosexuality in the age of enlightenment and revolution, 1680-1850', in *Gay Life and Culture: A World History*, ed. Robert Aldrich (New York, NY: Universe, 2006), 103–123.

10. Steven Soebbing, 'The fine line of friendship: Male homoerotic relationships in Mozart's Apollo et Hyacinthus', *The Journal of Men's Studies* 23, no. 1 (2015): 79–97.

11. Eugene Gates, 'Damned if you do and damned if you don't: Sexual aesthetics and the music of Dame Ethel Smyth', *Journal of Aesthetic Education* 31, no. 1 (1997): 63–71.

12. Virginia Woolf to Ethel Smyth, 24 December 1940, in *The Letters of Virginia Woolf*, ed. Nigel Nicolson and Joanne Trautmann, 6 vols (London: Hogarth, 1975–80) [henceforth Letters], 6:453.

13. It is essentially a *Singspiel*.

14. Quoted in Suzanne R. Stewart, 'The theft of the operatic voice: Masochistic seduction in Wagner's Parsifal', *The Musical Quarterly* 80, no. 4 (1996): 599–600.

15. Alfred Hickling, 'Soul's Rebirth', *The Guardian*, 22 February 2008, accessed 23 February 2022, https://www.theguardian.com/music/2008/feb/22/classicalmusicandopera.

16. Bob Gilmore, *Claude Vivier: A Composer's Life* (NY: University of Rochester Press, 2014).

17. Commonwealth of Australia, 'National Opera Review: Final report', 2016, accessed 12 April 2021, https://www.arts.gov.au/sites/default/files/national_opera_review_final_report.pdf.

18. Anne Midgette, 'The voice of American opera', *The Opera Quarterly* 23, no. 1 (2007): 81–95.

19. Barbara Gittings, 'Philadelphia Gay and Lesbian Pride Parade Speech, June 2, 1990', cited in Robert B. Ridinger, ed., *Historic Speeches and Rhetoric for Gay and Lesbian Rights (1892–2000)* (New York, NY: Routledge, 2012), 606.

References

Adames, Hector Y., Nayeli Y. Chavez-Dueñas, Shweta Sharma, and Martin J. La Roche. "Intersectionality in psychotherapy: The experiences of an AfroLatinx queer immigrant." *Psychotherapy* 55, no. 1 (2018): 73.

Adămuţ, Anton. "Philosophical aspects of homosexuality in Ancient Greek." *Philosophy, Social and Human Disciplines* 2 (2011): 11–22.

Alves, Bill, Brett Campbell, and Mark Morris. *Lou Harrison.* Bloomington: Indiana University Press, 2017.

Amidon, Kevin S. "What happens to countess Geschwitz? Revisiting homosexuality in Horkheimer and Adorno." *New York Journal of Sociology* 1 (2008): 1.

Anderson, Harriet. *Utopian Feminism: Women's Movements in Fin-de-Siecle Vienna.* New Haven, CN: Yale University Press, 1992.

Angert-Quilter, Theresa, and Lynne Wall. "The 'spirit wife' at Endor." *Journal for the Study of the Old Testament* 25, no. 92 (2001): 55–72.

Arenas, Reinaldo. *Antes que anochezca.* No. 863 A681b esp. Barcelona: Tusquets, 2013.

Arguelles, Lourdes, and B. Ruby Rich. "Homosexuality, homophobia, and revolution: Notes toward an understanding of the Cuban lesbian and gay male experience, part I." *Signs: Journal of Women in Culture and Society* 9, no. 4 (1984): 683–699.

Armstrong Percy III, William. "Reconsiderations about Greek homosexualities." *Journal of Homosexuality* 49, no. 3–4 (2005): 13–61.

Ashford, Chris. "Queer theory, cyber-ethnographies and researching online sex environments." *Information & Communications Technology Law* 18, no. 3 (2009): 297–314.

Baker, Joseph O., Christopher D. Bader, and Kittye Hirsch. "Desecration, moral boundaries, and the movement of law: The case of Westboro Baptist Church." *Deviant Behavior* 36, no. 1 (2015): 42–67.

Barrettara, Naomi. "Cyber-narrative in Opera: Three case studies." PhD diss., City University of New York, 2019.

Barry, Gerald, and Werner Fassbinder. *The Bitter Tears of Petra von Kant: Opera in Five Acts*. [Full score] London: Schott, 2004.

Barton, Bernadette. "'Abomination': Life as a Bible belt gay." *Journal of Homosexuality* 57, no. 4 (2010): 465–484.

Baum, L. Frank. "The road to oz." In *The Complete Works of L. Frank Baum, Part 6*. Hastings: Delphi Classics, 2017.

Beaucage, Réjean. "Kevin March and Les Feluettes: An American inspired by France." *La Scene Musicale*. April 1, 2016. Accessed, January 14, 2022. scena.org/lsm/sm21-6/sm21-6_march_en.html

Behar, Ruth, and David Bleich. *Autobiographical Writing Across the Disciplines: A Reader*. Durham, NC: Duke University Press, 2004.

Belk, Russell W., and Melanie Wallendorf. "Of mice and men: gender identity in collecting." In *Interpreting Objects and Collections*, edited by Susan M. Pearce, 252–265. Milton Park: Routledge, 2012.

Bell, Iain, and Mark Campbell. *Stonewall: Opera in One Act. [Full Score]*. Bury St Edmunds: Chester Music, 2019.

Belmonte, Juan Francisco. "Teenage heroes and evil deviants: sexuality and history in JRPGs." *Continuum* 31, no. 6 (2017): 903–911.

Bem, Sandra L., and Steven A. Lewis. "Sex role adaptability: One consequence of psychological androgyny." *Journal of Personality and Social Psychology* 31, no. 4 (1975): 634.

Benjamin, George, and Martin Crimp. *Lessons in Love and Violence: Opera in Two Acts. [Full Score]*. London: Faber Music, 2017.

Berg, Alban, arr. Erwin Stein. *Lulu. [Piano Reduction]*. Vienna: Universal Edition, 1936.

Bernheimer, Martin. "BLOOD SISTERS. (The works and career of Richard Strauss is discussed, in particular the two characters Salome and Elektra)." *Opera News* 64, no. 2 (1999): 10–14.

Bernstein, Charles. "Gertrude Stein views life and politics." *New York Times Magazine*, May 1934: 71.

Bernstein, Leonard, and Stephen Wadsworth. *A Quiet Place: An Opera in Three Acts [Full Score]*. Jalni Publications, Boosey & Hawkes, 1983.

Bérubé, Allan. *Coming Out Under Fire: The History of Gay Men and Women in World War II*. Chapel Hill, NC: University of North Carolina Press, 2010.

Bieber, Irving, Harvey J. Dain, Paul R. Dince, Marvin G. Drellich, Henry G. Grand, Ralph H. Gundlach, et al. *Homosexuality: A Psychoanalytic Study of Male Homosexuals*. New York: Basic Books, 1962.

Black, Jason Edward, and Charles E. Morris III. "Harvey Milk and the hope speech." *Voices of Democracy Journal* 6 (2012): 63–76.

Blaskie, Bryan, and Seth Christenfeld. *Outside. [Piano/Vocal Score]* Unpublished, 2019.

Boe, Joshua L., Valerie A. Maxey, and J. Maria Bermudez. "Is the closet a closet? Decolonizing the coming out process with Latin@ adolescents and families." *Journal of Feminist Family Therapy* 30, no. 2 (2018): 90–108.

Bonauto, Mary L., and Evan Wolfson. "Advancing the freedom to marry in America." *Human Rights Magazine,* 36 (2009): 11.

Borg, Kurt. *"Narrating Trauma: Michel Foucault, Judith Butler and the Political Ethics of Self-Narration."* PhD diss., Staffordshire University, 2019.

Boscardin, Steve. "David et Jonathas de Charpentier à Versailles: un Opéra à la chapelle." *ResMusica,* November 13, 2022.

Bouchard, Miche Marc. *Les Felluetes,* Unpublished libretto, 2015.

Boucher, Leigh, and Sarah Pinto. "'I ain't queer': Love, masculinity and history in Brokeback Mountain." *The Journal of Men's Studies* 15, no. 3 (2008): 311–330.

Bowen, Murray. "Family therapy and family group therapy." In *Treating relationships*, edited by David H. Olson, 219–274. Lake Mills: Graphic, 1976.

Bretonneau, François. *David et Jonathas.* Paris: Claude Thiboust, 1688.

Bretonneau, François. *David et Jonathas.* Paris: Louis Sevestre, 1706.

Brett, Philip. "Britten's bad boys male relations in the turn of the screw." In *Music and Sexuality in Britten*, 88–105. Berkeley: University of California Press, 2006.

Brett, Philip. "Eros and orientalism in Britten's operas." In *Queering the Pitch.* Milton Park: Routledge, 2013.

Brett, Philip. "Britten's dream." In *Musicology and Difference*, edited by Ruth A. Solie, 259–280. Berkeley: University of California Press, n.d, 1993.

Britten, Benjamin, and Myfanwy Piper. *The Turn of the Screw, Op. 54. An Opera in a Prologue and Two Acts.* [Vocal score]. London: Boosey & Hawkes, 1955.

Britten, Benjamin, and Myfanwy Piper. *Death in Venice, An Opera in Two Acts, Op. 88.* [Full Score] London: Faber Music Limited, 1979.

Britten, Benjamin, E.M. Forster, and Eric Crozier. *Billy Budd op. 50: An Opera in Two Acts.* [Vocal score] London: Boosey & Hawkes, 1961.

Brod, Harry. "They're bi shepherds, not gay cowboys: The misframing of Brokeback Mountain." *The Journal of Men's Studies* 14, no. 2 (2007): 252–253.

Bronski, Michael. *Culture Clash: The Making of Gay Sensibility.* Boston, MA: South End Press, 1984.

Burnett, William. "Opera advocating for human rights: An interview with 'Oscar' composer Theodore Morrison." Opera Warhorses, (September 10, 2013). Accessed January 5, 2022, https://operawarhorses.com/2013/09/page/2/

Butler, Judith. *Gender Trouble.* Milton Park: Routledge, 2002.

Cadrin, Paul, ed. "Education and musical culture in Szymanowski's writings." In *The Szymanowski Companion*, 93–96. Milton Park: Routledge, 2016.

Cameron, David R. "The hero in Rousseau's political thought." *Journal of the History of Ideas*, 45 (1984): 397–419.

Candey, Griffin. *Sweets by Kate.* [Piano/vocal score] Unpublished, 2016.

Cavanagh-Strong, Brian, and Benjamin Bonnema. *The Pomada Inn.* [Piano/vocal score] Unpublished, 2019.

Chamberlain, Jennifer. "Composer Mark Simpson on his debut opera, pleasure." *The Skinny.* April 22, 2016.

Charton, Anke. "Voicing challenge: Trans* singers and the performance of vocal gender." In *Under Construction: Performing Critical Identity,* edited by Marie-Anne Kohl, 107–126. Basel, Switzerland: MDPI, 2021.

Chauncey, George. *Gay New York: Gender, Urban Culture, and the Making of the Gay Male World, 1890-1940.* Paris: Hachette, 2008.

Chen, Justine F., and David Simpatico. *The Life and Death(s) of Alan Turing.* [Full score] Unpublished, 2019.

Chih-Yuan, Mai. "The knot garden: A mirror of 'love' and 'relationships' in the swinging 60's Britain." *International Journal of Languages, Literature and Linguistics* 4, no. 4 (December 2018): 298–302.

Choi, Mary H. K. "thefader.com." *The Fader*, Oct. 18, 2003. Accessed October 3, 2021, http://www.thefader.com/2013/10/18/interview-nico-muhly.

Chowrimootoo, Christopher. "Bourgeois opera: 'Death in Venice' and the aesthetics of sublimation." *Cambridge Opera Journal* 22, no. 2 (2010): 175–216.

Cohen, Cathy J. "Punks, Bulldaggers, and welfare queens: Radical potential of queer politics 201." In *Sexual Identities, Queer Politics*, edited by Mark Blasius, 200–228. Princeton: Princeton University Press, 2001.

Cohler, Bertram J., and Robert M. Galatzer-Levy. *The Course of Gay and Lesbian Lives.* Chicago: University of Chicago Press, 2000.

Cohn, Fred. "Fellow travelers." *Opera News.* (June 17, 2016). Accessed November 17, 2021, https://www.metguild.org/Opera_News_Magazine/2016/9/In_Review/CINCINNATI__Fellow_Travelers.html

Commonwealth of Australia. "National opera review: Final report." 2016. Accessed April 12, 2021, https://www.arts.gov.au/sites/default/files/national_opera_review_final_report.pdf

Cooper, John. "Finding Oscar." *The Wildean* 47 (2015): 109–117.

Cormier, Konor. "Increase the peace means increase the penalty: The impact of the James Byrd, Jr. hate crimes act in Texas." *Texas Tech Law Review* 34 (2002): 343.

Corral, Anna, and Ramon Lladó. "Opera multimodal translation: Audio describing Karol Szymanowski's Król Roger for the Liceu Theatre, Barcelona." *The Journal of Specialised Translation* 15 (2011): 163–179.

Corrigan, Patrick, and Alicia Matthews. "Stigma and disclosure: Implications for coming out of the closet." *Journal of Mental Health* 12, no. 3 (2003): 235–248.

Corse, Sandra, and Larry Corse, "Britten's 'Death in Venice': Literary and musical structures." *The Musical Quarterly* 73, no. 3 (1989): 344–363.

Corvino, John. ed., *Same Sex: Debating the Ethics, Science, and Culture of Homosexuality, Vol. 70.* Lanham, MD: Rowman & Littlefield, 1999.

Cox, John. "Truth art and life." *The Santa Fe Opera 2013 Season Program Book* (2013), 76–79.

Cram, E. "Pulse: The matter of movement." *QED: A Journal in GLBTQ Worldmaking* 3, no. 3 (2016): 147–150.

Crashaw, Richard. *Poems of Richard Crashaw.* Milton Park: Routledge, 1887.

Crompton, Louis. "Homosexuals and the death penalty in colonial America." *Journal of Homosexuality* 1, no. 3 (1976): 277–293.

Crompton, Louis. *Homosexuality and Civilization.* Cambridge, MA: Harvard University Press, 2009.

Cummines, Kevin, and Shoshana Greenberg. *The Community.* [vocal score] Unpublished, 2019.

Curtin, Adrian. "Alternative vocalities: Listening Awry to Peter Maxwell Davies's eight songs for a mad king." *Mosaic: A Journal for the Interdisciplinary Study of Literature* 42, no. 2 (2009): 101–117.

Cyrino, Monica Silveira. "Heroes in d(u)ress: Transvestism and power in the myths of herakles and achilles." *Arethusa* 31, no. 2 (1998): 207–241.

DaSilva, Julia. "Magic, lesbian sexuality, and the 'impossible possibility': Reading the early modern witch hunts and the cold war lavender scare for a politics of re-enchantment." *The Undergraduate Journal of Sexual Diversity Studies* 3, (2019): 68.

Davis, Daniel Thomas. *The Impossible She: Opera in Five Acts.* [Full score] Unpublished, 2019.

De Kuyper, Eric. "The Freudian construction of sexuality: The gay foundations of heterosexuality and straight homophobia." *Journal of Homosexuality* 24, no. 3–4 (1993): 137–144.

de Secondat Montesquieu, Charles-Louis. "De l'esprit des lois (1748)." *Œuvres complètes* (1964): 1949–1951.

Dellamora, Richard. *Masculine Desire: The Sexual Politics of Victorian Aestheticism.* Chapel Hill, NC: UNC Press Books, 1990.

Deutschman, Alan. "Cobb Canto: Sex, money, politics and acoustics: The Atlanta Opera's historic move to Cobb County is about more than mileage." *Atlanta* (September 2007), 144–145 + 168–175.

Devor, Aaron H. "Witnessing and mirroring: A fourteen stage model of transsexual identity formation." *Journal of Gay & Lesbian Psychotherapy* 8, no. 1–2 (2004): 41–67.

Dickinson, Tommy. *'Curing Queers': Mental Nurses and Their Patients, 1935–74.* Manchester: Manchester University Press, 2015.

Diethef, Carol. "Nietzsche and nationalism." *History of European Ideas* 14, no. 2 (1992): 227–234.

Doan, Laura. "Queer history queer memory: The case of Alan Turing." *GLQ: A Journal of Lesbian and Gay Studies* 23, no. 1 (2017): 113–136.

Doan, Petra L., and Harrison Higgins. "The demise of queer space? Resurgent gentrification and the assimilation of LGBT neighborhoods." *Journal of Planning Education and Research* 31, no. 1 (2011): 6–25.

Doane, Mary Ann. *Femmes Fatales.* Milton Park: Routledge, 2013.

Downes, Stephen. "Themes of duality and transformation in Szymanowski's' King Roger'." *Music Analysis* 14, no. 2/3 (1995): 257–291.

Downing, Christine. "Lesbian mythology." *Historical Reflections* 20, no. 2 (1994): 171.

Duberman, Martin Bauml. *Stonewall: The Definitive Story of the LGBTQ Rights Uprising that Changed America.* London: Plume, 2019.

Edel, Leon, and Adeline R. Tintner. "The private life of Peter Quin[t]: Origins of 'the turn of the screw'." *The Henry James Review* 7, no. 1 (1985): 2–4.

Ellison, Tom. "Lou Harrison centennial birthday celebration: 1917-2017." *The Diversity Center of Santa Cruz.* (April 24, 2017). Accessed September 12, 2021, https://www.diversitycenter.org/lou

Ellmann, Richard. *Oscar Wilde.* London: Hamish Hamilton Ltd: 1987.

Eötvös, Peter, and Mari Mezei. *Angels in America: Opera in Two Parts, Based on the Play by Tony Kushner.* [Full score] Mainz: Schott, revised version 2003-04, 2008/2012.

FemaleFirst.co.uk. "Rufus Wainwrights rape tragedy." March 1, 2005. Accessed December 15, 2021, https://www.femalefirst.co.uk/music/musicnews/Rufus +Wainwright-3238.html

Fernández, Eliecer Crespo. "Sex-related euphemism and dysphemism: An analysis in terms of conceptual metaphor theory." *Atlantis* 30, no. 2 (2008): 95–110.

Fitzsimons, Tim. "LGBTQ history month: The early days of America's AIDS crisis." *NBC News,* October 15, 2018. Accessed August 27, 2021, https://www .nbcnews.com/feature/nbc-out/lgbtq-history-month-early-days-america-s-aids-cri- sis-n919701

Foucault, Michel. *Archaeology of Knowledge.* Translated by A. M. Sheridan Smith. London and New York: Routledge, 2013.

Foucault, Michel. *Power: The Essential Works of Michel Foucault 1954-1984.* London: Penguin, 2019a.

Foucault, Michel. *The History of Sexuality: 1: The Will to Knowledge.* London: Penguin, 2019b.

Foucault, Michel. *The History of Sexuality: 1: The Will to Knowledge.* Translated by Robert Hurley. London: Penguin, 2019c.

Franco, Zeno E. Scott T. Allison, Elaine L. Kinsella, Ari Kohen, Matt Langdon, and Philip G. Zimbardo. "Heroism research: A review of theories, methods, challenges, and trends." *Journal of Humanistic Psychology* 58, no. 4 (2018): 382–396.

Frantzen, Allen J. "The handsome sailor and the man of sorrows: Billy Budd and the modernism of Benjamin Britten." *Modernist Cultures* 3, no. 1 (2007): 57–70.

Friedman, Andrea. "The smearing of Joe McCarthy: The lavender scare, gossip, and cold war politics." *American Quarterly* 57, no. 4 (2005): 1105–1129.

Frizzell, Nell. "How the Stonewall riots started the LGBT rights movement." *Pink News.* June 28, 2013. Accessed December 5, 2021, https://www.pinknews.co.uk /2013/06/28/feature-how-the-stonewall-riots-started-the-gay-rights-movement/

Gabriel, Paul. "Embracing our erotic intelligence." *Museums & Social Issues* 3, no. 1 (2008): 53–66.

Gage, Simon, Lisa Richards, and Howard Wilmot. *Queer: The Ultimate User's Guide.* London: MQ Publications, 2002.

Gahan, Peter. "Jitta's atonement: The birth of psychoanalysis and 'The fetters of the feminine psyche'." *SHAW the Annual of Bernard Shaw Studies* 24, no. 1 (2004): 128–165.

Gates, Eugene. "Damned if you do and damned if you don't: Sexual aesthetics and the music of Dame Ethel Smyth." *Journal of Aesthetic Education* 31, no. 1 (1997): 63–71.

Gedro, Julie, and Robert C. Mizzi. "Feminist theory and queer theory: Implications for HRD research and practice." *Advances in Developing Human Resources* 16, no. 4 (2014): 445–456.

George, Chauncey, and Carolyn Strange. "Gay New York: Gender, urban culture & the making of the gay male world, 1890-1940." *Labour* 39 (1997): 261.

Ghaziani, Amin. "Culture and the nighttime economy: A conversation with London's Night Czar and culture-at-risk officer." (2019). Accessed September 4, 2021, https://metropolitics.org/Culture-and-the-Nighttime-Economy-A-Conversation-with-London-s-Night-Czar-and.html

Gilmore, Bob. *Claude Vivier: A Composer's Life*. New York: University of Rochester Press, 2014.

Ginastera, Alberto, and Manuel Mujica Láinez. *Bomarzo Op. 34: Opera in 2 acts and 15 scenes*. [full score] Aldwych, London: Boosey & Hawkes, 1966–1967.

Ginastera, Alberto, and Mujica Láinez. "Origins of an opera." Joint lecture, reprinted in the *Central Opera Service Bulletin* 9, no. 5 (1967): 10–13.

Gittings, Barbara. "Philadelphia gay and lesbian pride parade speech, June 2, 1990." In *Historic Speeches and Rhetoric for Gay and Lesbian Rights (1892-2000)*. Edited by Robert B. Ridinger. 606. New York: Routledge, 2012.

Gluck, Christoph Willibald. *Iphigenie en Tauride: Tragédie en quatre actes* [Full score] Paris : Des Lauriers, 1780.

Goldman, Emma. *The Individual, Society and the State*. Chicago, IL: Free Society Forum, 1940.

Goldstein, Richard. "My country music problem—and yours." *Mademoiselle* 77, no. 2 (June 1973): 114.

Goodman, Jonathon. *The Oscar Wilde File*. London: W.H. Allen and Co., 1989.

Gordon, Ricky Ian, and Royce Vavrek. *27: An Opera in Five Acts*. [Piano/vocal score] Malvern, PA: Theodore Presser Company, 2014.

Graham, Michael. "Shakespeare and modern British opera: Into 'the knot garden.'" PhD diss., Royal Holloway, University of London, 2017.

Gratian, Margaret, Sruthi Bandi, Michel Cukier, Josiah Dykstra, and Amy Ginther. "Correlating human traits and cyber security behavior intentions." *Computers & Security* 73 (2018): 345–358.

Greenfield, Joanne. "Coming out: The process of forming a positive identity." In *Fenway: Guide to Lesbian, Gay, Bisexual, and Transgender Health*, edited by Harvey Makadon, Kenneth Mayer, Jennifer Potter, and Hilary Goldhammer, 45–74. Philadelphia: American College of Physician, 2008.

Grossman, Maxine L. "Jesus, Mama, and the constraints of salvific love in contemporary country music." *Journal of the American Academy of Religion* 70, no. 1 (2002): 83–115.

Gruenewald, Jeff. "Are anti-LGBT homicides in the United States unique?" *Journal of Interpersonal Violence* 27, no. 18 (2012): 3601–3623.

Gruenewald, Jeff, and Kristin Kelley. "Exploring anti-LGBT homicide by mode of victim selection." *Criminal Justice and Behavior* 41, no. 9 (2014): 1130–1152.

Guilbert, Georges-Claude. *Gay Icons: The (Mostly) Female Entertainers Gay Men Love*. Jefferson, NC: McFarland, 2018.

Gunther, Scott. "The indifferent ghetto." *Harvard Gay and Lesbian Review* 6, no. 1 (1999): 34–36.

Gvion, Liora. "Singing your way out of the closet: Young gay men in the operatic world." *YOuNG* 28, no. 4 (2020): 387–403.

Hagwood, Rod Stafford. "'Not in my town' revisits Matthew Shepard story." *South Florida Sun Sentinel.* June 1, 2016. Accessed January 28, 2022, https://www.sun-sentinel.com/entertainment/theater-and-arts/sf-lauderdale-opera-matthew-shepard-advance-20160601-story.html

Halbwachs, Maurice. *On Collective Memory.* Chicago: University of Chicago Press, 2020.

Haldeman, Douglas C. "Gay rights, patient rights: The implications of sexual orientation conversion therapy." *Professional Psychology: Research and Practice* 33, no. 3 (2002): 260.

Hale, Amanda. "Pomegranate: How my self-published chapbook became an opera." *Write* 44, no. 2, Summer (2016): 14–15.

Hall, William J. "Psychosocial risk and protective factors for depression among lesbian, gay, bisexual, and queer youth: A systematic review." *Journal of Homosexuality* 65, no. 3 (2018): 263–316.

Halperin, David M. "Is there a history of sexuality?" *History and Theory* 28, no. 3 (1989): 257–274.

Halperin, David M. "How to do the history of male homosexuality." *GLQ: A Journal of Lesbian and Gay Studies* 6, no. 1 (2000): 87–123.

Halperin, David M. "The normalization of queer theory." In *Queer Theory and Communication*, edited by Gust Yep, Karen E. Lovaas, and John P. Elia, 339–343. Milton Park: Routledge, 2014.

Hanson, Ellis. "Screwing with Children in Henry James." *GLQ: A Journal of Lesbian and Gay Studies* 9, no. 3 (2003): 367–391.

Harris, Daniel. *The Rise and Fall of Gay Culture.* New York: Hyperion Books, 1997.

Harrison, Lou. *Young Caesar: Opera in 14 Scenes.* [Full score, Revised Performing Edition] New York: Peermusic, 2021.

Haslam, Nick. *Psychology in the Bathroom.* New York: Springer, 2012. Uyeda, Leslie, and Rachel Rose. *When the Sun Comes Out.* [piano/vocal score] Toronto: The Avondale Press, 2020.

Heede, Dag. "Antinous: Saint or criminal?." *Lambda Nordica* 22, no. 4 (2017): 17–39.

Henderlight, Justin. "Marc-Antoine Charpentier's David et Jonathas: French Jesuit theater and the tragédie en musique." PhD diss., University of British Columbia, 2017.

Henry, Tri Keah, Brittany E. Hayes, Joshua D. Freilich, and Steven Chermak. "Comparison of honor killings to anti-LGBTQ homicides." *Journal of Aggression, Conflict and Peace Research* 10, no. 4, (2018), 272–282.

Herek, Gregory M., J. Roy Gillis, and Jeanine C. Cogan. "Internalized stigma among sexual minority adults: Insights from a social psychological perspective." *Stigma and Health,* 1 (S), (2015), 18–34.

Hickling, Alfred. "Soul's Rebirth." *The Guardian,* February 22, 2008, accessed February 23, 2022, https://www.theguardian.com/music/2008/feb/22/classicalmusicandopera

Higgins, Charlotte. "It's like being attacked by knives." *The Guardian.* September, 9, 2005.

Hindley, Clifford. "Love and salvation in Britten's "Billy Budd'." *Music & Letters* 70, no. 3 (1989): 363–381.

Hindley, Clifford. "Contemplation and reality: A study in Britten's 'death in Venice.'" *Music & Letters* 71, no. 4 (1990a): 511–523.

Hindley, Clifford. "Why does miles die? A study of Britten's 'the turn of the screw'." *The Musical Quarterly* 74, no. 1 (1990b): 1–17.

Hohmann, John. *"Orlando: Gender Bending and the Sound of Androgyny in Vienna." Schmopera.* Apr 27, 2020. Accessed December 4, 2021, https://www .schmopera.com/orlando-gender-bending-and-the-sound-of-androgyny-in-vienna/

Houston, Gail Turley. "'Oscar' the opera and the high-pitched life." *Victorian Literature and Culture* 43, no. 1 (2015): 182–188.

Howard, Patricia, ed. *Benjamin Britten: The Turn of the Screw.* Cambridge: Cambridge Opera Handbooks, 1985. https://www.aarp.org/entertainment/arts-leisure/ info-06-2009/tapping_the_muses.html

Hubbs, Nadine. "'Jolene,' genre, and the everyday homoerotics of country music: Dolly Parton's loving address of the other woman." *Women and Music: A Journal of Gender and Culture* 19, no. 1 (2015): 71–76.

Isay, Richard A. "Heterosexually married homosexual men: Clinical and developmental issues." *American Journal of Orthopsychiatry* 68, no. 3 (1998): 424–432.

James, Henry. "The turn of the screw." Dover Thrift Editions. New York: Dover Publications, 1991.

Janssen, Diederik F. "Karl Heinrich Ulrichs: First theorist of erotic age orientation." *Journal of Homosexuality* 64, no. 13 (2017): 1850–1871.

Johnson, Anne E. "'The impossible she': Lesbian romance tells moving story." *Classical Voice North America.* May 13, 2019. Accessed November 7, 2021, https://cla ssicalvoiceamerica.org/author/anne-e-johnson/

Johnson, David K. *The Lavender Scare: The Cold War Persecution of Gays and Lesbians in the Federal Government.* Chicago, IL: University of Chicago Press, 2009.

Johnson, Marguerite. "Eighteenth-and Nineteenth-Century Sapphos in France, England, and the United States." In *The Cambridge Companion to Sappho,* edited by P. J. Finglass, and A. Kelly, 361–374. (2021): 361.

Jung, Carl Gustav "II. The eros theory." In *Collected Works of CG Jung 7,* 19–29. Princeton: Princeton University Press, 2014.

Jung, Carl Gustav. *Letters of C. G. Jung: Volume I, 1906-1950.* Edited by Gerhard Adler. London & New York: Routledge, 2015.

Kaminsky, Laura, Mark Campbell, and Kimberly Reed. *As One: A Chamber Opera for Two Singers and String Quartet,* 31. [piano/vocal score] Brooklyn, New York: Bill Holab Music, 2015.

Kaptainis, Arthur. "Composer Kevin March says Les Feluettes was an opera all along." *Montreal Gazette.* June 3, 2020. Accessed May 5, 2022, https://montreal-gazette.com/entertainment/composer-kevin-march-says-les-feluettes-was-an-opera -all-along

Kelly, Christopher. "Rousseau's case for and against heroes." *Polity* 30 no. 2 (1997). 347–366.

Khan, B. Zorina. "Married women's property laws and female commercial activity: Evidence from United States patent records, 1790–1895." *The Journal of Economic History 56*, no. 2, (1996): 356–388.

Kim, Koeun. "Queer-coded villains (and why you should care)." *Dialogues@ RU* (New Brunswick, NJ: Rutgers University, 2017): 156–165.

Kimper, Paula, and Wende Persons. *Patience and Sarah: A Pioneering Love Story.* [Piano/vocal score] Brooklyn: Once in a Blue Moon Publishing Co., 1998.

King, George T. "A living tradition: Michael Tippett reaches 85 years." *Muziki 22*, no. 1 (1990): 64–73.

Kippax, Susan, and Gary Smith. "Anal intercourse and power in sex between men." *Sexualities 4*, no. 4 (November 2001): 413–434.

Kjaran, Jón Ingvar, and Ingólfur Ásgeir Jóhannesson. "Masculinity strategies of young queer men as queer capital." *Norma 11*, no. 1 (2016): 52–65.

Kobierzycki, Tadeusz, and Filip Maj. "Karol Szymanowskis opera king roger–Individuation, erotic transgression and musical aesthetics." *Scientific Yearbook of the University of Kuyavian-Pomeranian in Bydgoszcz* 14 (2020): 7–21.

Kohlmayer, Rainer. "From saint to sinner: The demonization of Oscar Wilde's Salome in Hedwig Lachmann's German translation and in Richard Strauss' opera." *Benjamins Translation Library* 20 (1997): 111–122.

Kostick, Conor. "Live reviews: The bitter tears of Petra von Kant." *The Journal of Music.* November 1, 2002. Accessed November 4, 2021, https://journalofmusic.com/criticism/live-reviews-bitter-tears-petra-von-kant

Kotnik, Vlado. "The adaptability of opera: When different social agents come to common ground." *International Review of the Aesthetics and Sociology of Music* 44, no. 2 (2013): 303–342.

LaBonte, Hillary. "Analyzing gender inequality in contemporary opera." PhD diss., Bowling Green State University, 2019.

Laird, Paul R. "Bernstein's monument to American diversity." In *Leonard Bernstein and Washington, DC*, NED - New edition, edited by Daniel Abraham, Alicia Kopfstein-Penk, and Andrew H. Weaver, 209–231. Woodbridge, England: Boydell & Brewer, University of Rochester Press, 2020.

Lam, George, and John Clum. *Heartbreak Express: Chamber Opera in One* Act. [Full score] Unpublished, 2015.

Latham, Clara Hunter. "How many voices can she have? Destabilizing desire and identification in American Lulu." *The Opera Quarterly* 33, no. 3–4 (2017): 303–318.

Leiner, Marvin. *Sexual Politics in Cuba: Machismo, Homosexuality, and AIDS.* Milton Park: Routledge, 2019.

Leppert, Richard. "Music 'pushed to the edge of existence' (adorno, listening, and the question of hope)." *Cultural Critique* 60 (2005): 92–133.

Leroux, Xavier. *Astarté.* [vocal score] Paris: Alphonse Leduc, 1901.

Leroy, Stéphane. "Gay Paris: Elements for a geography of homosexuality." *Annales de geographie* 6 (2005/6): 579–601.

Levitt, Heidi M., and Maria R. Ippolito. "Being transgender: The experience of transgender identity development." *Journal of Homosexuality* 61, no. 12 (2014): 1727–1758.

Lewes, Kenneth. "A special oedipal mechanism in the development of male homosexuality." *Psychoanalytic Psychology* 15, no. 3 (1998): 341.

Lewis, Rachel. "What's queer about musicology now?" *Women and Music: A Journal of Gender and Culture* 13, no. 1 (2009): 43–53.

Leyland, Winston, and Peter Garland. "Winston Leyland interviews Lou Harrison." *A Lou Harrison Reader* (1987): 70–84.

Lingel, Jessa. "Adjusting the borders: Bisexual passing and queer theory." *Journal of Bisexuality* 9, no. 3–4 (2009): 381–405.

Llorente, Elizabeth. "Tapping the muses: Jorge Martín's creative process for before night falls." *AARP.* June 11, 2009. Accessed February 7, 2022. Lyons, Richard D. "Psychiatrists in a shift. Declare homosexuality no mental illness." *The New York Times.* December 16, 1973.

Lon, Tuck. "The frenzy of 'a quiet place.'" *The Washington Post*, 1983, C1.

Longobardi, Ruth Sara. "Reading between the lines: An approach to the musical and sexual ambiguities of death in Venice." *Journal of Musicology* 22, no. 3 (2005): 327–364.

Macgillivray, Ian K., and Todd Jennings. "A content analysis exploring lesbian, gay, bisexual, and transgender topics in foundations of education textbooks." *Journal of Teacher Education* 59, no. 2 (2008): 170–188.

Maddocks, Fiona. "Lessons in love and violence review: A bolder, angrier, more tender George Benjamin." *The Guardian*, May 20, 2018. Accessed, December 15, 2021, https://www.theguardian.com/music/2018/may/19/lessons-in-love-and -violence-review-george-benjamin-royal-opera

Maddocks, Fiona. "Orlando world premiere review: A feast for ears and eyes." *The Observer.* December 14, 2019. Accessed December 5, 2021, https://www .theguardian.com/music/2019/dec/14/orlando-vienna-state-opera-review-olga-neu-wirth-world-premiere-virginia-woolf

Maffesoli, Michel. *The Time of the Tribes: The Decline of Individualism in Mass Society.* London: Sage, 1995.

Mann, Thomas. *Death in Venice, Tonio Krőger, and Other Writings.* New York: The Continuum Publishing Company, 2003.

Manning, Scott. "Revelation and dissimulation in André Gide's autobiographical space." *The French Review* (2004): 318–327.

Manternach, Brian. "Teaching transgender singers. Part 2: The singers' perspectives." *Journal of Singing* 74, no. 2 (2017): 209–214.

Marshall, Ky, and Amanda Hale, *Pomegranate* [Vocal score] Unpublished score, 2019.

Martin, Brian Joseph. *Napoleonic Friendship: Military Fraternity, Intimacy & Sexuality in Nineteenth Century France.* Hanover: University Press of New England, 2011.

Martin, Carol Lynn, Rachel E. Cook, and Naomi C. Z. Andrews. "Reviving androgyny: A modern day perspective on flexibility of gender identity and behavior." *Sex Roles* 76, no. 9 (2017): 592–603.

Martín, Jorge. "'The book, in my hands.' Music by Jorge Martín: A diary of musical thoughts and observations." February 8, 2010. Accessed December 12, 2021,

https://musicbyjorgemartin.blogspot.com/search?updated-max=2010-02-24T16
:20:00-08:00&max-results=7&start=7&by-date=false

Martin, Jorge. "Dreaming opera: Adapting before night falls." *The Gay & Lesbian Review Worldwide* 13, no. 5 (2006): 24.

Martin, Jorge, and Dolores M. Koch. *Before Night Falls: An Opera in Two Acts based on the memoir by Reinaldo Arenas.* [Full Orchestral Score] Atlanta: JMB Publishing, Fort Worth Opera Premiere Edition, 2009.

May, Thomas. "Hip to be hip: When early and new music intersect." *Early Music America* 24, no. 3 (2018): 22–27.

McDonagh, Michael. "Composer Nico Muhly on his 'gay opera'." (Bay Area Reporter, Jan 10, 2013), 13. Accessed August 13, 2021, https://issuu.com/bayareareporter/docs/january_10_2013

McKeever, Brooke W. "Public relations and public health: The importance of leadership and other lessons learned from 'Understanding AIDS' in the 1980s." *Public Relations Review* 47, no. 1 (2021): 102007.

McKenna, Neil (ed.). *The Secret Life of Oscar Wilde.* New York: Basic Books, 2003.

McKinnon, Arlo. "Three Way." *Opera News Magazine,* September 2017 - Vol. 82, No. 3.

McNeill, John J. *Both Feet Firmly Planted in Midair: My Spiritual Journey.* Louisville: Westminster John Knox Press, 1998.

Meiners, Christoph. *Vermischte philosophische schriften.* Vol. 1. Frankfurt: Weygandschen buchhandlung, 1775.

Melville, Herman. *Billy Budd, Sailor and Selected Tales.* New York: Oxford University Press, 1998.

Merrick, Jeffrey. "The Marquis de Villette and Mademoiselle de Raucourt: Representations of Male and Female Sexual Deviance in Late Eighteenth-century France." In *Homosexuality in modern France,* edited by Jeffrey Merrick, and Bryant T. Ragan Jr., 30–53. New York: Oxford University Press, 1996.

Meyer, Ilan H. "Resilience in the study of minority stress and health of sexual and gender minorities." *Psychology of Sexual Orientation and Gender Diversity* 2, no. 3 (2015): 209.

Meyers, Jeffrey. "For the love of Billy Budd." *The Gay & Lesbian Review Worldwide* 25, no. 4, July-Aug. (2018): 17–19.

Michaels, Sean. "Rufus Wainwright to compose opera about Roman emperor Hadrian." *The Guardian,* December 3, 2013. Accessed December 15, 2021, https://www.theglobeandmail.com/arts/theatre-and-performance/how-rufus-wainwright-is-turning-a-roman-emperor-into-a-coc-opera/article15677143/?page=all

Midgette, Anne. "The voice of American opera." *The Opera Quarterly* 23, no. 1 (2007): 81–95.

Milk, Harvey. *An Archive of Hope: Harvey Milk's Speeches and Writings.* CA: University of California Press, 2013.

Miller, Leta E., and Fredric Lieberman. "Lou Harrison and the American Gamelan." *American Music* 17, no. 2 (1999): 146–178.

Miller, Leta E., and Fredric Lieberman. *Composing a World: Lou Harrison, Musical Wayfarer.* Vol. 543, Champaign, IL: University of Illinois Press, 2004.

Miller, Leta E., and Fredric Lieberman. *Lou Harrison.* Champaign, IL: University of Illinois Press, 2006.

Milliet, Paul. "Astarte." *Le Monde artiste* 8 (February 24, 1901): 115–117.

Mitchell, Donald, and Richard Wagner, eds. *Benjamin Britten: Death in Venice.* Cambridge: Cambridge University Press, 1987.

Morrison, Theodore, and John Cox. *Oscar, An Opera in Two Acts.* [orchestral score] New York: G. Schirmer Inc. 2013.

Mozart, Wolfgang Amadeus. *Apollo et Hyacinthus: Lateinische Comoedie in I Acte.* Mozart's Werke, Serie V: Opern, Bd.1, no.2. Leipzig: Breitkopf & Härtel, 1879.

Muhly, Nico, and Craig Lucas. *Two Boys: An Opera in Two Acts.* [Full score] New York: St. Rose Music Publishing Co., 2013.

Muir, Cameron. "Misunderstood: The Matthew Shepard hate crime and its intercultural implications." *Proceedings of the New York State Communication Association* 2011, no. 1 (2012): 6.

Mulvey, Laura, ed. "Visual pleasure and narrative cinema." In *Feminism and Film Theory,* 57–68. Milton Park: Routledge, 1988.

Muñoz, José Esteban. *Disidentifications: Queers of Color and the Performance of Politics.* Vol. 2. Minneapolis: University of Minnesota Press, 1999.

Munro, Niall. "American decadence and the creation of a queer modernist aesthetic." In *Hart Crane's Queer Modernist Aesthetic,* 16–40. London: Palgrave Macmillan, 2015.

Neuwirth, Olga, and Catherine Filloux. "Orlando – eine fictive musikalische Biografie." [full score] Berlin: Ricordi, 2018.

New York Times. "THEATRE PADLOCK BILL REPORTED IN SENATE; Upper House Passes Rent Law Extension Measure and Fort Lee Bridge Bill." (March 22, 1927), 10. Accessed February 25, 2022, https://www.nytimes.com/1927/03/22/archives/theatre-padlock-bill-reported-in-senate-upper-house-passes-rent-law.html

Nichols, Margaret. "Lesbian relationships: Implications for the study of sexuality and gender." In *Homosexuality/Heterosexuality: Concepts of Sexual Orientation,* edited by David P. McWhirter, Stephanie Anne Sanders, and June Machover Reinisch, 350–364. Oxford: Oxford University Press, 1990.

Nicolosi, Joseph. *Reparative Therapy of Male Homosexuality: A New Clinical Approach.* Northvale: Jason Aronson, 1991.

Nicolson, Nigel, and Joanne Trautmann, eds. *The Letters of Virginia Woolf. 6 vols.* London: Hogarth Press, 1975.

Nietzsche, Friedrich. *Nietzsche contra Wagner.* Amsterdam: Singel Uitgeverijen, 2012.

NYC LGBT Historic Sites Project. "Various locations Manhattan: Central Park." 2016. Accessed April 13, 2022, https://www.nyclgbtsites.org/

Okin, Susan Moller. "Gender inequality and cultural differences." *Political Theory* 22, no. 1 (1994): 5–24.

Olive, Peter. "Reinventing the barbarian: Electra, sibling incest, and twentieth-century Hellenism." *Classical Receptions Journal* 11, no. 4 (2019): 407–426.

Osborne, Charles. *The Complete Operas of Richard Wagner.* Boston: Da Capo Press, 1993.

Osgood, Josiah. "Caesar and Nicomedes." *The Classical Quarterly* 58, no. 2 (2008): 687–691.

Pangle, Thomas L. ed. *The Laws of Plato.* Chicago: University of Chicago Press, 1988.

Parker, Sally, Helene Snihur, and Jan Waxman. "The story of the opera." *Rochester Review.* Accessed January 23, 2022, https://web.archive.org/web/20100624033107/http://www.patienceandsarah.com/URstory.html

Parra, Hèctor, and Händl Klaus. *Les Bienveillantes.* [Vocal score] Paris: Durand Editions Musicales, 2018.

Paterson, Robert, and David Cote. *Three Way: A Trio of One-Act Operas.* [Piano/vocal score] Brooklyn: Bill Holab Music, 2014.

Perdian, Rick. "Rhymes with opera explores loneliness and love in two world premieres." *Seen and Heard International.* May 20, 2019. Accessed September 12, 2021, https://seenandheard-international.com/2019/05/rhymes-with-opera-explores-loneliness-and-love-in-two-world-premieres/

Perle, George. "The music of 'Lulu': A new analysis." *Journal of the American Musicological Society* 12, no. 2/3 (1959): 185–200. Accessed May 26, 2021, https://doi.org/10.2307/829540.

Phillips, Sidney H. "Homosexuality: Coming out of the confusion." *The International Journal of Psychoanalysis* 84, no. 6 (2003): 1431–1450.

Picard, Anna. "The bitter tears of Petra von Kant, English national opera, London." *The Independent.* September 25, 2005. Accessed October 29, 2022, https://www.independent.co.uk/arts-entertainment/music/reviews/the-bitter-tears-of-petra-von-kant-english-national-opera-london-314718.html

Pines, Roger. "Dalibor. Bedřich Smetana." *The Opera Quarterly* 14, no. 1 (1997): 174–176.

Prod'homme, J-G. "Les Musiciens Français à Rome (1803-1903)." *Sammelbande der Internationalen Musikgesellschaft* (1903): 728–737.

Rajamani. Maya. "For a Bronx composer, opera rises out of identity struggles." The Riverdale Press, (August 28, 2014). Accessed November 23, 2021, https://www.riverdalepress.com/stories/for-a-bronx-composer-opera-rises-out-of-identity-struggles,55005

Raskauskas, Stephen. "7 American operas that put LGBTQ issues center stage." *WFMT.* June 20, 2017. Accessed October 25, 2021, https://www.wfmt.com/2027/06/20/7-american-operas-put-lgbtq-issues-center-stage/

Reed, Jennifer. "Queering Eleanor Roosevelt." *The Journal of American Culture* 39, no. 1 (2016): 9.

Richardson, Diane, Janice McLaughlin, and Mark E. Casey, eds. *Intersections between feminist and queer theory.* Basingstoke: Palgrave Macmillan, 2006.

Riddell, Fraser. "Queer music in the Queen's hall: Teleny and decadent musical geographies at the Fin de Siècle." *Journal of Victorian Culture* 25, no. 4, (2020): 593–608.

Riley, Sarah, Yvette More, and Christine Griffin. "The 'pleasure citizen' Analyzing partying as a form of social and political participation." *Young* 18, no. 1 (2010): 33–54.

Rio, Malcolm. "Architecture is burning: An urbanism of queer kinship in ballroom culture." *Thresholds* 48 (2020): 122–132.

Ritchey, Marianna. "Nico Muhly, two boys. Nonesuch records 7559795602, 2014, 2 CDs." *Journal of the Society for American Music* 9, no. 2 (2015): 252–255.

Robinson, Amy. "It takes one to know one: Passing and communities of common interest." *Critical Inquiry* 20, no. 4 (1994): 715–736.

Robinson, Paul. "The opera queen: A voice from the closet." *Cambridge Opera Journal* 6, no. 3 (1994): 283–291.

Robinson, Steven. "The contest of wisdom between Socrates and Agathon in Plato's Symposium." *Ancient Philosophy* 24, no. 1 (2004): 81–100.

Robson, Ruthann. "Assimilation, marriage, and lesbian liberation." *Temple Law Review* 75, no. 4. (2002): 709–820.

Ross, Michael. *Not in My Town*. [Piano/vocal score] Unpublished, 2016a.

Ross, Michael. *Not in My Town*. [Libretto] Unpublished, 2016b.

Rosser, B.R. Simon, William West, and Richard Weinmeyer. "Are gay communities dying or just in transition? Results from an international consultation examining possible structural change in gay communities." *AIDS Care* 20, no. 5 (2008), 588–595.

Rousseau, Jean-Jacques. *Considerations on the government of Poland and on its planned reformation. In the Collected Writings of Jean-Jacques Rousseau.* Vol. 11; Trans. C. Kelly & J. Bush. Hanover, NH: Dartmouth College Press, 2005.

Rubin, T.J., and Deepali Gupta, *Nightlife*. [Piano/vocal score] Unpublished, 2019.

Rubinstein, Arthur. *My Many Years*. London: Hamilton, 1987.

Salazar, David. "Q & A: Composer Laura Kaminsky on the development of 'as one,'" *Opera Wire*, March 14, 2018. Accessed October 25, 2021, https://operawire.com/q -a-composer-laura-kaminsky-on-the-development-of-as-one/

Salazar, David. "Honoring Stonewall: How Mark Campbell & Iain Bell came together to create an opera celebrating LGBTQ+ community." *OperaWire*. June 20, 2019. Accessed October 13, 2021, https://operawire.com/honoring-stonewall-how-mark -campbell-iain-bell-came-together-to-create-an-opera-celebrating-lgbtq-community/

Salzman, Leon. "The concept of latent homosexuality." *The American Journal of Psychoanalysis* 17, no. 2 (1957): 161–169.

Sanchez, Maria C., and Linda Schlossberg, eds. *Passing: Identity and Interpretation in Sexuality, Race, and Religion*, 29. New York: New York University Press, 2001.

Schildcrout, Jordan. *This Thing of Darkness: Reclaiming the Queer Killer in Contemporary Drama*. New York: City University of New York, 2005.

Schneider, Laurel C., and Carolyn Roncolato. "Queer theologies." *Religion Compass* 6, no. 1 (2012): 1–13.

Schott EAM. "Peter Eötvös's *Angels in America* at New York City Opera." June 1, 2017. Accessed April 13, 2022, https://www.eamdc.com/news/peter-eotvoss -angels-in-america-at-new-york-city-opera/

Scull, Andrew. *Hysteria: The Biography*. Oxford: Oxford University Press, 2009.

Sedgwick, Eve Kosofsky. *Epistemology of the Closet*. Los Angeles: University of California Press, 1990.

Seidl, Jan. *Queer Stories of Europe*. Edited by Kārlis Vērdiņš, and Jānis Ozoliņš. Newcastle upon Tyne: Cambridge Scholars Publishing, 2016.

Seidman, Steven. "Are we all in the Closet? Notes toward a sociological and cultural turn in Queer theory." In *Matters of Culture: Cultural Sociology in Practice*, edited by Roger Friedland and John Mohr, 255–269. Cambridge: Cambridge University Press, 2004.

Seutter, Ray A., and Martin Rovers. "Emotionally absent fathers: Furthering the understanding of homosexuality." *Journal of Psychology and Theology* 32, no. 1 (2004): 43–49.

Sibalis, Michael. "Male homosexuality in the age of enlightenment and revolution, 1680-1850." In *Gay Life and Culture: A World History*, edited by Robert Aldrich, 103–123. New York: Universe, 2006.

Simeonov, Jenna. "A lesbian chamber opera." *Schmopera*, 2019. Accessed January 5, 2022, https://www.schmopera.com/a-lesbian-chamber-opera-to-span-centuries-pomegranate/

Simpson, Mark, and Melanie Challenger. *Pleasure*. [Full score] London: Boosey & Hawkes, 2016.

Singh, Yumnam Oken, and Gyanabati Khuraijam. "Aestheticism, decadence and symbolism: Fin de siècle movements in revolt." *Journal of Literature, Culture & Media Studies* 4, 7/8 (2012): 71–84.

Sirin, Selcuk R., Donald R. McCreary, and James R. Mahalik. "Differential reactions to men and women's gender role transgressions: Perceptions of social status, sexual orientation, and value dissimilarity." *The Journal of Men's Studies* 12, no. 2 (2004): 119–132.

Sissa, Giulia. "Agathon and agathon. Male sensuality in aristophanes' Thesmophoriazusae and plato's symposium." *EuGeStA. Journal of Gender Studies in Antiquity* 2 (2012): 25–70.

Skinner, Graeme. "Szymanowski, Karol (1882 - 1937)." In *Who's Who in Gay and Lesbian History*. Edited by Robert Aldrich, and Garry Wotherspoon, 430–431. Milton Park: Routledge, 2002.

Smetana, Beidrich. *Dalibor. [Piano Reduction]*. Vaclav Juda Novotny: Umělecká Beseda, 1923.

Smith-Rosenberg, Carroll. "The hysterical woman: Sex roles and role conflict in 19th-century America." *Social Research* 39, no. 4 (1972): 652–678.

Soebbing, Steven. "The Fine Line of Friendship: Male Homoerotic Relationships in Mozart's Apollo et Hyacinthus." *The Journal of Men's Studies* 23, no. 1 (2015): 79–97.

Soebbing, Steven Eric. "The portrayal of male homoeroticism in selected early classical operas." PhD diss., ETD collection for University of Nebraska-Lincoln, 2012.

Solomon, Brin. "In review: The Stonewall operas." *National Sawdust*. May 18, 2019. Accessed November 27, 2021, https://nationalsawdust.org/thelog/2019/05/24/in-review-the-stonewall-operas/

Sontag, Susan. "Notes on 'Camp.'" *Partisan Review* 31 (1999): 515–530.

Soto, Francisco. "A gay Cuban activist in exile: Reinaldo Arenas." *Revista de Estudios Hispánicos* 42, no. 2 (2008): 380.

Spargo, Tamsin. *Foucault and Queer Theory.* Cambridge: Icon Books, 1999.

Spears, Gregory, and Greg Pierce. *Fellow Travelers: Opera in Two Acts.* [Full Score] New York: Schott, 2016.

Spitz, Brady Joseph. "Lou Harrison's 'Old Granddad': A composer's guide." PhD diss., Rice University, 2019.

Spreng, Sebastian. "An interview with 'before night falls' composer Jorge Martín." *Knight Foundation*, March 16, 2017. Accessed December 12, 2021, https://knightfoundation.org/articles/interview-before-night-falls-composer-jorge -martin/

Stadlen, Peter. "TV alters structure of Billy Budd." *Daily Telegraph*, December 12, 1966.

Staughton, George, Benjamin Nead, and Thomas McCamant. *Charter to William Penn, and Laws of the Province of Pennsylvania, Passed Between the Years 1682 and 1700.* Farmington Hills, MI: Gale, 1879.

Stearns, Patrick. "50 Years after Stonewall, classical music still fights the fight." *WQXR,* June 5, 2019, accessed November 23, 2021, https://www.wqxr.org/story/ stonewall-50-years-anniversary-classical-music-fight/

Stebbins, Amy. "Dramaturgical oper (an) ations: De-internationalization in contemporary opera libretti." In *Theatre and Internationalization*, edited by Ulrike Garde, and John R. Severn, 128–145. Milton Park: Routledge, 2020.

Stein, Gertrude. "The autobiography of Alice B. Toklas by Gertrude Stein-Delphi classics (Illustrated)." Vol. 24. Delphi Classics, 2017.

Stewart, Alan. "The early modern closet discovered." *Representations* no. 50 (1995): 76–100.

Stewart, Suzanne R. "The theft of the operatic voice: Masochistic seduction in Wagner's Parsifal." *The Musical Quarterly* 80, no. 4 (1996): 599–600.

Strauss, Richard. *Salome Op. 54 [Piano/Vocal Score by Otto Singer].* Berlin: Adolph Fürnster, 1903–1905.

Strauss, Richard, and Hugo von Hofmannsthal. *Elektra, Op. 58.* [Full score] Berlin: Adolph Fürstner, 1916.

Stuckenschmidt, Hans Heinz. "Karol Szymanowski." *Music & Letters* 19, no. 1 (1938): 36–47.

Suler, John. "The online disinhibition effect." *CyberPsychology & Behavior* 7, no. 3 (2004): 321–326.

Suresh, Devath. "Transgenders problems and administrative response." *Society for Public Welfare and Initiatives, Available at SSRN 3768221* (2016), https://doi.org /10.2139/ssrn.3768221

Sutherland, Andrew. *Children in Opera.* Newcastle Upon Tyne: Cambridge Scholars Publishing, 2020.

Symanowski, Karol, arr. Arthur Willner. *Król Roger: Opera in three acts.* [Piano/ Vocal Score] Vienna: Universal Edition, 1925.

Szymański, Karol. "Degeneration of the homosexual phantasm in normalised Czechoslovak cinema: From Václav Krška's the false prince (1956) to Stanislav Strnad's the bronze boys (1980)." *Studia z Dziejów Rosji i Europy Środkowo-Wschodniej* 52, no. 2 (2017): 77–141.

Telegraph, London, "Modest baritone made the role of Britten's Billy Budd his own." March 26, 2005. Accessed January 3, 2022, https://www.smh.com.au/national /modest-baritone-made-the-role-of-brittens-billy-budd-his-own-20050326-gdl05j .html

Terry, Jennifer. *An American Obsession: Science, Medicine, and Homosexuality in Modern Society.* Chicago: University of Chicago Press, 1999.

Theweleit, Klaus, and Timothy Nunan. "On the German reaction to Jonathan Littell's Les Bienveillantes." *New German Critique*, no. 106 (2009): 21–34.

Tippett, Michael. *The Knot Garden: An Opera in Three Acts.* [vocal score] London: Schott, 1970.

Tippett, Michael. *"Dreams of Power, Dreams of Love."* In *Tippett on Music*, edited by Meirion Bowen, 220–227. Oxford: Clarendon Press, 1995, 221.

Tommasini, Anthony. "Realism unvarnished for Gluck's bonded males." *The New York Times,* October 3, 1997, http://www.nytimes.com/1997/10/03/movies/realism -unvarnished-for-gluck-s-bonded-males.html

Town-Crier Editor. "April 4 fundraiser in Wellington to aid opera fusion project." *Town-Crier.* March 25, 2016. Accessed January 27, 2021, https://gotowncrier.com /2016/03/april-4-fundraiser-in-wellington-to-aid-opera-fusion-project/

Urtubey, Pola Suarez. "Ginastera's 'Bomarzo.'" *Tempo* 84 (1968): 14–21.

Venn, Edward. "Negotiating the labyrinth: Act II of Sir Michael Tippett's 'the knot garden.'" In *Second International Conference on Music and Gesture*, Unpublished, 2006.

Vermeulen, Timotheus, and Robin Van Den Akker. "Notes on metamodernism." *Journal of Aesthetics & Culture* 2, no. 1 (2010): 5677.

Von der Horst, Dirk. *Jonathan's Loves, David's Laments: Gay Theology, Musical Desires, and Historical Difference.* Eugene, OR: Wipf and Stock Publishers, 2017.

von Krafft-Ebing, Richard. "Über gewisse Anomalien des Geschlechtstriebes." *Archiv für Psychiatrie und Nervenkrankheiten* (1877): 291–312.

Voss, Georgina S. "'It is a beautiful experiment': Queer(y)ing the work of Alan Turing." *AI & Society* 28, no. 4 (2013): 567–573.

Wainwright, Rufus, and Daniel MacIvor. *Hadrian.* [Full score] London: Chester Music ltd., 2021.

Wallace, Stewart, and Michael Korie, *Harvey Milk Reimagined.* [Full score] New York: Sidmar Music, 2019.

Ward, Philip Marshall. "Hofmannsthal, Elektra and the representation of women's behaviour through myth." *German Life and Letters* 53, no. 1 (2000), 37–55.

Waters, Emily. *Lesbian, Gay, Bisexual, Transgender, Queer, and HIV-affected Hate Violence in 2009: A 20th Anniversary Report from the National Coalition of Anti-Violence Programs."* New York: National Coalition of Anti-Violence Programs (NCAVP), 2017. Accessed March 4, 2022, https://ncvc.dspacedirect.org/handle/20 .500.11990/257

Weber, Max, Hans Gerth, and C. Wright Mills. *From Max Weber: Essays in Sociology.* Milton Park: Routledge, 2009.

Weber, Shannon. "What's wrong with be(com)ing queer? Biological determinism as discursive queer hegemony." *Sexualities* 15, no. 5–6 (2012): 679–701.

Weininger, Otto. *Geschlecht und Charakter: eine prinzipielle Untersuchung.* Hamburg: Severus Verlag, 2014.

Weisbard, Eric. "Duets with modernity: Dolly Parton and country." In *Top 40 Democracy: The Rival Mainstreams of American Music*, 70–111. Chicago: University of Chicago Press, 2014.

Wenderoth, Valeria. "The making of exoticism in French operas of the 1890s." PhD diss., University of Hawaii, 2004.

Westphal, Carl. "Die conträre Sexualempfindung, Symptom eines neuropathischen (psychopathischen) Zustandes." *Archiv für Psychiatrie und Nervenkrankheiten* 2, no. 1 (1870): 73–108.

Whitesell, Lloyd. "Britten's dubious trysts." *Journal of the American Musicological Society* 56, no. 3 (2003): 637–694.

Whittall, Arnold. "'Twisted relations': Method and meaning in Britten's Billy Budd." *Cambridge Opera Journal* 2, no. 2 (1990): 145–171.

Wilde, Oscar. *Complete Works. With an Introduction by Vyvyan Holland.* London and Glasgow: Collins. 1987.

Wilde, Oscar. *Salome.* [Libretto] London: The Bodley Head, 1893.

Will, Barbara. *Unlikely Collaboration: Gertrude Stein, Bernard Faÿ, and the Vichy Dilemma.* New York: Columbia University Press, 2011.

Williams, Carla. "American art: Lesbian, nineteenth century." *GLBTQ Online Archive,* 2002. Accessed October 26, 2021, http://www.glbtqarchive.com/arts/am _art_lesbian_19c_A.pdf

Witty, Paul A., and Harvey C. Lehman. "Sex differences: Collecting interests." *Journal of Educational Psychology* 22, no. 3 (1931): 221.

Wuorinen, Charles, and Annie Proulx. *Brokeback Mountain: Opera in Two Acts.* [Orchestral Score] New York: C. F. Peters, 2011.

Yao, Shu-yi. *Tangzi: A Gay Sex Brothel and Opera Training Ground during the Late Qing.* Beijing: Chinese Academy of Social Science, 2004.

Yoshihara, Mari. "A quiet place in a not-so-quiet nation." In *Leonard Bernstein and Washington, DC*, NED - New edition, edited by Daniel Abraham, Alicia Kopfstein-Penk, and Andrew H. Weaver, 267–294. Woodbridge, England: Boydell & Brewer, University of Rochester Press, 2020. Quoted in "Benton for Mayor" letter, n.d., box 804, folder 3, Amberson Business Papers, Leonard Bernstein Collection, Library of Congress.

Yoshino, Kenji. "Covering." *Yale Law Journal* 111, no. 4 (2001): 769.

Yousef, Tawfiq. "Modernism, postmodernism, and metamodernism: A critique." *International Journal of Language and Literature* 5, 83, no. 1 (2017): 33–43.

Index

27, 65, 84–88

About the Author

Dr Andrew Sutherland is from Perth, Western Australia. He completed degrees in music at The University of Western Australia, Edith Cowan University and Monash University. He has published journal articles on a range of topics relating to music performance, music education and musicology. Having taught music at all levels in Australia, the United Kingdom and, more recently, Hong Kong, his interest for music performance by young people has consequently guided much of his research. Andrew's first monograph, *Children in Opera*, received critical acclaim, as did his edited volume, *Revolutions in Music Education*. Andrew is currently the director of Music at Methodist Ladies' College and an adjunct lecturer at the Western Australian Academy of Performing Arts.